Financial and Monetary Policy Studies

Volume 48

Series Editor
Ansgar Belke, University of Duisburg-Essen, Essen, Germany

More information about this series at http://www.springer.com/series/5982

Nazaré da Costa Cabral • Nuno Cunha Rodrigues

Editors

The Future of Pension Plans in the EU Internal Market

Coping with Trade-Offs Between Social Rights and Capital Markets

 Springer

Editors
Nazaré da Costa Cabral
CIDEEFF - Center for European,
Economic, Financial and Tax Law
Research
University of Lisbon, Faculdade de Direito
de Lisboa, Alameda da Universidade
Lisbon, Portugal

Nuno Cunha Rodrigues
CIDEEFF - Center for European,
Economic, Financial and Tax Law
Research
University of Lisbon, Faculdade de Direito
de Lisboa, Alameda da Universidade
Lisbon, Portugal

The European Commission support for the production of this publication does not constitute an endorsement of the contents which reflects the views only of the authors, and the Commission cannot be held responsible for any use which may be made of the information contained therein.

ISSN 0921-8580   ISSN 2197-1889   (electronic)
Financial and Monetary Policy Studies
ISBN 978-3-030-29499-1   ISBN 978-3-030-29497-7   (eBook)
https://doi.org/10.1007/978-3-030-29497-7

This Springer imprint is published by the registered company Springer Nature Switzerland AG.
The registered company address is: Gewerbestrasse 11, 6330 Cham, Switzerland

Contents

Part II   The Capital Markets Union (CMU) and the Future of Pension Plans: Opportunities, Risks and Drawbacks

The Capital Markets Union: Saving for Retirement and Investing for Growth

Ansgar Belke and Philipp Allroggen

Sustainable Pensions for European Citizens: How to Close the Gap?

Gabriel Bernardino

About the Editors

Nazaré da Costa Cabral Nazaré da Costa Cabral holds a license degree (1994), a master's (1998), and a PhD (2007) in law, from Lisbon School of Law (Faculdade de Direito, Universidade de Lisboa), and she holds a license degree in economics (2015), from Nova SBE—School of Business & Economics (Universidade Nova de Lisboa).

Nazaré is Associate Professor in tenure, in Lisbon School of Law.

She also lectures in other Universities, either in Portugal or abroad.

Nazaré is principal researcher of the Center for European, Economic, Fiscal and Tax Law Research (CIDEFF) of Lisbon School of Law (Group IV on 'Crises, Public Policies, Fiscal Policy and the Euro'). She is also a member of the Board of 'Instituto de Direito Económico, Financeiro e Fiscal' (IDEFF), of the same School, in which she also lectures. Nazaré is vice-president of the journal *Revista de Finanças Públicas e Direito Fiscal* (Public Finances and Tax Law Journal), published by IDEFF and Almedina Editors. She is also a member of the Executive and Editorial Board of the journal *Concorrência & Regulação* (Competition & Regulation), published by the Portuguese Competition Authority, IDEFF and Almedina Editors, and a member of the Editorial Board of the journal *Economia & Segurança Social* (Economics & Social Security), published by Diário de Bordo Editores.

Nazaré is author of several books, articles, and working papers, and her research areas are mainly on public finances, economic and monetary union, and social security.

Professional experience:

2019—Appointed by the Portuguese Government as Chair of the Senior Board of the Portuguese Public Finance Council

2018—Appointed as a member of High-Level Group of Experts on Pensions, by the Director-General for Employment, Social Affairs and Inclusion and the Director-General for Financial Stability, Financial Services and Capital Markets Union (under Commission decision C(2017)8523 of 18.12.2017 setting up a high-level group of experts on pensions)

2018—National expert at the EU project MoveS ('Network of independent experts in the fields of free movement of workers (FMW) and social security coordination').

2015–2017—National expert at the EU project FreSsco ('Network of Experts on Intra-EU Mobility—Free Movement of Workers and Social Security Coordination').

2015–2016—National expert at the EU project, developed by a scientific consortium led by CEPS (Centre for European Policy Studies) to the European Commission, and entitled 'National feasibility assessment of the different European unemployment benefit scheme options'.

2014—Appointed by the Ministry of State and Finance to integrate the Working Group charged with the reform of the Portuguese 'Budget Framework Law'.

1997–2002 and 2005–2007—Legal adviser in the Labor and Social Security Minister and Secretary of State Offices.

Nuno Cunha Rodrigues Bachelor (1995), Master in Laws (2003), and PhD (2012) in Law by the Faculty of Law of the University of Lisbon.

Associate Professor of the Faculty of Law of the University of Lisbon (FDL)

Non-executive member of the Board of Directors of Caixa Geral de Depósitos. Lawyer.

Vice-President of the European Institute of the FDL.

Investigator and Deputy Director of CIDEEFF (Center for Research in European Law, Economic, Financial and Fiscal)

Editor and member of the Advisory Board of the *Journal of Competition and Regulation*

Member of the Editorial Committee of the *Journal of Public Finance and Tax Law*

Member of the Scientific Council of the Faculty of Law of the University of Lisbon

Coordinator of the Jean Monnet (Erasmus +) module on Public Procurement, conferred by the European Commission (2015–2018)

Member of the Advisory Board of the *Journal of Regulation and Competition*

Member Editorial Committee of the *Journal of Public Finance and Tax Law*

Member of the Procurement Law Network

Head of a Jean Monnet Chair, awarded by the European Commission (since 2018)

Author of several books, articles and papers in the field of EU Law; Competition Law; Public Procurement; Economic Regulation and Public Finance.

List of Figures

What's New in the Debate About Pay-as-you-go Versus Funded Pensions?

The Coverage of Occupational and Personal Pension Plans

Sustainability and Adequacy of Pension Systems Across the OECD: Shocks, Robustness and Policies

List of Tables

**Pension Reforms After the Crisis: Bringing Adequacy Back
in the Domestic and EU Policy Equation?**

**How to Best Address Pension Adequacy and Financial Sustainability
in the Context of Population Ageing: The Labour Market as a Key
Determinant**

Introduction

Nazaré da Costa Cabral and Nuno Cunha Rodrigues

Abstract In this Chapter, the authors provide a global vision of this publication, *Pension Plans in the EU Internal Market*. It starts with a general description of the purposes of this academic project, led by the Centre for Research in European, Economic, Financial and Tax Law (CIDEEFF) of the University of Lisbon, to which the Editors—Nazaré da Costa Cabral and Nuno Cunha Rodrigues—are linked as researchers. Then it moves on to a description of each of the subsequent chapters, divided into three parts entitled: Part 1—Pay-as-you-go versus funded pension plans: Which way to better address common challenges in the EU?; Part 2—The Capital Markets Union (CMU) and the future of Pension Plans: opportunities, risks and drawbacks; Part 3—Pension Plans and the European Pillar of Social Rights: a new scope for EU social policy?.

1 General Description

The *Centre for Research in European, Economic, Financial and Tax Law* (CIDEEFF) of the University of Lisbon was created in the scholar year of 2014–2015 as a university research centre with the aim of monitoring and carrying out academic work, as well functioning as a centre for academic activity, through the medium of books, articles, working papers and organization of conferences and other thematic events especially in the fields of Law and Economics. One of its research groups is entitled "Crisis, Public Policies, Fiscal Policy and the Euro" and aims to conduct studies into the origins and characteristics of financial crises, public finance and monetary policies that the Eurozone has faced in recent years, and

N. da Costa Cabral (✉) · N. Cunha Rodrigues
CIDEEFF - Center for European, Economic, Financial and Tax Law Research, University of Lisbon, Faculdade de Direito de Lisboa, Alameda da Universidade, Lisbon, Portugal
e-mail: nazarecabral@fd.ulisboa.pt; nunorodrigues@fd.ulisboa.pt

© Springer Nature Switzerland AG 2019
N. da Costa Cabral, N. Cunha Rodrigues (eds.), *The Future of Pension Plans in the EU Internal Market*, Financial and Monetary Policy Studies 48,
https://doi.org/10.1007/978-3-030-29497-7_1

evaluate the effectiveness of the responses adopted in Europe (from 2008 until the present). An outcome of this research work was the 2017 publication, in this same Springer's Series (*Financial and Monetary Policy Studies*), of the important Book, entitled *The Euro and Crisis—Perspectives for the Eurozone as a Monetary and Budgetary Union*. Two of the Editors of this Book, Professors Nazaré da Costa Cabral and Nuno Cunha Rodrigues (the latter meanwhile having been awarded a *Jean-Monnet Chair*) are once again the Editors of this new publication.

For this Volume, the Editors invited a group of prestigious experts and academicians in the fields of pensions and social security to contribute, with diverse academic and professional backgrounds in Economics, Finance, Law and Political Science. This is indeed an interdisciplinary Book that embraces different scientific perspectives, even though linked to and focused on previously selected topics, in order to ensure its overall analytical coherence and coverage.

The Contributors were thus invited to analyse the different models of pension plans in European countries and the recent challenges, trends and prospects related to the design of such schemes. In the aftermath of the financial and Euro crisis, pension plans are more than ever at the intersection (possible even in the contradictory terms discussed) between, on the one hand, the development of the internal capital market and, on the other hand, the perspective of a new role for the EU regarding social policy, as demonstrated in the recent announcement made by President Juncker regarding the (new) 'European Pillar of Social Rights'—claiming a new approach to social policy at the European level as a response to common challenges, such as ageing and the digital revolution.

In Part 1, entitled *Pay-as-you-go versus funded pension plans: Which way to better address common challenges in the EU?*, the authors were challenged to: Identify major challenges in the design of pension systems: e.g. ageing, the digital revolution, employment/labour changes; Outline characteristics, advantages and shortcomings of both pay-as-you-go and funded systems; Analyse pay-as-you-go system reforms—major changes that have occurred in OCDE and European Union countries; Discuss with respect to funded systems major challenges and trends after the Great Financial Crisis (GFC) regarding the design of and respective prevalent instruments; Discuss the performance, return, and economic and social effects of public versus private systems.

In Part 2, titled *The Capital Markets Union (CMU) and the future of Pension Plans: opportunities, risks and drawbacks*, the Authors were confronted with several issues and questions to be discussed, notably the following: European and Monetary Union, the banking union and the CMU: completing the circle with the help of social security?; The CMU and enhancement of the internal market—coping with financial fragmentation in the EMU; The CMU: characterization; importance as a private risk sharing mechanism—major steps and elements; Funded pension plans as an instrument of the CMU—opportunities and risks; Funded systems and the 'search for yield' in a low interest rate environment; Funded systems, financial integration, and sovereign debt—discussing the home bias effect in the EMU; Funded systems, pension funds and sovereign debt—discussing the effects of quantitative easing (a 'balance-sheet approach'); Capital markets and pension plans/funds—effects on financial institutions and financial instruments; Using capital markets in pension provision: risks, dangers and shortcomings; Pension plans, pension funds, regulation and supervision: changes and trends after the GFC; Pension plans and taxation—savings and pension plan taxation, taxing pensions and social security financing; The GFC and new pension products; The Pan-European pension product and the integration of capital markets.

Finally, in Part 3, entitled *Pension Plans and the European Pillar of Social Rights: a new scope for EU social policy?* the Authors were invited to address a number of selected topics, such as: The EU and social policy: historical background and prospects for the future; Reflections on the Social dimension of Europe by 2025; Social policy and EU law: coordination, harmonization or what else?; EU social policy after the Crises: which areas to be reinforced?; Social policy between a rock (fiscal discipline and sustainability) and a hard place (coping with unemployment, inequality and social risks); The main features of the European Pillar of Social Rights: discussing its merits and shortcomings; The adequacy of pension plans: new trends in the EU (the EC's '*2018 Pension Adequacy Report*'); The EU and pension provision: discussing its timeliness, models and its role as an instrument of risk sharing and/or of solidarity and equality; Pension plans and pensions funds as a means for the 'financialization' of social rights: possible risks and dangers.

In short, for all these reasons, the Editors believe that this an essential and well-timed study, as it seeks to analyse the effects of ageing, changing labour markets and the digital revolution, and also the effects of the recent crises on the future evolution of pension systems in Europe. In fact, this Book intents to be milestone for the study and comprehension of on-going trends and policy responses, both at the financial and social levels, in response to common challenges and the uncertainties currently faced by European societies.

2   On the Structure of the Book

In Part 1, Miguel Coelho in the Chapter entitled *Old-age pension systems: Characterization and Comparability* starts with identifying the main old-age pension systems according to three criteria: (i) funded versus unfunded systems (pay-as-you-go—PAYGO), (ii) actuarial versus non-actuarial systems, and (iii) defined benefit (DB) versus defined contribution (DC) systems. The author then compares these various pension models, identifying, from a conceptual perspective, the advantages and disadvantages of each of them, in order to better address common challenges in the EU with regard to the protection of old age citizens in a sustainable manner.

Following this introduction, Hervé Boulhol and Marius Lüske in their Chapter pose the essential question *What's new in the debate about pay-as-you-go vs funded pensions?* In their answer, they start by assuming the actuarial equivalence between PAYGO and funded systems, then explain that the relative benefits and costs of moving away from the former to the latter mostly depend on whether the economy is dynamically efficient. The authors then stress that while the economic condition of dynamic efficiency (financial returns on pension assets higher that the rate of economic growth, $r > g$) was fulfilled in the past, the current economic scenario—with the perseverance of low interest rates—questions this assumption. Moreover, they point out that the benefits of risk-diversification should be weighed against the medium-term costs generated by the transition towards a multi-pillar system.

In turn, Yves Stevens, in the Chapter entitled *The role of the government in creating or enhancing access to funded or unfunded pensions in a modern welfare state* reflects on the financing techniques of funded or unfunded schemes not only from the classical point of view of risk sharing but also from the more historically and ideologically basis of different notions of pensions and their underlying meaning and/or significance. 'Pension' is a polysemic concept, with considerable variability of meanings across the world, leading to what the author names a 'national pension identity'. This different interpretation of the concept shapes different approaches to pension system reforms, whether systemic or parametric reforms. Indeed, as explained by the author, this "national pension identity' immediately explains why there are no so-called good or bad pension systems in the world from an ideological (or political) point of view. All pension systems reflect an identity that has historically (and ideologically) been shaped. This is also the reason why pension reforms are more successful when they are parametric instead of fundamentally and structurally reshaping the entire pension infrastructure."

In turn, Maria Teresa Garcia, in her Chapter entitled *The coverage of occupational and personal pension plans* analyses recent trends in both occupational and personal plans, highlighting in the former case the on-going shift from defined-benefit (DB) to defined-contribution (DC) plans, and identifying the main factors that can explain this modification.

Part 1 closes with the Chapter *Sustainability and adequacy of various pension systems across the OECD: shocks, robustness and policies.* The author, Falilou Fall, addresses the main challenges with which pension systems are today (and in the near future) confronted, investigating in particular the impact of demographic shocks both regarding the adequacy and sustainability of different types of pension plans. In this regard, automatic adjustment mechanisms are highlighted, as are the roles of prudential regulation and the buffering of reserve funds in the case of shocks.

Ansgar Belke and Philipp Allroggen contribute to Part 2 with the Chapter entitled *The Capital Markets Union: Saving for Retirement and Investing for Growth.* The authors start with a characterization of the capital markets union (CMU), highlighting its two main goals: enhancing investment opportunities across Europe and improving financing options for business. The authors then investigate the current situation in Europe with respect to savings, analysing the impact of the GFC on this matter. Through the CMU, the authors then explain why pension plans can and should be used in Europe to promote more investment and growth.

In the Chapter entitled *Sustainable Pensions for European Citizens: How to close the gap?* Gabriel Bernardino provides a detailed explanation of the challenges faced by pension plans, in the current post-crisis environment, with respect to their design, coverage, investment strategies and pay-out. The author then addresses the importance of increasing regulation and the role of supervisory authorities (in particular the European Insurance and Occupational Pensions Authority—EIOPA) to restore trust in these pension plans and products in the aftermath of the crisis. This is indeed a major condition for these plans to play their typical role of completing the first pillar with a proper and reliable pension provision.

Next, in the Chapter entitled *Welfare gains from a capital market union with capital-funded pensions*, Thomas Davoine and Susanne Forstner analyse the long-run effects for a country introducing a capital-funded pension pillar in two scenarios: The case of separate capital markets, on the one hand, and the case of integrated capital markets (a capital market union), on the other hand. The main conclusion is that, in the long run, the introduction of capital-funded pensions is more attractive in integrated capital markets than in separated capital markets, if other countries in the integrated capital market have pay-as-you-go pension systems.

In a rather innovative fashion, in the Chapter entitled *SeLFIES for Portugal—An Innovative Pan European Retirement Solution*, Robert C. Merton, Arun Muralidhar and Rui Seybert Pinto Ferreira propose a new type of Sovereign Contingent Debt Instrument (SCDI)—named SeLFIES (Standard-of-Living indexed, Forward-starting Income-only Securities)—and explain why this product can be an appropriate solution for countries with the characteristics of Portugal (an indebted economy with an ageing society). In the words of the authors, this new type of bond can greatly simplify retirement planning at the level of basic financial literacy, not only ensuring retirement security, but also improving the government's debt financing and funding for infrastructure.

In the following Chapter, entitled *The pan-European pension product and capital markets union—a way to enhance and complete the Economic and Monetary Union?* Nuno Cunha Rodrigues describes the main features of the PEPP, providing details of certain aspects that are discussed in the context of their application such as 'national compartments' and the problem of PEPP taxation. The author also discusses the role of the PEPP within the creation of the CMU, highlighting its virtues and possible insufficiencies as a way to enhance investment and growth.

In turn, Karel Lannoo, in his Chapter entitled *The final PEPP or how to kill an important EU Commission proposal* criticizes the outcome of the negotiation process regarding PEPP's design. In his opinion, and considering the initial intention—to make of PEPP a true generate large-scale portable, cost-efficient and simple long-term savings product—the final PEPP was disappointing: key elements of the proposal were watered down or replaced in response to heavy pressure from member states and certain organisations.

Closing Part 2, José Castro Caldas, in the Chapter *Deepening financialization within the EU: consequences for pension regimes*, presents a critical view of the process of the creation of the CMU, considering in particular its (negative) consequences for pension regimes. The author starts with an overview of 'financialization' and its meaning, and then focuses on deciphering the CMU as an institutional reconfiguration aimed at removing impediments to the circulation of capital and reviving the role of financial markets in the EU. In the author's opinion, "the revival of finance-friendly views and policies in the EU institutions, after the traumatizing experience of the Global Financial Crisis, is interpreted as the outcome of a political stalemate on 'fiscal unification' which opened the path for the advance of the idea of *private* risk-sharing through finance as a substitute for *public* risk-sharing in a Fiscal Union."

Part 3 opens with a similar insight. In the Chapter entitled *Pensions at a crossroad between social rights and financial markets: Which way to be chosen?*, Nazaré da Costa Cabral analyses two hypothetical alternatives for the future design of pension systems: the individual insurance model and the universal tax-financed model. Although motivated by common drivers—an ageing society and technological revolution—the responses and incentives are substantially (philosophically) different. Ultimately, there is a tension between social rights and financial markets that may end up with the predominance of one over the other. As noted by the author, "in the current (liberalizing) environment and considering past and recent EU policy guidance on this matter—the timidity of the social-rights centred strategy (contained in the European Pillar of Social Rights) in contrast with the impulse given to the development of the Capital Markets Union—may after all mean the triumph of a financial market-driven approach."

In the Chapter *From Paris to Lisbon: The ever-changing European social policy landscape*, Pedro Adão e Silva and Patrícia Cadeiras provide an historical overview of social policy in Europe, since the original Treaties until the present. Although social policy has been considered, since the foundation of the Economic Communities, as instrumental to other economic policies (e.g. trade unions and competition), in recent years, following the financial and economic crisis, European social policy has suffered a backlash and lost (even more) political salience. In these authors' opinion, nowadays the development of European social policy faces dilemmas that are parallel to those with which the European project is confronted. However, the soft nature of European Social Policy may prove to be a major asset to ensure the necessary flexibility in response to the differentiated national impacts of major trends in European societies, from demography to the future of work.

Following this, in the Chapter entitled *Pension reforms after the crisis: bringing adequacy back in the domestic and EU policy equation?* Slavina Spasova, Christos Louvaris Fasois, and Bart Vanhercke discuss the main trends in EU Member State reforms after the 2008 economic and social crisis and the links to the EU discourse on pensions. The authors propose a re-interpretation of the trends described in the Pension Adequacy Report, especially with regards to the conceptualization of adequacy. Then the authors show that Member States' reforms are mostly in line with the evolution of the discourse on pension policies at the EU level covering the years during and after the EU crisis from 2010 to 2019.

The next Chapter, *How to best address pension adequacy and financial sustainability in the context of population ageing. The labour market as a key determinant*, Josef Wöss and Erik Türk challenge conventional wisdom on pension system sustainability, bringing employment and jobs to the centre of the debate. The authors show that improving employment integration across all ages would help to significantly contain the future increase of economic dependency ratios and, thus, significantly support pension adequacy and financial sustainability.

Last, but not least, the closing Chapter *Pensions in the fluid EU-society: challenges for (migrant) workers*, authored by Ivana Vukorepa, Yves Joren and Grega

Strban, should be highlighted. The authors start by explaining how ageing societies and on-demand economies ('society fluidity') can affect pension plans and coordination rules at the EU level, both for the first and the second pillars of social protection. The article then proceeds to focus on three interlinked aspects: (1) necessary changes in pension systems due to new working arrangements, (2) the appropriateness of EU legislation on free movement and social security coordination in relation to public and supplementary (occupational) pension schemes, and (3) the importance of combating fraud and error.

Nazaré da Costa Cabral holds a license degree (1994), a Masters (1998), and a PhD (2007) in law, from Lisbon School of Law (Faculdade de Direito, Universidade de Lisboa), and she holds a license degree in economics (2015), from Nova SBE—School of Business and Economics (Universidade Nova de Lisboa).

Nazaré is Associate Professor in tenure, in Lisbon School of Law.

She also lectures in other Universities, either in Portugal or abroad.

Nazaré is principal researcher of the Center for European, Economic, Fiscal and Tax Law Research (CIDEFF) of Lisbon School of Law (Group IV on 'Crises, Public Policies, Fiscal Policy and the Euro'). She is also a member of the Board of 'Instituto de Direito Económico, Financeiro e Fiscal' (IDEFF), of the same School, in which she also lectures. Nazaré is vice-president of the journal Revista de Finanças Públicas e Direito Fiscal (Public Finances and Tax Law Journal), published by IDEFF and Almedina Editors. She is also a member of the Executive and Editorial Board of the journal Concorrência and Regulação (Competition and Regulation), published by The Portuguese Competition Authority, IDEFF and Almedina Editors, and a member of the Editorial Board of the journal Economia and Segurança Social (Economics and Social Security), published by Diário de Bordo Editores.

Nazaré is author of several books, articles and working papers, and her research areas are mainly on Public Finances, Economic and Monetary Union, and Social Security.

Professional experience:

2019—Appointed by the Portuguese Government as Chair of the Senior Board of the Portuguese Public Finance Council.

2018—Appointed as a member of High-level Group of Experts on Pensions, by the Director-General for Employment, Social Affairs and Inclusion and the Director-General for Financial Stability, Financial Services and Capital Markets Union (under Commission decision C(2017) 8523 of 18.12.2017 setting up a High-level group of experts on pensions).

2018—National expert at the EU project MoveS ('Network of independent experts in the fields of free movement of workers (FMW) and social security coordination").

2015–2017—National expert at the EU project FreSsco ('Network of Experts on Intra-EU Mobility—Free Movement of Workers and Social Security Coordination').

2015–2016—National expert at the EU project, developed by a scientific consortium led by CEPS (Centre for European Policy Studies) to the European Commission, and entitled 'National feasibility assessment of the different European unemployment benefit scheme options'.

2014—Appointed by the Ministry of State and Finance to integrate the Working Group charged with the reform of the Portuguese 'Budget Framework Law'.

1997–2002 and 2005–2007—Legal adviser in the Labor and Social Security Minister and Secretary of State Offices.

Nuno Cunha Rodrigues Bachelor (1995); Master in Laws (2003) and PhD (2012) in Law by the Faculty of Law of the University of Lisbon.

Associate Professor of the Faculty of Law of the University of Lisbon (FDL).

Non-executive member of the Board of Directors of Caixa Geral de Depósitos. Lawyer.

Vice-President of the European Institute of the FDL.

Investigator and Deputy Director of CIDEEFF (Center for Research in European Law, Economic, Financial and Fiscal).

Editor and member of the Advisory Board of the Journal of Competition and Regulation.

Member of the Editorial Committee of the Journal of Public Finance and Tax Law.

Member of the Scientific Council of the Faculty of Law of the University of Lisbon.

Coordinator of the Jean Monnet (Erasmus +) module on Public Procurement, conferred by the European Commission (2015–2018).

Member of the Advisory Board of the Journal of Regulation & Competition.

Member Editorial Committee of the Journal of Public Finance and Tax Law.

Member of the Procurement Law Network.

Holder of a Jean Monnet Chair, awarded by the European Commission (since 2018).

Author of several books, articles and papers in the field of EU Law; Competition Law; Public Procurement; Economic Regulation and Public Finance.

Part I
Pay-as-you-go Versus Funded Pension Plans: Which Way to Better Address Common Challenges in the EU?

Old-Age Pension Systems: Characterization and Comparability

Miguel Coelho

Abstract Old-age pension systems can be classified according to three aspects: funded versus unfunded systems (pay-as-you-go), actuarial versus non-actuarial systems, and defined benefit (DB) versus defined contribution (DC) systems.

Several European countries have (or had) public old-age pension schemes with defined benefits, financed by a pay-as-you-go (PAYGO) scheme, where old-age pensions are determined by a formula not related to actuarial principles.

However, given the existence of several structural problems, such as the decrease in employment, ageing of the population and decline in fertility rates, these systems have reached their maturity, showing certain signs of difficulties as regards sustainability and/or the capacity to meet social goals.

In this context, in order to guarantee the sustainability of the systems, some countries have introduced structural reforms in their pension system architecture adopting alternative solutions as regards the funding of the system and/or the calculation of the pension benefit value.

This article intends to compare the main pension models, trying to identify, from a conceptual perspective, the advantages and disadvantages of each one of them, in order to identify how to better address common challenges in the EU with regard to the protection of old age citizens in a sustainable manner.

1 Introduction

The main objective of Social Security is to smoothe consumption profiles over a person's lifetime and to reduce the poverty rate particularly among the elderly. According to Rofman (2005) "this vision is the synthesis of two initially distinct criteria, seeking to replace earned income or to reduce poverty, respectively". Given

M. Coelho (✉)
Universidade Lusíada, Lisbon, Portugal
e-mail: mtcoelho@montepio.pt

© Springer Nature Switzerland AG 2019
N. da Costa Cabral, N. Cunha Rodrigues (eds.), *The Future of Pension Plans in the EU Internal Market*, Financial and Monetary Policy Studies 48,
https://doi.org/10.1007/978-3-030-29497-7_2

11

these objectives, the "pure" systems could be classified as contributive and non-contributive".[1]

Contributive old-age pension systems can be traditionally classified according to three aspects: funded *versus* unfunded systems; defined benefit *versus* defined contribution systems; and actuarial *versus* non-actuarial systems (see Lindbeck and Persson 2003).

The first aspect is the degree of funding (which is a continuous variable).[2] In this aspect we make a distinction between a funded and an unfunded system (pay-as-you-go system—PAYGO). In a funded system the pension benefits are financed by a pool of assets (usually the contributions from current workers are used to accumulate assets and these assets are used in part or in full to pay benefits in the future) whereas a PAYGO system is financed by current contributions from the working population (its main feature is intergenerational solidarity).

The second aspect of analysis is related to "adjustment methods to financial realizations" (Diamond 2006), and can be divided into defined contribution (DC) and defined benefit (DB) schemes. According to Lindbeck (2006), in the first scheme (DC) "the contribution rate is fixed, which means that the pension benefits must be (endogenously) adjusted from time to time to ensure that the pension system remains financially viable" and the second scheme (DB) "promises either a lump-sum pension benefit or a specific relationship between earnings and subsequent pension benefits (often expressed as a promised replacement rate)".

The third aspect is related to the actuarial fairness of the system. A pension system is completely nonactuarial if there is no link between the individual's own contributions and his or her future pension benefits (Lindbeck 2006). On the other hand, a pension system is actuarial if "the capital value of the individual's expected pension benefits is equal to the capital value of his or her own contribution" (Lindbeck 2006).

Figure 1 shows the taxonomy of an old-age pension system that can be illustrated by the extreme points (I–VIII).

Position I corresponds to an unfunded (PAYGO) and non-actuarial old-age pension system with defined benefits (An example of this kind of system is the Portuguese old-age pension system).[3]

---

[1]The main objective of a contributive scheme is to replace the income of those who leave the market for reasons of age and is financed by the participants (current or former participants). On the other hand, non-contributive systems usually take the form of public programmes for the alleviation of poverty, invalidity or sickness in old age and their financing should come from general taxation not linked to the labour market.

[2]According to Valdés-Prieto (2002), the "degree of funding is obtained dividing the market value of the pension fund by the expected discount value of accrued liabilities on the same date".

[3]In Portugal, old-age individuals with at least 15 years of earnings are entitled to an earnings-related pension (contributory system). The calculation of pensions is based on the number of contribution years and the average wage of the employee (however, there is no actuarial analysis to calculate pension benefits, with the exception of the so-called sustainability factor where the pension benefit has been adjusted in accordance with the evolution of average life expectancy of the Portuguese population since 2007).

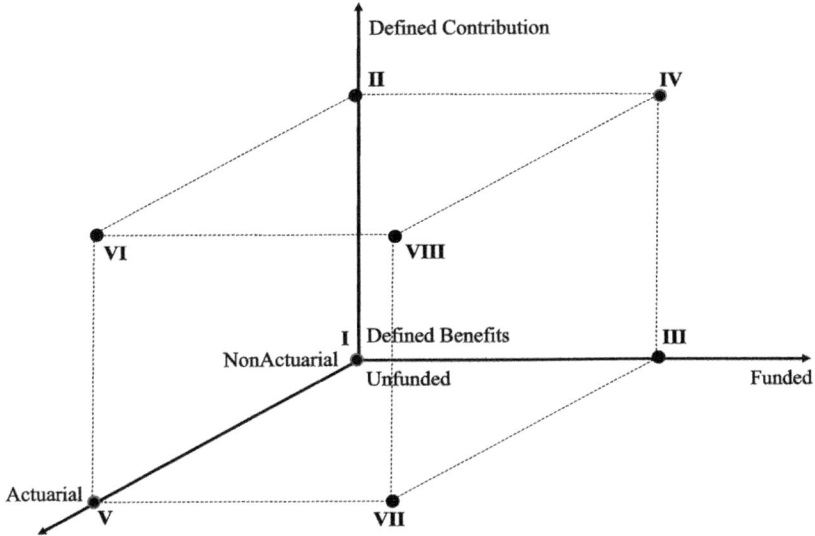

Fig. 1 Taxonomy of old-age pension system. Source: Based on Lindbeck and Persson (2003) proposal

The other extreme position (Position VIII), corresponds to a funded system with defined contributions and where the pension benefits are calculated with actuarial fairness. An example of this kind of system may be seen in some private pension funds where the employees make a regular and constant contribution to the pension fund and when reaching retirement age an annuity is calculated based on a mortality table and a discount rate (appropriate to the mortality and interest rate conditions on that date).

An unfunded (PAYGO) notional defined contribution (NDC)[4] system may be found between Position II and Position VI, because it is a quasi-actuarial system insofar as the individual's pensioner contributions may be registered in an abstract (notional) account and capitalized over time through a composite capitalization rate, rather than an actual financial account capitalized over time through a market discount rate.[5]

---

[4]An example of an NDC system is the Swedish model where part of the contributions of employees/firms are transferred to an account of the beneficiary (abstract or notional account), which is capitalized over time through a composite capitalization rate (incorporating, among other variables, the growth rate of the economy). The accumulated value (Notional) is transformed at retirement date into an annuity according to actuarial rules prevailing at the time—Defined Contribution systems. The payment of the annuity is made through the contributions of employees/employer in business—a PAYGO system.

[5]The Swedish system of notional accounts has a buffer fund that is financed by the surplus between contributions and pension disbursements and charged in the opposite situation. This Fund consists of financial assets that are invested in capital markets and therefore are credited or debited depending on their gains or losses, respectively (The Portuguese system also has a buffer fund).

It is important to highlight that several European countries have (or had) public old-age pension schemes of defined benefits, financed as a pay-as-you-go (PAYGO) scheme, whereby old-age pension is determined by a formula unrelated to actuarial principles (Position I in Fig. 1).

However, given the existence of several structural problems, such as the decrease in employment, the ageing of the population and the decline in fertility rates, these systems have reached their maturity showing certain signs of difficulties with regard to sustainability (*i.e.*, current flows of contributions are lower than current expenses in pension benefits) and/or the capacity to meet social goals (*i.e.*, a pension benefit is insufficient to maintain the living standard of the pensioner).

In this context, in order to guarantee the sustainability of these systems, some European countries have introduced structural reforms within their pension system architecture, adopting alternative solutions as regards the funding of the system and/or the calculation of the pension benefit value.

This article compares the main pension systems, trying to identify, from a conceptual perspective, the advantages and disadvantages of each one of them, in order to identify how to best address common challenges in the EU with regard to the protection of old-age citizens in a sustainable manner.

2 Contributive Old-Age Pension Systems: Aspects to Analyse

2.1 Degree of Funding

In this aspect, I make a distinction between an unfunded (PAYGO) and a funded system.

A PAYGO system is financed by current contributions from the working population (its main feature is intergenerational solidarity).

For the purposes of assessing the balanced conditions of a PAYGO system, let us consider the following assumptions:

- One period model;
- Contributors (beneficiaries) of the system represented by a representative employee (pensioner);
- Contributions to the system are a fraction (k) of the annual gross average wage (W) of the employee (*i.e.*, contribution rate);
- Pension benefits are a fraction (δ) of the annual gross average wage (W) of the employee (*i.e.*, replacement rate);
- The payment of pension benefits depends on the existence of revenues from the contributions to the old-age pension system (*i.e.*, no transfers are allowed from the state budget or other sources to the system).

In this context, the system's revenue with contributions (C) from a representative employee is given by the following expression:

$$C = k \times W \tag{1}$$

The system's overall revenue (R), with the total number of employees in the system (n), is given by:

$$R = n \times k \times W \tag{2}$$

On the other hand, the expenditure of the system with the pension benefit (P) of a representative pensioner is given by:

$$P = \delta \times W \tag{3}$$

The overall expenditure of the system (D) with all the pensioners (m) is given by:

$$D = m \times \delta \times W \tag{4}$$

Given that the system has to be balanced at each moment ($D = R$), and assuming also that the total population (L) corresponds to the sum of employees (n) and pensioners (m), the equilibrium of this is graphically shown in Fig. 2.

With the number of pensioners equal to m_1, the balance of the system ($R = D$) occurs when the number of employees contributing to the system is equal to n_1 (equalling expressions 2 and 4):

$$n \times k \times W = m \times \delta \times W \tag{5}$$

This results in a replacement rate given by:

$$\delta = \frac{n}{m} k \tag{6}$$

Fig. 2 Balance in a PAYGO system. Source: Coelho (2013)

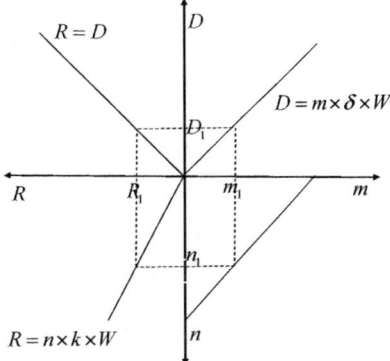

Therefore, for a given replacement rate, contribution rate and number of pensioners, the system will be balanced if the number of employees equals:

$$n = \frac{\delta}{k}m \tag{7}$$

In this context, the System is in imbalance if:

$$n > \frac{\delta}{k}m \rightarrow R > D \; (surplus) \tag{8}$$

$$n < \frac{\delta}{k}m \rightarrow R < D \; (deficit) \tag{9}$$

Graphically, we can represent the (im) balanced situation as follows (Fig. 3):

Based on the steady state given by Eq. 7, the balanced relationship between the number of beneficiaries and employees for different replacement rates (δ) and contribution rates (k), is given in Table 1.

To keep the system in balance, and assuming that the ratio between the number of employees and pensioners (n/m) is constant, the greater the replacement rate, the greater the contribution rate (*i.e.*, the old-age risk component of the global contribution rate).

For instance, with a replacement rate of 45% and a contribution rate of 15%, the system will be balanced only with a ratio of three employees per pensioner. If the replacement rate increases to 75%, in order to maintain the ratio of employees per pensioner constant (3), the contribution rate must rise to 25%.

In the same way, to maintain a constant replacement rate in a context of a declining ratio between employees and pensioners, the contribution rate must be raised.

In this context, assuming that in most developed countries the number of pensioners grows at an increasing rate and the number of employees grows at a

Fig. 3 Balanced relationship between number of employees and pensioners. Source: Coelho (2013)

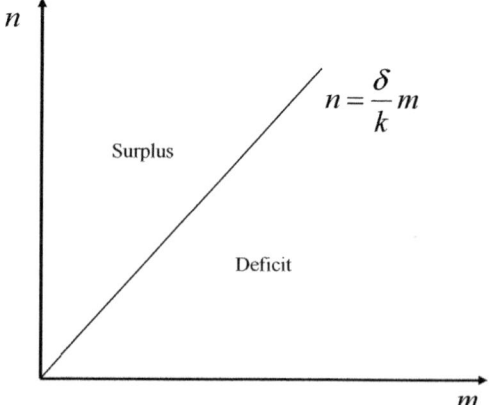

Table 1 Balanced relationship between the number of employees and pensioners (numerical example)

Contribution rate for the system	Replacement rate												
	90%	85%	80%	75%	70%	65%	60%	55%	50%	45%	40%	35%	30%
30%	3.00	2.83	2.67	2.50	2.33	2.17	2.00	1.83	1.67	1.50	1.33	1.17	1.00
29%	3.10	2.93	2.76	2.59	2.41	2.24	2.07	1.90	1.72	1.55	1.38	1.21	1.03
28%	3.21	3.04	2.86	2.68	2.50	2.32	2.14	1.96	1.79	1.61	1.43	1.25	1.07
27%	3.33	3.15	2.96	2.78	2.59	2.41	2.22	2.04	1.85	1.67	1.48	1.30	1.11
26%	3.46	3.27	3.08	2.88	2.69	2.50	2.31	2.12	1.92	1.73	1.54	1.35	1.15
25%	3.60	3.40	3.20	**3.00**	2.80	2.60	2.40	2.20	2.00	1.80	1.60	1.40	1.20
24%	3.75	3.54	3.33	3.13	2.92	2.71	2.50	2.29	2.08	1.88	1.67	1.46	1.25
23%	3.91	3.70	3.48	3.26	3.04	2.83	2.61	2.39	2.17	1.96	1.74	1.52	1.30
22%	4.09	3.86	3.64	3.41	3.18	2.95	2.73	2.50	2.27	2.05	1.82	1.59	1.36
21%	4.29	4.05	3.81	3.57	3.33	3.10	2.86	2.62	2.38	2.14	1.90	1.67	1.43
20%	4.50	4.25	4.00	3.75	3.50	3.25	3.00	2.75	2.50	2.25	2.00	1.75	1.50
19%	4.74	4.47	4.21	3.95	3.68	3.42	3.16	2.89	2.63	2.37	2.11	1.84	1.58
18%	5.00	4.72	4.44	4.17	3.89	3.61	3.33	3.06	2.78	2.50	2.22	1.94	1.67
17%	5.29	5.00	4.71	4.41	4.12	3.82	3.53	3.24	2.94	2.65	2.35	2.06	1.76
16%	5.63	5.31	5.00	4.69	4.38	4.06	3.75	3.44	3.13	2.81	2.50	2.19	1.87
15%	6.00	5.67	5.33	5.00	4.67	4.33	4.00	3.67	3.33	**3.00**	2.67	2.33	2.00

Source: Coelho (2013)

Note: In this table we present the minimum number of employees for each pensioner so that the system is balanced, considering global contribution rates and alternative replacement rates. For example, for a contribution rate of 25% (15%) we will need three employees for each pensioner (values in bold) in order to ensure a pension equal to 75% (45%) of the wage

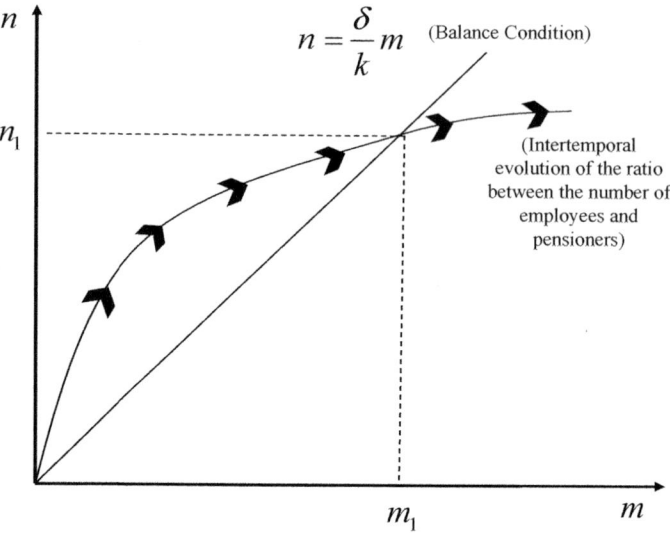

Fig. 4 Balance conditions and intertemporal evolution of the ratio between the number of employees and pensioners. Source: Coelho (2013). Note: This graph represents the state of balance of the System and the estimated intertemporal evolution between the number of employees and pensioners in a developed country

decreasing rate, we will inevitably have an unbalanced situation if we maintain stable replacement rates and contribution rates, as can be observed in Fig. 4.

Population ageing in developed countries, associated with low fertility rates, leads to a deterioration of the ratio between employees and pensioners (n/m). In order to keep the system in balance, *ceteris paribus*, it is necessary to increase the contributory rate (k), and/or to reduce the replacement rate (δ).[6]

In a funded system the pension benefits are financed by a pool of assets (usually the contributions from current workers are used to accumulate assets and these assets are used in part or in full to pay benefits in the future).

To illustrate the mechanics of a funded system, consider the following assumptions:

- Two time-period model: working period (n_w) and retirement period (n_r);
- Contributors (beneficiaries) of the system represented by a representative employee (pensioner);

---

[6]In his model, Samuelson (1958) shows that, if the population grows at a rate of m, the system is able to pay m interest ('biological' interest rate) and pensions can increase accordingly, thus supporting the necessary condition, *ceteris paribus*, for a PAYGO model to be sustainable. According to Banyár (2016) the solution to the longevity problem can be solved by "the regular indexation of the pensionable age" (This has already been introduced in several countries and was also recommended by the European Commission in its Pension White Paper).

- Defined contributions (DC) to the system are a fraction (k) of the annual gross average wage (W) of the employee and are registered in an individual financial account capitalized over time through a market discount rate (i). The individual financial account is collateralized by a pool of assets (*i.e.,* bonds, stocks, real estate, etc);
- The annual gross average wage (W) is constant during the whole working period (n_w);
- Pension benefits are a fraction (δ) of the gross average wage (W) of the employee;
- Contributions to the system and the payment of the pension benefits are made annually (at the end of the year);
- The payment of pension benefits depends on the pool of assets that was built based on the contributions of the pensioners during the working period (*i.e.,* no transfers are allowed from the state budget or other sources to the system).

With these assumptions, the capitalized value of all contributions at retirement age (CV_{n_w}) can be expressed by the following equation:

$$CV_{n_w} = k \times W \frac{(1+i)^{n_w} - 1}{i} \qquad (10)$$

Figure 5 shows the evolution of financial account value over time for different values of the discount rate.

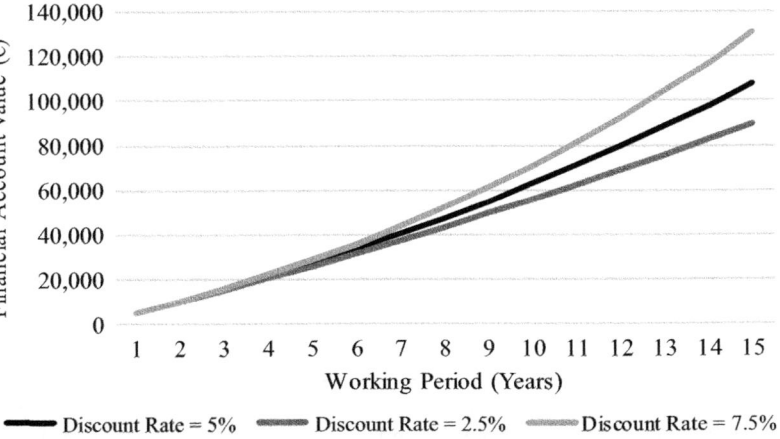

Fig. 5 Evolution of financial account with different discount rates (Working period). Source: Own calculation. Note: Assuming an annual average gross wage (W) of €25,000, a contributive rate (k) of 20%, a working period of 15 years and an discount rate of 5%, the financial account value at retirement age will be €107,893. Once the contributions are allocated to an individual financial account for the pensioner and capitalized over time through a market discount rate, the amount allocated to the payment of pension benefits at retirement age will be €107,893. For the same contributive rate and wage, a change in the discount rate has a significant impact on the evolution on the financial account value. With a discount rate below (above) 5% the financial account value, at the end of the 15th year, it will be below (above) €107,893

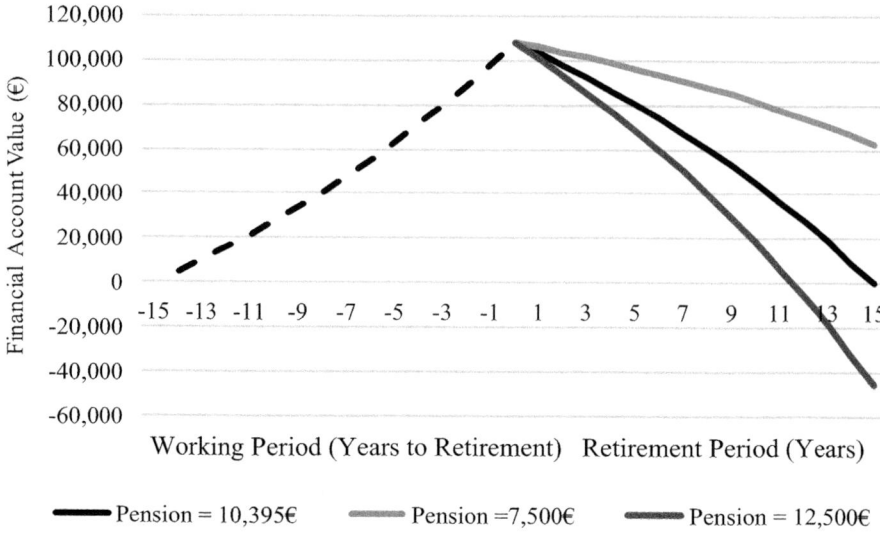

Fig. 6 Evolution of financial account for different values of pension benefits. Source: Own calculation. Note: Assuming a financial account value at retirement age equal to €107,893, a discount rate equal to 5% in the retirement period and a longevity of the pensioner after retirement of 15 years, the system's ability to pay pensions fully depends on the value of the pension benefits. With annual pension benefits equal to (or below) €10,395 the system is sustainable. On the other hand, with annual pension benefits above €10,395 the system is unsustainable (with annual pension benefits of €12,500 the system collapses in the 12th year)

As we can see, changes in the discount rate, *ceteris paribus*, will have an impact on the evolution of the financial account value. An increase (decrease) in the discount rate raises (reduces) the financial account value.

On the other hand, in a funded pension system, the payment of pension benefits is conditional on the existing financial account value (collateralized by a pool of assets) Fig. 6.

For a given financial account value at retirement age, discount rate in the retirement period and life expectancy, the ability of a funded system to pay pensions fully depends on the value of the pension benefits. This means that for pension benefits above a certain value the system becomes unsustainable.

In short, in a PAYGO system the equilibrium of the system for a certain contributory and replacement rate depends on the relationship between the number of employees (contributors to the system) and the number of pensioners (beneficiaries of the system), which means that it depends on intergenerational solidarity.

On the other hand, a funded system does not appeal to intergenerational solidarity, given that the pool of asset that supports the payment of pension benefits to the pensioners was built based on the contributions of those pensioners (during their working period). In this kind of system, the payment of pension benefits will cease when the pool of assets is exhausted.

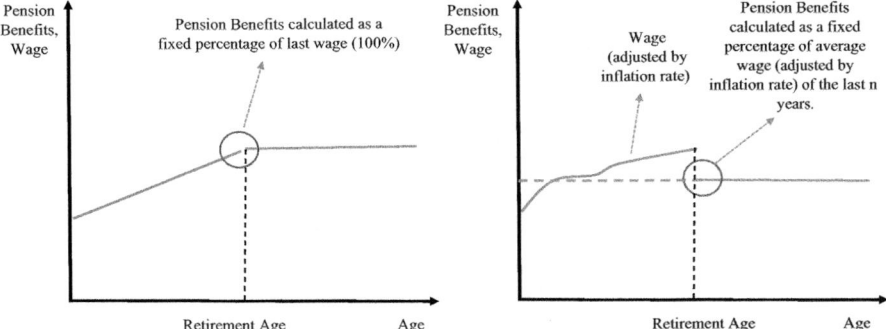

Fig. 7 Wage and pension benefits in a non-actuarial system. Source: Own calculation. Note: This figure, shows two examples of a non-actuarial old-age pension system. In some systems the pension benefits are calculated as a percentage (in some cases 100%) of the last wage (left-hand figure). In other systems the value of pension benefits is calculated as a percentage of average wage (adjusted for the inflation rate) of the last n years (right-hand figure)

2.2 Actuarial Fairness

Regarding the actuarial fairness of the system, we can distinguish two schemes: non-actuarial versus actuarial systems.

A pension system is completely non-actuarial if there is no link between the individual's own contributions and his or her future pensions benefits (Lindbeck 2006) (Fig. 7).

In this type of system, the value of pension benefits is usually calculated as a fixed percentage of the last wage or a fixed percentage of the average wage (adjusted for the inflation rate).

A pension system is actuarial if "the capital value of the individual's expected pension benefits is equal to the capital value of his or her own contributions" (Lindbeck 2006).

To illustrate the mechanics of an actuarial system, consider the following assumptions:

- Two-time periods model: working period (n_w) and retirement period (n_r);
- Contributors (beneficiaries) of the system represented by a representative employee (pensioner);
- The life expectancy of the representative pensioner is well known on the date of retirement and is equal to the retirement period (n_r);
- Defined contribution (DC) to the system is a fraction (k) of the annual gross average wage (W) of the employee and is registered in the individual financial account capitalized over time through a market discount rate (i);

- The annual gross average wage (W) is constant during the whole working period (n_w);
- Pension benefits are a fraction (δ) of the gross average wage (W) of the employee;
- Contributions to the system and the payment of pension benefits are made annually (at the end of the calendar year);
- The payment of pension benefits depends on the pool of assets that was built based on the contributions of the pensioners during their working period (*i.e.* no transfers are allowed from the state budget or other sources to the system);
- The capital value of the individual's expected pension benefits (PV_{n_r}) is equal to the capital value of his or her own contributions (CV_{n_w}), which means that pension benefits (in a DC system) must be endogenously adjusted from time to time in order to guarantee this equality.

With these assumptions, the capitalized value of all the contributions at retirement age (CV_{n_r}) can be expressed by the following Eq. [11]:

$$CV_{n_w} = k \times W \frac{(1+i)^{n_w} - 1}{i} \tag{11}$$

On the other hand, the capital value of the individual's expected pension benefits at retirement age (PV_{n_r}) can be expressed by the following equation:

$$PV_{n_r} = \delta \times W \frac{1 - (1+i)^{-n_r}}{i} \tag{12}$$

Given that on retirement date in an actuarial system the capital value of the individual's expected pension benefits (PV_{n_r}) must be equal to the capital value of his or her own contributions (CV_{n_w}), the replacement rate (δ) is given by the following equation:

$$\delta = \frac{CV_{n_w}}{W \frac{1-(1+i)^{-n_r}}{i}} \tag{13}$$

In financial terms, on retirement date, the financial account value (collateralized by the pool of assets) must be equal to the capital value of the individual's expected pension benefits.[7] The financial account value will progressively decrease as the pension payments are made and will be exhausted on the date of death of the beneficiary (if the discount rate and the retirement period used for the calculation correspond to reality).

---

[7]The financial account value (collateralized by a pool of assets) corresponds (approximately), for a life insurance company, to mathematical provisions (*i.e.* the difference between the present value of all future obligations of life insurance contracts and the present value of future policy-holder obligations on these contracts).

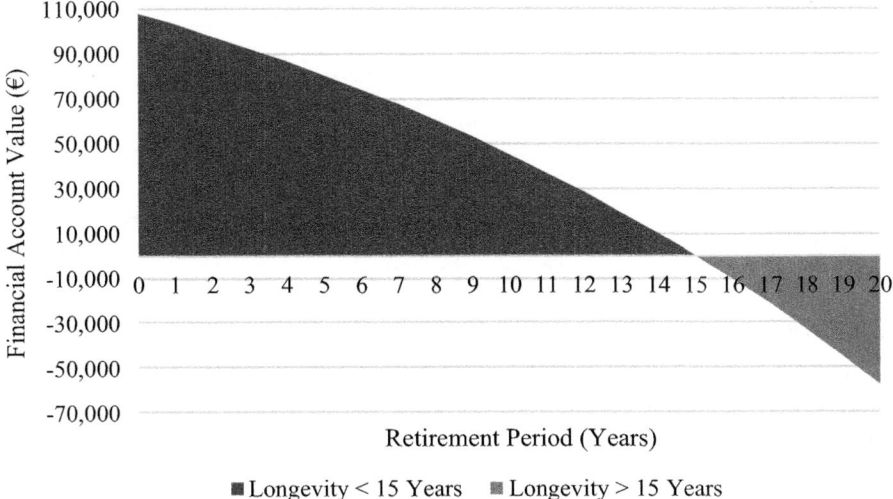

Fig. 8 Evolution of the financial account with changes in life expectancy. Source: Own calculation. Note: Assuming that the financial account value on retirement date is €107,893, the life expectancy is 15 years and the discount rate is 5%, the value of pension benefits (actuarial) will be €10,395 (annuity) and the pool of assets (financial account value) will be consumed by the end of the 15th year. For the same annuity, a change in life expectancy has a significant impact on the balance of old-age pension systems. If the longevity of pensioners is higher (lower) than 15 years, the old-age pension system will be in deficit (surplus)

The financial account value in year n_r (FA_{n_r}), can be expressed by the following equation:

$$FA_{n_r} = CV_{n_w}(1 + i)^{n_r} - (\delta \times W) \sum_{t=1}^{n_r} (1 + i)^{t-1} \qquad (14)$$

Figure 8 shows the evolution of the financial account value (that will decrease as the payments of pension benefits are made) with changes in life expectancy.

For a certain financial account value at retirement age, an increase (decrease) in life expectancy, *ceteris paribus*, has a negative (positive) impact on the sustainability of the old-age pension system. Figure 9 shows the evolution of the financial account value considering different discount rate levels, *ceteris paribus*.

As we can see, in an actuarial system, if the "actual" discount rate (*i.e.,* discount rate that is actually observed) is higher (lower) than the discount rate that was used to calculate the pension benefits, the financial account value will be (will not be) enough to keep the system balanced.

Considering the above, it is clear that the calculation of the value of pension benefits is important to ensure the sustainability of the system. In fact, for a given financial account value on retirement date, an increase (decrease) of life expectancy

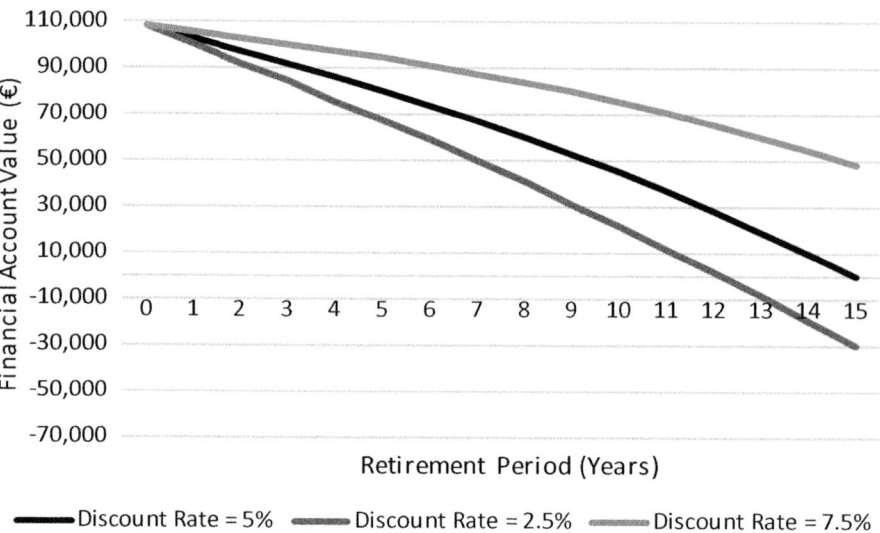

Fig. 9 Evolution of the financial account with changes in discount rate. Source: Own calculation. Note: Assuming that, on retirement date, the financial account value is €107,893; life expectancy is 15 years; and the discount rate is 5%, the value of pension benefits (actuarial) will be €10,395 (annuity) and the pool of assets (financial account value) will be consumed by the end of the 15th year. For the same annuity, a change in the discount rate has a significant impact on the evolution of the financial account value. With a discount rate below (above) 5%, the financial account value, at the end of the 15th year, will be below (above) zero, which means that the old-age pension system will be in deficit (surplus)

and/or a decrease (increase) in the discount rate implies a decrease (increase) in the value of pension benefits to restore the actuarial balance.

In short, in a non-actuarial system there is no relationship between contributions and pension benefits. In this type of system, the life expectancy of the pensioner, the level of contributions or the discount rate do not affect the pension benefits (that are usually calculated based on wage).

On the contrary, in an actuarial system the pension benefits depend positively on the discount rate and the contributions made by the pensioner to the system and, negatively, on the expected longevity of the pensioner.

2.3 Adjustment Methods to Financial Realizations

The "adjustment methods to financial realizations" (Diamond 2006) can be divided into a defined contributions (DC) and a defined benefits (DB) system.

According to Lindbeck (2006), in a defined contribution system (DC) "the contribution rate is fixed, which means that the pension benefits must be

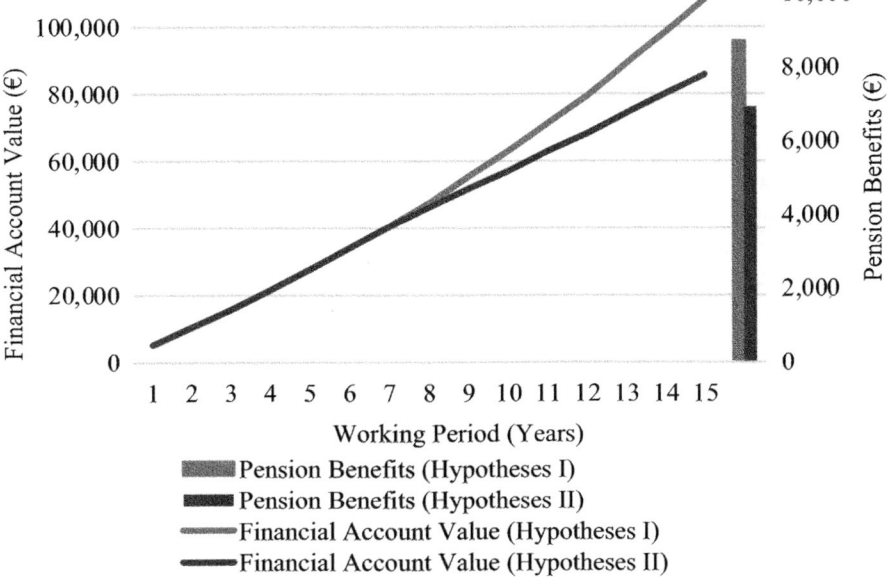

Fig. 10 Evolution of the financial account and pension benefits (DC System). Source: Own calculation. Note: With a fixed contribution value, the pension benefits must be (endogenously) adjusted from time to time, in response to changes in interest rate and longevity, to ensure that the pension system remains financially viable. With an annual contribution of €5000 and a discount rate of 5%, the financial account value in the 15th year will be €107,893. For a longevity of 15 years and a discount rate of 2.5% (during the retirement period), the annual pension benefits will be €8714 (Hypotheses I). With an annual contribution of €5000 and a discount rate of 5% (1%) during the first 7 years (during the second 8-year period), the financial account value in the 15th year will be €85,512. In this situation, for a longevity of 15 years and a discount rate of 2.5% (during the retirement period), the annual pension benefits will decrease to €6907 (Hypotheses II)

(endogenously) adjusted from time to time to ensure that the pension system remains financially viable".

To illustrate this, consider the assumptions of an actuarial system (see Sect. 2.2) with defined contributions (DC). Figure 10 shows the evolution of the financial account value in two scenarios (hypotheses I and II) as well as the associated pension benefits.

As expressed in Fig. 10, the evolution of the financial account value, *ceteris paribus*, has an impact on the value of pension benefits. For example, a decrease (increase) in the interest rate during the working period, *ceteris paribus*, will reduce (raise) the financial account value and, consequently, will reduce (raise) the pension benefits at retirement age.

According to Lindbeck (2006), a defined benefit system (DB) "promises either a lump-sum pension benefit or a specific relationship between earnings and subsequent pension benefits (often expressed as a promised replacement rate)". In this context, and assuming that the pension benefit is calculated with actuarial fairness, the contribution to the system must be (endogenously) adjusted from time to time to ensure that the pension system remains financially viable.

Figure 11 expresses the evolution of the financial account value in two scenarios (hypotheses I and II) as well the contributive effort of the employee (consider the assumptions of an actuarial system with defined benefits expressed in Sect. 2.2).

As expressed in Fig. 11, a decrease (increase) in the discount rate must be compensated for by an increase (decrease) in contributions in order to maintain the pension benefit unchanged. Likewise, an increase (decrease) in life expectancy after retirement, *ceteris paribus*, must be compensated for by an increase (decrease) in contributions and/or an increase (decrease) in the working period.[8]

In short, in a defined contribution (DC) system, given that "the pension benefits must be (endogenously) adjusted from time to time to ensure that the pension system remains financially viable" (Lindbeck 2006), the uncertainty occurs on retirement date as it is only then that the pensioner knows the value of the pension benefits that he or she will receive.

On the other hand, in a defined benefit system (DB), the uncertainty occurs during the working period if the pension benefit is calculated with actuarial fairness, given that the contribution to the system must be (endogenously) adjusted to ensure that the pension system remains financially viable.

3 Comparison of Old-Age Pension Systems

3.1 *The Unfunded Versus Funded System: An Example*

From a numerical point of view, to explain the difference between the two extreme examples of old-age pension systems (Points I and VIII in Fig. 1), I considered the actual case of a worker who made social security contributions for 41 years and retired in August 2007 (Individual A).[9]

---

[8]An equivalent conclusion could be reached with a PAYGO system with defined benefits if we assume actuarial fairness. In fact, the impact of a reduction in the discount rate on the value of contributions during the working period is "equivalent" to the effect of a future deterioration in the relationship between the number of employees and the number of pensioners, *ceteris paribus*. On the other hand, a future deterioration in the relationship between the number of employees and the number of pensioners, *ceteris paribus*, will create an implied debt in the system that in the future will correspond to real debt. This system's implied debt can be compensated for by an increase in current contributions which can be used to reduce the current public debt, and consequently, reduce future public debt.

[9]Individual A it is a real pensioner of the Portuguese social security system who retired on 26 August 2007. The total amount of remuneration received by the worker during his/her 41-year working life (adjusted for inflation) corresponded to €1,003,662.02 (€1,002,244.85 during the last 40 years).

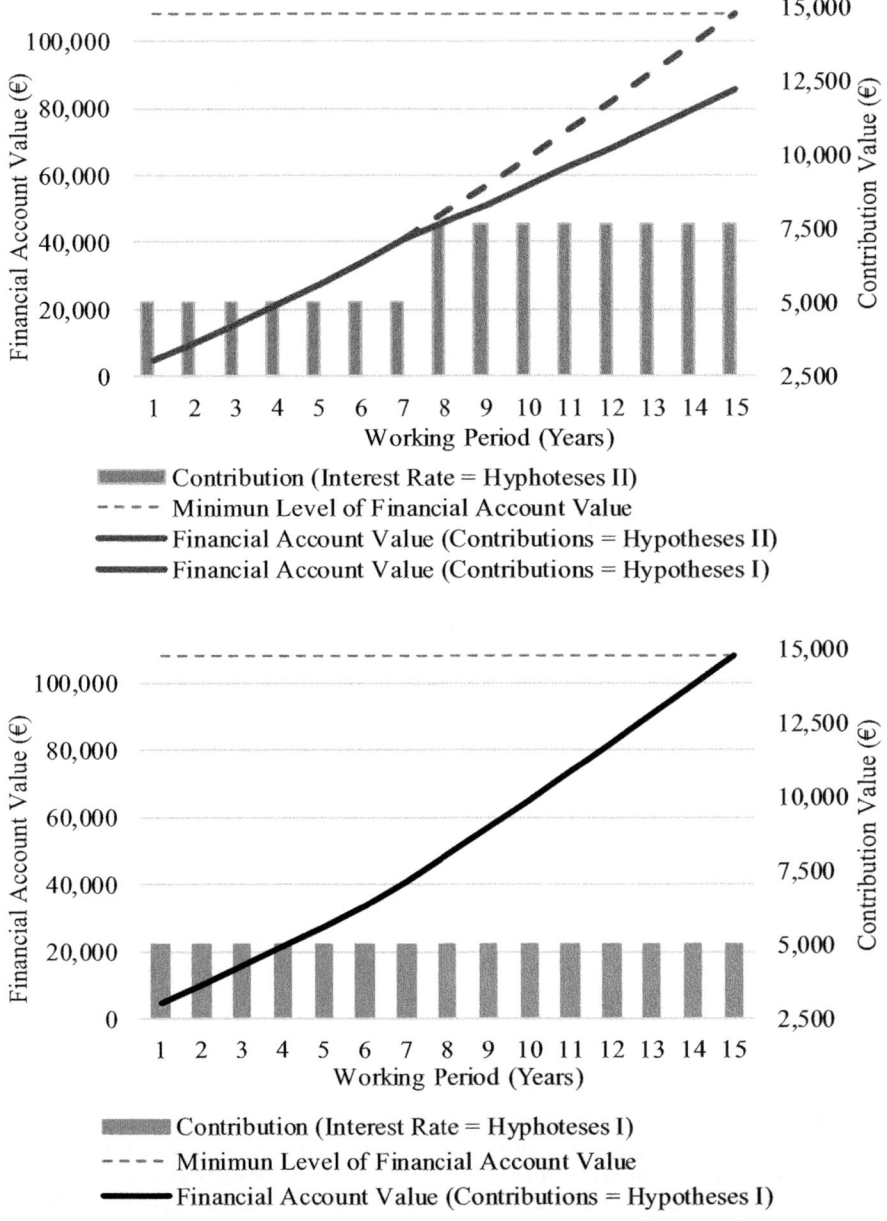

Fig. 11 Evolution of the financial account and contributions (DB System). Source: Own calculation. Note: With a defined benefit, the contribution to the system must be (endogenously) adjusted from time to time to ensure that the pension system remains financially viable. Consider (left-hand graph) that the required financial account value to generate annual pension benefits of €8714 is equal to €107,893 (this value was obtained with an annual contribution of €5000, assuming an

3.1.1 Unfunded, Defined Benefits and Non-actuarial System

To illustrate an unfunded (PAYGO) and non-actuarial system with defined benefits, the formula for calculating the old-age pension was considered in accordance with Decree-Law No 187/2007 of 10 May (pensions starting up to 31 December 2016 with social security registration until 31 December 2001).

$$Pension\ Benefits = \frac{P_1 \times n_w^1 + P_2 \times n_w^2}{n_w} \qquad (15)$$

Where P_1 corresponds to the pension benefits calculated according to the best 10 years of the last 15 years of discounts; P_2 to the pension benefits calculated according to the whole working period with a cap of 40 years; n_w^1 to the working period (in years) until 31 December 2006; n_w^2 to the working period (in years) after 1 January 2007; and n_w the number of years of social security contributions.

$$P_1 = RR_1 \times 2\% \times n_w = \frac{TR_{10/15}}{140} \times 2\% \times n_w \qquad (16)$$

Where RR_1 corresponds to reference earnings (wage) of subperiod 1 and $TR_{10/15}$ to the sum of wages (adjusted for inflation) of the best 10 years of the last 15 years of contributions.[10]

$$P_2 = (1.1IAS \times 2.3\% \times n_w) + (0.9IAS \times 2.25\% \times n_w)$$
$$+ (2IAS \times 2.2\% \times n_w) + [(RR_2 - 4IAS) \times 2.1\% \times n_w] \qquad (17)$$

Where $RR_2 = TR/(n_w \times 14)$ corresponds to the reference earnings (wage) for the whole working period; TR to the sum of wages (adjusted for inflation) for the whole working period with a limit of 40 years; and IAS the Index of Social Support.

Based on data relating to Individual A, the amount of the pension benefit according to Decree-Law No. 187/2007 of 10 May shall be calculated on the basis of components P_1 and P_2:

Fig. 11 (continued) interest rate of 5% for 15 years—Hypotheses I). With a decrease in the discount rate, *ceteris paribus*, the financial account value at the end of the period will decrease, forcing a reduction in the pension benefits. However, since we have a defined benefit, the endogenous variable is the contribution to the system. To maintain the pension benefit (right-hand graph), in a context of a reduction in the discount rate from the 8th to the 15th year from 5% to 1%, the annual contribution to the system must increase from €5000 to €7701 in the same period (Hypotheses II)

---

[10] $P_1 \leq 12 \times IAS$

$$P_1 = \frac{€441,591}{140} \times 2\% \times 40 = €3154 \times 2\% \times 40 = €2523 \qquad (18)$$

$$P_2 = (1.1(€397.86) \times 2.3\% \times 40) + (0.9(€397.86) \times 2.25\% \times 40)$$

$$+ (2(€397.86) \times 2.2\% \times 40) + \left[\left(\frac{€1,002,244}{40 \times 14} - 4\,(€397.86) \right) \times 2.1\% \times 40 \right]$$

$$= €1591 \qquad (19)$$

Thus, the monthly amount of the pension benefits will be:

$$Pension\ Benefits = \frac{€2523 \times 40 + €1591 \times 1}{41} = €2500 \qquad (20)$$

Assuming that in Portugal a monthly payment of €2500 is made 14 times a year, the annual pension benefits will be €35,000.

3.1.2 Funded, Defined Contribution and Actuarial System

To illustrate a funded and actuarial system with defined contributions, we will consider that the contributions to the system (old-age risk component)[11] are registered in an individual financial account capitalized over time through a discount rate (i).[12]

The capitalized value of all contributions at retirement age (CV_{n_w}), calculated according Eq. [10] is transformed into an annuity (R), according to the following formula:

$$R = \frac{CV_{n_w}}{a_x^{(m)}} \qquad (21)$$

Where $(a_x^{(m)})$ is expressed through the following equation:

$$a_x^{(m)} = \frac{N_{x+1}}{D_x} + \frac{m-1}{2 \times m} \qquad (22)$$

---

[11]In Portugal the overall contributory rate is 34.75 percentage points (p.p.) (23.75 p.p. for employees and 11 p.p. for employers) and the old-age risk component is 20.1 p.p. (excluding administrative costs), according to Law No. 110/2009, 16 September. The old-age risk component, excluding administrative costs, was 13.34 p.p. between 1993 and 1998 (Decree Law No. 326/93, 25 September), and 15.57 p.p. between 1999 and 2009 (Decree Law No. 200/99, 8 June. It should be noted that before 2000 there was no breakdown of the overall rate. In this context, we will assume in our example that the contributions to the system (old-age risk component) correspond to 13.34 p.p. of the wage between 1967 and 1998 and 15.57 p.p. between 1999 and 2007.

[12]It is assumed that the discount rate is equal to the monetary adjustment factor published annually by the Portuguese Government.

With N_x and D_x equal to:

$$N_x = \sum_{k=0}^{w-x} D_{x+k} \tag{23}$$

$$D_x = I_x \times v^x = [I_{x-1} - (I_{x-1})(q_{x-1})] \times v^x \tag{24}$$

Where x corresponds to the age of the pensioner at retirement age, w to the maximum age in the mortality table; m is the number of payments of the pension in a year ($m = 1, 2, 3, 4, 6$ or 12); i the discount rate; v to the discount factor ($v = 1/(1 + i)$) and q_x to the probability of the pensioner dying before the end of age x, assuming that the pensioner is alive at the beginning of that age x.

Considering the data of Individual A,[13] assuming an annual discount rate equal to 3% and the TV 99/01 mortality table, the annual pension benefit (with m = 1) according to Eq. [25] will be:

$$R = \frac{C}{a_{65}^{(1)}} = \frac{€142,433}{14.69169} = €9695 \tag{25}$$

If we assume that the annual discount rate is 2% (4%), the annual pension benefits in a funded and actuarial system with defined contributions will be €8709 (€10,725).

When we compare these values with those obtained in a PAYGO system like the Portuguese for the same Individual A (annual pension benefit of €35,000), we can conclude that the pensioner will suffer a decrease in pension benefits of more than 70% (this means that with the new system the capitalized value of the contributions must increase 3.5 times, from €142,433 to €498,515 to maintain the annual benefits of the Portuguese PAYGO system).

Even if we assume that the entire contribution rate is used to pay old-age pension benefits,[14] with a discount rate of 3%, the annual pension benefits are €23,739[15] (32% below the value calculated according to Portuguese PAYGO rules).

3.2   Advantages and Disadvantages of Alternative Systems

The determinants of income and expenditure of the social security system have undergone profound changes in recent years. In fact, according to Billari (2016),

---

[13]The capitalized value of contributions at retirement age is €142,433. The retirement age of the pensioner was 65 years of age.

[14]Assuming a global contribution rate of 34.75 p.p., the capitalized value of the contribution at retirement age is €348,773.

[15]If we assume that the annual discount rate is 2% (4%), the annual pension benefits in a funded actuarial system with a defined contribution will be €21,325 (€26,263).

"European societies face profound demographic changes with effects that are both immediate and enduring. These changes include accelerated population ageing, declining fertility, heterogeneous family structures, reconfigured relationships between women and men and across generations, and surges in geographical mobility and migration".

Some authors advocate the need to change pension systems. Banyár (2016), for example, states that "very few countries in the world can boast about having a pension system which will be able to work more or less in its present form when today's children retire. Instead, most countries can be certain of quite the opposite: their systems will not last for another generation (*i.e.*, major transformation and reforms are necessary)".[16]

The economic crisis that began in 2007 had an impact on the process of reforming pension systems in Europe leading, according to some authors, to a reduction in the social protection levels of public systems. According to Colàs-Neila (2016), the measures that were adopted "have impacted on pension systems, which have undergone various reforms to reduce public expenditure. The EU has played an influential role in this field, insisting, despite a lack of competence, on the promotion of complementary private retirement savings to ensure adequate incomes. Consequently, the protection levels of public social security systems are being eroded".[17]

Orenstein (2005) argues that these changes are part of a wider process of a global nature, that has "been pursued by a transnational advocacy coalition that seeks to revolutionize social protection on a global scale".

For this author, the current reform makes it possible to conclude that: firstly, "the new pension reform model of state-mandated but privately managed pension insurance appears to be popular among policy makers. There is no sign that this trend is abating". Secondly, "it appears likely that more developed countries will adopt new pension reforms in coming years. Middle-income developing countries have led the way in implementing the new pension reforms, with the help of a broad transnational advocacy coalition led by the World Bank". Thirdly, "the impact of such reforms will be to further consolidate a growing trend towards neoliberal economic policy;

---

[16]According to Banyár (2016), assuming that the PAYGO system is still valid, there are several possibilities of reform which, however, have several limitations:

- To adopt temporary solutions that "include the parametric adjustments of the existing pension system, such as slightly raising the retirement age (or, more radically, continuously indexing it to increases in life expectancy), increasing contributions, cancelling earlier benefits, making the indexing rule less generous and so on".
- "To fund the deficit of the system, which is not impossible, but has some limits: In fact, this solution worked well in countries where the PAYGO pension system (and the implicit government debt) was of a relatively small scope, but very difficult in countries where the implicit government debt corresponds to the GDP of several years".

[17]According to Brimblecombe and McClanahan (2019), "recent reforms have increased the number of years required for entitlement to a full and/or minimum social security pension", and it is the case that "Meeting these requirements is particularly challenging for women workers who spend on average significantly less time in the workforce than their male counterparts".

however, it may not seriously undermine the importance of state-mandated social insurance". Fourthly, "with the new pension reforms, the design of guaranteed minimums, state regulation of private managers and investment fees, annuity schedules, and many other aspects can substantially alter the welfare impact of these systems".

It should be pointed out that the replacement of a pension system does not only bring advantages, but this can also present some disadvantages that need to be identified.

Given this, consider Table 2 showing the advantages and disadvantages of the two extreme examples of pension systems identified in Fig. 1 (Point I and VIII).

It should be noted, that, during the 1990s, countries like Sweden (Palmer 2000), Italy (Franco and Sartor 2006), Latvia (Palmer et al. 2006) and Poland (Chlon et al. 1999) introduced structural reforms in their pension system architecture, trying to optimize certain advantages/disadvantages of the traditional solutions (unfunded, defined benefits and non-actuarial system versus funded, defined contributions and actuarial system).

Though in very distinct ways, each of the aforementioned countries outlined a path to achieve a common objective: the implementation of a financially sustainable public pension system in the long run. These transitions have led to the abandonment

Table 2 Alternative old-age pension system (advantages and disadvantages)

	Advantages	Disadvantages
Unfunded DB non-actuarial (Position I in Fig. 1)	• Generous model with regard to the benefits (favourable relationship between contributions and pension benefits); • Independent of capital market risks; • Less exposed to inflation; • Protects smaller contributory careers	• Depends on a favourable demographic path[a]; • Depends on a favourable labour market[b]; • Does not encourage savings; • Can generate the creation of implicit debt within the social security system; • Increases the politicization of the pension system
Funded DC actuarial (Position VIII in Fig. 1)	• Better able to deal with ageing of the population; • Limited fiscal liabilities; • Removes some labour market distortions; • Increases capital market development and even possibly savings; • Reduces the politicization of the pension system	• Dependent on the capital market (and associated risks); • Less generous model with regard to benefits (i.e. The relationship between contributions and pension benefits is less favourable than in a PAYGO); • Penalizes smaller contributory careers; • Exposed to inflation; • Increase the uncertainty of the worker as regards pension benefits

[a]According to Baynar (2017), in order to keep a PAYGO system balanced, it is necessary that "demographic tendencies are always favourable (*i.e.* there is no pension problem relating to demography ('demographic problem')"
[b]According to Baynar (2017), in order to keep a PAYGO system balanced "everybody in the labour market at an active age can find work, so that they are able to pay their contributions (*i.e.* there is no labour market problem)"

of a defined benefit system and to the adoption of notional account defined contribution systems (NDC), financed on a PAYGO scheme (a solution between position II and VI in Fig. 1).

This "hybrid" system is better able to deal with ageing of the population and reduces fiscal liabilities compared with a "pure" PAYGO system. It is also independent from capital market risks and reduces the politicization of the pension system.

However this system also has some disadvantages: it is a less generous model with regard to benefits (*i.e.,* the relationship between contributions and pension benefits is less favourable than in a "pure" PAYGO system but more favourable than in a funded, DC and actuarial system); it raises the uncertainty of the worker as regards pension benefits; and it does not (completely) eliminate the relationship between system sustainability and demographics.[18]

It should noted that there are strong barriers to pension reform (Banyár 2017), particularly those resulting from the stability and growth pact—SGP (the so-called Maastricht criteria). According to the author, "the main problem with the SGP is that it only deals with explicit government debt and ignores implicit debt. Although it renders reforms politically palatable, it will increase overall debt in the course of reducing the explicit one".

These reform processes should consider the context in which they are carried out, since the adoption of a given model may have different impacts depending on the country (a good solution for one country may not be a good solution for another country).

In fact, Schoyen and Stamati (2013) shows that "reform processes do not end with legislation. The post-adoption policy trajectory depends on a number of factors related to policy design, economic context and political ownership."

4   Conclusion

European societies face profound demographic changes, particularly those related to accelerated population ageing, declining fertility, heterogeneous family structures, reconfigured relationships between women and men and across generations, and surges in geographical mobility and migration. These demographic changes have had a major impact on European PAYGO systems.

In order to identify how to better address common challenges in the EU with regard to the protection of citizens during old age in a sustainable manner, I have

---

[18]According to Brimblecombe and McClanahan (2019) "the introduction of defined contribution systems (notional or funded) for first pillar (social security) provision has penalized women beneficiaries in a number of ways. Most significantly, the lower salary and greater incidence of part time working amongst women translates directly into lower pension entitlements at retirement".

In this context, Brimblecombe and McClanahan (2019) argue that "policymakers should therefore assess systems on the distribution of outcomes rather than average outcomes".

compared the main pension models, trying to identify the advantages and disadvantages of each one of them from a conceptual perspective.

The analysis carried out enables us to conclude that a funded system (with defined contributions and actuarial fairness) has some advantages over a PAYGO system. In fact, it allows for a better approach to demographic issues, has limited fiscal liabilities, increases capital market development and reduces politicization of the pension system.

It should be noted that this model also has some disadvantages compared to the PAYGO system. In addition to the greater reliance on capital markets (and associated risks), it is also a less generous model with regard to benefits (*i.e.*, the relationship between contributions and pension benefits are less favourable than in a PAYGO system), penalizing smaller contributory careers.

In order to mitigate some of these disadvantages, some European countries have adopted a notional account defined contribution system (NDC), financed through a PAYGO scheme. This "hybrid" system is better able to deal with ageing of the population compared to a "pure" PAYGO system but less generous (but more generous than a funded, DC and actuarial system).

It should be noted that there are no perfect pension systems and the reform process should consider the context in which it is being carried out, since the adoption of a given model may have different impacts, depending on the context.

References

Banyár J (2016) Possible reforms of pay-as-you-go pension systems. Eur J Soc Secur 18 (3):286–308

Baynar J (2017) European handling of implicit and explicit government debt as an obstacle to the funding-type pension reforms. Eur J Soc Secur 19(1):45–62

Billari F (2016) The "Timing of life": the organisation of the life course in Europe. The European Social Survey Round 9 Question Module Design Teams (QDT) Stage 2 Application

Brimblecombe S, McClanahan S (2019) Improving gender outcomes in social security retirement systems. Soc Policy Admin 53(3):327–342

Chlon A, Góra M, Rutkowski M (1999) Shaping pension reform in Poland: security through diversity. Pension Reform Primer, SP Discussion Paper No. 9923, The World Bank, Washington, DC

Coelho M (2013) Balanced conditions of a pay as you go public system with defined benefit: an analysis of the Portuguese public system. Working Papers in Economics, E/n° 63/2013, Universidade de Aveiro

Colàs-Neila E (2016) Reconfiguring the employment pension connection in times of austerity. Eur Labour Law J 7(3):461–478

Diamond P (2006) Conceptualization of non-financial defined contribution systems. Pension Reform Issues and Prospects for Non-Financial Defined Contribution (NDC) Schemes, Proceedings of the NDC Conference in Sandhamn, Sweden, September 28–30, 2003, World Bank, pp 76–80

Franco D, Sartor N (2006) NDCs in Italy: unsatisfactory present, uncertain future. Pension Reform Issues and Prospects for Non-Financial Defined Contribution (NDC) Schemes, Proceedings of the NDC Conference in Sandhamn, Sweden, September 28–30, 2003, World Bank, pp 467–493

Lindbeck A (2006) Conceptualization of non-financial defined contribution systems. Pension Reform Issues and Prospects for Non-Financial Defined Contribution (NDC) Schemes, Proceedings of the NDC Conference in Sandhamn, Sweden, September 28–30, 2003, World Bank, pp 71–75

Lindbeck A, Persson M (2003) The gains from pension reform. J Econ Lit 41(1):74–112

Orenstein M (2005) The new pension reform as global policy. Glob Soc Policy 5(2):175–202

Palmer E (2000) The Swedish pension reform model – framework and issues. World Bank's Pension Reform Primer Social Protection Discussion Paper No. 0012. The World Bank, Washington, DC

Palmer E, Stabin S, Svensson I, Vanovska I (2006) NDC strategy in latvia: implementation and prospects for the future. Pension Reform. Issues and Prospects for Non-Financial Defined Contribution (NDC) Schemes, Chapter 15, The World Bank, pp 397–424

Rofman R (2005) Social security coverage in Latin America. Social Protection Discussion Paper Series, Social Protection Unit Human Development Network, The World Bank, No. 523

Samuelson P (1958) An exact consumption-loan model of interest with or without the social contrivance of money. J Polit Econ 66(6):467–482

Schoyen M, Stamati F (2013) The political sustainability of the NDC pension model: the cases of Sweden and Italy. Eur J Soc Secur 15(1):79–101

Valdés-Prieto S (2002) Pension policies and pensions markets: a university textbook for Latin America. Ediciones Universidad Católica, Santiago

Miguel Coelho is an Assistant Professor in Universidade Lusíada (Lisbon) and an Invited Professor in IDEFE/ISEG/ULisboa (Lisbon). He have a PhD in Economics and a Masters Degree in International Economics from ISEG/ULisboa.

Chief Economist in Banco de Empresas Montepio, he was chairman of Montepio Gestão de Ativos, SGFI (Asset Management Company) between 2017 and 2019 and executive board member in Montepio Geral Associação Mutualista (MGAM) between 2016 and 2019.

Board member in Montepio Valor (Asset Management Company) between 2013 and 2016, vice-president of Instituto da Segurança Social between 2011 and 2013, board member in Futuro (Pensions Funds Management Company) and MGA (Asset Management Company) between 2009 and 2011.

He has held executive positions in the Financial Department, Research Department and Risk Department in Caixa Económica Montepio Geral between 2004 and 2009.

Economist of the Studies Department in the Portuguese Securities Market Commission (CMVM) between 2001 and 2004 and in the Research Department in Macroeconomics and Financial Markets in the Banif—Investiment Bank between 2000 and 2001, having collaborated yet, as an external consultant with the Portuguese Economic and Social Council (CES) between 1997 and 2000.

Author of the book "Social Security—Current Situation and Prospects of Reform" and co-author of the books "Markets—Are They the Great Responsibles for the Crisis?" and "Financial Mathematics—A Handbook for Understanding the Principles of Financial Mathematics—Vol. I and Vol. II".

What's New in the Debate About Pay-as-you-go Versus Funded Pensions?

Hervé Boulhol and Marius Lüske

Abstract Recent history has shown that with tight public finances the costs associated with a transition from a PAYGO to a diversified pension system with funded and PAYGO components can be high. A number of countries backtracked on previously decided transitions, highlighting that the political risk of policy reversals is considerable. There is an actuarial equivalence between PAYGO and funded schemes. While, when an economy is dynamically efficient, a move from PAYGO to funding can boost future pension levels, it creates both winners and losers, thus implying some form of redistribution. Hence, choosing one type of financing over the other is essentially a political decision. While the economic condition for dynamic efficiency was typically fulfilled without ambiguity in the past, the current economic context questions whether this is still the case, suggesting to revisit the trade-off between PAYGO and funded schemes. Risk diversification remains a key argument for combining PAYGO and funded elements, but the benefits of risk-diversification should be weighed against the medium-term costs generated by the transition towards a multi-pillar system.

1 Introduction

Few policy areas have moved up on political agendas as much as pensions over the last decades. Countries have come up with manifold approaches to organising retirement systems, trying to reconcile financial sustainability and social adequacy as far as possible. One of the most fundamental questions in this context relates to

The opinions and arguments expressed herein are those of the authors and do not necessarily reflect the official views of the OECD or its member countries. The authors are grateful to Maciej Lis for his comments.

H. Boulhol (✉) · M. Lüske
OECD's Directorate for Employment, Labour and Social Affairs, Paris, France
e-mail: herve.boulhol@oecd.org

© Springer Nature Switzerland AG 2019
N. da Costa Cabral, N. Cunha Rodrigues (eds.), *The Future of Pension Plans in the EU Internal Market*, Financial and Monetary Policy Studies 48,
https://doi.org/10.1007/978-3-030-29497-7_3

financing. Should pensions be organised as pay-as-you-go (PAYGO) systems, funded systems or as a combination of both?

In PAYGO systems, current contributions are handed down directly from contributors to beneficiaries, i.e. there is a transfer from today's workers to today's retirees. Contributing today buys the right to benefit from future generations' contributions later on. Conversely, in funded schemes, current contributions are used to build up a stock of savings, i.e. there is no direct transfer from today's young to today's elderly, but each generations saves by itself while in working age. Funds are invested in the financial market and eventually used to pay pension benefits when people retire.

While commonly mentioned in one breath, the choice between PAYGO and funded systems is a different question than choosing between private and public pensions or between defined benefit (DB) and defined contribution (DC) schemes (OECD 2017). PAYGO and funded pensions can both be DB and DC and may be organised publicly or privately. In the Netherlands and Switzerland for example, funded DB pensions exist while some countries, including Italy and Poland, have PAYGO-financed DC pensions, so-called notional (non-financial) defined contribution (NDC) pensions. PAYGO schemes do not always have to be public, but can also be private, as in the case of some occupational schemes in Germany, and funded schemes may be public, as in Latvia or Sweden. Comparing funded DC (FDC) with NDC, and PAYGO DB with funded DB based on the same promised benefits can help identify the main questions at stake. By contrast, discussions about opportunities to shift from DB to DC or from public PAYGO DB to private FDC are not the topic of this article.

Similarly, the issue analysed in this paper should not be confused with questions about redistribution within generations. Some public PAYGO schemes possess a wide range of redistributive mechanisms, which are absent from pure funded DC systems. Whether this kind of redistribution should take place is a matter of debate. If some forms of redistribution are considered undesirable, they can be adapted within the PAYGO design even without shifting to a funded system (Orszag and Stiglitz 2001). The comparison between PAYGO and funded pension is conceptually unrelated to redistribution within generations.

This article has two main objectives. The first is to summarise the main issues at stake in the debate about financing old-age pensions through PAYGO versus funded schemes. The second is to bring new insights in this debate by taking into account some relevant recent developments. These include the experience of countries which partly moved from PAYGO to funded pensions and had to face the related transition costs. Transition costs cannot simply be considered as something that lowers long-term gains. They can be large and their burden might be difficult to accept politically. The faster pace of population ageing, high public debt levels, persistently low interest rates and the possibilities of secular stagnation can also affect how one might think about those issues.

2 Moves from PAYGO to Funded Schemes in Recent History

Historically, many countries relied on PAYGO systems to organise their pensions. Especially after World War II, industrialised countries built up PAYGO pension systems or extended already existing PAYGO schemes. At the time, population growth was fast and the economy developed quickly, both of which made PAYGO systems financially attractive, at least in the short and medium run. On average across OECD countries, the size of the working-age population aged 20–64 grew by almost 20% in just 15 years between 1950 and 1965—this compares with 7% over the last 15 years and an expected decrease of 2% over the next 15 years. As the baby boom set in, high fertility rates fuelled the expectation of many that also in the future the labour force would continue to grow for a long time. In addition, the Post World War II economic expansion boosted employment, resulting in a high number of contributors. In such a context, transferring funds from a large and growing number of workers to a small number of pensioners was politically easy and brought immediate results, as the first generation of retirees received benefits even without having contributed.

In a number of OECD countries, including Canada, Denmark, the Netherlands, Switzerland and the United States, funded occupational pensions built up over time in addition to PAYGO schemes. These schemes often started out in specific sectors before becoming progressively widespread, eventually covering large parts of the labour force. Today, these countries usually have a high ratio of pension assets as a share of GDP, exceeding the OECD average by far. In Denmark, for instance, total assets in funded and private pension arrangements summed up to 208% of GDP in 2017, against 51% on average in the OECD (OECD 2018a).

Demographic, economic and political developments prompted further countries to move away from pure PAYGO systems. Numerous Latin American and Central and Eastern European countries, which had been undergoing deep economic transformations, added a mandatory funded component to their retirement system or even replaced their PAYGO system entirely from the 1980s onwards. One of the most salient factors behind this development were long-term demographic trends. While remaining life expectancy at age 65 kept growing continuously, from 13.7 years in 1960 to 17.2 years in 2000 in the OECD, fertility rates plummeted from 3.2 to 1.7 children per woman, raising questions regarding the long-run financial sustainability of PAYGO pensions, which were typically organised as public DB schemes.

The finances of PAYGO DB systems are indeed directly affected by demographic developments while in funded DC systems the impact is primarily on benefit levels. In funded DB schemes, ageing might indirectly lower the returns on pension assets through its impact on GDP growth while longer life expectancies would require higher returns. In NDC pensions, adjustments to life expectancy are automatically built in while employment growth is accounted for if the notional interest rate is properly set (Boulhol 2019). Many countries wanted to use the so-called demographic dividend to move towards a more diversified system, i.e. to introduce a funded component at times when the size of the working-age population is large compared to young and old population groups and the contribution rate needed to finance the PAYGO scheme is low. Another argument raised by advocates of funded pensions was that under certain conditions the rate of return on funded pensions may exceed that of PAYGO systems, potentially leading to higher pensions, as discussed below.

Chile was the first country to proceed to a sharp move from a PAYGO to a funded system. In 1981, the country established a system in which workers accumulate savings in individual accounts which are invested by pension funds. Other countries, including Argentina (1994), Bolivia (1997), and Mexico (1997) followed suit and introduced funded schemes. In Argentina, where a unified PAYGO system covering most workers had existed for several decades, the 1993 reform introduced a multi-pillar system combining PAYGO and fully funded components. Workers could choose between joining a newly implemented PAYGO scheme or a fully funded scheme with individual accounts (Rofman et al. 2010). To improve financial sustainability, the reform also increased the retirement age and the length of contribution periods, and abolished special regimes for a number of job families.

In Central and Eastern Europe, where pension schemes were often fragmented, a wave of pension reforms introducing funded pensions took place in the late 1990s and early 2000s. This was the case in Bulgaria (2002), Estonia (2002), Latvia (2001), Lithuania (2004), Hungary (1998), Poland (1999), Romania (2008) and Slovakia (2005). In most cases, the introduction of a funded component came along with a downscaling of the financially unsustainable PAYGO component. In order to limit the increase in contribution rates, mandatory contributions to the PAYGO system were partially transformed into mandatory contributions to the funded systems. Enrolment in the funded schemes was usually mandatory for new entrants or younger workers while it was voluntary for older groups in most cases.

3   Economic and Financial Turbulence as well as Tight Public Finances Shed New Light on the Trade-off Between PAYGO and Funding

The move towards systems combining PAYGO and funded components were often welcomed and praised as a good way of organising pensions. Not only would pension finances—but not pension benefits—become more resilient to population ageing, especially when funded pensions are constructed as DC schemes, the introduction of a funded component would also transfer money to financial markets. The view was that this would develop financial markets, increase domestic savings and in the end improve economic prospects. In 1994, the seminal World Bank report *Averting the Old-Age Crisis,* for example, encouraged multi-pillar retirement system with strong funded components (World Bank 1994). Combining PAYGO and funded components would also help diversify risks, as both types of systems are not equally exposed to different types of risks.

Moving towards such a diversified system was not an easy step, however. Starting from a PAYGO system, building up a funded component involves high transition costs. Pension funding needs to be sufficiently high not only to pay current pensions within the PAYGO scheme, but also to accumulate additional savings for the funded component. These transition costs can be covered from different funding sources, most notably higher contributions, higher taxes, an increase in government debt or a decrease in pension levels. Depending on how heavily each of these sources is used, the burden is split differently across generations. Higher pension contributions, for instance, affect current workers while lower pensions would affect retirees. Especially in economically difficult times, such transition costs can become problematic as neither current workers nor current retirees can carry such a high financial burden without major sacrifice and governments' capacity to finance the transition through higher debt levels may be limited.

In Argentina, the caveats of funded systems became apparent when the economy deteriorated in the 1990s and then collapsed from 1998 to 2002. In 2001–2002, pension assets plummeted. The move towards a multi-pillar system with a strong funded component, which had started in the 1993 reform, began to be progressively reverted. In 2001, special regimes for a certain number of job families, which had been abolished previously, were re-established as PAYGO. Furthermore, starting in 2007, individual accounts of older workers with low levels of savings were transferred back to the PAYGO system unless they actively refused. Finally, at the end of 2008, the funded system was stopped entirely and all funds were transferred to a newly created PAGYO scheme (Rofman et al. 2010).

Several countries modified or revoked their plans of introducing funded pensions as the financial crisis severely affected economies around the globe from 2007, leading to high public deficits and deteriorated long-term public finance prospects. In OECD countries, gross general government debt amounted to 85% of GDP in 2018, against 64% in 1995 (Fig. 1). When public debt is low, issuing new debt is one way of financing transition, thus permitting to spread the burden of transition costs over long-time horizons. However, in times of tight public finances, this option is limited and transition costs have to be borne when they occur, either through lower pensions, higher contributions or redistribution from other sources, such as taxes. The high transition cost, sometimes combined with other factors such as high administrative costs, pushed many Central and Eastern European countries to reduce, temporarily stop or even entirely reverse their reforms. OECD (2018b) concludes that countries wishing to diversify their pension systems should introduce funded arrangements gradually and that policymakers should carefully assess the transition as it may put an additional strain on public finances.

Decreasing interest rates pose challenges for pension funds and financial institutions offering life insurance policies that promise pre-crisis and fixed nominal returns (OECD 2016). Shrinking returns on accumulated capital erode the strengths of funded systems, bearing the risk of lower pensions later on. Due to monetary policy intervention during the economic crisis and its aftermath, interest rates dropped

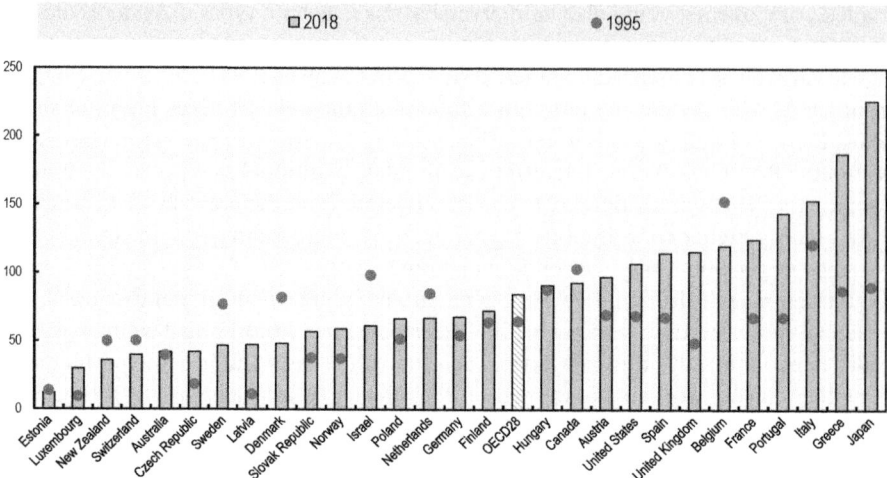

Fig. 1 General government gross financial liabilities as a percentage of GDP. Source: Economic Outlook No 104—November 2018

significantly in many areas, reaching record low levels. In the Euro area, for instance, bank interest rates for deposits from households dropped from over 4% in 2008 to almost 0% today. In other countries, including in Central and Eastern Europe, similar developments took place. In funded DB plans, prolonged low interest rates affect solvency both through low returns on the asset side and through the liability side as a fall in the discount rate increases the present value of DB products (OECD 2016) while benefits are not automatically adjusted downwards. Yet, declining interest rates generally raise bond prices while risks on the liability side could (have) be (en) covered by adjusting DB promises to take account of the price of hedging these risks.

In 2009, Estonia decided to temporarily suspend contributions to the funded pension scheme, thus slowing down the transition process to a multi-pillar system. Instead, contributions were redirected to the PAYGO scheme. Latvia and Lithuania chose to partially reduce contributions to their funded schemes in the same year. Poland and Hungary took even stronger policy action. In Poland, contributions to the funded system, which had initially been set to 7.3%, were reduced to 2.3% in 2011 and 2.92% in 2014 while contributions to the PAYGO scheme increased. In addition, assets in the funded system were partially transferred back to the PAYGO system. While enrolment in the funded scheme was mandatory before the reform reversal, opt-out options were introduced in 2014 (Bielawska et al. 2016). In Hungary, where contributions used to lie between 6% and 8% after the funded system was introduced in 1998, all contributions were stopped in 2011 and assets were transferred to the PAYGO system, i.e. the move towards a funded scheme was entirely and permanently reversed (ILO 2017).

Beyond the financial difficulty during the transition, moving from only PAYGO to multi-pillar systems can be very challenging politically as these country examples highlight. Introducing funded systems should only be implemented as a policy option if the change can be sustained in the long run. Even so, there may still be valid arguments for introducing funded pensions, including potentially higher returns on contributions in funded schemes and the opportunity to diversify risks. These arguments have been widely discussed in the economic literature, but often through the prism of the economic conditions prevailing at the time and without recognising the full consequences of the transition costs. Today, in a context of population ageing, low interest rates, high public debt and low economic growth in a number of countries, both types of financing are exposed to difficulties.

4 Pensions as an Actuarial Zero-Sum Game in the Aggregate, Whether Funded or Unfunded

One central motivation supporting the development of funded pensions to at least partly replace PAYGO systems has been that funded schemes may benefit from higher returns, thereby generating higher pensions. The internal rate of return of PAYGO pensions, i.e. the return that delivers pension promises in a financially sustainable way, corresponds to the growth rate of the contribution base (Samuelson 1958), which is equal to the sum of the employment growth rate and the wage growth rate (that is, the growth rate of the wage bill) under a stable contribution rate. Assuming a constant labour share in GDP, this means that the internal rate of return of PAYGO pensions is equal to the output growth rate.

One of the key arguments in favour of funded schemes thus hinges on the assumption that financial returns on pension assets (r) are larger than GDP growth (g), $r > g$. A common perception was that ageing would weigh on labour supply, lowering output growth and widening the gap between market rates and output growth rates. This relation is discussed at great length below. Moreover, it should be clear from the outset that the variables considered here are net rates, taking into account fees in funded schemes and administrative costs in both funded and PAYGO schemes.

Extensive literature has highlighted since the seminal article by Breyer (1989) that, even if financial returns are greater than output growth rates, funded schemes cannot be considered as a conceptually better arrangement nor that PAYGO should be replaced by funded pensions based on the financial returns argument alone. While contributors can expect higher pensions in funded schemes if $r > g$, this surplus is actuarially equal to the "gift" made to the first generation of PAYGO pensioners who did not contribute fully, and to the contributions that would have been accumulated from the first generation of contributors if no gift had been provided. There is no free lunch and someone must pay for this gift.

Sinn (2000), building on Breyer (1989), shows in a simple and elegant setting that the implicit debt, which is equal to the gift to the first generation of pensioners when the PAYGO scheme is created, is also equal to the discounted value of the tax share included in the contributions. This tax is the difference between paid contributions and the funded savings that would generate the same pension entitlements. Sinn (2000) shows that this implicit tax is $\tau = \frac{r-g}{1+r}$, with g being the growth rate in the contribution base (proxied here by GDP growth).[1] This illustrates that the introduction of a PAYGO system essentially amounts to an intergenerational transfer providing a gift to the first generation of pensioners. The gift generates an implicit debt that is paid back by all cohorts of contributors through implicit taxes. From that standpoint, whether the system is PAYGO or funded, the present value of all contributions equals the present value of all pensions (Sinn 2000).

There are of course welfare implications inherent in PAYGO and funded pensions, but these implications involve redistribution at the individual level over the life cycle, and possibly among individuals of the same generation and across generations. However, there is no intrinsic value in a pure actuarial sense in choosing to contribute during working age to get pensions when old, whether the system is funded or unfunded.

5   Implications for the Transition from PAYGO to Funded

The same mechanisms are at play when analysing the transition from PAYGO to funded systems, as experienced by some OECD countries. The gains achieved by future pensioners from the excess return on pension financial assets over output growth ($r > g$) are offset by foregone contribution revenues through the transition phase, during which PAYGO pensions that had accrued before the transition must be paid. The transition just makes implicit liabilities—which can remain implicit forever—explicit, requiring higher taxes or lower spending today, or issuing debt. In short, no economic value results from investing contributions in financial assets rather than financing current spending for example. Recent experiences discussed above have shown that these transition costs can be large and politically difficult to finance, especially in a context where fiscal space is heavily constrained.

One related question arises when a government considers that future pensions are too low and decides to raise contribution rates. Should these additional contributions be directed to a funded or a PAYGO scheme? The answer to this question depends on the objective. If the sole objective is to maximise future pensions and if $r > g$, the funded scheme is the best option. On the other hand, if PAYGO is chosen for the additional contributions, future pensioners will get lower additional pensions than with funding (again assuming $r > g$), but the additional contributions create some fiscal space over a generation, which can be used in many ways and actuarially offset the lower returns.

---

[1]To get an order of magnitude of that implicit tax, r and g are not here annual rates but compounded over the working life.

Replacing PAYGO by a funded system generates losers, namely those who have to finance already accumulated PAYGO entitlements. Hence, the choice between funded and PAYGO cannot be directly reduced to a question of efficiency, but is a distributional matter, implying that the problem of equity among generations inevitably arises (Breyer 1989). However, there might be some indirect effects from the way pensions are financed which would support the choice to fund schemes. Three channels through which funding itself might increase output growth are worth discussing.

First, funding is likely to increase private savings although there might be substitution effects between private savings instruments. Moreover, additional private savings might be offset, as discussed above, by less public saving (more public borrowing) and the total impact on national saving is unclear. In turn, even if total saving increases, in the absence of efficiency gains this might result from lower consumption, with an ambiguous impact on welfare. Indeed, an increase in national saving is not beneficial in all circumstances (Barr and Diamond 2008). In particular, the total welfare impact depends upon whether the initial savings rate is too low, which is not the case in all countries and at all times. In addition, if both total saving and output growth increase, r tends to decrease (while g grows), thus reducing $r - g$.

Second, funding might help develop financial markets. This argument applies especially to countries with underdeveloped financial markets, but cannot be extended to all countries. Moreover, if the objective is to optimise future pension benefits, pension assets should be diversified, and small countries in particular would gain little in terms of financial market development. In addition, here also the question arises whether financial deepening is beneficial by itself, which in part depends on how the development of financial markets is managed. The initial transformation of Poland's public PAYG system into a multi-pillar DC approach helped Warsaw's development as a financial centre, while the introduction of funded DC pensions in Chile encouraged the growth of Chilean financial markets (OECD 2018b).

Third, assuming $r > g$, PAYGO pensions generate an implicit tax on labour earnings—as most redistribution devices—and this implicit tax might restrict labour supply. This cost in terms of lower labour supply should be weighed against potential losses generated by the shift to funding. As the implicit debt becomes explicit, it has to be paid back, possibly involving other types of distortive taxes.

6 Dynamic Efficiency: Are Market Rates Larger than Growth Rates ($r > g$)?

The comparison of market rates and output growth rates is central for the analysis of the welfare impact of public debt. The $r > g$ relation is generally referred to as dynamic efficiency. Dynamic efficiency means that no generation can be made better off without making any other generation worse off $r > g$ implies that the marginal product of capital is sufficiently large such that increasing saving and investment generates returns, thereby contributing to economic growth. In textbook economic models, the optimal amount of capital, i.e. the amount of capital that maximises consumption, is obtained when the golden rule $g = r$ applies (see e.g. Diamond 1965). If r is lower than g, however, capital exceeds the golden rule level. This means that the capital stock is too large, which is dynamically inefficient: consuming the surplus capital would be Pareto improving and debt would be self-financing.

When assessing whether the economy is in an efficient or inefficient equilibrium one key question relates to the market rate the comparison should be based upon. The risk-free rate (typically long-term government bond as the time horizon is long-term) or financial rates of return? The latter include a risk premium to compensate for risk-taking, and there is a large range of financial assets based on a large range of financial risks. Another question is which growth rate also enters the comparison given uncertainty. Abel et al. (1989) developed a testable criterion of dynamic efficiency based on whether capital income exceeds investment, thus overcoming the problem of choosing the most appropriate measure of capital returns and growth rates—in seven OECD countries and concluded that these economies were dynamically efficient. However, these results have been questioned by more recent research by Geerolf (2018) indicating that Japan and South Korea have accumulated too much capital, supporting the "savings glut" hypothesis according to which savings are too high. Using the criterion developed by Abel et al. (1989), Kajitani et al. (2018) also question whether China is in a dynamic efficient equilibrium.

Diamond (1965) characterises $r < g$ as dynamic inefficiency in a model with no uncertainty such that it is impossible to determine within this setting whether r should be the safe or the risky rate. In a recent paper, Blanchard (2019) introduces uncertainty to analyse the impact of a transfer from the young to the elderly (introduction of a PAYGO scheme) on welfare and shows that both the risk-free rate and the marginal product of capital (risky rate) matter. There are two mechanisms at play, as in Diamond (1965), but the effect of each of the two market rates on welfare works through a different channel. The risk-free rate has a direct effect when factor prices are constant (partial equilibrium effect). If the risk-free rate is lower than output growth, contributing to a PAYGO scheme generates returns exceeding the returns on savings, as in Diamond (1965), and introducing a PAYGO scheme is beneficial for everyone through this effect. The risky rate comes into play through changes in factor prices (marginal product of capital relative to wages) in the general equilibrium. The transfer from the young to the elderly increases the risky rate as private savings diminish due to the contributions to the PAYGO scheme; Blanchard shows that if the marginal product of capital is lower than output growth the increase in the risky rate raises welfare.

To sum up, in order to assess economic (in)efficiency, both the risk-free and risky rates matter. When the risk-free rate is lower than GDP growth and GDP growth, in turn, is lower than the risky rate, the two effects go in opposite directions and the overall effect of a transfer from the young to the elderly is unclear. Based on US historical data, Blanchard (2019) shows that the risky rate has exceeded output growth, contributing to dynamic efficiency through the general equilibrium effect.

Table 1 10-year government bond rates and nominal GDP growth, selected countries, average by periods

	Bond yields (r) 1992–2005	GDP growth (g) 1992–2005	Bond yields (r) 2006–2018	GDP growth (g) 2006–2018	r–g 1992–2005	r–g 2006–2018	r–g 1992–2018
Australia	6.8	6.2	4.1	5.3	0.6	−1.2	−0.2
Canada	6.2	5.2	2.7	3.6	1.0	−1.0	0.0
France	5.6	3.5	2.4	2.3	2.1	0.2	1.2
Germany	5.4	2.7	2.0	3.1	2.7	−1.1	0.9
Italy	7.2	4.6	3.7	1.3	2.6	2.3	2.5
Japan	2.5	0.6	0.8	0.4	1.8	0.4	1.2
Sweden	6.5	4.2	2.2	4.0	2.3	−1.8	0.3
UK	6.2	5.0	2.9	3.3	1.3	−0.4	0.5
USA	5.6	5.5	2.9	3.6	0.1	−0.6	−0.2
Average	5.8	4.2	2.6	3.0	1.6	−0.3	0.7

Source: Economic Outlook No 104—November 2018; https://stats.oecd.org/index.aspx?queryid=51396#

However, he emphasises that the current situation, in which the risk-free rate is lower than the growth rate, has become common and pushes towards dynamic inefficiency through the partial equilibrium effect, which lowers the cost of public debt.

Table 1 compares the average of long-term government bond rates and GDP growth rates for G7 countries, Australia and Sweden since 1992, breaking the whole period into two sub-periods. During 1992–2005, this measure of the risk-free rate was higher than GDP growth rate on average, pointing to dynamic efficiency without ambiguity. However, since 2006, the case has been a lot less clear as the risk-free rate has been lower than output growth except in Italy, and to a much lesser extent in France and Japan. Averaging over the whole period 1992–2018, the $r > g$ relation holds unambiguously in all countries except Australia, Canada and the United States. On average across countries, long-term government bond yields exceeded GDP growth rate by 0.7% point.

The OECD pension model uses key economic parameters to project future pension benefits. The set of economic assumptions in the pension model were revised in 2015 to reflect major economic developments since 2000; this update led to lower values for price inflation, real-wage growth and financial returns (OECD 2015, Chap. 4). The real risk-free rate used for discounting is 2% while the risky rate used for valuing funded defined contribution assets is 3%. Real wages are assumed to grow by 1.25% per year and the annual inflation rate is set at 2%. GDP enters in the pension modelling for a limited number of countries only, and when it does, the labour share is assumed to be constant, implying that real-GDP growth is equal to real-wage growth plus labour-force growth. The growth rate of the working-age population, defined as the population aged between 20 and 64 years, permits to approximate labour-force growth. On average in the OECD, the working-age population is projected to be roughly stable (−0.1% per year) over the next three decades

Projected average annual change in the population aged 20-64 in OECD countries between 2015 and 2045

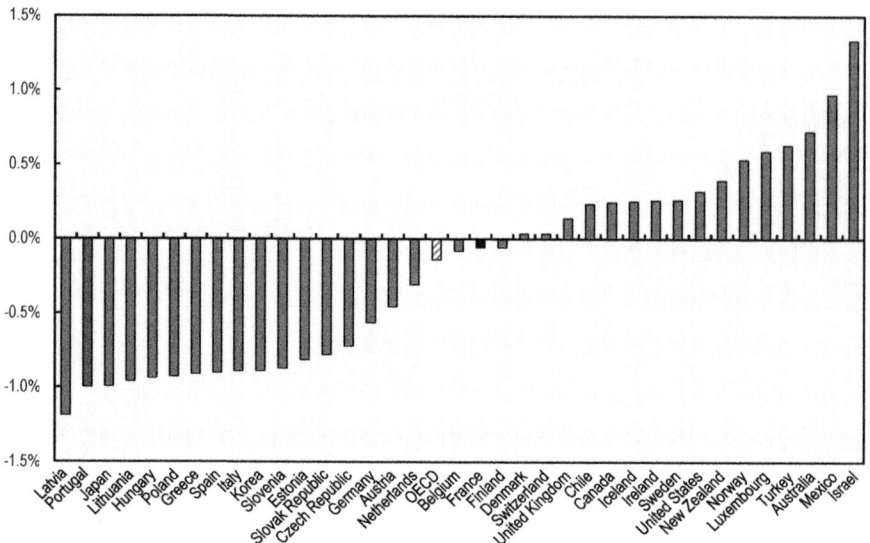

Fig. 2 Projected average annual change in the working-age population, 2015–2045. Projected average annual change in the population aged 20–64 in OECD countries between 2015 and 2045. Source: United Nations, World Population Prospects—2017 Revision

(Fig. 2). Its expected evolution ranges between an average fall of about 1% per year in Central, Eastern and Southern European countries, Japan and Korea and an increase of more than 1% per year in Israel. These numbers imply that based on the parameters used in the OECD pension model, real GDP would grow by 1.1% per year on average, which is less than the risk-free rate of 2% and the risky rate of 3%. The difference between assumed GDP growth and the discount rate is therefore equal to 0.9% point on average, which is in line with the average for the nine countries in Table 1 since 1992 but much larger than what has been observed in recent periods.

7   Are the Same r and g Variables Needed to Assess Dynamic Efficiency and to Compare Returns of PAYGO and Funded Pensions?

In Sinn (2000), r stands for the expected financial returns on savings in a funded scheme. However, his framework does not account for uncertainty. In reality, the question at stake is broader as depending on their design pensions are exposed to different types of risks. Pension contributors investing in FDC may have some aversion to risk, so expected financial returns should be adjusted, taking account of risk taking. This reasoning suggests using the risk-free rate as r for the computation of the implicit tax embedded in PAYGO schemes. In that case, the implicit tax is likely to be small or even negative in the recent past—akin to dynamic inefficiency—implying that introducing a PAYGO scheme and providing a gift to one first generation would generate a "free lunch".

On the other hand, a key question for the computation of the implicit tax is what the contributor would expect from the PAYGO pension. Using g abstracts from any social and political risks associated with holding PAYGO pension promises. In other words, it is correct to use the risk-free rate only if the PAYGO was designed in a financially sustainable way, automatically adjusted to various shocks and with a credible political commitment to keep pension rules unchanged. In addition, using g assumes away the uncertainty around the growth rate of the wage bill itself. This means that r and g should both be adjusted to account for uncertainty as their expected values might not match actual values.

8 Secular Stagnation

Current demographic trends might reduce GDP growth and the internal rates of return of PAYGO schemes as they slow down the growth of the working-age population. As Fig. 2 shows, the quantitative impact of these trends is very different across countries. However, the impact of ageing on output growth will to a large extent depend on how labour productivity is affected and in particular on how much capital intensity increases. There is no consensus among economists on this question (Crafts 2019). It has generally been considered that the ageing of the baby boomers has contributed to lower interest rates, but that market rates will rise once they start to retire and draw down their wealth. However, there has been little empirical evidence of such an effect (Poterba 2004).

In any case, long-term interest rates and capital returns are related to GDP trend growth. Interest rates have been falling over the last three decades, boosting asset prices. The natural rate of interest is not directly observable but can be estimated. Holston et al. (2017) find that the natural interest rate has declined considerably since 2000 and has been close to zero since 2008. They infer from macroeconomic modelling that this is associated with lower potential output growth, which has fallen over the past 10 years, and eventually translates into low real wage growth. Demographic trends might have been one of the key drivers of the so-called secular stagnation hypothesis. Carvalho et al. (2016) estimate that demographic trends lead to a reduction of the equilibrium interest rate of 1.5% points in the United States between 1990 and 2014. Börsch-Supan et al. (2016) find based on a calibrated CGE model that the return on productive capital declines with the increase in the so-called old-age dependency ratio, but that this decline is lower than the decrease in output growth.

What happens if market rates become so low that they fall below growth rates? More precisely, if the risk-adjusted financial returns are lower than the risk-adjusted

PAYGO internal returns? Just as debt finances itself under such conditions, financial assets in pension plans should be used to make a "gift" to retirees and pensions should be PAYGO financed, generating higher returns than financial assets. In such a dynamically inefficient case, there is no trade-off between PAYGO and funded pensions because the implicit tax in the PAYGO scheme is negative. Replacing funded by PAYGO pensions as a Pareto improvement would appear as an unusual, almost provocative proposition. However, $r < g$ does not seem to be a realistic assumption in the long run, which is what matters here. Homburg (2014) argues that accounting for land, a non-reproducible factor, rules out dynamic inefficient options.

9 Diversification of Risks

The above discussion highlighted that, *from an actuarial standpoint*, when the economy is dynamically efficient the choice between PAYGO and funded is a normative issue dictated by the policy objectives that are pursued as it essentially involves redistributional issues. There is no magic bullet and maximising future pensions without considering how these long-term outcomes are achieved should not be the main consideration in this debate, and certainly not the only one.

One appealing argument in favour of combining funded and unfunded schemes lies in the advantages produced by diversifying the nature of risks that people face both before and after retirement. Financial versus political, social or purely labour market risks. International versus domestic developments. In particular, the determinants driving financial-market uncertainty are substantially different from those generating uncertainty about wage and employment trends. Improving the risk-reward ratio of contributing to the pension system, at both the individual and aggregate level, given the different sources of risks is helped by having both a funded and unfunded component.

PAYGO and funded pensions can thus be complementary. A mixed system provides a diversification of risks of very different nature, which is likely to improve the overall risk-adjusted returns of the pension system. Diversification is important because the mechanisms through which shocks work into different pension arrangements vary (OECD 2018b).

10 Conclusion

Recent history has shown that the transition from a PAYGO to a diversified system with funded and PAYGO components comes with high costs. In times of high public debt and a constrained fiscal space, such high costs are a major financial burden. In a number of Latin American and Central and Eastern European countries, transitions from PAYGO to multi-pillar systems were stopped due to these high transition costs, showing that the political risk of policy reversal is high. One lesson learned is that policymakers should carefully assess such transitions as they may put an additional strain on public finances over the medium turn (OECD 2018b).

From the late 1980s, the economic literature has shown that PAYGO and fully funded systems are equivalent from an actuarial point of view. PAYGO systems make a transfer—a "gift"—to the first generations of retirees, permitting them to receive benefits without having (fully) contributed to the system. The cost of this gift is borne by future retirees who contribute (fully) to the PAYGO system. Indeed, when the economy is dynamically efficient, i.e. in a framework abstracting from uncertainty when market rates are larger than GDP growth rates, which are good proxies for internal rates of return of PAYGO pensions, future retirees end up with pensions below the level they would receive if their contributions were invested in financial markets. The actuarial equivalence means that the cumulated losses for future retirees are actuarially equivalent to the gift made to the first generation of retirees.

Choosing one mode of financing pensions over the other is hence a political choice that involves various types of redistribution. When the economy is dynamically efficient, pensions cannot be shifted from PAYGO to funding without generating losers bearing the cost of higher future pensions. In other words, there is no free lunch, the gift creates an implicit debt which becomes explicit when retirement systems are shifted from PAYGO to funded systems, leading to transition costs. By contrast, when the economy is dynamically inefficient, PAYGO pensions are permanently higher than funded pensions and in addition the first generation of retirees benefits from the gift. Creating a PAYGO scheme is beneficial for every generation as it leads to a stable implicit debt that can be indefinitely rolled over.

The dynamic efficiency condition was usually fulfilled in the past. However, the prolonged period of low interest rates, feeding the secular stagnation hypothesis, raises the question whether the dynamic efficiency condition fails to hold in the current environment, and how this will evolve in the foreseeable future. Over the last fifteen years, government bond yields have been lower than GDP growth rates on average. However, both risk-free and risky rates matter to assess dynamic efficiency (Blanchard 2019), and observing long-term bond yields below output growth, even over long periods, is by far not sufficient to conclude that economies are dynamically inefficient and that PAYGO systems would be preferable in terms of welfare.

One key argument remains that combining PAYGO and funded systems generates benefits from risk diversification. The two types of financing are exposed to different risks, such as risks arising from low interest rates, population ageing, economic shocks and political uncertainty. Financial returns are subject to a large volatility. Internal rates of return in PAYGO schemes—i.e. the growth rate of the wage bill—are uncertain as well. Combining both types of financing pensions can help raising the risk-adjusted returns of contributions to the retirement system. However, as discussed in this article, the transition from a PAYGO to a diversified system can be challenging, especially in a context of difficult economic conditions.

References

Abel AB, Mankiw NG, Summers LH, Zeckhauser RJ (1989) Assessing dynamic efficiency: theory and evidence. Rev Econ Stud 56(1):1–19

Barr N, Diamond P (2008) Reforming pensions: principles and policy choices. Oxford University Press, Oxford

Bielawska K, Chlon-Dominczak A, Stanko D (2016) Retreat from mandatory pension funds in countries of the Eastern and Central Europe in result of financial and fiscal crisis: causes, effects and recommendations for fiscal rules. Warsaw School of Economics, Warsaw

Blanchard O (2019) Public debt and low interest rates. American Economic Association Presidential Address

Börsch-Supan A, Härtl K, Leite DN (2016) Chapter 13: Social security and public insurance. In: Handbook of the economics of population ageing, vol 1B. Elsevier, Amsterdam, pp 781–863

Boulhol H (2019) Objectives and challenges in the implementation of a universal pension system in France. OECD Working Papers, forthcoming

Breyer F (1989) On the intergenerational Pareto efficiency of pay-as-you-go financed pension schemes. J Inst Theor Econ 145:643–658

Carvalho C, Ferrero A, Nechio F (2016) Demographics and real interest rates: inspecting the mechanism. Eur Econ Rev 88:208–226

Crafts N (2019) The future growth path for Europe and Ireland. Third annual conference of the Irish fiscal advisory council, path for the public finances, 2019: long-term fiscal sustainability: winter is coming!. https://www.fiscalcouncil.ie/path-for-the-public-finances-2019-long-term-fiscal-sus tainability-winter-is-coming/

Diamond P (1965) National debt in a neoclassical growth model. Am Econ Rev 55:1126–1150

Geerolf F (2018) Reassessing dynamic efficiency, *mimeo*

Holston K, Laubach T, Williams JC (2017) Measuring the natural rate of interest: international trends and determinants. J Int Econ 108:1

Homburg S (2014) Overaccumulation, public debt and the importance of land. Ger Econ Rev 5:4

ILO (2017) World Social Protection Report 2017–2019: Universal social protection to achieve the sustainable development goals. Geneva

Kajitani K, Kinugasa T, Lun K (2018) Dynamic efficiency in world economy, Discussion Paper No. 1801. Graduate School of Economics, Kobe University

OECD (2015) Pensions at a glance. OECD Publishing, Paris

OECD (2016) OECD economic outlook 2016 2. OECD Publishing, Paris. https://doi.org/10.1787/eco_outlook-v2016-2-en

OECD (2017) Pensions at a glance. OECD Publishing, Paris

OECD (2018a) Pension markets in focus. OECD Publishing, Paris

OECD (2018b) Pensions outlook. OECD Publishing, Paris

Orszag P, Stiglitz JE (2001) Rethinking pension reform: ten myths about social security systems. In: Holman R, Stiglitz JE (eds) New ideas about old age security: toward sustainable pension systems in the twenty-first century. World Bank, Washington, D.C., pp 17–56

Poterba J (2004) Impact of population aging on financial markets in developed countries. Econ Rev 89:43–53

Rofman R, Fajnzylber E, Herrera G (2010) Reforming the pension reforms: Argentina and Chile. CEPAL Rev (101):83–106

Samuelson P (1958) An exact consumption-loan model of interest with or without the social contrivance of money. J Public Econ 66:467–482

Sinn HW (2000) Why a funded pension system is useful and why it is not useful. Int Tax Public Financ 7:389–410

World Bank (1994) Averting the old agee crisis: policies to protect and promote growth. Washington, DC

Hervé Boulhol has been a Senior Economist in the Directorate for Employment, Labour and Social Affairs of the OECD, responsible for the work on pensions and population ageing since March 2014. Previously he worked in the Economics Department of the OECD, heading the France and Poland Desks. Prior to joining the OECD in 2007, he had worked as an Economist in Natixis (2001–2007) and in financial markets (1989–2000) including as Head of Interest Rate and FX Exotic Options.

He graduated as a Statistician, Economist and Actuary from the Ecole Nationale de Statistique et d'Administration Economique (ENSAE 1989), and holds a Ph.D in Economics from Université Paris Panthéon-Sorbonne (2007) on International competition and labor market interactions in developed countries under Lionel Fontagné. Author and co-author of numerous publications at the OECD and in highly-ranked periodicals.

Marius Lüske is an economist and social policy analyst at the OECD's Directorate for Employment, Labour and Social Affairs. His work focuses on topics related to social policies, especially in the area of pensions and population ageing. Recent projects include analyses of the transition from work to retirement and of the barriers to longer working lives.

Before joining the OECD, Marius worked in research and as an actuarial consultant in the private sector. He holds a Ph.D. on the design of social security systems from the Swiss Federal Institute of Technology in Zurich (ETH Zürich), a master's degree from Paris School of Economics (PSE) and a bachelor's degree from Goethe University Frankfurt.

The Role of the Government in Creating or Enhancing the Access to Funded or Unfunded Pensions in the Modern Welfare State

Yves Stevens

Abstract Due to ageing, governments have put into place parametric pension reforms during the last two decades. Consequently pension systems have become extremely complicated. Whether statutory, occupational or personal all pension forms are remarkably difficult to understand in depth. Nonetheless this huge complexity people are connected to their national pension system due to the existing underlying pension concepts. Each country possesses thus a unique own national pension identity. Every national pension landscape is created by or composed of the various pension forms occurring and operating concurrently, resulting in an aggregate pension concept that is tailored to a specific national context. It is this uniqueness that makes transposition of reforms from one country to another so complicated or at least deeply problematic. Changes from PAYG to funded schemes are therefore far from self-evident to be successful.

1 Introduction

A modern and ambitious welfare state tends to do much more than just poverty alleviation. Such a state shapes society by creating social rights and duties covering all kinds of social risks. The coverage and the coverage rate of pension schemes can be seen in this light. Many factors and parameters eventually thus determine the coverage and its' rate. When implementing parametric reforms, there is a kind of bandwidth for governments in which to handle the different parameters determining the duties and rights, similar to the range of frequencies within a given waveband used for an electronic signal. This bandwidth refers not only to changes within the pension schemes but also to the broader policy aspect defining the schemes themselves. The broadening or narrowing of rights and/or duties is thus clearly of a determinative, prescriptive and formative nature. This text reflects on the financing

Y. Stevens (✉)
Law Faculty KU Leuven, Leuven, Belgium
e-mail: yves.stevens@kuleuven.be

© Springer Nature Switzerland AG 2019
N. da Costa Cabral, N. Cunha Rodrigues (eds.), *The Future of Pension Plans in the EU Internal Market*, Financial and Monetary Policy Studies 48,
https://doi.org/10.1007/978-3-030-29497-7_4

55

techniques of funded or unfunded schemes not only from the classical point of view of risk sharing but also from the more historically and ideologically set-up of different notions of pensions and their underlying meaning and/or significance. This set-up or perspective has a clear impact on the range of possible tools a government has when trying to adapt the coverage of pension schemes.

2 Funded or Unfunded: The Aaron Condition and Governmental Choices

It goes without saying that there are vast differences between funded and unfunded pension schemes. The sponsoring, the time horizon, the investment (culture), the accounting rules for pension providers and employers alike,[1] the liabilities and the structure of the administration of the schemes are but simple examples in which these two basic financing techniques differ essentially and fundamentally.[2] In many western countries the domestic national pension landscape knows varieties between these two basic financing techniques types. Most statutory pensions are for example unfunded or PAYG while most personal pensions are funded. Occupational pensions are more often funded than unfunded in most western countries, although there are some countries such as notably France that have occupational pension in PAYG schemes (Agirc-Arcco).

From an historical point of view, many European statutory pensions schemes evolved from funded to unfunded just before or after the Second World War.[3] A lot of European member states started out with a funded obligatory pension scheme for all. These schemes were often unsuccessful due to very high inflation rates after World War One as well as due to the enduring lack of constant resources from the working population that was confronted with (high levels of) unemployment or lack of stable income. The strong and fundamental structural reforms from funded schemes to PAYG schemes were possible because of the exceptionally hard times people endured during two successive wars with a financial meltdown in between. Hard times often lead to full-sized structural reforms that are quasi impossible in more normal or common circumstances.

In any case the pension landscape nowadays is very divers with all kinds of statutory, occupational or personal pensions that exist in funded, unfunded or hybrid systems. Over the years, it seems as if a univocal and universal pension proverb has emerged saying that "a good national pension landscape" should have both funded and unfunded elements. Following this maxim, the combination of the two methods of financing has been preached as if they are balancing some unseen or invisible pension imbalance. However, there is no sound economic reason to believe this to be

---

[1]Roels (2010), pp. 1–23.

[2]Schmähl (2000), pp. 195–207; Davies (2000), p. 114.

[3]Peemans-Poulet (1995), pp. 29–65.

the case.[4] The collapse of many funded (obligatory of quasi obligatory) schemes in CEE countries has shown that the previously advocated favorable macroeconomic advantages of funded schemes such as risk diversification, better investment portfolios, increased savings, capital market development and better labour market incentives were often false.[5]

When it comes to the discussion between funded or unfunded schemes it is useful to go back to the principles that theoretically underpin this divide. Arguably the most influential set of principles in this regard are the ones set out in 1966 by Henri Aaron in the *Canadian Journal of Economics and Political Science*.[6] Ever since this publication on the equation between funded or unfunded pension schemes this equation is known as the Aaron condition.[7] The Aaron condition is based on an economic presumption that economic efficiency in any pension system—regardless of PAYG or funded—means that the pension benefits should be financed with the smallest possible contribution rate.[8] Economically this makes sense: how to get the highest pensions at the lowest cost for society?

According to the Aaron condition, a PAYG system is financed entirely by actual and current contributions while a funded scheme is characterized by actual and current contributions plus a return on investment over a period of time. Aaron was one of the first to make the economic comparison.[9] Depending on the real net return on investment, the average wage increases, the average (societal) employment ratio it is possible to ascertain economically when PAYG is more efficient than funding at least from a governmental point of view. The Aaron condition states that funding is more efficient than PAYG if the real net return on investment is higher than the sum of the average wage increases and the average increases of employment ratios over a given time.[10] The time horizon of 30–40 years is crucial in the Aaron condition.[11] From the point of view of the premium payer (i.e. microeconomic), the pay-as-you-go system is more attractive if the sum of the growth of participants together with the average income growth for each individual exceeds the real net return on investment.[12]

---

[4]Banyar (1991), p. 58.

[5]Hirose (2011), p. 5.

[6]Aaron (1966), pp. 371–374.

[7]Sometimes it is also refered to as the Samuelson scenario. This refers to Paul Samuelson who taught Aaron in the 1960s. See for example: Banyar (1991).

[8]Gollier speaks about the financial efficiency in this respect, while the economic efficiency also refers to the role of the pensionners as consumers. Gollier (1989), pp. 285–293.

[9]$Bt . Pt = c . Wt . Lt. (1 + r) = c. W0 . L0. (1 + m) . (1 + l)$ Whereby: B = average amounf of pension; P = number of people eligible for a pension; c = contribution rate; W = the average salary; L = working population; 0 = period of pension accrual; t = period of payment of pensions; r = rate of return over period 0 to t; l = growth in the working population between periods 0 and t; m = growth of the average salary between period 0 and t.

[10]Aaron (1966), p. 93.

[11]Deleeck (2000), p. 16.

[12]Hemming (1994), p. 561.

Since the 1980's PAYG public systems have been a particular focus of a number of neoclassical economists. Ever since the Chilean experiment whereby a full PAYG system was replaced by a funded scheme, it was argued that funding might lead to positive impacts both at a micro-economic and a macro-economic level. Nowadays, these findings are considered rather too blunt because of the assumptions of rational expectations and perfect information[13] in funded schemes.[14] The OECD now acknowledges that funded and unfunded schemes both have merits and shortcomings.[15] The Chilean experiment has in the meantime been reversed and elements of PAYG have been reinstated.

The choice that a government has to make between PAYG or funding is per definition biased and not made as if there is some kind of policy vacuum. This is due to an inherent generational choice.[16] Every starting or ending pension system has a generational problem depending on the chosen financing technique.[17] In a PAYG system, it is possible to give full pension benefits from the starting date of the system. The first generation of beneficiaries in this plan receive benefits that are often not proportional to possible contributions made within that same system. At least this is true when looking at the pension scheme from a social insurance (infra) point of view. Technically however, there is not a real finance problem in the sense of a monetary deficit for this first generation in a PAYG system, even if full benefits are given from the first day onwards. The problems are rather of a political or ideological nature and concerns fairness and justice.[18] After all, to a certain extent such a first generation gets a "free lunch". The question is fundamentally about societal acceptability. In the past many Western countries have opted for PAYG and have started the scheme right after the Second World War by taking over or nationalizing the existing but underfunded funded schemes.

Even if the start may not raise financial but rather political problems, terminating a PAYG system is a highly arduous and thorny task. PAYG is based on an intergenerational contract whereby current generations of pensioners depend on the current payers of contributions. If a generation stops paying, this can be construed as a breach of social contract. But this is inherent in all social security schemes where solidarity plays a role: people are (or must be) trusted to pay compulsory contributions or taxes to pay out those who are in need, whereby the payment of these contributions or taxes gives them a possible future entitlement. In pension schemes it is up to the government to determine how and when such an

---

[13]Correct information and transparency about cost and charges are just one element in this respect but is happens to be a rather thorny and difficult subject, see on this matter: OECD, "Pension costs in the accumulation phase: policy options to improve outcomes in funded private pensions" OECD Working Party on Private Pensions, Paris, OECD 2018, 34 p.

[14]Ferreiro and Serrano (2012), pp. 317–323.

[15]OECD (2018), pp. 19–20.

[16]Worth reading in this respect is: Hoff (2015), 82 p.

[17]Behrendt (2000), pp. 3–26; Chand and Jaeger (1996), 42 p; Orszag and Stiglitz (1999), 46 p.

[18]On the link between social justice and social law, see: Stroobant (2018), pp. 641–665.

intergenerational income transfer through distribution will take place, is upheld or cancelled in the future. This political insight can lead to generational frictions or even conflicts. The only way forward is either the acceptance or refusal by society in the generational transfers. With an ageing society it is certain that the balancing of generations can be hazardous from a political point of view.

At the same time, making a choice between PAYG or funded schemes is becoming more and more troubled, complex or even discomposed. This is due to the nature of investments in funded schemes. If a funded scheme takes government bonds as investment vehicle than there is a mixture of what I would call pure PAYG and pure funding. After all, government bonds are debts paid by a national population at large. Hence the nature of the financing is no longer "pure". The time horizon might differ[19] and pension providers might have some costs on the asset allocation side, however there is no clear doubt about the final debtor: the people.

The analysis on the financing techniques funding and PAYG goes far further than the mere debate of financing techniques or budgetary implications. The real debate is about spreading risks and thus responsibilities.[20] Who should carry which risks in what type of pension scheme? Fundamentally it is the role of a government to decide on the spread of these risks.[21] This spreading of risks is naturally linked with how a given country sees the different pension forms and the concepts it has historically envisaged and embedded in its' national welfare state or social policies (infra). The risks involved in setting up and running pension schemes are numerous, well known, miscellaneous and often (strongly) intertwined. The most commonly referred to risks include

- Longevity;
- Demography;
- Inflation or deflation including the low interest environment[22];
- Investment risk[23];
- Insolvency of the pension provider (including even a national government);
- Insolvency of an employer;
- Political instability and thus regulatory unpredictability;
- Economic instability;
- Labour market fluctuations.

All these elements are definitely worthwhile separate analyses but the way in which is dealt with them is also reflected in different pension concepts and notions

---

[19]This also shifts the intergenerational transfer or redistribution that is classically attributed to PAYG. See also: Davies (2000), p. 114. Davies concludes even that funded pension schemes may incur the same intergenerational effects as unfunded schemes (pg. 118–119).

[20]For an inspiring text, see Schokkaert and Van Parijs (2002), pp. 491–515.

[21]Bovenberg and Nijman (2016), p. 289; Gelissen (2001), pp. 495–523.

[22]For an interesting view, see: Ebinghaus and Wiss (2011), pp. 15–28.

[23]For a detailed analysis on the underlying risks related to investment in DC, DB or hybrid schemes, see: Ghilarducci (2009), 127 p.

used by countries. The analysis of these pension concepts is less well studied than the study of the risks themselves.

3   Underlying Pension Notions and the Significance of Historically Embedded Pension Concepts: A National Pension Landscape Is Defined in Many Ways

When studying pensions, one realizes quickly that pensions are a highly technical topic. Actuarial calculations and complex legal structures define elements such as acquired or vested rights, age cohorts, solvency, sustainability, transferability, (demographic) reserve funds, accounting standards, taxation and in some schemes investment policies. For the average citizen, all of this mathematical and legal technicality is often difficult to grasp without further education or reading. However, it is important to note that the technical nature of the subject matter does not imply its neutrality from a normative point of view: behind this veil of legal and actuarial technicality lies a distinctly ideological dimension which shapes pensions in a specific and contingent way. From a bird's eye view, organizing pensions in practice might seem like a purely technical matter, but a lot of the "small" rules point to a real ideological course.

Pensions remain a highly national competence in an ever globalizing world. As an element of the welfare state nations tend to keep pensions close at the heart of their national interest. Even within the EU for example there are no significant political powers pleading the case for an overall, general and overarching competence to develop a common European pension system replacing various national pension systems. Pensions thus always reflect a vision of the national welfare state. Consequently the pension landscape (even within the EU) is and remains very diverse. It is obvious that this diversity is historically embedded.

Although current governments might have some outspoken ideas on how their national pension systems should look like and how the pension systems should be further developed, almost no government preaches revolution by abolishing the existing legal structures and replacing them by entirely new structures. Apart from some Eastern European countries such as Hungary or Poland that have significantly altered the configuration of their pension systems most countries tread very softly when adopting legislation. Pension reforms are therefore known to be mainly parametric reforms. Structural and fundamental modifications are rather rare because they tend to alter existing rights or limit legitimate expectations of people. For most politicians preaching pension revolutions is out of the question due to the possible political instability of backlash that it will entail for themselves or the constituencies they represent.

This political inclination to parametric reforms is not only linked to a possible fear of political instability or strong negative reactions by the public. There is more to it. As a part of the welfare state, pensions are embedded in a—historically justified—vision on what a pension actually is or should represent. Every nation has a kind of pension landscape whereby the existing pension forms actually reflect an underlying "pension vision". It can be construed as a sort of "national pension identity". Although the word "pension" might at first sight seem to be univocal in meaning a kind of "money transfer at retirement", the underlying and primary idea can and often is multivocal even within a country. In any national context the word pension can thus reflect an assortment of underlying concepts or notions. With parametric reforms these concepts remain (roughly) intact. However structural pension reforms can upset the underlying concepts and implement fundamental alterations. As this can impact the political and societal support for pension reforms, structural pension reforms are often also seen as long term engagements whereby the changes into the system are put forward long before coming into force. Structural pensions reforms are known to work when they are very gradual or even slow. In order not to upset the legitimate expectations of people and by the creation of such stability pension notions tend to be very constant or even irreversible in countries.

In my opinion ten such different underlying pension concepts can be identified. These concepts are all used and referred to as "pension" but they (can) lead to very different understandings of how a pension system operates or should function. Hence it is important to recognize the exact meaning when someone uses the word "pension". In pension policy debates opponents of proposed reforms are inclined to use another concept of the word pension than the reformers themselves, as this enables them to criticize reforms without having to engage with the actual subject matter at hand. For example, reforms that wish to strengthen the link between pensions and previously earned wages can be criticized from a the perspective of a universal pension on the basis of citizenship. Neither forms are inherently right or wrong: they are simply expressions of different underlying ideas on what a pension should look like. In my opinion a better understanding of this polylithic structure of the word pension enhances the policy dialogue.

The pension concept can refer to:

1. A form of deserved rest. In this pension concept people will use the word pension to indicate that they have earned their retirement income after working. The pension is in this concept literally earned for a period in which people are entitled to rest. The concept reflects a dichotomy between the active and the passive life.
2. A compensation for the physical impossibility to work any longer. In this pension concept there is an underlying idea of (temporary) incapacity to work or even (permanent) invalidity for a pensioner. The pension is considered a consequence of a (presumed or real) inadequacy to work any longer and often even irrespective of a certain age or required seniority.
3. A part of the wage structure. This pension type refers to the contributory basis of the pension and is more often linked to funded schemes. The pension reflects the calculation basis on which the pension rights are based. As a part of the wage structure the pension is seen as a more negotiable remuneration.

4. A deferred remuneration. In this pension concept the idea is to have a postponed wage. The pension is thus seen as a part of the salary but not negotiable as such. This concept is often seen or used when the average salary is low but compensated by a relatively higher pension amount. It is more common in PAYG systems and often more used in civil servants schemes.

5. A reward for services paid to the country. This pension concepts occurs often in pension types of civil servants or military personnel. The pension refers to personal sacrifices an individual has incurred due to his or her service to the nation to which he or she belongs. Pensions in this regard are construed as an expression of gratitude on behalf of the nation.

6. A form of savings. Many statutory pensions have their legal origins in this concept. Pensions often started as funded personal savings schemes on individual accounts. Only after the first world war the first nationwide PAYG systems occurred often on the basis of the existing individual accounts. Ever since a lot of people think they have "saved" for their pension even if their statutory pension is PAYG. The savings concept is clearly present in some forms of occupational and unequivcally in personal pensions.

7. A form of property. This pension concept is often used in the jurisprudence of the European court of human rights. Some pensions can indeed reflect a property idea. Hence pension reforms can violate personal property rights. The use of the word pension as a property concept is often defensive in order to avoid the lowering of benefits in politically or regulatorily unstable environments.

8. A form of individual or collective life insurance. Many statutory pensions started as life insurances organized by national insurers working under the strict supervision of the state. Many occupational and personal pensions take the legal form of a life insurance. As a life insurance notion, people view their pension as risk sharing product.

9. A form of social insurance. Over the last 2 centuries many individual or collective life insurances became social insurances. These insurances are mainly characterized by two features. First there is a subsidy from the state or government. For each individual payment or payment by the employer there is a tax credit or a true subsidization. Hence the financial risk is socialized in the form of solidarity by all those participating in the scheme. Secondly, there is compulsory participation in the scheme. On the condition of fulfilling all prerequisites, a participant is legally obliged to pay into the scheme and be solidary with the other participants. This pension concept is well established in countries with a more Bismarckian social security tradition and social dialogue.

10. A form of shared citizenship. This form of pension is mainly present in countries that are historically more oriented towards the Beveridge type of social security. The mere fact of being legally recognized as a citizen is sufficient to claim pension rights. Few to no social contributions are involved in the financing. This more universal approach of pension form is often exclusively based on tax expenditure.

It goes without saying that these pension types are not (mutually) exclusive. On the contrary, often these various pension forms occur simultaneously in a given country and are often connected to one another. In my opinion it is exactly this unique mixture of the pension forms occurring at a certain moment in a given country that explains the uniqueness of each national pension landscape. Every national pension landscape is created by or composed of the various pension forms occurring and operating concurrently, resulting in an aggregate pension concept that is tailored to a specific national context. It is this uniqueness that makes transposition of reforms from one country to another so complicated or at least deeply problematic.[24] This is even more so if we recognize that pension forms are historically and ideologically embedded in this national "pension identity" of a nation or welfare state. The various national combinations of the ten pension forms consequently reflect a kind of identity in which people recognize their pension system as being their own.[25]

This "national pension identity" explains why, from an ideological (or political) point of view, there are no so-called "good" or "bad" pension systems in the world. All pension systems reflect an identity that has historically (and ideologically) been shaped. This is also the reason why pension reforms are in the short term perspective more successful when they are parametric instead of fundamentally and structurally reshaping the entire pension infrastructure. Pension reforms that are revolutionary by altering the pension identity require a structural accompanying by way of communication (e.g. Sweden) or budgetary injections. Even if pension reforms are "really necessary" from an economic point of view, this fact should not be forgotten from a political point of view. So even if the adequacy and sustainability of the pension system is under a large amount of economic pressure due to increasing poverty amongst the elderly or declining average income replacement ratios the changing of the system will be easier if the reforms do not conflict with the various existing pension forms defining the "national pension identity" of a country.[26]

The "national pension identity" is a patchwork reality.[27] The so-called three pillar model that has been promoted by the World Bank in the 1990s is an illusion from a legal perspective.[28] Nations around the world have developed pension schemes

---

[24]Mesa-Lago (2009), pp. 602–617.

[25]From a broader perspective on this identiy idea, see: Morris (2014), pp. 14–24; Van Oorschot et al. (2012), pp. 181–197.

[26]In Belgium for example a structural reform of the pension system was proposed in 2014. Although governments wanted to reform, it never succeeded and this was due to the shift in pension identity.

[27]This is recognized even in countries such as the Netherlands who have developed pension schemes that are very close to the so-called three pillar model. E.g. Jacobs (2017), p. 4.

[28]World Bank (1994), 402 p. Since the mid-1990s, the CEE countries have carried out structural reforms of their pension systems. Notably, several countries have introduced a Chilean-type of mandatory, privately managed pension system (the so-called second-pillar pension system). The CEE countries that implemented this type of pension system include Hungary (1998), Kazakhstan (1998), Poland (1999), Latvia (2001), Bulgaria (2002), Croatia (2002), Estonia (2002), the Former Yugoslav Republic of Macedonia (2003), the Slovak Republic (2005), and Romania (2008) (the numbers in brackets indicate the years of implementation). As these countries had pre-existing state

whereby all different pension notions are present in different schemes that are often hybrid.[29] Pension systems are by nature polylithical.

4 Governments Determining the Coverage Rate of Certain Pension Types Dispose of Several Tools in Their Kit

From a governmental point of view, pension policy is thus not only between choices involving PAYG or funded schemes, more importantly it also requires the managing of (all the above mentioned) risks while upholding the national pension identity. As a result, pension policy in reality boils down to a careful balancing act, modifying in a controlled fashion the parameters shaping various pension schemes. When it comes to the parametric reforms the government disposes of a kind of toolkit to define the specific bandwidth of their reforms. The broadening or narrowing of rights and/or duties is thus clearly of both a prescriptive and normative nature. I distinguish the following tools as the most critical for determining coverage:

- The level of organization
- The presence or absence of legal compulsion
- The taxation system
- The role of the social partners
- The labour market policy

These tools are intrinsically intertwined with the different pension notions in a country. As such they are part of or even shape the pension identity of a country.

4.1 Level of Organization

Pension coverage can be determined at several levels. The scope of the coverage is mainly determined by the kind of pension scheme and the competent organizer. A distinction can be made between:

---

pension systems, the reforms resulted in scaling down the state pension systems and partially replacing them with privately managed individual savings accounts. At the same time, the state pension systems (now called the first-pillar pension systems) were also reformed by changing some key scheme parameters (e.g. the extension of the qualifying period for pensions, the increase in the pensionable age, and the transition from wage indexation to price indexation). Some countries (including Poland, Latvia, Sweden and Italy) introduced notional defined-contribution accounts (sometimes referred to as non-financial defined-contribution accounts) for their state pension systems. The multi-pillar pension reform strategy advocated for in a seminal report by the World Bank (1994) played a very influential role in the policy debate. Hirose (2011), pp. 4–5.

[29]The same applies for the wording of "private" or "public" schemes. Most schemes are hybrid and the words "public" or "private" are contested and entails methodological research questions. See on this issue: De Deken (2013), pp. 270–286.

- Nationwide schemes;
- Regional schemes;
- Sectoral schemes applicable to certain branches of industry or certain professions;
- Company schemes;
- Employee related schemes;
- Purely personal schemes.[30]

The scope of the coverage is mainly reflected by the legal competence of the level on which the scheme is organized. This link between the scope of the coverage and the competence of the organizer is well known, clear, understandable and even self-evident. A national government will for example obviously be able to operate a national scheme.

These different levels of organization reach further than the so-called three pillar model promoted by the world bank (first pillar: nationwide; second pillar: sectoral or company; third pillar: personal).[31] The levels of organization reflect the state structure and the position of the different actors such as social partners involved in the social policy of a country. For example the creation of a regional pension fund only for inhabitants of that region or employees working for a certain region is often a clear sign of the regional constitutional freedom.[32] Countries with a high degree of centrifugal powers and requests for more independence from the central government will increasingly develop regional social policies. Another example is strength of labour unions. Countries with traditionally strong trade unions will often put less emphasis on personal or individual pension schemes. The organizational level of coverage is in these cases often also reflected by a more paritarian approach in pension policy.[33]

4.2 Compulsion

From a member's point of view, pension schemes can be mandatory (often the case in nationwide statutory schemes or company occupational schemes), quasi-mandatory (often the case in sectoral occupational pension schemes such as in the

---

[30]See for example the website of EIOPA with all possible variants in occupational schemes.

[31]For a very good and comprehensive overview of the role of the world bank in the promotion of the three pillar model, see Orenstein (2008), 216 p.

[32]Some European regions in Europea such as Flanders in Belgium, Catalonia in Spain or Trentino Alto Adige in Italy have regionally develop supplementary funds for certain employees or civil servants.

[33]The lack of social consensus in the pension reform process of many CEE countries raised for example serious concerns. A well-informed and participatory reform process is critical for making rational decisions based on broad consensus. Yet social dialogue was weak or sometimes absent in the pension reform processes of many countries, and many workers' and employers' organizations attempted to search for ways to influence pension policy with only limited success. Hirose (2011), pp. 4–5.

Netherlands, Denmark or Germany), quasi-voluntary (in the case of auto-enrolment as in the UK) or voluntary (often the case in personal (saving) pension plans) (e.g. Germany).

Although there are some clear preferences for countries, there is no clear link between the type of compulsion and the kind of pension scheme at hand. Some personal plans are mandatory (e.g. PKK in Poland for employers) and some nation-wide schemes are voluntary (e.g. German Riester rente). This is even true for the kind of funding. PAYG is not solely organized on a nationwide level but can also be found in sectoral professional schemes (e.g. some Belgian civil servants employed by local communities or the French system of AGIRC-ARCCO).[34]

It is an unmistakable fact that compulsion leads to higher degrees of coverage. Nearly all social security schemes globally operate on a compulsory basis for increasing the level of solidarity and reducing the administrative cost per head. Compulsion can therefore be seen—together with solidarity—as a main feature of social security. It leads to governmentally guaranteed protection and (social) welfare. In the same way it is clear that compulsion is far less obvious for personal pensions and savings. The choice to consume later by saving for retirement income or to consume today[35] is mostly left to individual choice. If the resources are present and the savings capacity it allows for it, the individual is considered to be personally capable and sufficiently knowledgeable to distinguish between his or her actual personal needs versus the future needs at retirement. In most Western free market economies, this individual liberty is esteemed logical and therefore governments should not intervene too heavily with obligatory membership.[36]

More complex than the question about implementing forms of compulsion in statutory (yes) or personal (no) schemes is the question of compulsion in occupational schemes. Ideologically speaking, occupational pensions are often seen as being in between statutory and voluntary when it comes to compulsion. Faced with increasing budgetary constraints in the statutory pension schemes many governments are gradually looking into widening all forms of supplementary pensions (occupational or personal). Consequently, the coverage of the new or renewed supplementary scheme is central.

Two elements are therefore important. The first one is taxation (see below). In my opinion the correct focus on the targeted group of beneficiaries or members is fundamental and essential when allocating tax incentives. If tax incentives are given these inducements should be given to those people having the highest needs to additional retirement income and this should be in balance with the overall fiscal cost for a country. Solidarity means in this respect that the strongest shoulders should bear the burden of the weaker members of society. If not, tax incentives

---

[34]www.agirc-arrco.fr

[35]This includes all forms of actual savings including e.g. homes (mortgages) or cars.

[36]Nonetheless legal protection of savings amounts is a prerogative for most Western countries. Savings are seen as forms of property requiring adequate protection.

just encourage people to shift money they would have saved anyhow into tax-advantaged accounts.[37]

The second element is the nature of the compulsion. The idea of compulsion in supplementary pensions differs strongly from the same idea in statutory pensions. When it comes to social security, it is more or less generally accepted that compulsion and obligation are "natural" or at least inherent components.[38] However, in a free market economy the presence of compulsion into occupational pensions can be and is questioned from two angles. The first angle is the one of the member who is compelled to forfeit a part of his actual remuneration (and thus direct consumption) for future benefits. The freedom to dispose of one's wages is often legally embedded. An employee can freely decide on his wages. The second angle is one of the employer having to step into a scheme that is being run by others than himself. Both angles reflect the same idea: the freedom to decide whether and how to deal best with income is disregarded. In the past employers in the Netherlands have tried to reject the legal obligation to adhere to a sectoral pension fund by claiming that they could get higher returns on investment and thus better pensions if there would not be any form of compulsion.[39] The ECJ overruled this reasoning by stating clearly that it was a matter of social policy to keep these compulsions in place.[40] At the same time, a very comparable idea can be presented by employees who do not have any say in the choice by their employer for a certain pension provider being a pension fund, insurance company, asset manager or any other financial institution that runs the employers occupational scheme.

Both angles reflect a similar ideological theme present in the shaping of the welfare state being the scope and depth of the paternalistic welfare state.[41] How far is a policy of legal paternalism legitimate? The justifications to instate more or less compulsion or freedom in pension schemes goes hand in hand with the underlying pension identity. Auto-enrollment in the UK is a good example. The classical British welfare state was and is far less interventionist than for example the German social security system. Ever since SERPS (the state earnings related pension scheme) was installed in 1978, individual freedom to choose has been important. When the scheme was established, employers with final-salary pension schemes could indeed choose to contract-out of SERPS, provided they gave scheme members a Guaranteed Minimum Pension. This freedom conflicts with the idea of compulsory solidarity in many continental European countries. In the British context however it is reasonable to assume that the auto-enrollment into occupational pension schemes is considered

---

[37]Ellis et al. (2014), p. 123.

[38]For an interesting analysis, see: Jaime Castillo (2013), pp. 390–405.

[39]Heemskerk et al. (2016), p. 340.

[40]Three judgements were made on the 21 September 1999 by the ECJ in this respect (Brentjens' (C-115/97, C-116/97 and C-117/97, ECR 1999 p. I-6025), Albany (C-67/96, ECR 1999 p. I-5751), Drijvende Bokken (C-219/97, ECR 1999 p. I-6121).

[41]Wyper (2017), pp. 352–375.

a success. Having a possibility to opt-out of the default option lies closely with the pension notion being a kind of remuneration.

An increasing number of countries are looking into the possibility of implementing auto-enrolment (Ireland, Poland, Turkey). However, the installation of such scheme might not always be as successful as in the UK due to the historically embedded pension notion. After all, in an auto-enrollment system an individual can be asked to take active decisions. This active outlook on individual responsibility is not self-evident in all countries. It can mean a mentality shift in the underlying pension notions.

4.3   Role of the Social Partners

In countries where the pension notions of remuneration or deferred salary are strongly present there is often also a link to social insurance. Historically, these countries also have well-established trade unions and social dialogue.

When it comes to occupational pensions in more Bismarckian oriented welfare states the social partners have played and are still playing an important role in governing, organizing, managing, supervising and dealing with pension schemes in the broadest sense of the word. Social partners are used to work in dialogue and making compromises. Countries such as Belgium, Sweden, the Netherlands, Finland or Germany with long traditions of social dialogue can use the paritarism (i.e. the social dialogue between employers and employees on company level, in a branch of industry or for a certain profession) to determine the coverage or coverage rate.[42]

4.4   Taxation

As in all social policies, taxation is also influential when it comes to coverage.[43] Indeed, one of the most if not the most important tool for a government to influence coverage and coverage rate is taxation. Many countries have installed tax incentives for occupational or personal pensions. The fiscal treatment of the contributions, the return on investment and the final benefits is seen as key for the development of any pension type or scheme.

Personal pension savings are for example often mainly present in countries where fiscal incentives are worthwhile. The effectiveness of these fiscal incentives is often questioned.[44]

---

[42]Steinmeyer (2000), pp. 163–165; Davies (1994), pp. 29–42.

[43]Peeters (2014), pp. 249–265.

[44]OECD (2018), pp. 51–55; Ellis et al. (2014), p. 123; De Witte et al. (2009), pp. 151–175.

4.5 Labour Market Policy

In many ways, a lot of pension forms are a factual derivative of the labour market. This is in any case true for many forms of statutory pensions[45] and occupational pensions. Personal pensions are often individually based forms of savings that operate legally apart from the labour status. The coverage in pensions is indeed in many ways a derivative of the labour market. The working status (employee, self-employed, civil servant) or the non-working status (unemployed, sick, houseman or housewife, parental leave, etc.) determine together with the number of working hours and the remuneration the (kind of) membership to a pension scheme. As a derivative of the labour market it is clear that any possible discrimination of unequal treatment in the one leads to possible questions in the other.

As such a derivative of the labour market, pension policies are consequently shaped by labour market policy. If for example the number of self-employed rises compared to the number of employees or civil servants this can affect the statutory pension budget, the social security budget, the budget on tax incentives for occupational or personal pensions. In some countries there are substitutive effects between different forms of pensions (e.g. a decline in statutory pensions can be influence by a rise in occupational or personal pensions). These effects should be taken into account by government looking at their labour market policies. Unfortunately this is often not the case.

The best example of the close link between labour policy and pension policy is the rise in the retirement age. Together with the average increase of the pensionable age many European member states have installed incentives for working longer with a clear intention and focus for a more general labour market participation. The knife thus clearly cuts both ways: on the one hand the contributions and taxes towards pensions increase and the benefits have to be paid less long due to the increasing longevity. It is clear that for example many European governments—mainly with a Bismarckian tradition—have been strengthening some kind of "insurance principle" in their statutory schemes by trying to clarify some kind of link between the contributions paid and pensions received. Examples along the same legislative lines are the review mechanisms of benefits and the decreasing of (automatic) indexing mechanisms.

5 Evolution: Background of a Silent Pension Pillar Implosion

In order to understand "the role of the government in creating or enhancing the access to funded or unfunded pensions in a modern welfare state" the background of pension reforms should be highlighted.[46] A distinction should be made between the

---

[45]Exception being the citizenships pensions such as for example the AOW in the Netherlands.
[46]Hoff (2015), 82 p.

so called structural reforms whereby the pension system of a country is profoundly and structurally altered by for example changing the financing from PAYG to funded or the introduction of new so-called pillar type of pension (supra). Apart from structural reforms there are also parametric reforms. These reforms do not change the underlying structure of the pension scheme but change some parameters within the calculation method (such as pensionable age) or the administrative process (e.g. sending emails instead of paper envelopes).

Structural pension reforms alter the so-called pension identity of a country. From a political point of view, these reforms are really complex and challenging. Structural reforms such as switching from funded to unfunded, are generally hard to sell because they change the underlying pension notions and forms of a country (supra). There are but a few successful examples such as Sweden with the notional defined contributions (NDC). There are many more examples of countries that have not been able to alter their system structurally and are hence on the drift (e.g. Poland or Hungary).

However, it is not because parametric reforms such as raising the pensionable age or the number of years required in a pension calculation that parametric reforms are to be viewed as merely symbolic. This is definitely not the case. Parametric reforms can have huge effects and consequences on the pension outcome, the income replacement ratio or the administrative process. Parametric reforms however do not change the existing structure of the existing pension forms or the general pension landscape. As a matter of speaking the identity of the pension structure is not altered and the public still recognizes its' unique pension identity.

Where structural reforms require smoothing and time with very gradual implementation (even decades to come into full force) parametric reforms are easier in the sense that the general level of understanding the consequences is a lot higher and thus leading to higher degree of (possible) broad public acceptance. Structural reforms tend to attract far more opposition because of the difficulty of understanding the changes. In other words a well-informed and participatory reform process is critical for making rational decisions based on broad consensus.

The creation or enhancement of the access to funded or unfunded pensions in a modern welfare state can be both structural or parametric. It depends on the national context how the access is historically embedded in certain pension types and thus whether a reform of creation or enhancement is to be seen parametric or structural. Whether parametric or structural though, one cannot deny that for the last years changes have taken place in a lot of pension systems, be they statutory, occupational or personal in nature. Although it is difficult to see general or overall tendencies some observations can be made on these reforms.

The first observation is clearly that occupational and personal pensions have clearly been impacted by the (very) low interest environment. The second observation is that the role of the social partners has unequivocally declined and that collective bargaining is less prevalent in pension schemes than it used to be. The third observation is the stabilization of the sovereign debt crisis. When the European member states were hit by the economic crisis of 2009 their respective governments had trouble keeping their sovereign debt stable. Due to interventions such as those by the ECB the economic stability for governments has increased. The fourth observation is that more and more pension schemes have shifted the risks towards the individual.[47] This shifting of the risks can been seen as a silent pension pillar implosion.[48]

The role of occupational pensions is changing in a lot of countries. Due to de-risking or risk shifting in occupational pensions, occupational pensions are increasingly being individualized.[49] Employers back away. This withdrawal occurs just as the task of accumulating adequate retirement income has gotten harder. The world grapples with low or even negative interest rates. For years the general increases in voluntary pensions have been said to alleviate the (financial and budgetary) pressure on the publicly managed and state provided pension schemes. However if the risks are gradually individualized after retirement then the question arises whether the types of individualized pension schemes are truly pensions in the sense of an element of the welfare state or mere (fiscally subsidized) saving accounts.

6 Conclusion: Reforms on Coverage Require Trust

Whatever pension system a government may envisage, pensions have proven to be a very sensitive political debate for a great deal of people. Changes to existing schemes are often difficult from a political point of view. A national government that acts wisely thus tries to teach evolution and never preaches revolution. Some eastern European countries such as Hungary and Poland have not been good students in this class. An overall turnover of the system leads to a decline in the overall trust in the pension system. This should be avoided as people need to be able to trust their pension system.

This trust seems to be difficult when it comes to altering the coverage and the coverage rate of the schemes. The clear analysis is that pension systems have become extremely complicated systems. Whether statutory, occupational or personal all pension forms are remarkably difficult to understand in depth. No wonder that in pension legislation the devil is often in the detail. In my opinion pension legislation has rapidly increased in complexity over the last two decades in many western countries. I believe this complexity is mainly linked to the awareness of the ageing society inviting governments to reform their schemes. These parametric changes have steered to a great amount of new legislation with regard to coverage in various

---

[47] Jacobs (2017), p. 7.

[48] Stevens (2017), pp. 98–117.

[49] See for a very detailed analysis on the US but with many similar valid lessons for other countries: Stevens (2017), pp. 98–117.

ways. Most governments have upheld their national pension identity by installing justifiable parametric instead of structural reforms but at a price of complexity. This leads to a paradox: in order to maintain the trust in the existing schemes it is vital not to change too abruptly the underlying pension concepts and notions in a country. However by not changing things fundamentally but rather parametric, the pension legislation has become very difficult to grasp and understand. The paradox being of course that this can lead to distrust of the system as the sheer complexity and opaqueness of the pension system can lead to the erosion of trust.

For many countries, the ageing of society is still an ongoing challenge. The parameters defining the bandwidth of coverage of funded or unfunded schemes will therefore remain at the heart of pension policies in the coming decade. My personal prediction is that more countries will start looking towards funded schemes with an increased responsibility for the individual for personal pension savings. Simultaneously, auto-enrollment in occupational schemes will likely be ever more an object of study.

References

Aaron H (1966) The social insurance paradox. Can J Econ Polit Sci 32(3):371–374

Banyar J (1991) "Possible reforms of PAYG pension systems", in E.J.S.S. 2016/18, 286–308. In: Deleeck H (ed) Zeven lessen over sociale zekerheid. ACCO, Leuven

Behrendt C (2000) Private pensions – a viable alternative? Their distributive effects in a comparative perspective. ISSR 53(3):3–26

Bovenberg L, Nijman T (2016) Persoonlijke pensioenrekeningen met risicodeling. In: Van Ewijk C, Heemskerk M, Maatman H, Nijman T (eds) Pensioen 2020. Kluwer, Deventer

Chand SK, Jaeger A (1996) Aging populations and public pension schemes, paper 147. International Monetary Fund, Washington

Davies B (1994) Participation des syndicats aux régimes complémentaires. La Revue de L'IRES 15:29–42

Davies B (2000) Equity within and between generations: pension systems and equity. In: Hughes G, Stewart J (eds) Pensions in the European Union: adapting to economic and social change. Kluwer, London

De Deken J (2013) Towards and index of private pensions provision. J Eur Soc Policy 23 (3):270–286

De Witte K, Stevens Y, Roels P (2009) The Matthew effect: why current pension policy helps the rich get richer. In: Stewart J, Hughes G (eds) Personal provision of retirement income, meeting the needs of older people? Edward Elgar, Cheltenham, pp 151–175

Deleeck H (2000) De betaalbaarheid van de pensioenen. In: CSB Berichten. UFSIA, Antwerpen, p 16

Ebinghaus B, Wiss T (2011) Taming pension fund capitalism in Europe: collective and state regulation in time of crisis. Transfer 17(1):15–28

Ellis C, Munnell A, Eschtruth A (2014) Falling short: the coming retirement crisis and what to do about it. Oxford University Press, Oxford

Ferreiro J, Serrano F (2012) Uncertainty and pension system reforms. J Econ Issues 45 (2):317–323

Gelissen J (2001) Old age pensions: individual or collective responsability. Eur Soc 3 (4):495–523

Ghilarducci T (2009) The plan to save American Workers' retirements. In: Orenstein M (ed) Pensions, social security and the privatization of risk. Columbia University Press, New York

Gollier J-J (1989) Les problèmes de pension vus dans la perspective des trois pilliers. Reflets perspectives de la vie économique 4:285–293

Heemskerk M, Maatman R, Werker B (2016) Heldere en harde pensioenrechtechten onder een PPR. In: Van Ewijk C, Heemskerk M, Nijman HM e T (eds) Pensioen 2020. Kluwer, Deventer

Hemming R (1994) "Should public pensions be funded?", I.S.R.R. 1999/2, 3–29. In: Kune J (ed) De controverse kapitaaldekking versus omslagfinanciering, S.MA

Hirose K (2011) Pension reform in central and Eastern Europe in times of crisis, austerity and beyond. ILO, Budapest

Hoff S (2015) Pensions: solidarity and choice: opinions of working people on supplementary pensions. SCP, The Hague

Jacobs A (2017) Pensioenrecht: de sociaalregelijke en sociaalpolitieke aspecten. Kluwer, Deventer, p 4

Jaime Castillo A (2013) Public opinion and the reform of the pension systems in Europe: the influence of solidarity principles. J Soc Policy 23:390–405

Mesa-Lago C (2009) Re-reform of Latin American private pensions systems: Argentinian and Chilean models and lessons. Geneva Pap Risk Insur 34(4):602–617

Morris M (2014) Values as the essence of culture: foundation or fallacy. J Cross Cult Psychol 45 (1):14–24

OECD (2018) OECD Pension outlook 2018. OECD, Paris

Orenstein M (2008) Privatizing pensions: the transnational campaign for social security reform. Princeton University Press, Oxford

Orszag P, Stiglitz J (1999) Rethinking pension reform: ten myths about social security systems. World Bank, Washington

Peemans-Poulet H (1995) Sociale zekerheid: de 70ste verjaardag van de werknemerspensioenen. In: Belgium Ministerie van Sociale Voorzorg (ed) En toen kwam het pensioen. Bruylant, Brussel, pp 29–65

Peeters H (2014) The invisible tax system: how taxation impacts pension outcomes in Belgium. In: Van Oorschot W, Peeters H, Boos K (eds) Invisible social security revisited. Lannoo, Leuven, pp 249–265

Roels P (2010) Myths with respect to accounting for pensions. In: Stevens Y (ed) Protecting pension rights in times of economic turmoil. Intersentia, Cambridge, pp 1–23

Schmähl W (2000) PAYG versus capital funding: towards a more balanced view in pension policy. In: Hughes G, Stewart J (eds) Pensions in the European Union: adapting to economic and social change. Kluwer, London, pp 195–207

Schokkaert E, Van Parijs P (2002) Pension policies for a just Europe: individual versus collective responsibilities. Belg J Soc Secur 44(3):491–515

Steinmeyer HD (2000) The decision making process in the German pension system. In: Hughes G, Stewart J (eds) Pensions in the European Union: adapting to economic and social change. Kluwer, London, pp 163–165

Stevens Y (2017) The silent pension pillar implosion. Eur J Soc Secur 19(2):98–117

Stroobant M (2018) Ideologie en sociaal recht: over de ideologieën als verborgen rechtsbronnen en over de eenheid en diversiteit in de sociaalrechtelijke structuren. In: Liber Amicorum Willy Van Eeckhoutte. Kluwer, Mechelen, pp 641–665

Van Oorschot W, Reekens T, Meuleman B (2012) Popular perceptions of welfare state consequences: a multilevel, cross-national analysis of 25 European countries. J Eur Soc Policy 22 (2):181–197

World Bank (1994) Averting the old age crisis: policies to protect the old and promote growth. Oxford University Press, Oxford

Wyper A (2017) Pensions auto-enrolment: unintended consequences of regulation and private law remedies. Edinb Law Rev 21:352–375

Yves Stevens is a graduate of the Universities of Namur (French speaking), Leuven (Dutch speaking), Brussels (ULB—French speaking) and London (Queens college). He holds a PhD in law from the University of Leuven.

Current positions

Currently, Yves is a full time law professor at the University of Leuven where he is also the coordinator of the specialized pension law program and the director of the legal post-academic training programs. Yves is an executive professor at the Antwerp Management School (Financial Planning).

Yves Stevens is the Chair of the editorial board of the Belgian Journal for Social Security and a member of the Scientific Committees for the judgement of the academic quality of projects and researchers of:

– The FNRS: Fonds de la Recherche Scientifique (Scientific Research Fund) of the Wallonia-Brussels Federation (www.fnrs.be);

– The Netspar's Scientific Council (www.netspar.nl).

Yves is a member of:

– The ENRSP (European Network For Research On Supplementary Pensions) (I'm also treasurer of this organization);

– The Belgian academic council for pensions (previously known as the expert commission for pension reform 2020-2040);

– The editorial board of the Journal for Social Law (dutch);

– The advisory council for pensions for independent workers within the Financial Services Market Authority (FSMA);

– European Institute on Social Security (EISS);

– The scientific council of the AEIP.

The Coverage of Occupational and Personal Pension Plans

Maria Teresa Medeiros Garcia

Abstract Expanding private pension plans coverage is seen as an alternative to address the growing pension gap. Indeed, due to recent reforms, lower public pension system replacement rates are expected for future generations of retirees. However, in most countries, private provision remains voluntary and the coverage rates observed are still very low. Several factors might explain this evidence and several policy options have been suggested to increase coverage in private pension plans. Yet, the issues concerning both the decision of the occupational pension plan type, defined benefit or defined contribution, and the characteristics of the personal pension plans, are most important and complex, as the implications for attaining the expected retirement income adequacy are diverse. This paper reviews these issues and the coverage of these pension plans.

1 Introduction

Corporate and personal private pension plans are suppose to fulfil the provision needs of income at retirement. Indeed, the financial pressure on public social security systems calls for proposals to restructure these systems, which are not consensual (Beattie and McGillivray 1995; Diamond and Orszag 2004; Orenstein 2011). In the case of promoting voluntary or compulsory employer-organized retirement savings plans, a key aspect of the decision to offer a pension plan is the choice of what type of pension plan to establish. On the other hand, participation in a personal pension

REM, Research in Economics and Mathematics; UECE (Research Unit on Complexity and Economics) is financially supported by FCT (Fundação para a Ciência e a Tecnologia), Portugal. This article is part of the Strategic Project (UID/ECO/00436/2019).

M. T. M. Garcia (✉)
ISEG, Lisbon School of Economics and Management, Universidade de Lisboa, Lisbon, Portugal
e-mail: mtgarcia@iseg.ulisboa.pt

© Springer Nature Switzerland AG 2019
N. da Costa Cabral, N. Cunha Rodrigues (eds.), *The Future of Pension Plans in the EU Internal Market*, Financial and Monetary Policy Studies 48,
https://doi.org/10.1007/978-3-030-29497-7_5

plans depends on individual circumstances (such as age, income, education), tax incentives, and on herd behavior, faulty logic, and defective information.

Section 2 presents the differences in the attributes of these structures regarding sponsor liability, funding, benefit assurance, and the risks for sponsors and employees, as well as a brief analysis concerning large declines in defined benefit plans in many countries. Section 3 reviews the main issues about personal pension plans.

Section 4 gives evidence on the coverage of occupational and personal pension plans in the EU. Finally, Sect. 5 concludes.

2 Occupational Pension Plans: Defined-Benefit (DB) Versus Defined-Contribution (DC) Pension Plans

Private pension systems design is experimenting significant changes worldwide (Antolín et al. 2012; DWP 2017). Accordingly, the provision of retirement income is increasingly relying on private employer-provided defined contribution (DC) pension plans. Traditionally, defined benefit (DB) pension plans have provided employees with relevant part of retirement income. However, among private sector, those plans have declined while defined contribution plans have increased.

The attributes of the two structures are significantly different and worth mentioning (Davis 1995).

In a DB plan the member's pension benefit entitlement is determined by a formula which takes into account wages or salary, years of service for the employer[1] and, in some cases, other factors. Many defined benefit formulas also take into account the social security benefits to which an employee is entitled. These are the so-called integrated plans (Bodie et al. 1988). The DB plan framework focuses on the flow of benefits which the individual will receive upon retirement. Hence, the calculation of the funding status of DB plans is complex and controversial. If the plan's assets are invested in traded securities, their market value is relatively easy to ascertain. The source of difficulty is in measuring the sponsor's liability. From a strictly legal point of view the sponsor's liability is the present value of the accrued vested benefits which would be payable if the plan was immediately terminated. But many pension experts contend that sponsors have an implicit semicontractual obligation which makes it more appropriate to take account of projected future salary growth in the computation of the firm's pension liability. The contention of a further obligation beyond the legal one makes it unclear whether a real or nominal interest rate should be used in discounting future benefits (either with or without salary growth projections) to compute their present value. The major advantage of DB plans is the potential they offer to provide a stable replacement rate of final income to

---

[1]Length of employment.

workers. If the replacement rate is the relevant variable for worker retirement utility, then DB plans offer some degree of insurance against real wage risk. Of course, protection offered to workers is risk borne by the firm. As real wages change, funding rates must correspondingly adjust. However, to the extent that real wage risk is largely diversifiable to employers, and nondiversifiable to employees, the replacement rate stability should be viewed as an advantage of DB plans. On the other hand, employers have used defined benefit plans in competitive labour markets to attract and retain skilled employees. The anticipated shortage of skilled workers accompanying the retirement of the baby boom generation raises the possibility that defined benefit plans might make resurgence, if the regulatory environment were to facilitate such a development.

Under a DC plan each employee has an account into which the employer and, if it is a contributory plan, the employee make regular contributions. Benefit levels depend on the total contributions and investment earnings of the accumulation in the account. Often the employee has some choice regarding the type of assets in which the accumulation is invested and can easily find out what its value is at any time. Defined contribution plans are, in effect, tax deferred savings accounts in trust for the employees, and they are by definition fully funded. At retirement, the employee either receives a lump sum or an annuity, the size of which depends upon the accumulated value of the funds in the retirement account. The employee thus bears all of the investment risk and the firm has no obligation beyond making its periodic contribution. Valuation of the DC plan is straightforward: simply measure the market value of the assets held in the retirement account. However, as a guide for personal financial planning, the DC plan sponsor often provides workers with the indicated size of a life annuity starting at retirement age that could be purchased now with the accumulation in their account under different scenarios. The actual size of the retirement annuity will, of course, depend upon the realized investment performance of the retirement fund, the interest rate at retirement, and the ultimate wage path of the employee (Antolín et al. 2009; Antolín et al. 2010). Defined contribution plans cannot be used to retain long-service workers because their account balances are fully portable once vested so they provide workers no incentive to stay with their current employer. Yet, Munnell et al. (2018) note that the retirement savings of those with a 401(k) plan[2] is often hindered by portability and leakage problems.

The shift from DBP to DCP is a phenomenon spread throughout most of the OECD countries (OECD 2005a). Indeed, with pension systems reforms undertaken worldwide, retirement and financial risks are increasingly being shifted to individual households (European Commission 2003; OECD 2002, 2003a, b, 2005b; World Bank 1994; Holzmann and Stiglitz 2001).

The causes of the decline in defined benefit plans and the move toward defined contribution plans have been evaluated (Broadbent et al. 2006; Turner and Hughes 2008). Those reasons can be divided into two categories: changes in the economy and changes in regulations. The first category can be divided into changes in

---

[2]A type of employer-sponsored retirement plan in United States.

the characteristics of workers, changes in the characteristics of employers, and macroeconomic changes. Regulatory changes include changes in laws and regulations and changes in accounting requirements, which affect the cost of providing pensions.

Changes in the characteristics of workers that may affect their demand for defined benefit pensions include a decline in unionism and an increase in job mobility. Unions traditionally have favored defined benefit plans over defined contribution plans. On the other hand, more mobile workers generally fare better in defined contribution plans than in defined benefit plans. Workers' account balances in defined contribution plans, once vested, are fully portable. By comparison, the accrued benefits in defined benefit plans generally are not portable, and are reduced in value for job changers. In addition, the greater numbers of women in the labor force may be a factor in the reduced demand for defined benefit plans. Women may have less attachment to a particular employer than men because they have greater responsibility for care-giving. Also, they are more likely to be influenced by job changes of their husband than the reverse because they tend to have lower salaries than their husbands, though that tendency is declining. Consequently, these factors suggest that an increasing proportion of workers would favor pensions that do not penalize job change, which would include defined contribution plans and cash balance plans.

Further, employers also have reasons for wanting to provide defined benefit pensions namely to enforce a long-term implicit contract with employees that can importantly affect productivity (influencing the type of worker attracted to the job and shaping behavior while on the job) and retirement decisions (Ippolito 1997). However, changes in characteristics of employers that may affect their demand for defined benefit plans include a decline in manufacturing, which has been associated with the provision of defined benefit plans, and a growth in the service industry, which has been associated with the provision of defined contribution plans. Manufacturing firms may have a greater need to retain experienced employees than service firms where skills are more transferable across employers, perhaps explaining the greater demand for defined benefit plans by manufacturing firms.

Changes in the costs of providing pensions are another reason to explain the international transition towards DC plans. Factors affecting costs of providing defined benefit pensions relative to defined contribution pensions can be categorized into three groups: changes in asset markets, increasing longevity, and changes in regulations.

The low interest rates, which raise the value of pension liabilities, and the stock market declines during the early years of the 2000s, have highlighted for employers the macroeconomic risks they face in financing defined benefit plans. The decline in asset markets means greater contributions are needed to provide a given level of assets at retirement. The decline in interest rates means that a larger asset base is needed when converting to an annuity to achieve the same level of annuitized benefits.

The increase in life expectancy means that a larger asset base is needed to provide the same level of benefits over the longer retirement period. The effect of this change can be large. Employers bear the cost of increases in life expectancy, and they bear the risk of unexpected increases in life expectancy.

Finally, frequent changes in legal requirements and increased reporting requirements and administrative burdens have raised the compliance costs for defined benefit plans (OECD 2004). Defined benefit plans require actuarial valuations, which is an aspect of costs not required for defined contribution plans. Hence, the decreasing trend of the defined benefit plans type and the increasing trend of the defined contribution plans type is probably the result of the accounting rules and regulatory changes (Yermo 2007).

In this context, the role and the impact of accounting and regulatory changes should be reviewed regularly fostering the development of better risk management and investment strategies better aligned with the liability structure of pension funds. Better information disclosure should also be required to assess the extent to which management institutions act in members' interests.

3   Personal Pension Plans

Personal pension plans[3] are a type of defined contribution pension scheme. They are individual contracts between the member and the pension provider, which is an insurance company or an independent provider. These were created by governments, with tax incentives, in many countries, to address personal saving rates decreases (Attanasio and Banks 1998; World Bank 1994; Holzmann and Stiglitz 2001). They expected that, by exempting contributors from certain taxes, personal savings would increase more than the tax revenue loss. Yet, this expected effect is not straightforward. Skinner (1991) concluded that IRAs may not be effective in increasing savings because the degree of adhesion for these accounts is relatively small. Furthermore, it seems that most of the tax benefits have gone to high-income households (Gale and Scholz 1994; McCarthy and Pham 1995; Skinner and Hubbard 1996; Antolin et al. 2004).

Furthermore, a significant percentage of individuals often shows an astonishing ignorance of the most basic provisions determining future retirement incomes (Burtless 2004). Therefore, greater attention should be put on education and regulation issues (Mitchell and Utkus 2003). Ghilarducci and Pavlakis (2016) suggest that the optimal policy solution is Guaranteed Retirement Accounts (GRAs): mandatory, professionally managed accounts that supplement social security.

The high degree of risk might be one of the factors that discourages people from enrolling in IRAs (Casey 2004).

---

[3] Also known as Individual Retirement Accounts (IRAs).

4 Coverage of Funded and Private Pension Plans

The coverage rate[4] of pension plans is a relevant measure of the importance of its role of fulfilling the provision needs of income at retirement within each country. OECD (2018) notes that, as expected, the coverage rates are usually higher among countries with mandatory plans. However, some caution is due concerning available data as individuals may be counted as members several times if they hold accounts in several funds and there is no way to match duplicate records. Therefore, coverage data only provide an estimate of the upper limit of what the true coverage is.

A plan is mandatory when employers have to set up a plan for their employees (e.g. Norway) or when employees have to contribute to a state funded pension scheme (e.g. Denmark, Latvia) or a private pension fund of their choice (e.g. Chile, Mexico). OECD (2018) data consider a plan as quasi-mandatory when employers are requested to set up a plan for their employees as a result of labour agreements (e.g. Korea, Netherlands). A plan is voluntary if there is no compulsion for employers to set up a plan nor for employees to participate in a plan (e.g. Portugal, Lithuania). In the United States, most pension plans in the private sector are provided through an employer on a voluntary basis (Munnell et al. 2018). However, at any moment in time, about half of private sector workers are not participating in an employer-sponsored pension plan and the percentage of workers covered has not improved since the late 1970s. Finally, in some countries, employers have to enrol their employees in a pension plan under certain conditions, but employees have the option to opt out of the plan within a certain timeframe. These automatic enrolment programmes are set up at the national level in New Zealand, Italy, Turkey and the United Kingdom.

In 2017, in countries where participation in a plan was mandatory, the coverage of funded and private pension plans is higher than 70% (the highest level ever), e.g. Australia, Chile, Denmark, Estonia, Finland, Iceland, and Israel (Fig. 1).

The coverage rate is lower in some OECD and non-OECD countries for various reasons. The coverage rate of mandatory plans was still relatively low in Armenia in 2017 (16%) as mandatory plans were only introduced recently. High rates of informal work in Mexico and Peru (ILO 2016) may explain the relatively lower participation in mandatory plans (covering formal workers) compared to other OECD countries. In Malawi, the coverage rate was also low in 2017 at 3.1%, as the Reserve Bank of Malawi reported that a considerable number of employers have not joined the mandatory pension system yet. In the case of the Slovak Republic, the coverage rate of mandatory plans may be lower than in other OECD countries as members have been given several opt-out windows since the inception of mandatory plans in 2005.

---

[4]The coverage rate is measured by the number of active members of a pension plan over the working age population (i.e. individuals aged 15–64 years old). Active members are individuals with assets in a pension plan and who are not retired yet. They may be actively contributing or may be holding rights in a plan.

As a percentage of the working age population

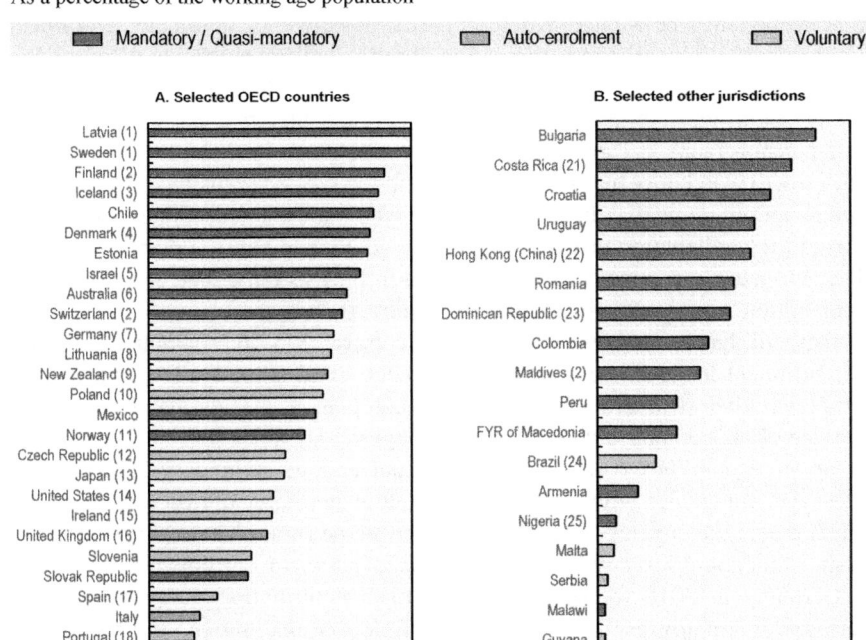

Fig. 1 Coverage of funded and private pension plans, latest year available (As a percentage of the working age population). Source: OECD (2018); OECD Global Pension Statistics. Notes: Data refer to 2017, unless stated otherwise. (1) The coverage is close to 100%. (2) Data refer to 2016. (3) The coverage rate includes foreign workers in Iceland. (4) This result is the ratio of ATP members below the retirement age and paying contributions in 2017 over the population aged 15–64. (5) Data refer to new pension funds only. A saver can be an active member in more than one pension fund. (6) Source: ABS Survey of Income and Housing 2015–2016. (7) Source: Federal Ministry of Labour and Social Affairs (Survey on Pension Provision 2015). The coverage rate refers to 2015 and is expressed with respect to employees aged 25–64 subject to social insurance contributions. (8) Data refer to the membership of the second pillar only. (9) Source: KiwiSaver website. Data include individuals below 18. (10) Data refer to members of open pension funds only. (11) Source: Finance Norway. The coverage rate of mandatory plans is based on the number of active members in private group pensions and municipal group pensions. It is compulsory for government employees (who represent a significant part of the Norwegian working population) to be members of the Norwegian Public Service Pension Fund, financed by the Norwegian State Budget. This Fund is out of the scope of this report and members of this Fund are therefore not taken into account in this chart. (12) The coverage of pension plans in the Czech Republic is calculated over the population below 65 as children may be members of plans opened by their parents. (13) Source: Ministry of Health, Labour and Welfare. (14) Chap. 4 of the OECD Pension Outlook 2012. (15) Source: Quarterly National Household Survey, Module on Pensions Q4 2015. The coverage rate represents the proportion of workers aged between 20 and 69 with a pension plan. (16) Data come from DWP's Family Resources Survey 2016/2017. (17) Source: Spanish Survey of Household Finances (EFF) 2014 by Bank of Spain. The result shows the percentage of households with a pension scheme (or a unit-linked or mixed life insurance product). (18) Source: Inquérito à Situação Financeira das Famílias (ISFF) (2013 edition). The value refers to the proportion of

The introduction of automatic enrolment led to higher coverage rates in New Zealand and the United Kingdom. The objective of automatic enrolment programmes is to increase the participation of individuals in a pension plan, relying on behavioural economics (e.g. inertia). The number of KiwiSaver members has kept increasing over the last years (FMA 2017), and the coverage of funded and private pension plans in New Zealand (68%) was close in 2017 to most OECD countries with mandatory plans. The Department for Work & Pensions (DWP) in the United Kingdom found that the introduction of automatic enrolment in October 2012 improved the participation rate of working-age adults in a pension plan.

The automatic enrolment was more limited in Italy as only 20% of the working age population was covered by a pension plan in 2017.

Turkey still has a relatively low coverage compared to other countries as automatic enrolment has only been introduced recently and is gradually being phased in. Employees below 45 are enrolled in a pension plan at different dates depending on the size of the company, starting with the largest companies (i.e. companies with 1000 or more employees) in January 2017 and ending in January 2019 for the smallest (i.e. companies with 5–9 employees). It is therefore still too early to know to which extent the coverage of funded and private pension plans will rise.

Some other countries have also just introduced automatic enrolment programmes (e.g. Germany in 2018 for occupational defined contribution pension plans for private sector employees in the case of deferred compensation, if specified in collective agreements) or are preparing legislation in this respect (e.g. Ireland, Lithuania and Poland).

5 Conclusion

Private pension systems are going through changes. However, large declines in DB plans are not inevitable. They can be prevented or reversed by public policy if governments decide that preserving defined benefit plans as an important part of the retirement income system is desirable. Public policy changes in this respect can be grouped into three categories: (1) changes that reverse policies that have lead to the decline in defined benefit plans, (2) innovative policies that strengthen defined

---

Fig. 1 (continued) households having a voluntary pension plan. (19) Data refer to 2016. (20) The coverage rate for Turkey shows the number of individuals who are members of a private pension plan and/or an auto-enrolment plan among the working age population. Individuals who are members of several plans are only counted once. (21) Data refer to the number of members of mandatory supplementary pension schemes only. (22) Data refer to the number of members of MPF schemes and other retirement schemes. The coverage rate would be 85% if the employed population was used as the denominator instead of the working age population. (23) Data refer to all the affiliates of the private pension system. Only half of the affiliates were contributing in 2017. (24) Data refer to the active participants of open pension funds only. (25) Data refer to the number of members of contributory pension schemes

benefit plans by shifting some of the cost and risk to workers, and (3) policies that level the playing field with defined contribution plans by providing stricter regulation of defined contribution plans.

Concerns with accumulating assets through personal pension plans, in order to address the growing pension gap, are exclusive to few people as just a minority seems to be able to plan effectively for retirement. Policy makers should consider the individual characteristics that influence the participation in personal pension plans when addressing pension reform. Indeed, less-educated and lower income individuals seem not to be able to supplement decreasing public retirement provision through personal pension plans. On the other hand, many workers in developed and developing markets still lack easy access to pension plans and saving products (World Economic Forum 2017). The self-employed and informal sector workers are least likely to have access to a workplace savings plan. Also, those working at smaller companies, where regulation may make providing a plan overly burdensome for employers, are also at a disadvantage. Munnell et al. (2018) summarize options to expand retirement savings among traditional workers with and without access to workplace plans in order to substantially shrink the coverage gap in the United States. In this context, they conclude that the challenge in the coverage area is not just providing pension plans for the uncovered population but doing so in a cost-effective way.

Furthermore, spurring individual choice in the context of retirement security has an implicit assumption about behavior, namely that the individual to whom the responsibility of choice has been handed to is a well-informed economic agent, who acts rationally to maximize their self-interest. In contrast, in the real world, individuals' decisions are subject to several restrictions, namely: bounded self-interest or bounded selfishness, in the sense that many individuals seek to maximize their personal welfare, yet they prove far more cooperative and altruistic than economic theory predicts they will be; bounded self-control, in the sense that individuals have the right intentions or beliefs, but they lack willpower to carry out the appropriate changes in behavior; and bounded rationality, in the sense that certain types of decisions and problems may be simply too complex for individuals to master on their own (Banks and Oldfield 2007; Garcia 2009). The way that defined contribution pension plans are designed puts a high level of responsibility on individuals to manage their retirement savings. This includes deciding how much to save each year, which investments to choose, how long they are likely to live, when they should retire, and how to withdraw their savings when they do decide to retire full-time. All these constraints should be considered in the design, management, and regulation of personal retirement savings plans. Policy makers should be more aware of these issues and take actions toward consumer education and regulation.

Moreover, pension privatization policies, implemented in a number of countries, as a consequence of the concern with the pattern of increasing pension expenditure, did not deliver the expected results, as coverage and benefits did not increase, systemic risks were transferred to individuals and fiscal positions worsened (Orenstein 2011; ILO 2018). Consequently, several countries are reversing privatization measures and returning to public solidarity-based systems.

In addition, recent austerity or fiscal consolidation trends affected even more the adequacy of pension systems and general conditions of retirement, putting at risk the fulfilment of the minimum standards in social security and, consequently, the contribution of public pension systems to the Sustainable Development Goals (SDGs) (Casey 2014; ILO 2017, 2018; Garcia and Silva 2019).

Acknowledgment The author wishes to thank the anonymous reviewer for the careful reading and the pertinent comments and suggestions.

References

Antolin P, de Serres A, de la Maisonneuve C (2004) Long-term budgetary implications of tax-favored retirement savings plans. OECD Economic Studies, 2(39)

Antolín P, Blome S, Karim D, Payet S, Scheuenstuhl G, Yermo J (2009) Investment regulations and defined contribution pensions. OECD Working Papers on Insurance and Private Pensions, No. 37. OECD publishing, © OECD, Paris

Antolín P, Payet S, Yermo J (2010) Assessing default investment strategies in defined contribution pension plans. OECD Working Papers on Finance, Insurance and Private Pensions, No. 2. OECD Publishing, Paris. https://doi.org/10.1787/5kmdbx1nhfnp-en

Antolín P, Payet S, Yermo J (2012) Coverage of private pension systems: evidence and policy options. OECD Working Papers on Finance, Insurance and Private Pensions, No.20. OECD Publishing, Paris

Attanasio O, Banks J (1998) Trends in household saving don't justify tax incentives to boost saving. Econ Policy 13(27):548–583. https://doi.org/10.1111/1468-0327.00040

Banks J, Oldfield Z (2007) Understanding pensions: cognitive function, numerical ability and retirement saving. Fisc Stud 28(2):143–170

Beattie R, McGillivray W (1995) A risky strategy: reflections on the World Bank report averting the old age Crisis. Int Soc Secur Rev 48(3–4):5–23

Bodie Z, Marcus AJ, Merton RC (1988) Defined benefit versus defined contribution pension plans: what are the real trade-offs? In: Bodie Z, Shoven JB, Wise DA (eds) Pensions in the U.S. Economy. University of Chicago Press, Chicago

Broadbent J, Palumbo M, Woodman E (2006) The shift from defined benefit to defined contribution pension plans - implications for asset allocation and risk management. Prepared for a Working Group on Institutional Investors, Global Savings and Asset Allocation established by the Committee on the Global Financial System

Burtless G (2004) Social norms, rules of thumb, and retirement: evidence for rationality in retirement planning. The Brookings Institution, Washington, DC

Casey HB (2004) Why people don't choose private pensions: the impact of 'Contagion'. Discussion Paper PI-0503. The Pensions Institute, London

Casey BH (2014) From pension funds to piggy banks: (Perverse) consequences of the stability and growth pact since the Crisis. Int Soc Secur Rev 67:27–48. https://doi.org/10.1111/issr.12029

Davis EP (1995) Pension funds - retirement-income security, and capital markets - an international perspective. Clarendon Press, Oxford

Diamond A, Orszag PR (2004) A summary of saving social security: a balanced approach. MIT Department of Economics Working Paper No. 04-21. Available at SSRN: http://ssrn.com/abstract=544244. https://doi.org/10.2139/ssrn.544244

DWP (2017) Security and sustainability in defined benefit pension schemes

European Commission (2003) Occupational pensions: Commission welcomes European Parliament approval of proposed Directive, IP/03/360, Brussels, 12th March 2003

FMA (2017) KiwiSaver annual report 2017

Gale W, Scholz JK (1994) IRAs and household saving. Am Econ Rev 84(5):1233–1260

Garcia MTM (2009) Pension reform and individual responsibility, 7th International Workshop on Pension. Insurance and Saving, Bratislava

Garcia MTM, da Silva AFRR (2019) Assessing pension expenditure determinants – the case of Portugal, REM Working Paper 068-2019. REM – Research in Economics and Mathematics

Ghilarducci T, Pavlakis A (2016) The states of reform. Schwartz Center for Economic Policy Analysis and Department of Economics, The New School for Social Research, Working Paper Series 2016-1

Holzmann R, Stiglitz JE (eds) (2001) New ideas about old age security: toward sustainable pension systems in the 21st century (English). The World Bank, Washington, DC

ILO (2017) World Social Protection Report 2017–19: Universal social protection to achieve the Sustainable Development Goals. International Labour Office, Geneva

ILO (2018) Social protection for older persons: policy trends and statistics 2017–19. Social Protection Policy Papers, Paper 17, International Labour Office, Social Protection Department. ILO, Geneva

International Labour Office (ILO) (2016) Social contract and the future of work: inequality, income security, labour relations and social dialogue. The Future of Work Centenary Initiative Issue Note Series (No. 4) (Geneva)

Ippolito RA (1997) Pension plans and employee performance: evidence, analysis, and policy. University of Chicago Press, Chicago

McCarthy J, Pham HN (1995) The impact of individual retirement accounts on savings. Current Issues in Economics and Finance, September Vol. 1, Number 6, FRBNY

Mitchell OS, Utkus SP (2003) Lessons from behavioral finance for retirement plan design. Pension Research Council WP

Munnell AH, Belbase A, Sanzenbacher GT (2018) An analysis of retirement models to improve portability and coverage. Center for Retirement Research at Boston College and Summit Consulting, LLC, Special Report, March

OECD (2002) Guidelines for pension fund governance. Financial Market Trends, No. 83

OECD (2003a) Strengthening private pensions – international standards, data and analysis. The OECD Working Party on Private Pensions

OECD (2003b) Private pensions: OECD classification and glossary

OECD (2004) Guidelines for the protection of rights of members and beneficiaries in occupational pension plans. Financial Market Trends, No. 87

OECD (2005a) Pensions markets in focus. Newsletter June 2005, Issue 1

OECD (2005b) Ageing and pension system reform: implications for financial markets and economic policies. Supplement to Financial Market Trends, November 2005

OECD (2012) OECD pensions outlook 2012

OECD (2018) Pension markets in focus

Orenstein MA (2011) Pension privatization in Crisis: death or rebirth of a global policy trend? (July–September 2011). Int Soc Secur Rev 64(3):65–80. Available at SSRN: https://ssrn.com/abstract=1879020. https://doi.org/10.1111/j.1468-246X.2011.01403.x

Skinner J (1991) Individual retirement accounts: a review of the evidence. NBER, WP 3938

Skinner J, Hubbard RG (1996) Assessing the effectiveness of saving incentives. J Econ Perspect 10 (4):73–90

Turner JA, Hughes G (2008) Large declines in defined benefit plans are not inevitable: the experience of Canada, Ireland, the United Kingdom, and the United States. Discussion Paper PI-0821. The Pensions Institute, Cass Business School, City University

World Bank Policy Research Report (1994) Averting the old age Crisis. In: Policies to protect the old and promote growth. Oxford University Press, Oxford

World Economic Forum (2017) We'll Live to 100 – How Can We Afford It? Geneva, Switzerland

Yermo J (2007) Reforming the valuation and funding of pension promises. OECD Working Paper on Insurance and Private Pensions No. 13

Maria Teresa Medeiros Garcia holds a PhD degree in Economics from ISEG, Technical University of Lisbon. Research interests include pension economics and finance, applied economics, microeconomics and financial economics. Currently, she is assistant professor at the Department of Management at ISEG, Universidade de Lisboa. http://orcid.org/0000-0001-8683-2112

Sustainability and Adequacy of Pension Systems Across the OECD: Shocks, Robustness and Policies

Falilou Fall

Abstract Demographic developments are unfavourable for the financing of pension schemes in most OECD countries, implying continued growth in pension expenditure in virtually all OECD countries. This chapter examines the vulnerability of pension systems, with an emphasis on financial sustainability and adequacy. Policy trade-offs and complementarities are reviewed and flanking policies, which could underpin successful pension reforms, are examined. Automatic adjustment mechanisms are highlighted, as are the roles of prudential regulation and buffer or reserve funds in the case of shocks.

1 Introduction and Main Findings

Pension schemes have been reformed in most OECD countries over the last 20 years to cope with the demographic trend towards ageing populations. However, more efforts are needed to ensure the long run financial sustainability of pension schemes while preserving pension adequacy. Moreover, pension systems face challenges related to structural factors, such as productivity or migration trends, that can have important impacts on their financing. Short-run developments, as illustrated by the 2008–2009 crisis, can also have significant impacts on pension schemes. For instance, investment returns of private funded schemes were hard hit during the crisis.

Demographic shocks are a main source of vulnerability of pension systems. Demographic developments are unfavourable to the financing of pension systems

The author is member of the Economics Department of the OECD. The author thanks Corinne Chanteloup for statistical assistance and Peter Hoeller for comments on earlier drafts. Regretted Debbie Bloch contributed to an earlier version. The opinions expressed in this paper are the author's and do not necessarily correspond to those of the OECD or its member countries'.

F. Fall (✉)
Economics Department, OECD, Paris, France
e-mail: falilou.fall@oecd.org

in most OECD countries, because of rising life expectancy and declining fertility rates. The resulting decline in the old age support ratio is particularly challenging for pay-as-you-go (PAYG) pension schemes as pension spending is financed by contributions of current workers. This is compounded by lasting effects of the recent crisis and slowing productivity growth.

The sustainability of pension systems can be ensured by a combination of different policy measures. Many countries are phasing in increases in the retirement age to restore the financial health of pension schemes. Adjusting key parameters automatically to cope with changes in structural variables can increase the financial robustness of pension systems. Many countries have introduced adjustment mechanisms to take into account changes in life expectancy. The adjustment can link the pension level, retirement age or contribution period to life expectancy. Increasing the contribution rate would improve financial sustainability, but could have a negative impact on labour markets.

Various policy levers exist that can bolster the sustainability of funded pension schemes. In particular, a sound prudential regulatory framework for private and defined-contribution schemes is needed to protect individuals' pensions. Prudential regulation should aim to balance the trade-off between the prevention of excessive risk-taking and the goal of high returns on investments. In addition, buffer and reserve funds, which exist in many countries, can play an important role as smoothing tools in the case of shocks. They can be used to avoid annual parametric changes of pension schemes, thereby limiting uncertainties.

Pension reforms already enacted to ensure financial sustainability raise pension adequacy issues as replacement rates from mandatory pension schemes are expected to decrease in the future in some countries. The adequacy of pensions is already an issue in some OECD countries with regard to old age poverty. On average, 12% of the over 65 year olds in OECD countries live in poverty.

Different policies can improve the adequacy of pensions. For instance, indexation and revaluation rules of pensions play an important role in determining the pension level. They should be designed in a way that balances their sustainability and adequacy impact. Too high indexation and revaluation rates increase pension spending while too low indexation of pensions will create adequacy issues in the long run, particularly among the older pensioners. However, specific rules can guarantee that pension levels for pensioners with full contribution periods remain above the poverty line. Finally, increasing coverage of voluntary private pensions should be a prime objective in countries where they represent an important complement to (relatively low) public or mandatory pensions.

In most countries, the retirement age has been increased and early retirement schemes phased out to improve the financial sustainability of pension schemes. The success of these policies depends on well-functioning labour markets, in particular for older workers. In many OECD countries, the effective age of labour market exit is lower than the official retirement age. However, older workers employment have been increasing driven by increasing retirement age. To raise the employment rate of older workers, reforms should include a better screening of access to long-term disability schemes, changes to the implicit tax on continued work by increasing the bonus for deferred retirement up to the actuarially neutral level, favouring the development of part-time work for older workers and enabling the combination of work with pension receipt.

Section 2 of this chapter presents the patterns of population ageing in the OECD and the main shocks that affect pension schemes. Section 3 presents the policy levers to enhance the financial sustainability of pension systems and Sect. 4 discusses the adequacy of pension schemes, drawing out policy trade-offs and complementarities.

2 Shocks to Pension Systems and Sustainability

Pension schemes are exposed to trend changes of productivity and migration, which have long lasting transitory effects (Fall 2014). Over the long run, population ageing puts upward pressure on spending along with longevity and investments risks for funded pension schemes.

2.1 Population Ageing Remains the Main Challenge to Pension Sustainability

The ageing of societies has two components: the decrease of fertility rates and the increase of life expectancy. In all OECD countries, life expectancy has increased since the 1970s (Fig. 1). One striking feature of this ageing trend is the gain in life expectancy at 65 years. In most OECD countries, life expectancy at 65 reaches 20 years for women and 15 years for men.

The rise in life expectancy has induced an increase in the duration of retirement even if the retirement age has been raised progressively in many countries. If retirement ages remain at the same level, more time will be spent in retirement and, with unchanged benefits, pension expenditure will rise. In addition, larger cohorts are entering retirement with the labour market exit of the baby boom generation and fewer people will contribute because of low fertility rates.

Life expectancy gains are combined with a decrease in fertility rates in almost all OECD countries. These two phenomena are jointly lowering the old-age support ratio. It is projected that between 2015 and 2050, the average OECD old-age support ratio will double in the next 35 years (Fig. 1, Panel B).

Moreover, the changing age structure of the population will exert downward pressure on GDP per capita growth. The slowing growth of working-age populations will exert pressure on potential growth of GDP per capita, and may lead to durably slower increases in living standards if policies do not adjust rapidly enough. Assuming no changes in institutional and policy settings, global growth will decline in the next decades, mostly due to demographics in OECD countries (Guillemette and Turner 2018). The falling share of the working-age population is projected to drag

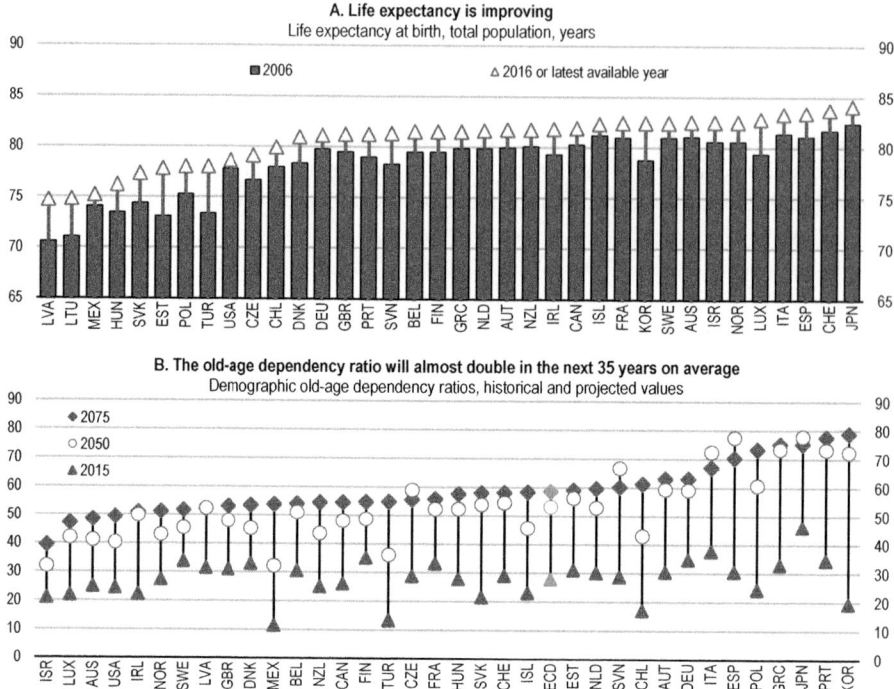

Fig. 1 Ageing remains the main challenge. *Source*: OECD Health Statistics; OECD (2017), Pensions at a Glance 2017. *Note*: The demographic old-age dependency ratio is defined as the number of individuals aged 65 and over per 100 people of working age defined as those aged between 20 and 64

down real GDP per capita by up to ½ percentage point per year in the euro area. Lower growth leads to lower wage bill, which is the base for pension contributions.

Moreover, population ageing is suspected to have contributed to the "productivity slowdown", and may continue to weigh on labour productivity growth in decades to come. First, the age profile of employment will continue shifting towards older workers whose skills are more at risk of becoming obsolete as digitalisation transforms labour market needs. Evidence from the OECD Survey of Adult Skills confirms that older workers score lower on literacy and numeracy proficiency than younger adults, reflecting both lower initial education and age-related declines (Paccagnella 2016). Second, an older labour force may be less entrepreneurial, less creative and less innovative than a younger one, though evidence is mixed in this regard. Third, a larger share of elderly population will shift the structure of consumption, and therefore of production, towards lower-productivity services such as personal care. These composition effects may reduce aggregate productivity growth. Lower productivity will also have negative impact on pension sustainability or adequacy depending on the type of pension schemes (see Box 1).

Box 1 Key Features of Two Stylised Pension Models and Their Reaction to Shocks

The PAYG DB scheme

In the PAYG defined-benefit scheme, employees contribute to the financing of the scheme during their career. At retirement, the pension is calculated by applying a pension rate to the reference salary, which is the average career salary. The reference salary depends on the revaluation index used to up-rate past salaries at the retirement year, which is the growth rate of wages. During retirement, pensions are indexed to the inflation rate.

At the scheme level, each year's contributions pay current pensions. The annual balance depends, on the financing side, on the size of the payroll and the contribution rate and, on the spending side, on the number of retirees and on the average pension. If pension spending exceeds total contributions the scheme is in deficit. The actuarial balance of the scheme is the discounted sum of the expected annual balances of the scheme over the projection period.

The PAYG DC point scheme

The accumulated rights of an individual are calculated in terms of the number of points accumulated over the working life. The number of points acquired is determined by dividing contributions paid by the purchasing value of the point, which is determined as the price of one unit of differed life annuity. The pension at retirement is calculated by multiplying the number of points by the service (or selling) value of the point, which is the balancing value of the scheme. The service value of the point is identical for all insured individuals. It converts the points into monetary values at the retirement year and also during retirement. Thus, pension levels during retirement are revalued with respect to its development.

The purchasing value of the point and the service value of the point are the two key parameters for the steering of the scheme. They are adjusted to ensure that the scheme remains in balance. Point prices depend on the projection of life expectancy by age cohort.

Both schemes are in steady state in the baseline scenario and balanced. In the baseline demographic scenario the mortality rate is constant. There is thus no ageing and the number of retirees is constant. Alternative scenarios show the effect of various shocks as deviations from the baseline.

Notional defined-contribution (NDC) schemes (as in Sweden and Italy) are not modelled, but their functioning is close to a point scheme with the difference that contributions are recorded in individual accounts. In particular, the internal rate of return on accumulated capital is set to guarantee the actuarial balance of the scheme. It has the same function as the adjustment mechanisms of the point scheme. In both cases, the determination of the adjustment mechanisms takes into account the evolution of life expectancy.

(continued)

Box 1 (continued)

The impact of a negative productivity shock

The stylised model was used to simulate the impact of a productivity shock on a DB scheme. Under the assumption that productivity and real wages move in tandem over longer periods, the productivity shock is simulated as a permanent reduction in the growth rate of the real wage by 1 percentage point.

Due to the shock, the balance of the DB scheme moves gradually into deficit up to year 40 (−17% of baseline revenues) and then it improves gradually to −5% of baseline revenues in the long run (Table 1). As initial pensions are tied to wage developments, the average pension decreases considerably in the long run in comparison with the baseline average pension. Revenues go down by even more, as revenues depend on the wage bill, which is much larger than the pension bill.

The PAYG DC point scheme is balanced by definition. As the revenues of the scheme decrease, pension benefits shrink progressively leading to a reduction in the average pension by 50% compared with the baseline average pension. The service value of the scheme decreases in line with the revenues of the scheme. In the long run as the cohorts entering into retirement are affected by the productivity shock and therefore have accumulated less capital points, the decrease of the service value necessary to balance the scheme is lower than that the one in the medium term.

The impact of a migration shock

The migration shock is a permanent negative shock. From the initial year of the shock, the size of the cohort entering the labour market (aged 20) is lowered permanently by 5%. 40 years later all working cohorts are 5% smaller than in the baseline. The support ratio (contributors per pensioner) decreases continuously from the initial year of the shock to year 40 as the cohorts of lower size age. 40 years after the shock, these smaller cohorts start retiring which improves the support ratio progressively. 70 years after the shock, all retired cohorts are 5% smaller than in the baseline.

The impact of the negative migration shock on the balance of the DB scheme follows the evolution of the support ratio and is temporary. From the initial year of the shock to year 40 the balance of the scheme deteriorates. Then, as these cohorts of lower size retire, the support ratio improves and so does the balance of the scheme. In the long run, the DB scheme reverts to balance.

The DC point scheme is balanced by definition. The negative impact of the migration shock is absorbed by declining pensions. As revenues of the scheme decline, the service value of the point is reduced to balance the scheme. The average pension decreases in line with contributions and stays below the baseline in the long run.

(continued)

Box 1 (continued)

The impact of ageing

The demographic shock scenario corresponds to a longevity shock. The longevity shock induces a fall of the support ratio from 2.3 to 1.5 in the long run.

In the DB scheme, ageing induces a progressive deterioration of the balance of the scheme. The average replacement rate (the ratio of the average pension to the average wage) in the ageing scenario is lower than in the baseline due to a decline in the average pension, reflecting the fact that pensions are averaged among all cohorts in retirement, with the oldest pensioner cohorts having lower pensions than younger cohorts as pensions are indexed to prices, rather than wages.

The DC point scheme is balanced by definition. The negative effect of the same ageing process is reflected in a decline in the replacement rate. The decline in the replacement rate is larger than for the DB scheme. Also, the service value of the point diminishes in line with the support ratio whereas the purchasing value of the point—defined as the price of one unit of differed life annuity—increases with life expectancy. Therefore, individuals gain a lower number of points at a lower service value. The adjustment of the point values keeps the scheme in balance.

Source: Fall, F. (2014), "A Framework of Comparing the Robustness of PAYG Pension Schemes", *OECD Economics Department Working Papers*, No. 1134, OECD Publishing, Paris.

Ageing will be the main driver of increases of public expenditure on pensions. The projected increases of pension spending has led to many reforms in advanced countries to ensure the sustainability of pension schemes. In particular, in European countries where main pension schemes are public. These reforms have mainly resulted in reducing pension spending, as seen in Fig. 2, which compares projections of pension spending in 2050 realised in 2009 and in 2050 for European countries. The main reforms have been to increase retirement age, reduce pension entitlements and in some case, increase contribution rates.

2.2 Longevity Risk and Defined-Benefit Schemes

Defined-benefit plans are exposed to uncertainties surrounding future life expectancy developments. Public pension systems and private pension funds providing defined pension benefits need to assess the number of future pensioners based on long-term projections. Longevity risk is the risk that actual life spans of individuals or of whole populations will exceed expectations.

Table 1 Vulnerability of PAYG schemes to shocks. Difference with respect to the baseline

	Year 10 after the shock	Year 30 after the shock	Year 40 after the shock	Year 70 after the shock
Productivity shock				
DB scheme				
Difference in balance (in % of baseline revenues)	−0	−7	−17	−5
Difference in average pension (in %)	−3	−13	−16	−44
Difference in average pension (in %)	−3	−20	−33	−50
Difference in point service value (in % of baseline value)	−2	−17	−30	−22
Migration shock				
DB scheme				
Difference in balance (in % of baseline revenues)	−2	−5	−7	0
Difference in average pension (in %)	0	0	0	−2
Point DC scheme				
Difference in average pension (in %)	−2	−5	−7	−2
Difference in point service value (in % of baseline value)	−2	−4	−6	0
Ageing shock				
DB scheme				
Difference in balance (in % of baseline revenues)	−7	−23	−26	−29
Difference in average replacement rate (in % points)	−4	−3	−4	−5
Point DC scheme				
Difference in average replacement rate (in % points)	−7	−10	−12	−13
Difference in service value (in %)	−4	−14	−18	−21

Note: The scheme is balanced in the baseline scenario. The productivity shock is a reduction in the growth rate of the real wage by 1 percentage point. The migration shock is a permanent negative shock. The size of the cohort entering the labour market (aged 20) is lowered permanently by 5%. In the long run the labour force is 5% lower than in the baseline. The ageing shock induces a fall in the support ratio from 2.3 to 1.5 in the long run. The average pension is the annual average of pensions among all pensioners. The average replacement rate is the average pension over the annual average wage among all workers

IMF (2012) and Antolín (2007) show that projections consistently under-estimated improvements in mortality and life expectancy in the past. The underestimation pertains partly to the projection method and the lack of data for the very old (those aged 85 and above). Studies show that, on average, life expectancy has been underestimated by 3 years. According to IMF (2012) estimates, the additional cost of providing individuals of age 65 and over with a 60–80% replacement rate for those additional 3 years adds between 1.5 and 2.0 percentage points of GDP to the annual cost of ageing in advanced economies in 2050.

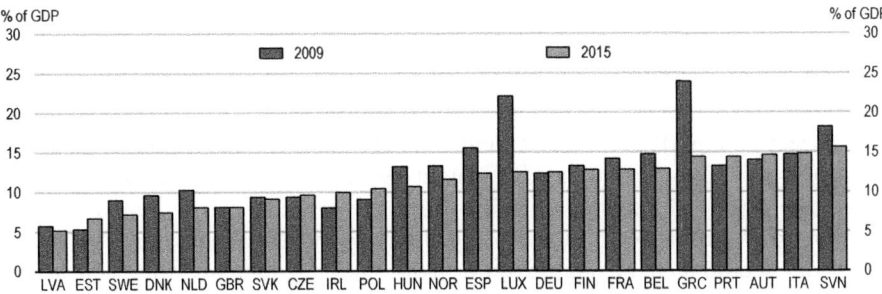

Fig. 2 Projections of public expenditure on pensions in 2050. *Source*: OECD (2017), Pensions at a glance 2017; European Commission (2009), 2009 Ageing Report

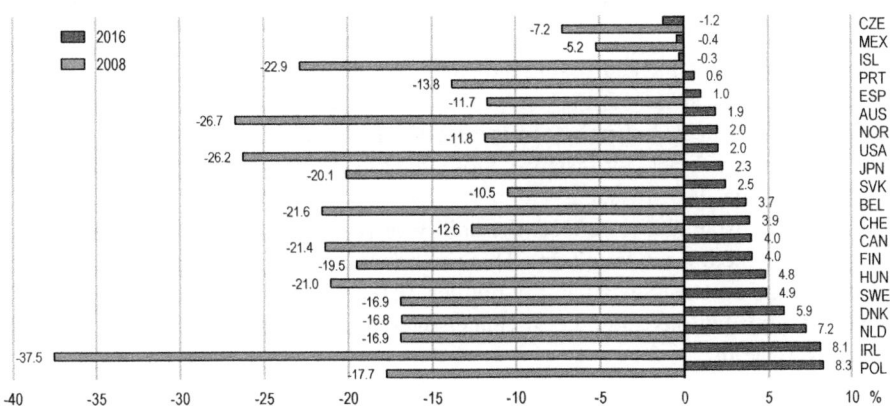

Fig. 3 Net real investment returns of pension funds in selected countries, 2008 and 2016. *Source*: OECD Global Pension Statistics; OECD Pension Markets in Focus 2013 and Pensions at a Glance, 2017

The uncertainties about future life expectancy are not fully taken into account by pension funds. In some countries, pension funds incorporate an allowance for uncertainty about future improvements in mortality, while others use tables that relate to past mortality developments, without accounting for future gains in life expectancy (Belgium, Denmark, Norway, Sweden, and Switzerland) (Antolín 2007).

2.3   Investment Risks

Private pension plans are exposed to investment risks as they seek to maximise investment returns. The recent 2008–2009 crisis illustrated the high uncertainty and risks surrounding investment in stocks (Fig. 3). OECD (2009) estimates that pension funds lost 23% of their value in 2008, worth about USD 5.4 trillion. While in 2015–2016 investment returns of pension funds were positive in all countries in Fig. 3.

D'Addio et al. (2009) using historical data on returns on equities and bonds in major OECD economies over the past quarter century show a median real return of 7.3% a year on a portfolio equally weighted between equities and bonds (averaging across the countries studied). It might be expected that, over a very long period, the degree of uncertainty in investment returns is small. A few bad years in the market are likely to be offset by boom years. However, they found the degree of uncertainty to be large, even with the relatively long investment horizons of pensions.

3 Policies Favouring the Sustainability of Pension Schemes

Policy reforms aimed at addressing the effects of shocks on pension systems need to balance financial sustainability and adequacy concerns. Both sustainability and adequacy are critical, but policy reforms often face a trade-off between these two goals. Flanking policies, for instance, those that raise employment, ease the trade-off as more revenues are provided.

Financial sustainability reflects the ability of pension systems to meet their liabilities in the medium to long term. This can be measured by the long-term actuarial balance of the system. Sustainability implies that the discounted present value of the stream of contributions and other revenues over a long horizon is sufficient to cover projected benefits.

3.1 Actuarial Neutrality

The actuarial neutrality of pension schemes' rules affects defined-benefit (DB) and defined-contribution (DC) schemes differently. The actuarial balance of pension schemes depends primarily on the actuarial balance at the individual level, which is reached when lifetime pensions received are equal to overall career contributions. There is thus no redistribution: what people receive in retirement is the same as what they paid in when working, together with the investment returns on the accumulated assets before retirement.

However, the balance between contributions and pensions also depends on the parameters (contribution rate, rate of return, official retirement age) of the pension schemes and on individual choices (retirement age decision) and characteristics (wage profile and life expectancy). The parameters of the scheme should be chosen carefully to ensure that for the average individual actuarial neutrality is guaranteed, in order to encourage individual choices that satisfy overall actuarial neutrality.

Different pension schemes are exposed differently to the risk of not satisfying the actuarial neutrality principle. Defined-contribution schemes and notional defined-contribution Schemes (NDC) are less exposed to non-actuarial neutral pricing (setting of the parameters of the scheme), because there are less options for individual choice or characteristics that affect the balance. In DC schemes, as all contributions are taken into account in defining the pension level, it is the market rate of return, which affects the pension level. Instead, in point and NDC schemes the rate of return has to be selected so as to ensure the actuarial balance and has to be eventually adjusted to take into account the evolution of life expectancy.

Defined-benefit schemes are more prone to violate the actuarial neutrality principle, because pension benefits are not strictly linked to contributions. In many countries, the whole career is not taken into account when determining the reference wage. In France, for instance, it is the best 25 years that are chosen for private sector workers, while in other countries it is sometimes only the final years. In general, this implies a reference wage over which the pension benefit is calculated which is higher than the average wage. This reduces the contributory dimension of the scheme and undermines actuarial neutrality. Also not adjusting the retirement age to rising life expectancy can alter actuarial neutrality.

Moreover, actuarial neutrality at the margin can be important, if pension reforms seek to provide incentives for individuals to delay their retirement. One way to define actuarial neutrality at the margin is that marginal contributions (one additional year of work, for instance) equal marginal benefits and bonuses for delaying retirement or penalties for early retirement should be set accordingly (See Queisser and Whitehouse 2006). The difficulty is to set up a unique scale for individuals with different characteristics (life expectancy differences by sex or income level).

3.2 Automatic Adjustment Mechanisms

Automatic adjustment of pension system parameters allows pension financing to be closely aligned with demographic and economic trends. Like other pre-commitment mechanisms in economic policymaking—in monetary and fiscal policy, for example—it is designed to enhance credibility and provide assurance that public pension schemes will not place an unexpected burden on public finances in the future (Barr and Diamond 2011).

The financial sustainability of a pension scheme is governed by the relationship between its parameters (contribution rates and periods, retirement age, valorisation and indexation) and demographic dependency variables. Current or expected prolonged deficits can occur due to a mismatch between spending (overly generous pensions, ageing populations) and funding (too low contribution rate, slump in payroll or income base and employment or lower productivity). Given the difficult process of pension reform, many countries have introduced automatic adjustment mechanisms to cope with trend changes or shocks that threaten the actuarial equilibrium. Automatic adjustment mechanisms can be an alternative to frequent and difficult pension reforms.

3.3   Adjustment of Benefit Levels

Pension benefits in payment can be reduced through automatic factor rules, which take into account financial imbalances (Canada, Germany, Japan and Sweden). In Finland, the life expectancy coefficient automatically adjusts the amount of pensions in payment as life expectancy changes. In Sweden, indexation of pension benefits and of accumulated notional capital, are adjusted automatically, when the balancing ratio (current liabilities of the pension system) is below one. However, the way the adjustment is realised can lead to unintended intergenerational redistribution.

3.3.1   Pension Indexation

Changing the indexation method (adjustment to reflect changes in living standards between the time that the pension entitlement was earned and when it is paid) from wage to price indexation will lower the relative pension level. In Japan, the switch from wage to inflation indexation was an integral part of the automatic balancing mechanism introduced in 2004. In Germany, the revaluation of retirement points (which determine the pension level) takes into account the evolution of the demographic dependency ratio.

3.3.2   Adjusting for Life Expectancy Developments

Many countries have introduced adjustment mechanisms to take into account changes in life expectancy. The adjustment can link the pension level, the retirement age or the contribution period to life expectancy. In notional defined-contributions schemes (Sweden, Chile, Estonia, Mexico and Italy) and some defined-contributions plans, accumulated contributions and investment returns are converted into a pension or annuity in retirement, with the conversion factor depending on life expectancy. Denmark, Greece and Italy have introduced reforms to index the retirement age to life expectancy. In France, the automatic adjustment mechanism targets the contribution period, which is adjusted according to life expectancy gains in order to maintain a constant ratio between the duration of activity (2/3) and the expected duration in retirement (1/3).

Most countries have chosen to link pension benefits rather than retirement age to life expectancy, as the retirement age has already been raised in many countries and it is expected that individuals will delay their retirement in the face of declining pensions. However, as demographic and economic dependency ratios are both affected by life expectancy gains, and as these are the major determinants of pension scheme balances in PAYG systems, linking retirement age to life expectancy would better restore the balance of these schemes.

3.3.3   Indexation and Revaluation Rules of Pensions

The indexation and revaluation rules of pensions play an important role in determining the level of pensions. First, they determine the level of the pension as they are used to up rate past contributions or income to determine the reference wage in DB schemes or the accumulated contributions in NDC schemes. Second, they determine the evolution of pensions during retirement. In many countries, pension indexation has shifted from the average nation-wide wage growth rate to inflation. Pensions are indexed to price inflation in 13 OECD countries, with a mix of wage and price weighting in six countries, with wage or part of wage inflation in five countries and a mix of price and GDP indexation in two countries.

However, governments tend to systematically override these rules (OECD 2012), changing pension levels by larger or smaller amounts than implied by indexation. In the recent period, several countries chose to freeze pensions rather than reduce them (Finland, Slovenia and Austria and Italy for higher pensions) and they were sharply reduced in Greece.

As prices tend to rise at a slower pace than earnings, indexing pensions to price developments increases financial sustainability. Indeed, it disconnects the growth rate of the funding base from the growth rate of spending. However, in the long run and for future generations, there is a risk of creating an important income gap between workers and older retirees. In some cases, it can increase the poverty rate of pensioners as increases in pension benefits are smaller than those of earnings.

3.4   Buffer and Reserve Funds

Short-run economic fluctuations and temporary demographic shocks can create imbalances and deficits in pension schemes. In order to avoid frequent parametric changes of pension schemes bringing about uncertainties, buffer or reserve funds can be built up as smoothing tools. One can distinguish at least three different functions for buffer and reserve funds (Fall and Ferrari 2008). First, they can be used to smooth the effects of fluctuations of the demographic dependency ratio along its long run trend. In the case of temporary demographic shocks (such as a transitory drop in the fertility rate, for example), it may be desirable to adapt the financial equilibrium constraint by introducing reserves. In that sense, a reserve fund is a means for smoothing the effects of temporary demographic shocks. Second, a reserve fund can be used to smooth temporary over-spending (compared to trend) resulting from any shock that affects the pension balances (temporary slump of payroll or arrival of large cohorts of pensioners at retirement). Such a fund would naturally fall to zero once the shock has been smoothed. Finally, a pension reserve fund can be designed as a permanent means of additional funding for the old-age insurance system. After the fund's build-up phase, its capital is preserved and its investment income contributes to the financing of pension spending. The returns from the fund act as a substitute to individual contributions or government transfers.

3.5 Prudential Regulation and Investment Strategies to Preserve the Sustainability of Funded Schemes

The goal of pension regulation is to protect the rights of pension fund members and occupational plan stakeholders (firms and members). Financial prudential regulatory bodies exist in almost all OECD countries (OECD 2013b). Investment by pension funds should be adequately regulated to ensure solvability (OECD/IOPS 2011). The approach should take into account the investment characteristics of the scheme (diversification, maturity and currency matching) given its assets and liabilities. In the case of funded defined-benefit plans and DC schemes, the goal of investment strategies is to generate the highest possible returns consistent with the liabilities and liquidity needs of the pension plan.

Since the crisis, pension fund investment strategies have become more regulated. Some investment limits on the different asset classes have been put in place. In a large number of OECD countries, pension funds were not constrained in their allocation between bills, bonds and shares (OECD 2013b). In 2012, restrictions on the allocation of bills and bonds were in place in 4 OECD countries, while 14 OECD countries had restrictions on investments in shares.

Private occupational plans should be well-funded. While defined-contribution plans should be fully funded, other types of plans should be subject to minimum funding rules or other mechanisms to ensure adequate funding of pension liabilities (OECD 2010). The funding ratio requirements should be flexible given the long-term liabilities of pension plans. The funding ratio or activation for additional capitalisation is normally stricter for defined-benefit pension plans. In addition, countries may need to have funding rules that seek to ensure that plan assets at least equal all promised benefits to date if the plan were to be terminated/wound-up (the accumulated benefit obligation or termination liability). About 60% of OECD pension assets are in defined-benefit and other plans, which offer return or benefit guarantees.

The funding standard has an important impact on the investment strategy followed by private pension plans. In particular, for occupational defined-benefit plans, where the liabilities are borne ultimately by the sponsors, clear rules and guidance should be in place to avoid the under-estimation of the liabilities. Prudential ratios require the sponsors to adjust the funding in line with liabilities and the performance of the plans. In defined-benefit plans, the expected investment returns necessary to cover the liabilities of the scheme need to be followed carefully.

Guarantee funds are essential to protect members of occupational and private pension plans. In some countries, private and occupational pensions represent an important part of pension income (Ireland, the United States and the United

Kingdom, for instance). Moreover, some of the private plans are sponsored by firms or public pension plans and are directly managed by employers. Individuals covered by such pension plans face various risks, such as the risk of the collapse of an enterprise, important losses on investment or underfunding of pension plans.

A guarantee mechanism is in place in some countries but to work effectively, these schemes must be independent and have powers to set and collect risk-adjusted premiums (Stewart 2007). Such mechanisms also need to be complemented by other benefit protection policies (notably effective funding rules). For instance, the Pension Benefit Guaranty Corporation (PBGC) in the United States is running deficits since 2002, because it is not independent enough to control the benefits paid or the premiums charged.

3.6　Protecting Pension Assets of Old Workers

Different pay-out options exist in defined-contribution schemes: a life annuity that pays a constant nominal stream of income throughout retirement; an inflation-indexed life annuity where payments are indexed to inflation and are thus constant in real terms; a fixed programmed withdrawal where the assets accumulated at retirement are divided by the life expectancy at retirement; a variable programmed withdrawal where payments vary according to capital gains of the remaining assets and life expectancy at each year in retirement; and, finally, a combined arrangement mixing a variable programmed withdrawal and a deferred inflation indexed life annuity that starts paying at some age (Antolin et al. 2010).

In private funded pension schemes, older workers or retired individuals can be disproportionately hit by a reversal of asset returns. Some cohorts may be strongly negatively affected in the short run. Those closest to retirement with pension capital invested in the stock market face the greatest risk in case of a market reversal, as they may begin pension withdrawals before the market can recoup. Retired individuals with a life annuity payment are protected from the stock market shock (the life annuity provider bears the risk). The recent crisis has shown the high exposure of private plans to adverse market movements and their consequences on old age living standards.

As individuals move closer to retirement or are already in retirement (if their pensions are not annuities) a high proportion of their pension capital should be invested in safer assets even though these investments have lower returns. Investment strategies based on the life-cycle approach are the appropriate default investment strategies. Life-cycle investment strategies suggest that the amount of assets accumulated to finance retirement allocated to risky assets (e.g. equities) should fall, as people get closer to retirement. However, the risk-adjusted performance of the different investment strategies depends on the type of benefit during the pay-out phase. Life-cycle investment strategies perform better than, for instance, dynamic investment strategies when benefits are paid as life annuities.

Also, in voluntary and occupational private plans, including life insurance, individuals should be encouraged to annuitise their withdrawal from schemes as a protection against longevity risk. Individuals tend to under-estimate the longevity risk and unexpected costs related to ageing. In DC pension plans, individuals bear the longevity risk and only by using the assets accumulated in these plans to buy life annuities can they be insured against longevity risk.

However, there are barriers to annuitisation. In particular, life annuities are illiquid and they do not allow for bequests. Also, life annuities are not flexible to allow people to address unexpected shocks requiring important outlays, like health or old age care. Still life annuities present an advantage in providing protection against longevity risk. Therefore, in countries where mandatory DC schemes represent the largest part of the pension system, mandatory annuitisation should be put in place to guarantee that individuals will have an adequate pension during retirement. Some degree of annuitisation of capital accumulated in voluntary DC pension plans, at least as the default arrangement, may also be appropriate.

Balancing these various aspects, the main recommendation for a default arrangement for the pay-out phase is to combine programmed withdrawals with a deferred life annuity (buying today a life annuity to be paid at a future date). Programmed withdrawal provides some flexibility and liquidity to face any contingencies, as well as potential portfolio investment gains, and the deferred annuity insures against longevity risk at the cost of only a relatively small portion of the assets accumulated in DC plans. The pay-out phase should include protection against inflation. The lack of inflation indexation could reduce the purchasing power of retirement income by as much as one third over a 20-year period, but indexing retirement income to inflation requires a greater saving effort.

4   Policies Affecting the Adequacy of Pensions

4.1   Replacement Rates and Poverty

Pension adequacy can be assessed by the pension replacement rate calculated as the share of either life-time earnings or final earnings that the pension benefit replaces. Pension adequacy can also be defined relatively to poverty. It is then based on the comparison of the pension level with the poverty threshold (proportion of the median income). However, to assess whether retired people are at risk of poverty, one has to take into account all income in retirement and not only pensions.

The outlook for mandatory pension replacement rates shows that adequacy may be an issue in the coming years for some countries (Fig. 4). The average replacement rate from mandatory schemes for a full-career average earner is equal to 53%. For the 15 OECD countries where the calculations of entitlements only cover mandatory public pensions, the average replacement rate for an average worker earner is 59%; for the 12 OECD countries with both public and mandatory private provision, the average replacement rate is 56%; and for the last eight countries, where the only

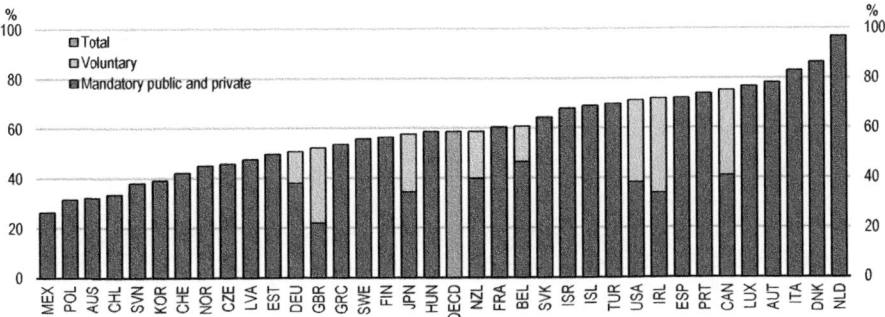

Fig. 4 Gross pension replacement rate for an average earner. *Source*: OECD (2017), OECD Pensions at a glance 2017

mandatory part is public but with significant voluntary pensions, the replacement rate from the mandatory component alone is 37%. For all 35 OECD countries, including voluntary (private) pensions raises the average total replacement rate for the average earner from 53% with mandatory schemes to 59%.

In some countries, high replacement rates and pension poverty coexist. This is largely due to weak labour market performance over the last 20 years in many countries and, in particular, for low skilled workers. Indeed, a weak labour market performance may generate poor pension entitlements in countries where there is a tight link between contributions and pension benefits. In many countries, public transfers comprising earnings-related pensions and means-tested benefits are the main source of income for pensioners. However, capital returns play an important role in some countries, while in others the elderly have to rely on revenues from work.

The adequacy of public transfers can be gauged by the old age poverty rate. On average, 12.5% of the over 65 year olds live in income poverty, defined as an income below half the national median (Fig. 5). In 2014, poverty rates of people aged over 65 were very high in Korea (46%), Latvia (26%) and high in Australia and Mexico (26%), Mexico (28%). At below 2%, Denmark, France and the Netherlands had the fewest poor elderly. On average, poverty is higher among older generations (+75) than among younger cohorts of retirees (66–74) due to regressive indexation rules. Korea's very high old-age poverty rate is primarily because the public pension scheme was introduced only in 1988, so retirees in the late-2000s had little or no entitlements.

Pension coverage of the working-age population is a significant policy concern in some OECD countries. Lower income countries with many workers in the informal sector not enrolled in a pension scheme have a low coverage rate. Only about 60% of the labour force is covered in Chile and Turkey, and less than 50% in Mexico (OECD 2012). This means that many people reach the pensionable age with little or no pension entitlement.

Safety net allowances exist in almost all OECD countries to prevent poverty. Old age safety nets are in general means-tested and serve to complement pensions.

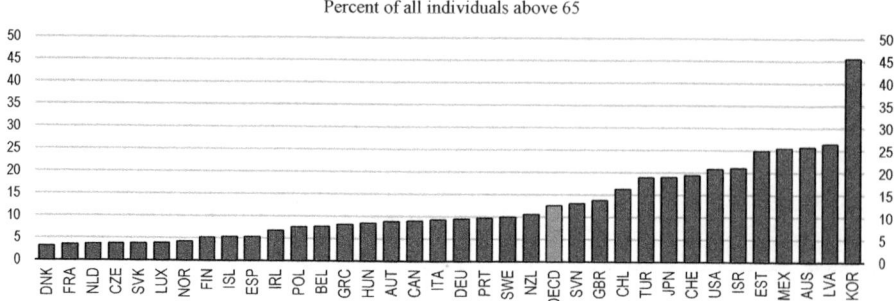

Fig. 5 Poverty among older people. *Source*: OECD (2013a, b, c), Pensions at a Glance 2013: OECD and G20 Indicators; OECD (2013a, b, c), "Income Distribution", OECD Social and Welfare Statistics (database)

There are three types of benefits: a non-contributory benefit in 21 countries including the Netherlands and New Zealand, where basic pensions are residency-tested; a targeted safety-net income in 13 countries; and a contributory minimum pension defined as the minimum income of a low-earning, full-career worker. In many countries, there are several programmes and benefits, which may be complementary or substitutable.

Incentive effects and adequacy issues arise for the three types of social benefits. If non-contributory benefits are too low relative to the poverty threshold, they will increase the poverty rate. In Australia, for example, this benefit was below the poverty threshold in the late-2000s. By contrast, the basic pension in New Zealand was slightly higher than the country's poverty threshold. The incentive issue is related to the "making work pay" principle. Means-tested benefits should provide less revenue than work-based income.

In many countries, the replacement rate decreases with earnings. Therefore, low-income earners with a weak saving capacity have a higher replacement rate during retirement. Specific rules can be set to guarantee that all pensioners with full contribution periods will have a pension level above the poverty line. For instance, in France, the objective of the contributory minimum pension is to guarantee that a pensioner with a full contribution period at full time work at the minimum wage should get a pension corresponding to 85% of the minimum wage.

4.2   Public-Private Mix and Extending Private Pension Coverage

The private provision of pensions could be increased in most countries to provide a better diversification of old age income risks and to increase pension adequacy (level and coverage). In many countries old age income is a mix of a national public pension and a private or occupational funded pension. However, in some countries, the public pension represents a very important share of pension income, thus limiting risk diversification for individuals. A good mix of public and private pensions would allow a better diversification of pension risks between idiosyncratic risks on investments of pension funds and macroeconomic risks to national pension schemes.

In 21 OECD countries, replacement rates offered by public PAYG pensions to new entrants to the labour force are not expected to reach 60% for workers on average earnings. Funded private pensions already play an important complementary role for pension adequacy in Canada, Ireland, the United Kingdom and the United States. Income from capital, predominantly private pensions, accounts for between 25% of income of over-65 year olds (Ireland) and 40% (Canada). Among countries with low mandatory replacement rates, some already have old age poverty rates above the OECD average (Australia, Mexico, the United States, Chile, Japan, Slovenia), illustrating the need to increase coverage of low income earners or workers in the informal sector.

4.3   Preventing Early Retirement and Exit from the Labour Market

Increasing the official retirement age has been one prominent feature of pension reforms in almost all countries to cope with ageing. The normal pension age is expected to be at least 65 for most countries (Fig. 6). However, the effective retirement age is lower than the pensionable age in many OECD countries due to early retirement schemes and distortions to retirement decisions (Fig. 6). In order to close the gap between the actual and the statutory retirement age, early retirement has been limited in many countries (Denmark, Hungary, Ireland, Israel, the Netherlands, New Zealand, Turkey and the United Kingdom) (OECD 2013c). Also, the tightening of retirement provisions, in particular penalties in pension rates when the contributed periods are below a minimum at retirement age, are affecting more women than men in many countries (France, Korea, Spain and Turkey).

The different pension reforms, the phasing out of early retirement schemes and the tightening of eligibility criteria for other social transfer programmes that operated as de facto early retirement schemes are having an impact on retirement decisions. As a result, the recent performance of older individuals in the labour market has improved. Employment rates of people aged 55–64 have improved in most OECD countries, from 44.0% in 2000 to 58.4% in 2016. Reforms should include a better screening of access to long-term sickness, phasing out of early retirement schemes, changes to the tax on continued work by increasing the increment to pensions for deferred retirement up to the actuarially neutral level, favouring the development of part-time work for older workers and enabling the combination of work with pension receipt.

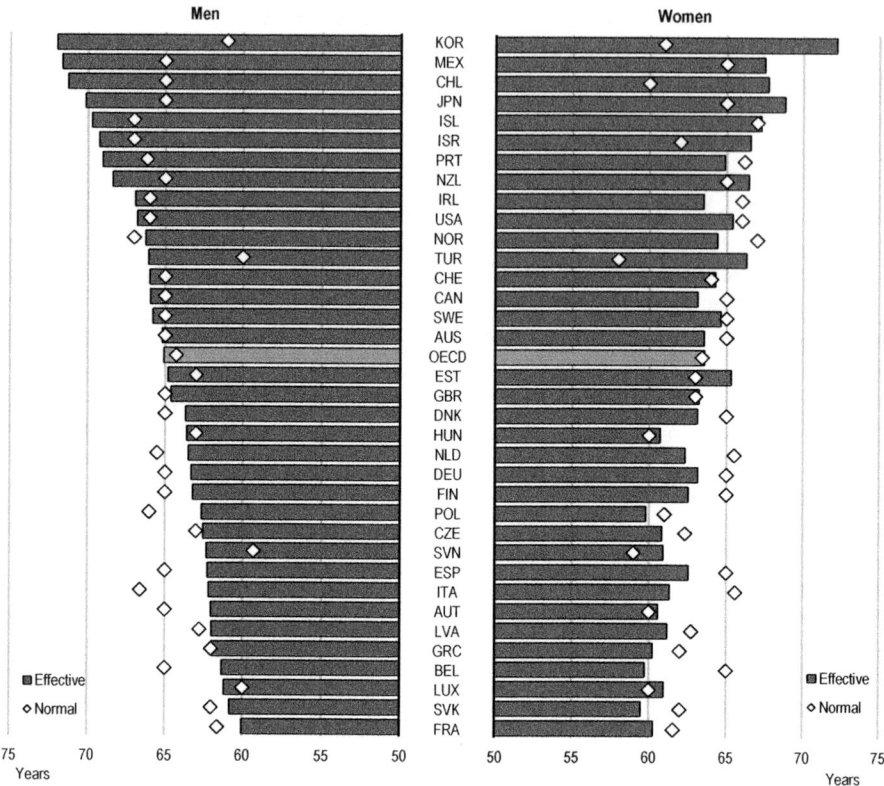

Fig. 6 Average effective age of labour-market exit and normal pensionable age in 2016. *Source*: OECD Global Pension Statistics; OECD Pension Markets in Focus 2013 and Pensions at a Glance, 2017. *Note*: Effective retirement age shown is for 5 year period 2011–2016. Pensionable age is shown for individuals retiring in 2016 and assuming labour market entry at age 20

5   Concluding Remarks

In the face of the great recession, pension schemes in Europe and most OECD countries appeared robust and resilient. Most schemes absorbed the negative revenue shock without reducing pension levels. However, pay-as-you-go pension schemes, in particular defined benefit ones, are exposed to economic trend developments like ageing and slowing down of productivity.

Reforms started 20 years ago in many countries to address the financial sustainability challenge posed by ageing. Despite these important reforms, as ageing continues, funding of pension schemes does not match expected pension liabilities in many countries. Moreover, pension reforms have mostly affected pension benefits exposing in particular low earners to poverty risk.

There is no place for complacency. Many challenges are lying ahead. In addition to ageing, slowing down of productivity will affect pension financing compared to liabilities built under higher productivity growth. Second, current labour market developments with non-regular forms of work or contracts (uberisation), development of new forms of self-employment, pose new challenges in terms of accumulation of pension rights and adequacy of future pensions.

Going forward, new or more flexible forms of accumulating pension rights need to be developed. Younger generations must be educated to save and accumulate wealth for their retirement and financial literacy enhanced.

References

Antolín P (2007) Longevity risk and private pensions. OECD Working Papers on Insurance and Private Pensions, No. 3. OECD Publishing, Paris

Antolin P, Payet S, Yermo J (2010) Assessing default investment strategies in defined contribution pension plans. OECD Journal: Financial Market Trends 2010(1):87–115

Barr N, Diamond P (2011) Improving Sweden's automatic pension adjustment mechanism, issue in brief, no. 11-2. Center for Retirement Research at Boston College, Newton, MA

D'Addio AC, Seisdedos J, Whitehouse ER (2009) Investment risk and pensions: measuring uncertainty in returns. OECD Social, Employment and Migration Working Papers, No. 70. OECD Publishing, Paris

European Commission (2009) European economy no. 2/2009 — The 2009 ageing report : economic and budgetary projections for the EU-27 member states (2008–2060)

Fall F (2014) A framework of comparing the robustness of PAYG pension schemes. OECD Economics Department Working Papers, No. 1134. OECD Publishing, Paris

Fall F, Ferrari N (2008) The outlook for pension spending and the role of a reserve fund. Tresor-Economics, No. 39

Fall F et al (2014) Vulnerability of social institutions: lessons from the recent crisis and historical episodes. OECD Economics Department Working Papers, No. 1130. OECD Publishing, Paris

Guillemette Y, Turner D (2018) The long view: scenarios for the world economy to 2060. OECD Economic Policy Papers, No. 22. OECD Publishing, Paris

IMF (International Monetary Fund) (2012) Chapter 4: The financial impact of longevity risk. In: Global financial stability report. April 2012, Washington, DC

OECD (2009) Pensions at a glance 2009: retirement-income systems in OECD countries. OECD Publishing, Paris

OECD (2010) OECD principles of occupational pension regulation: methodology for assessment and implementation. OECD Publishing, Paris

OECD (2011) OECD/IOPS good practices for pension funds' risk management systems. OECD Publishing, Paris. www.oecd.org/site/iops/principlesandguidelines/46864307.pdf

OECD (2012) OECD pensions outlook 2012. OECD Publishing, Paris

OECD (2013a) Pension markets in focus. OECD Publishing, Paris

OECD (2013b) Annual survey of investment regulations of pension funds. OECD Publishing, Paris. www.oecd.org/daf/fin/private-pensions/InvRegPensionFunds2013.pdf

OECD (2013c) Pensions at a glance 2013: OECD and G20 indicators. OECD Publishing, Paris

OECD (2017) Pensions at a glance 2017: OECD and G20 Indicators. OECD Publishing, Paris. https://doi.org/10.1787/pension_glance-2017-en

Paccagnella M (2016) Age, ageing and skills: results from the survey of adult skills. OECD Education Working Papers, No. 132. OECD Publishing, Paris

Queisser M, Whitehouse ER (2006) Neutral or fair? Actuarial concepts and pension-system design. OECD Social, Employment and Migration Working Papers, No. 40. OECD Publishing, Paris

Stewart F (2007) Benefit security pension fund guarantee schemes. OECD Working Papers on Insurance and Private Pensions, No. 5. OECD Publishing, Paris

Falilou Fall is Senior Economist at the Economics Department of the OECD. Previously, he was the head of the office for economic analysis of globalization at the French Ministry of Foreign and European affairs. He has also worked for the French National Treasury.

Dr Fall has written a dozen peer reviewed articles on macroeconomics, pensions, inequality and African issues and has taught at leading universities and business schools. He was a Marie Curie fellow at Université Catholique de Louvain (Belgium). He holds a PhD from Université Panthéon-Sorbonne (France).

Part II
The Capital Markets Union (CMU) and the Future of Pension Plans: Opportunities, Risks and Drawbacks

The Capital Markets Union: Saving for Retirement and Investing for Growth

Ansgar Belke and Philipp Allroggen

Abstract Very recently, the European Institutions made progress on the Capital Markets Union (CMU). The CMU is part of the so called "Juncker-Plan" which aims to boost investment across Europe. In our contribution we focus on retirement savings and investment for growth aspects of the CMU. We find that Europeans indeed accumulate savings but do not invest and thus do not prepare for retirement. Additionally, long-term investment could foster growth in the European Union (EU). We argue that the CMU is a step in the right direction as it introduces a new pan-European Pension Scheme, reduces bank reliance of enterprises, especially SMEs, and represents a key complement to Banking Union. However, CMU focuses mainly on the demand side, although functioning capital markets need (potential) investors who a willing and open to invest in capital markets products. Transparency, a stronger regulatory framework and better financial literacy could help overcome this shortfall.

1 What Is the Capital Markets Union About?

One priority of the Juncker Commission is, or has been, to boost employment, growth and investment across the European Union (EU). As an important pillar of the Investment Plan for Europe, often referred to as the "Juncker Plan", the

A. Belke (✉)
University of Duisburg-Essen, Essen, North Rhine-Westphalia, Germany

CEPS, Brussels, Belgium

King's College, London, UK

IZA, Bonn, Germany
e-mail: ansgar.belke@uni-due.de

P. Allroggen
University of Duisburg-Essen, Essen, North Rhine-Westphalia, Germany
e-mail: philipp.allroggen@stud.uni-due.de

© Springer Nature Switzerland AG 2019
N. da Costa Cabral, N. Cunha Rodrigues (eds.), *The Future of Pension Plans in the EU Internal Market*, Financial and Monetary Policy Studies 48,
https://doi.org/10.1007/978-3-030-29497-7_7

Capital Markets Union (CMU) is set up to overcome an investment shortage and diversify funding for businesses and firms within the EU. In September 2015, the Commission passed an action plan setting out over 30 actions and measures to establish the fundamentals of an integrated capital market in the EU by 2019. The CMU shall address several challenges in the Economic and Monetary Union: investment in Europe heavily relies on banks and SMEs and Start-ups have limited access to finance. Furthermore, financing conditions vary significantly between EU countries. Additionally, investors are prone to a home bias, meaning buyers and shareholders of corporate debt rarely go beyond their home country and even though EU households save a lot, they do not make the most out of their savings. Besides there are differences in the regulatory framework and market practices for finance and investment products, hindering cross-border investment.

Taking this as a starting point, the CMU aims for a more stable and resilient financial sector through deeper integration. A completed CMU could potentially absorb adverse shocks on the European economy. Unlike the Banking Union, it covers all Member States and not only those which are members of the Euro area (European Commission 2018a, b).

The action plan was updated in a mid-term review in June 2017, but the key elements are still the ones originally set out already in 2015: creating a single market for capital by removing barriers to cross-border investments, improving access to financing for all business around the EU with special focus on SMEs and start-ups and diversifying the funding of the economy and reducing its cost, as well as fostering retail and institutional investments. Furthermore, the CMU shall help Europe to attract more investment from other parts of the world and become more competitive (Brender et al. 2015; European Commission 2015).

There is no doubt, that the CMU is a complex and extensive project that includes many facets and various aspects of policies and legislation. However, it ultimately shall contribute to further boost jobs and growth in the European Union.

Brender et al. (2015) also acknowledge that a single capital market could be useful in the EU. However, shifting their focus towards Economic and Monetary Union (EMU), they argue that it is extremely dangerous to conduct one and the same monetary policy in an area with broadly varying financial practices and structures— as the first 15 years of the euro area's history have vividly shown. They conclude that financial integration of the countries in EMU must receive top priority in a process that the rest of the European Union may then subsequently join.

The authors also put into doubt the European Commission's call for the "liberalisation" of capital flows. In their perspective, the problem faced by the Euro area specifically does not just present a matter of suppressing or eliminating barriers to allow capital to circulate more freely. What is more, it is an issue of building new channels that will allow economies to more fully mobilise and more efficiently allocate the savings potential in the E(M)U. This is exactly the focus of our contribution.

We thus narrow the purpose of the CMU down to two main aspects: enhancing investment opportunities across Europe and improve financing options for business. Thus, from a fully-fledged CMU, households and businesses would profit alike.

Within the context of this book, in our contribution we focus on retail investment linked to financing opportunities for businesses. For this purpose, we first look in detail on the status quo of retirement saving and long-term investment in Europe. Then we check what has been achieved and sketch the way forward.

2   Retirement Saving and Long-Term Investment in Europe

When talking about pension plans, retirement and investment from the perspective of the CMU, it is first of all helpful to look at the demographic situation in Europe (The Economist 2017a). According to all accounts, the population is shrinking and ageing significantly over the next few decades (Fig. 1).

While a shrinking population itself does not necessarily represent a threat for a pension system, the *composition* of the former certainly does have an impact. The share of elderly people who are no longer available to the labour market but enjoying their retirement will increase significantly (Fig. 2).

These stylised demographic developments put increasing pressure on the various pension systems across the EU (The Economist 2017a, b). As pension systems vary, they usually have some sort of capital-focused pillar. A recent study by Aviva (2016) quantifies the pension gap at €2 trillion a year, i.e. the amount that must be saved additionally to achieve an adequate living standard after retirement. While the responsibility for "saving for retirement" tends to be shifted more and more towards the individual, policymakers should at least provide better access, stability, capability and information to savers and investors. In this regard, CMU could contribute to

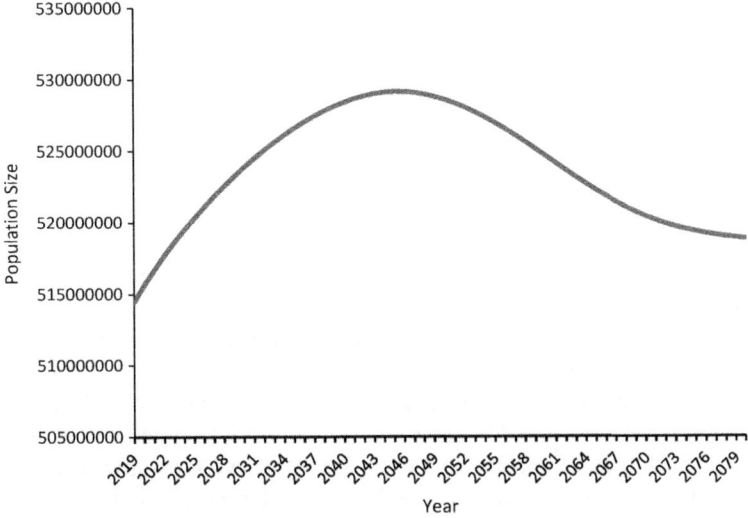

Fig. 1 Population size projection in Europe according to Eurostat. *Source:* Eurostat

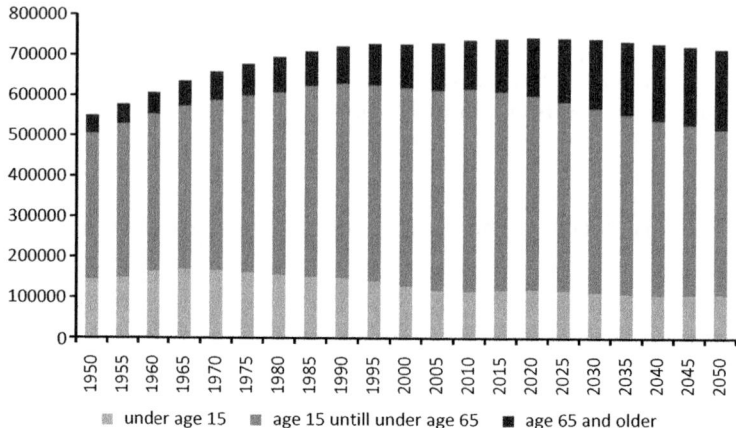

underage 15   ■ age 15 untill under age 65   ■ age 65 and older

Fig. 2 Changes in the age structure in Europe. *Source:* United Nations—Department of Economic and Social Affairs, Population Division (2017)

Table 1 Percentage shares households save from their disposable income

	BEL	UK	FRA	DEU	GRE	IT	NL	ESP	SWE
2008	10.01	2.93	9.25	10.48	−3.84[b]	7.83[b]	3.63	1.57	11.76
2012	5.69	4.54	10.00	9.29	−10.92[b]	1.98[b]	8.30	2.35	14.38
2017	3.70[a]	−0.91	8.47[b]	9.88	−16.95[a,b]	2.30[b]	8.99[b]	−0.83	15.08

Source: OECD, Household savings indicator
[a]Value of 2016
[b]Estimated value

gradually and partially move more of the national pension schemes in Europe which are usually organised in a "defined benefit" system, to a funded "defined contribution" system (Deutsche Bank Research 2015, p. 12).

However, Europeans are indeed saving, even though savings decreased in the aftermath of the financial crisis. According to OECD data, households throughout Europe usually are able to save a certain share of their disposable income. However, citizens in countries hit hard and financially distressed by the Global Financial Crisis and also by the European debt and banking crisis represent an exemption from this rule (Table 1). Additionally, the United Kingdom (UK) is an outlier according to 2017 data. The envisaged Brexit may be one driver in this regard.

Next, we take a look at the financial assets of households, to better understand what Europeans are using their savings for. Figure 3 shows in what type of assets households invest as percentage of total financial assets (data from 2017).

It becomes obvious that the majority of household's financial assets are in currencies ("cash") and deposits. Only few savings have been invested in pension funds and the share of shares and equity of total financial assets is mediocre. Apparently, there are some exceptions. Households in the UK, Scandinavia and the Netherlands are investing significantly more relative to just transferring their

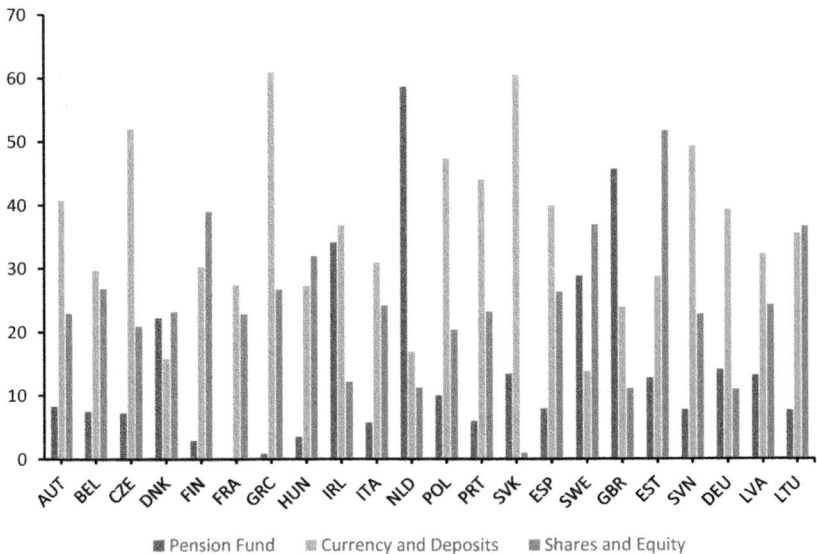

Fig. 3 Pension funds, currency and deposits, shares and equity, % of total financial assets of households. *Source:* OECD, household financial assets (indicator)

Table 2 Results of Investor Pulse Survey—European savers and investors

	Belgium (%)	France (%)	Germany (%)	Italy (%)	Netherlands (%)	Spain (%)	Sweden (%)	UK (%)	Average (%)
Survey respondents who have savings	83	87	75	79	78	81	75	79	80
Survey respondents who invest	42	33	44	45	27	44	61	43	43

Source: Blackrock (2017), Investor Pulse Survey 2017

savings into their deposit accounts. However, since almost a decade interest rates find themselves at the lower zero-bound, resulting in exceptionally low interest gains for deposits. In the light of increasing inflation and negative real interest rates, savers basically "loose" money that is located in bank accounts. Furthermore, other interest rates based products are not very profitable either. A recent survey conducted by Blackrock (2017) reveals complementary facts: Europeans "have" savings, but few of them tend to invest in direct stocks or bonds (Deutsche Bank Research 2015, p. 10). Table 2 shows the results of the Investor Pulse Survey 2017.

Before looking at the product that are usually offered to retail investors, we examine how many products are available to individuals. Figure 4 displays the total number of share classes (including passive investment funds) available for sale to retail investors in 2017. Data shows that there are substantial discrepancies

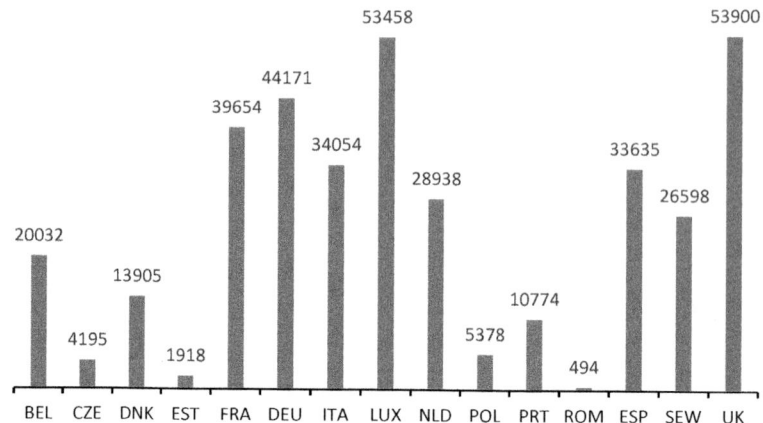

Fig. 4 Total number of share classes available for sale to retail investors in 2017. *Source:* European Commission (2018a, b) based on the Morningstar database (2017)

between different Member States. However, it seems that the number of share classes correlates with the size of the country. For listed bonds and equities, retail investors can have access to products worldwide, therefore a count of such securities being available would be rather difficult to make. Furthermore, the amount of life insurance and/or pension products available to households is difficult to estimate.

A detailed and in-depth study of the European Commission (2018a, b) analyses the products offered to retail investors throughout the websites of (big) banks and insurance companies as well as products offered by advisors to two types of investors finds, unsurprisingly, that potential retail investors are offered and proposed almost exclusively in-house products. Furthermore, they find that mixed funds are the most offered product by advisors across Member States and the investment profile does not play a major role. The study concludes that there is a big mismatch between supply and demand. In addition, comparing and interpreting fees across providers and products is rather difficult for the average retail investor. The information provided to potential clients is neither transparent nor standardised across Member States. A reason here probably is that product development is supply-driven instead of demand-driven. Most citizens heavily relay on their local banks and financial institutes when it comes to savings and investment.

The European market for retail investors is highly fragmented and diverse. In addition to the shortcomings described above, (potential) retail investors refrain from investing in investment products and keep their savings on in their deposits. Another noteworthy aspect is, that fees are relatively high in the majority of Member States, thus deterring retail investors from investing (Lannoo 2018a).

At this point, we feel legitimised to summarise that European citizens generally have savings, but are not investing, which however would prepare them for retirement. Among the reasons are a lack of transparency, high fees and a fragmented market.

Now we are turning to the investment side, an outspoken key priority of the Juncker Commission. As one of the key aspects of the CMU is to provide savers with better investment opportunities, we have to look at the current investment options for savers. A top priority for today's savers is the preparation for retirement, so they usually face a long investment horizon. Thus, we feel legitimised to look especially at the availability of long-term investment options. From the macroeconomic perspective, long-term investment drives the economic capacity of an economic area. Long-term investing is a multi-facetted topic. In this regard, Manuel Aramendía and Lannoo (2013, p. 13) provide a useful overview of definitions of long-term investment by important institutions, which are depicted in Table 3.

The Group of 30 and the European Commission propose a similar definition of long-term investment, following the concept of gross fixed-capital formation in national accounting. Infrastructure, equipment etc. (tangibles) as well as all forms of education and research (intangibles) fall under this concept. The definitions of the other organisations are usually closely related to these concepts but focus precisely und the length of the investment.

The gross fixed-capital formation in millions of € (at current prices) within the European Union is presented in Fig. 5.

After a decrease in 2008 after the financial crisis, gross fixed-capital formation accelerated again and is now reaching a new high. Gross fixed-capital formation (GFCF) describes the net capital accumulation during an accounting period. It measures the net increase in fixed capital, sometimes referred to as net investment. In other words, it refers to additions to the capital stock such as land improvements,

Table 3 Definitions of long-term investment

Group of 30 (2013)	*Long-term financing* refers to the provision of long dated funds to pay for capital-intensive undertakings that have multi-year payback periods. *Long-term investment* is spending on the tangible and intangible assets that can expand the productive capacity of an economy
European Commission (2013)	*Long-term investment* is the formation of long-lived capital, covering tangible assets and intangible assets that boost innovation and competitiveness
OECD (2011) Yermo et al. (2011)	*Responsible and longer-term investment* among institutional investors shares the following features: more patient capital that acts in a counter-cyclical manner; ongoing and direct engagement as shareholders and consideration of environmental and other longer-term risks; and an active role in the financing of long-term, productive activities that support sustainable growth
WEF-OW (2011)	*Long-term investing* can be usefully defined as investing with the expectation of holding an asset for an indefinite period of time by an investor with the capability to do so
Kay (2012)	Portrays a broad distinction between investing, focused on the activities of the company (business, strategy, profits) and trading, focused on the market for shares of a company (order flow, short-term correlations, arbitrage opportunities)

Source: Manuel Aramendía and Lannoo (2013)

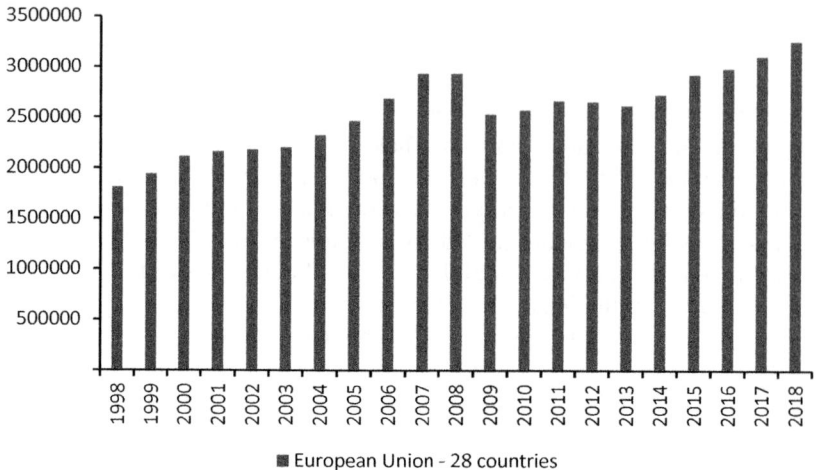

Fig. 5 Gross fixed-capital formation within the EU. *Source:* Eurostat

machinery, construction of roads and railways. Economies need capital goods to replace the ones used and depreciated to produce goods and services. However, as the growth outlook for EU countries currently tends to be corrected downwards systematically, future investment which is dominantly influenced by growth expectations may suffer and could not fit with this positive trend anymore.

Beyond the general view, that institutional investors are "the most natural providers of long-term finance in the financial system" (FSB 2013, p. 1) one should not neglect the potential of the mobilisation of household wealth. Individuals who save for the purpose of retirement undoubtedly have a longer-time horizon. Admittedly, the line between retail investment and institutional investment might not be as sharp as expected at first sight, because households often invest in products which are managed and/or offered by institutional investors.

However, Manuel Aramendía and Lannoo (2013, p. 1) point out, that households are direct owners or indirect beneficiaries of around 60% of financial assets in Europe. Even though, the study is a few years old. However, to all our knowledge that ratio did not change much. Given this background, the European Commission tries to explore the potential of an integrated single market for retail investors with the CMU.

3   A Need for Action?

In the previous section we have already shed some light on investment in Europe since the mid-90s. In the following we will take a closer look at it and present a more detailed analysis with an eye on the pension issue.

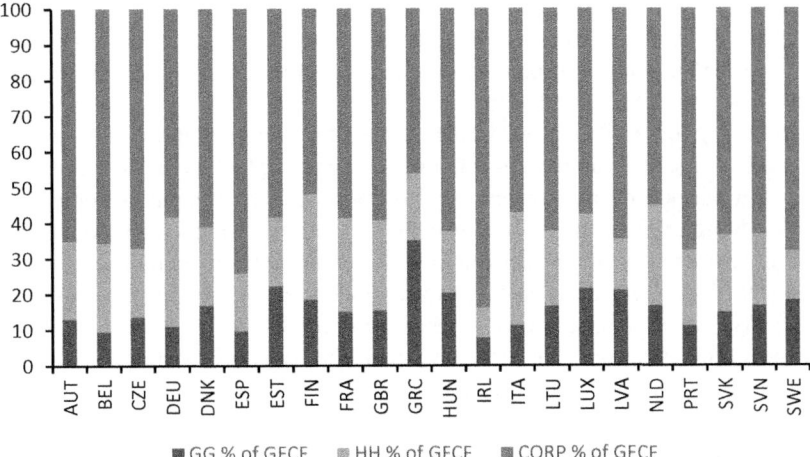

Fig. 6 Gross fixed-capital formation, as % share of total amount. *Source:* OECD, Investment by sector (indicator)

We have a glance of the composition of investment across Europe. Figure 6 displays the gross fixed-capital formation according to sectors as shares of the total amount.

The data retrieved from the OECD is from 2017. Investment is split into three sectors, the general government (GG), households (HH) and Corporations (CORP). In all Member States, the business sector is the main contributor to gross fixed-capital formation. The simple reason is that the EU is a market-based economy and investing is essential for profit-orientated and competitive businesses. However, looking at the remaining two sectors, households and government, the picture is not so clear. Especially the share of the government varies highly across countries. It is important to note that data on public investment and capital has some limitations which should be taken into account when interpreting and comparing across Member States.

The difference between investment and other government expenditure is not always as clear with regard to their particular effects on the productive capacity of the economy. For instance, public investment also includes expenditure on sport stadiums and military equipment, which have questionable effects (or no effects at all) on the productive capacity of an economy. Furthermore, the distinction between public and private investment is not always clear in practise as it may seem in theory. Consider when private companies participate in infrastructure projects through Public Private Partnership (PPP) projects with budgetary risks for the government due to guarantees. In addition, difficulties occur because the delineation between the public and private sector differ between Member States. Last, public capital stock data are not observed but constructed, based on investment flow data and other (ECB 2016).

Despite these limitations it is worth taking a look at governments' contribution to investment, respectively gross fixed-capital formation. Greece is an exception with a share of 34.88%, while the share of the other Member States rarely exceeds 20%. The share is lowest in Ireland with 7.76%.

Reasons for these distinctions in the compositions are structural differences and historical heritage. To start with, it is not per se a good or bad matter of fact, to have a high or low proportion of government and household investment as percentage of gross fixed-capital formation. However, the possibility of a crowding-out effect of private investment due to government investment has to be taken into account in any assessment, depending on what the prior is regarding the "better" investor and on whether investment is regarded as a public good or not.

In the previous section we presented data, that proved that gross fixed-capital formation in total terms is increasing. However, that was not the full story. If one does put it in relation to GDP, the picture turns out to be rather different. Figure 7 shows the gross fixed-capital formation as percentage of GDP in the EU.

The share of investment at GDP has risen in the past years, but still is below the post-crisis level. However, in the light of an increase of gross fixed-capital formation in total terms, the question emerges, if investment is really high enough to feed economic growth.

Following standard growth theory, investment is the vital driver for growth in an economy. The main narrative behind this statement is that investment itself is part of aggregated demand and, at the same time, a higher capital stock increases potential output (supply side). However, at some point output will stop growing, once a higher capital stock is reached. So, in the long-run more accumulated investment results in a higher capital stock and an increased level in output per capita, but not in a permanently higher growth rate (Gros 2014).

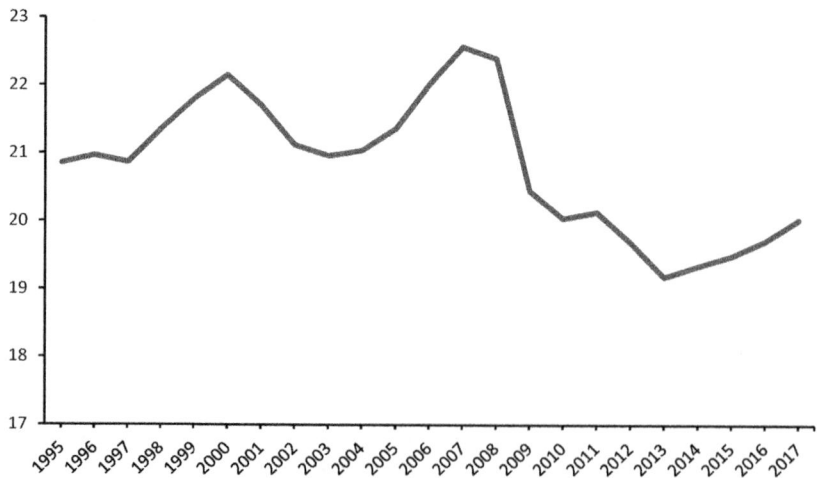

Fig. 7 Gross fixed-capital formation as percentage of GDP in the EU. *Source:* World Bank national account data and OECD national accounts data files

Along these lines, Gros (2014) argues that, admittedly, investment has declined in the Euro area since the start of the economic and financial crisis. However, this does, according to his view, not imply the existence of an 'investment gap'. This is because investment in the Euro area was most probably above a sustainable level caused by the credit boom before 2007. What is more, the fall in the Euro area's potential growth—caused by a combination of a sharp demographic slowdown and lower total factor productivity growth—should also lead to a permanently lower investment rate. Increasing the investment rate, as suggested by the proponents of a Capital Markets Union, might thus represent the wrong target for economic policy. Increasing infrastructure investment might be justified in some Member Countries. However, it cannot be regarded as 'free lunch' when efficiency levels are low, which is apparently the case in some of the financially stressed Euro area countries (Gros 2014).

Furthermore, empirical evidence indicates that an increase of capital stock per worker causes decreasing returns. Thus, after a certain point even a much higher investment effort will not generate a much higher output per worker once the transition period has ended. Notably, the transition period, in which investment indeed has a significant effect on growth can be rather long, depending heavily on the starting point (Gros and Alcidi 2013, p. 20; Gros 2014).

However, the European Commission apparently is not mainly focused on these kinds of caveats but is striving for a general "boost in investment". As mentioned above, there are basically three sectors which could invest more, namely governments, businesses and households. High national government debt in the Euro area's periphery and unwillingness to finance investment with debt instead of current tax revenue in the core Member Countries and also northern Europe are reasons why one should not expect a significant rise of investment on the government side.

Anyway, from a public choice point of view, one should not expect the government to be the "best" of all investors. Instead, it should define and enforce areas of investment where market failure prevails, and trans-national spill-overs can be expected. What is more, the currently low interest rates should, due to the risk of later rate hikes and the existence of other important drivers of investment beyond just interest rates, not serve as the main argument for more public investment. Finally, in a scenario of interest rates at the lower zero-bound, the probability is high that also low-yielding investment is supported by governments.

Businesses instead are free in their investment decisions, and incentives in the form of reduced taxes for more investment or other measurements to stimulate corporate investment mainly lie within the hands of national government. In general, for Capital Markets Union, one needs to have a clear idea of to whom those channels should convey the funds. In that regard, the European Commission's approach is surprisingly lopsided: it is almost exclusively focused on companies, and in particular on SMEs. This is an unjustified bias for several years now since, in the Euro area as well as in the other developed economies, *household* debt has been as important and has been growing as fast, if not faster, than corporate debt (Brender et al. 2015). Thus, seen on the whole, the European Commission should eye also on households, respectively retail investors, to boost investment.

4   What Has Been Achieved and the Way Forward

In the previous sections we pointed out the desire of the European Commission to boost investment for the sake of future economic growth and jobs. This initiative, if interpreted and conducted properly, contains a lot of potential benefits not only for businesses and institutional investors but also for European citizens.

But will the CMU deliver as promised? The European Commission seems rather optimistic and emphasises the possible positive effects for savers, who are enabled with better investment opportunities. The need to overcome the fragmentation of European capital markets is widely accepted (EPRA 2017; Lannoo 2018a) and from the newly introduced pan-European Pension Scheme one can expect benefits for savers.

So indeed, the proposed initiatives could generate more funding through lesser fragmentation and easier access to capital markets and investment flows. Due to the transformation from a "defined benefit" to a "defined contribution" system retirement savings could be channelled into capital markets (Deutsche Bank Research 2015, p. 12). Undoubtedly, it is a step in the right direction to go beyond the one-sided reliance on bank financing and focus on SME financing through, for instance, venture capital (Deutsche Bank Research 2015, p. 4). The Capital Markets Union is a key complement to Banking Union (Belke and Gros 2016; Martinez et al. 2019), to foster development and integration of European capital markets and diminish, as an important lesson from the recent European banking and debt crisis, the high dependency of European businesses on banks. The main focus should be on reinforcing resilient forms of financing, primarily in the form of equity (German Council of Economic Advisors 2018).

However, if we assess the prospects for funded pension schemes as a component of balanced retirement savings, we must also ask how the regulatory framework could become more supportive within the EU's nascent Capital Markets Union (German Council of Economic Advisors 2018). Harmonising insolvency law and safeguarding an equal tax treatment of debt and equity should be important elements of promoting the development of an integrated capital market. What is more, the competencies assigned to the European Securities and Markets Authority (ESMA) should be expanded. Finally, measures should be implemented to increase the supply of capital, such as by *strengthening private and occupational pension systems* and additionally improving financial literacy and education. Also, in the context of CMU one may call for better availability and comparability of data from areas like accounting and credit reporting, and for stronger enforcement tools in common supervision and insolvency proceedings (Valiante 2015).

We have shown above that Europeans indeed "save high amounts money" but are not making the best out of their savings especially in an around-zero interest rate scenario. But to get European citizens to become retail investors and to invest the European Commission would necessitate to change the playing field. Since the first step in late 2015 tremendous progress has been made so far. Ten out of 13 proposals developed by the European Commission related to CMU have been agreed on by the

Council and the European Parliament or have even been adopted (European Commission 2019).

Two proposals are utterly important for retail investors to *support their preparations for retirement*. First, "simple, standardised and transparent securitization" as a policy is already adopted and expected to broaden opportunities to invest and additionally boost lending to households as well as businesses.

Secondly, the European Parliament and the Council recently agreed on a *Pan-European personal pension product* (PEPP) which appears to be a major step forward for savers across Europe (The Economist 2017a, b; Nieminen and Eatock 2018). It provides savers with better options to save efficiently for retirement. The PEPP is inspired by the Swedish Investment Savings Account (ISkonto). ISkonto was introduced by the Swedish government in 2012 to make savings easier and more benefitting. It makes it simpler for households to invest in shares and funds in Sweden. So far, this long-term saving scheme has been a great success. The PEPP is set out to make large-scale and cost-efficient saving product available across Europe. It is a useful buy-side initiative with high potential for savers. It is expected to become an important investment vehicle in support of the EU economy, supposedly overtaking the UCITS, which was first adopted back in 1985 (Lannoo 2018b).

The German Council of Economic Experts (GCEE) in its recent report pointed out (GCEE 2018, p. 235) that the idea underlying PEPP is to establish *a framework under which different private providers*, such as life insurers, banks and asset managers, *can develop pension products*. The main product features are to be *standardised*, e.g., in relation to transparency requirements, investment provisions, rules for switching between providers and portability. The existing options for statutory, occupational and private pensions are to be supplemented, not replaced, by the PEPP (European Commission 2017). One should note here, that insurance companies and pension funds need predictable and long-term cash flows, to meet their obligations to pensioners and insurance policy holders. Thus, they have a low tendency to invest in potentially higher yielding assets, which are more risky and volatile, but are more driven to invest in bonds (Deutsche Bank Research 2015, p. 11).

Notably, the GCEE has supported the creation of a standard product offered by private-sector providers for private and occupational pensions in previous years (GCEE 2016, p. 325). Developing such a product at European level is a step forward in the right direction as far as the key objective of an integrated European capital market is concerned and could boost competition among private-sector providers, so that clients could benefit.

Overall, it is worth to mention that almost all of the measures planned in connection with Capital Markets Union are aimed at the demand side (GCEE 2018, p. 271). Functioning Capital Markets Union, however, also requires (potential) investors to be more willing and open to invest in capital markets products and not just to leave their savings in deposits. Considering the demographic trend in most EU Member States, it would be sensible and advisable to further strengthen pension schemes funded by capital (The Economist 2017a, b). In this vein, the GCEE has previously proposed various alternative approaches for Germany (GCEE 2016, 327 ff).

Not to forget, *fostering financial literacy* in school education could boost investment in European capital markets products, particularly investment funds. However, this is a long-term project that can be managed at European level merely to a limited extent, as educational matters are often dealt with on a regional level across European countries. Both private pensions and occupational pension schemes could support capital markets because they create a more important role for pension funds that invest in European capital market products.

As The Economist (2017a, b) states, we feel legitimized to conclude: "Any attempt to encourage Europeans to make adequate provision for their old age is welcome. The combination of ageing populations, falling birth rates and generous state pensions could leave future generations footing the bill, unless people work for longer. Especially in countries such as Italy and Greece, where the state is the main pension provider, encouraging people to make personal savings for their retirement would be sensible".

References

Aviva (2016) Mind the gap. Quantifying the pensions gap in Europe. European Public Real Estate Association, London

Belke A, Gros D (2016) On the shock absorbing properties of a banking union – Europe compared with the United States. Comp Econ Stud 58(3):359–386

Blackrock (2017) Investor pulse survey. London

Brender A, Pisani F, Gros D (2015) Building a capital markets union....or designing a financial system for the euro area? CEPS Commentary, 2 June 2015

de Manuel Aramendía M, Lannoo K (2013) Saving for retirement and investing for growth. In: Emerson M, Flôres R (eds) Report of the CEPS-ECMI task force on long-term investing and retirement savings. Centre for European Policy Studies, Brussels

Deutsche Bank Research (2015) Capital markets union: an ambitious goal, but few quick wins. Frankfurt (Main)

ECB (2016) Public investment in Europe. European Central Bank, Frankfurt (Main). (ECB Economic Bulletin, 2/2016)

EPRA (2017) Is capital markets union the answer to Europe's pension crisis? (News, 59) European Public Real Estate Association

European Commission (2013) Green paper on the long-term financing of the European economy. Brussels

European Commission (2015) Action plan on building a capital markets union. Communication from the Commission to the European Parliament, the Council, the European Economic and Social Committee and the Committee of the Regions. European Commission. Brussels

European Commission (2017) Pan-European personal pension product (PEPP) – frequently asked questions. Brussels (European Commission – fact sheet)

European Commission (2018a) Distribution systems of retail investment products across the European Union – final report. Brussels

European Commission (2018b) Capital markets union, Brussels. https://ec.europa.eu/commission/news/capital-markets-union-2018-mar-08_en. Accessed 6 Apr 2019

European Commission (2019) Factsheet: delivering on the capital markets union. Brussels

FSB (2013) Financial regulatory factors affecting the availability of long-term investment finance. Report to G20 Finance Ministers and Central Bank Governors. Financial Stability Board. Basel

GCEE (2016) Zeit für Reformen. Jahresgutachten. German Council of Economic Experts, Wiesbaden

GCEE (2018) Vor wichtigen wirtschaftspolitischen Weichenstellungen. Jahresgutachten. German Council of Economic Experts, Wiesbaden

Gros D (2014) Investment as the key to recovery in the euro area? In: CEPS policy brief. Centre for European Policy Studies, Brussels. 18 November

Gros D, Alcidi C (2013) The global economy in 2030. In: Trends and strategies for Europe. Centre for European Policy Studies, Brussels

Group of Thirty (G30) (2013) Long-term finance and economic growth. Working group on long-term finance. Washington, D.C.

Kay J (2012) The Kay review of UK equity markets and long-term decision making. HM Government, London

Lannoo K (2018a) Funds, fees and performance. ECMI, Brussels. (ECMI Commentary, 54)

Lannoo K (2018b) The PEPP could become the new UCITS. ECMI, Brussels. (ECMI Commentary, 57)

Martinez J, Philippon T, Sihvonen M (2019) Does a currency union need a capital market union? Risk sharing via banks and markets. NBER Working Paper No. 26026

Nieminen R, Eatock D (2018) Pan-European pension product. European Parliament, Brussels, March. http://www.europarl.europa.eu/RegData/etudes/IDAN/2018/615656/EPRS_IDA%282018%29615656_EN.pdf. Accessed 6 Apr 2019

OECD (2011) Promoting longer-term investment by institutional investors: selected issues and policies. OECD Discussion Notes, Paris

The Economist (2017a) Pepped up – the EU proposes pan-European pension products, 6 July

The Economist (2017b) The new old – getting to grips with longevity, Special Report: The Economics of Longevity, 6 July

Valiante D (2015) Europe's untapped capital market – rethinking financial integration after the crisis, CEPS European Capital Markets Expert Group (ECMEG) final report. Rowman & Littlefield, London

World Economic Forum and Oliver Wyman (2011) The future of long-term investing. World Economic Forum, Geneva

Yermo J, Della Croce R, Stewart F (2011) Promoting longer-term investment by institutional investors. OECD J: Financ Mark Trends 2011(1):145–164

Ansgar Belke is Full Professor of Macroeconomics and Director of the Institute of Business and Economic Studies (IBES) at the University of Duisburg-Essen. Since 2012 he is (ad personam) Jean Monnet Professor. Moreover, he is Associate Senior Research Fellow at the Centre for European Policy Studies (CEPS), Brussels, Senior Research Fellow at the Centre for Data Analytics for Finance and Macroeconomics (DAFM), King's Business School, London, member of the Adjunct Faculty Ruhr Graduate School in Economics (RGS Econ) and visiting professor at the Europa-Institut at Saarland University, Saarbrucken. Ansgar Belke was visiting researcher at the IMF in Washington/DC, CentER Tilburg, CEPS Brussels, IfW Kiel, DIW Berlin and OeNB Vienna. Furthermore, he was member of the "Monetary Expert Panel" of the European Parliament, Research Director for International Macroeconomics at the German Institute for Economic Research (DIW), Berlin, and Visiting Professor at the Hertie School of Governance, Berlin.

He is President of the European Economics and Finance Society (EEFS), and member of the Scientific Advisory Council of IAW Tubingen, the Councils of "Arbeitskreis Europäische Integration" (AEI), the "Institut für Europäische Politik" (IEP), the Executive Committee of the International Atlantic Economic Society (IAES) and the Scientific Committee of the International Network for Economic Research (INFER).

He serves as editor-in-chief of "Credit and Capital Markets—Kredit und Kapital", "Konjunkturpolitik—Applied Economics Quarterly" and as co-editor of "International Journal of Financial Studies", "Empirica", "International Economics and Economic Policy", "Journal of Economic Studies", "Vierteljahreshefte für Wirtschaftsforschung", "Aestimatio—The International IEB Journal of Finance","Economist's Voice", "E-conomics" (Kiel Institute of the World

Economy), as editor of the book series "Financial and Monetary Policy Studies", Springer, as a guest editor of renowned journals such as Energy Economics, the European Journal of Political Economy, the Open Economies Review, the Review of International Economics, and as a co-editor of the book series "Quantitative Ökonomie", Eul Verlag.

He published widely in international refereed journals and other outlets, has regular appearances in the printed press, and in national as well as international TV broadcasts.

His main areas of interest are in the fields of international macroeconomics, monetary economics, European integration and applied econometrics.

Philipp Allroggen studied Economics at University of Duisburg-Essen and Universidad Autónoma de Madrid. After participating in a post-graduate program of the Centre for European Policy Studies (CEPS), in Brussels and short stint at the Chair of Economic Policy at University of Duisburg-Essen, Philipp Allroggen is currently working as a graduate research assistant at the ad personam Jean Monnet Chair of Prof Belke. His research interests lie particularly in Monetary Policy and Capital Markets.

Sustainable Pensions for European Citizens: How to Close the Gap?

Gabriel Bernardino

Abstract Living considerably longer than ever before is certainly a positive fact, but at the same time, this presents a number of challenges and opens up questions how to reserve for retirement. Projections show that there will be fewer and fewer people paying into the pensions systems to support an ever-increasing number of pensioners. People living longer and low birth rates in developed countries, paired with low interest rates, mean that there is pressure on any pensions system, as funds have to cater for much longer periods. For a number of years, the growing gap between what people perceive as what they will receive as retirement income and what they will actually receive—as well as the basic adequacy of retirement income—has been on the agenda of governments, policy makers and regulators. There have been a number of studies showing that in Europe, yet also in many other developed and developing countries, not just the pensions gap, but also the funding gap of pension funds, is increasing and will be hard to close.

1 Introduction: The Challenge

1.1 Demographic and Labour Market Changes

Adequate retirement income—or the prevention of old age poverty—has been a constant concern of the European human rights agenda in the context of increasing life expectancy and low birth rates. Social security systems and national budgets are feeling the pressure of more and more pensioners depending on the contributions of less and less workers. Further, the implications of migration on social security and pension systems are mostly unknown. Consequently, the vast majority of European

I thank Sandra Hack, Carine Pilot-Osborn and Giulia Conforti for their contributions to this article.

G. Bernardino (✉)
European Insurance and Occupational Pensions Authority (EIOPA), Frankfurt am Main, Germany
e-mail: OfficeEIOPASeniorManagement@eiopa.europa.eu

© Springer Nature Switzerland AG 2019
N. da Costa Cabral, N. Cunha Rodrigues (eds.), *The Future of Pension Plans in the EU Internal Market*, Financial and Monetary Policy Studies 48,
https://doi.org/10.1007/978-3-030-29497-7_8

Member States—and equally most countries around the world—have considered supplementing the pressured, traditional social security systems by incentivising private pension savings.

Traditionally, pension systems are based on the idea of citizens contributing to their pension rights or future retirement income by saving a part of current income for future consumption or to support current pensioners. However, drastic changes in the labour market and the way individuals build their careers can be observed. Considering the implications of the recent financial crises—resulting in high unemployment rates and unprecedented levels of youth unemployment of up to 60% in certain European countries[1]—on individuals and their careers, it is obvious that traditional pension systems cannot cater for these recent challenges.

Potentially due to the recent, dire economic situation in a number of countries and exacerbated by the digital age, individuals were driven to access new forms of labour, choosing to become temporarily or permanently self-employed or part-time employed, commuting or moving across borders. Those modern ways to work are difficult to cover by any one national pension system that is solely reliant on full-time work income and corresponding contributions.[2]

Most vulnerable to the inherent shortcomings of work-based pension systems are non-permanent migrant workers—who are at risk of not being sufficiently covered by security systems in their home or host countries of employment, and women—who suffer from a stable 'gender gap' in replacement ratios of, on average, 10% in the EU,[3] mostly due to breaks in female careers to care for children and relatives.

1.2   Economic Environment

The disruptions caused by the 2008 financial crisis and the following sovereign debt crisis in Europe during 2011 and 2012 affected both European governments and investors, and subsequently European citizens to a significant extent. Consumers' disposable income declined by up to 30% (in aggregate) in a few EU Member States in the years immediately after the financial crisis and since then has been only slowly increasing to pre-2008 figures.[4]

The recent phase of weak growth and low interest rates, not only in Europe but in many mature economies, has put private pension providers, be they pension funds or life insurers, particularly under pressure, as the guaranteed interest on their long-term obligations are expected to significantly exceed the yields to be gained from financial markets.

---

[1]See Eurostat (2019a). Since 2008 the youth unemployment rates have steadily decreased, yet remain at high levels of up to 34% in certain EU Member States.

[2]See for example Rutkowski (2018), pp. 10–13.

[3]See Eurostat (2019b).

[4]See Eurostat (2019c).

Both, EIOPA's 2015 and 2017 stress tests showed that, even prior to applying a stressed scenario, on average European Defined Benefit pension funds are underfunded, so that the available assets are insufficient to cover the actual liabilities. In line with national arrangements, these shortfalls in funding are usually addressed by mitigating mechanisms, such as increasing sponsor or member contributions, benefit reductions and, where available, by involving pension protection schemes.[5] The impact of consequently increased funding contributions by sponsors—and of benefit reductions to members and beneficiaries—depends on the financial strength of the sponsor and the degree of dependency of members and beneficiaries on the retirement income stemming from those pension funds, but may be significant and may further affect already challenged financial markets. Corporate failures in recent years have highlighted the risk of pension fund members to lose a substantial amount of retirement income and have shown that the potential effects of current underfunding are not to be underestimated.[6]

In response to these economic challenges, it is not surprising that the private pension funds and products are transforming from Defined Benefit (DB) to Defined Contribution (DC) systems or substantially decreasing—if not cancelling—guarantees in life insurance contracts towards pure unit-linked contracts.[7] This shift of financial, investment risk from the (institutional) investor to the consumer requires re-thinking the regulatory framework of these pension providers—and their products—and so to address potential conflicts of interests as well as to prevent consumer detriment.

However, on a positive note, pension providers have been acknowledged as having the potential to play a central role as drivers of efficient capital markets—as providing genuinely long-term financing, based on long-term savings of their customers. Incentivising long-term financing and investing, so called 'sustainable investments'—and their promotion amongst institutional investors—are at the centre of current policy considerations, with the appreciation of 'ESG' factors (Environmental, Social and Governance) as one of the European Commission's flagship initiatives.[8]

1.3 Learnings from Behavioural Economics

Behavioural Economics[9] help to understand how human behaviour may affect financial decision-making and may shape individuals' decisions regarding private retirement saving. In the focus of those considerations are human 'shortcomings'

---

[5] See EIOPA (2017), pp. 7–8.
[6] See for example Financial Times (2019).
[7] See EIOPA (2018a), pp. 6 and 37.
[8] European Commission (2018a).
[9] See for example Kahneman et al. (1982).

that contrast with the often-cited financial theories' economic assumption of individuals acting rationally. Several behavioural patterns and biases influence people's thinking and are most relevant for potentially affecting financial decision-making, such as:

- Procrastination/inertia: a tendency to avoid decisions for fear of regret and—in face of complexity, choice or information overload—resulting in choosing the path of the least resistance, also known as 'status quo bias'. This is closely linked to the so-called 'present bias' and individuals' preference for consumption now over saving for future consumption.
- Loss aversion: it is easier for individuals to give up a gain rather than to accept a loss. In practice, this means that people may put more effort into preventing a loss than trying to achieve a gain. Prospect theory[10] presents evidence of risk aversion as a consequence of individuals' inherent bias to unfairly weight gains and losses. A gain of €10 is seen as less pleasant than a loss of €10 is unpleasant, and the possibility of a €10 gain is less appealing than the possibility of losing €10 is unattractive.
- Rule of thumb: a means of estimating according to a rough and ready practical rule, not based on science or exact measurement, which can lead to errors and mistakes. For instance, people may hold a naïve idea of portfolio diversification, which leads to, for example, dividing their contributions evenly across all the funds offered in the pension plan or finding median portfolios (e.g. constructed on the statistical average of a peer group's behaviour).

Accordingly, consumers face significant cognitive barriers when planning long-term savings for future retirement income. This is exacerbated by the inherent complexity of such financial decisions and the—on average—limited financial literacy, in particular regarding the understanding of the impact of inflation, required saving or future replacement rates.

In addition to the already existing biases and human preferences to avoid or delay planning for old age, current pension systems, be they occupational or personal pensions, are often very complex, opaque in cost and investment structures and simply difficult to understand. Consequently, the perceived reliability of private pensions is deteriorating, as evidenced in consumer market studies that show persistently low ratings of personal pension products in terms of consumer trust.

Obviously, consumers' views, expectations and trust in private pensions are shaped by the importance and relative significance of individuals' saving decisions regarding financial planning and private personal pensions. Potential pension savers' detriment, such as risk and sizable value of an incurred loss on retirement savings, which can severely reduce the future replacement rate[11]—or even pension fraud, the

---

[10]See in particular Kahneman and Tversky (1979), pp. 313–327.

[11]After applying a stressed, yet plausible, scenario, replacement rates of DC members fell by more than 11% on average and up to nearly 20% for those members close to retirement, see EIOPA (2017), pp. 67–68.

difficulty or highly charged possibility to switch providers and the lack of comparability of features and costs, contribute to the negative perception of private pensions.[12]

2 Complementary Private Pensions

On average 15% of the working population in the European Economic Area are active members of Institutions for Occupational Retirement Provision, so-called IORPs, or other occupational pension scheme arrangements and only 27% of Europeans between 25 and 59 years are saving in personal pension products.[13] Even though these are aggregate figures, which need to be read in light of a highly diverse pension system in Europe, there is clearly scope to further promote private pensions in Europe, complementing social security or state pension designs.

Considering the challenges described in the first chapter, stemming from demographic and socio-economic developments, complementary private pensions have to address the demands of current and future generations. Further, they need to be attractive to consumers—considering individuals' 'natural' biases and often little ability to save due to low disposable income—as well as to private pension providers, so that such schemes or products are actually available to consumers.

2.1 Flexible, Adaptive Solutions

Successful complementary private pensions necessitate solutions that can address socio-economic challenges. Consequently, these solutions should be sufficiently flexible to adapt to variable and discontinued career paths as well as harness human shortcomings and help to overcome people's cognitive and behavioural biases.

For European pension solutions and considering the EU citizens' freedom of movement, portability is a key feature, which is a challenge due to the wide diversity of prudential, social and tax regulated pension systems in Europe.

Following an 'unconventional' career path requires the private pension savings to be adaptable to continue to contribute in times of unemployment or self-employment. Yet any modern and future career path will benefit from flexible and adaptive pension solutions. Secure and easy digital technology and its everyday use by consumers may foster the engagement in financial and pension-specific planning

---

[12]Private personal pension products being one of the services lowest graded in consumer trust in the European Commission's regular surveys of consumer markets. Please see in particular European Commission (2018b), p. 17.

[13]See EIOPA (2018b), p. 3; European Commission (2017), p. 1.

and may increase the willingness to save more for future retirement income, in particular if the pension solutions are adaptable to personal needs.

2.1.1 Nudging

Ensuing from the fact that consumers cannot fully rely on social security and state pension systems to reach an adequate retirement income in the future, consumers have to contribute an appropriate share of their current disposable income to supplement their future retirement income. As most individuals' disposable income is limited and individuals are biased to favour higher available income in the present over higher income in the future, contribution levels need to be set in a meaningful way, taking into account future needs and ideally the future income from other sources.

Automatic enrolment of EU citizens in complementary private pensions, also known as auto-enrolment,[14] can effectively encourage pension savings by changing the choice architecture[15] and harnessing people's inertia and tendency to procrastinate when they face difficult and complex decisions such as planning and saving for their retirement. Auto-enrolment may be either mandatory or semi-compulsory with the possibility for EU citizens to opt out of pension saving within a limited time-period or stop contributing at any point in time.

The success of auto-enrolment initiatives implemented nationally, in specific sectors or at company level, also depends on setting appropriate contribution levels, which are adapted to individuals' career path. This means designing solutions that prompt EU citizens to review regularly their contributions and make it easy on them to choose appropriate levels. Such follow-up actions are necessary, as individuals continue to procrastinate following auto-enrolment and remain disengaged with retirement planning—and may feel a false sense of security being automatically enrolled and being 'taken care of'.[16]

In practice, unless prompted or via automatically stepping up contributions with increases in disposable income, they will not review regularly the adequacy of their contribution levels, especially as they tend to show a preference for the present. Pre-committing people to increase gradually their contributions with each future pay rise can be an effective way to encourage them to save more (SMART[17]). Necessary adjustments to the contribution levels, due to expected insufficient pension outcomes, need to be very transparent towards the consumer and ideally should be

---

[14]Auto-enrolment refers to a system whereby an individual is made a member by default, and automatic enrolment has to actively decide to leave the scheme.

[15]This term introduced by Thaler and Sunstein refers to the practice of influencing choice by changing the way in which options are presented to people. Thaler and Sunstein (2008).

[16]See World Economic Forum (2018), p. 12.

[17]Benartzi and Thaler (2004), pp. S164–S187.

linked to changes in the individuals' lives, such as salary increases and career progression.

2.1.2   Adapting to Personal Needs

Pensions and annuities—these are two concepts with which individuals struggle to fully understand their intricacies and—even more concerning—their respective value for the individual. Individuals' preference for the present, as well as the inflexibility and illiquidity of most pensions and annuities, constitute the main reasons for that lack of understanding. Pension savings cannot be accessed or collateralised before retirement; and annuities do not allow for bequests. Making private pensions more attractive and more adaptable to personal needs could help encourage retirement savings and may help people to engage more in financial pension planning and thereby (re-)gain consumers' trust and confidence in pensions.

In order to achieve an adequate level of future retirement income, it is necessary to build up sufficient savings and to enable the pension provider to invest long-term, reaching higher yields. However, smart designs of pension solutions, matching certain quality criteria, could make pension savings more flexible and tailored to individuals' circumstances, demands and eventually may facilitate important changes in individuals' lives. Solutions seeking to improve the flexibility of private pensions should above all discourage unintended consequences and behaviours that could jeopardise secure, stable and adequate income in retirement.

Several jurisdictions have looked into ways to make private pensions more flexible and liquid, for instance, by allowing people to use their accrued pension savings as a collateral to borrow money, e.g. for home purchase, funding of training or education) or to take loans from their own pension funds, which they must pay back with interest e.g. US 401(k) plans.[18] Other solutions provide for the option to withdraw funds permanently under certain circumstances, e.g. qualifying criteria such as severe financial hardships, with no obligation to repay e.g. Kiwisaver in New Zealand.[19]

Further, also to incentivise additional voluntary savings, the accounts could distinguish between such that are accessible—after reaching a certain threshold and after a certain investment period—and such that remain inaccessible, so that there is access to a certain amount of liquid savings. For instance, the pension account could feature a more liquid element e.g. instant access savings account for emergency spending. Once the level of savings reaches a satisfactory threshold, contributions may be fed into the liquid part of the pension account. If at any point withdrawals from the liquid account goes below the savings cap, future contributions

---

[18]www.finra.org/investors/highlights/what-you-need-know-about-401k-loans

[19]www.kiwisaver.govt.nz/already/get-money/early/hardship/

would start again being divided between the liquid and illiquid accounts e.g. NEST sidecar savings trial.[20]

In order to make private pensions more attractive—and to encourage private pension savings in excess of the minimal adequate level—regulating possibilities for early access or usability of the pension savings may be a crucially effective tool. The size of such lump sum payments or the proportion in relation to the entire pension savings, as well as certain conditions like minimum age, value of the accrued pension, maximum ceiling amount, have to be regulated so as to ensure the adequacy of the future retirement income and the long-term investment of the pension savings.

Further, flexibility with regard to portable solutions or switching savings between occupational to personal pensions (or vice versa) are deemed beneficial to cater for changing career paths and labour markets. These considerations to enhance the flexibility of pension solutions should also extend into the decumulation—retirement—phase, for example to provide for more flexible retirement income strategies suited to future personal needs in retirement in contrast to full mandatory annuitisation at retirement.

2.2   Standardisation: Quality Features

Standardising key features of pension solutions can have three benefits: firstly, it can be ensured that basic components are designed in a way to safeguard good pension outcomes, secondly, it helps consumers to better understand and to compare and benchmark pension solutions offered to them and thirdly, it brings efficiency gains and cost savings to pension providers.

Standardised quality features of private pensions should meet conditions that will benefit consumers and providers through the realisation of economies of scale, lower costs and an environment fostering both open and fair competition as well as innovation. As a result, it is important to achieve the right balance in a way that the mandatory standardised elements protect the interest of savers and lower information costs for providers, yet leaving sufficient room for innovation. Developing an overly prescribed product or scheme may deter providers from offering private pensions due to lack of profitability or making it too expensive for employers or consumers.

Further, due to their inertia, individuals will want to decide upon complex, long-duration and long-term decisions, like private pensions, 'once and for all', without reconsidering options or monitoring the performance of the product or scheme. Therefore, choosing the most suitable pension product or scheme or feature from the outset is crucial. This is an important consideration for the design of private pensions and in particular for default products.

---

[20]www.nestinsight.org.uk/wp-content/uploads/2017/12/Liquidity-and-sidecar-savings-discussion-paper.pdf

2.2.1 Designing 'Defaults' and Standardised Elements

To promote private pension savings, consumers need to be made aware of the necessity to contribute privately for retirement income. At the same time, consumers should be supported to understand the offered pension solution and its features. As discussed before, consumers' trust in such products and schemes—and their providers—need to be built to promote further savings. Private pension savings can positively influence and enable adequate replacement rates in the future, only if the products and schemes are fair and when savings are indeed safe. Safety here is meant as trust enhancing, fair, cost-effective and transparently designed with the objective of ensuring stable and superior pension outcomes. At the same time, the pension solutions should be sufficiently flexible to cater for a European labour market that is characterised by increasing unconventional careers and heightened mobility of workers. Building on these views, EIOPA developed the idea and the regulatory outline to create a Pan-European Personal Pension Product (PEPP),[21] which exhibits standardised features mirroring the specific objective of a personal pension product to provide for future retirement income, alongside some flexible elements taking into account national specificities.

Transparency about the product features is crucial to encourage procrastinating individuals to engage in pension planning. High complexity is often seen as inherent to the nature of any long-term savings. In order to enable a consumer to make well-informed decisions about taking up and maintaining long-term savings, relevant and easy accessible information on those products need to be provided. Experience shows that individuals cannot necessarily rationalise an estimate of the need to save for pensions and the extent to which additional savings are required. The nature, frequency and presentation of relevant information are crucial in this regard. By reducing the diversity and number of pension product characteristics e.g. choice of investment options, standardisation can lead to economies of scale and hence lower costs. Furthermore, simplifying and reducing the number of pension product characteristics through standardisation can help market players better focus on their target market through a better alignment of savers' needs. This, in turn, helps facilitate market take-up for private pensions.

Cost-effective pension solutions are in high demand, as the disposable income in Europe is limited and it needs to pay off to save even small amounts. Determinants of administration costs are the level of distribution, information and manufacturing costs, which are intrinsically linked to the complexity of products—and the lack of standardisation. Efficiency gains are needed, particularly at a time of low asset returns, to build a stronger market for private pensions. Economies of scale and risk diversification contribute to lowering costs and reaping efficiency gains. A well-functioning market without obstacles to cross-border activities, facilitating healthy competition and financial innovation, is a pre-condition for realising such gains.

---

[21]EIOPA (2016).

Standardisation is not just about generating efficiency gains; it also helps to overcome information asymmetry. The economic rationale for standardisation typically stems from the need to reduce both transaction costs and information asymmetries. Whilst lower transaction costs result in decreasing production and distribution costs, they also reduce search costs, time and effort spent for savers by setting benchmarks, signalling on the product quality, which should help improve trust and confidence in pensions.

Product standardisation also facilitates information standardisation and assists savers with valuable and transparent information to evaluate and compare product characteristics. As the information is standardised, specific and tailored features can be presented specifically and tailor made—yet in a comparable fashion, making the product features—and their effects—transparent to the consumer. In this context, EIOPA has identified several principles for the design of pension information documents throughout the career and life of a consumer.[22] These principles cover for example the requirement to design the information documents with a behavioural purpose and to respond to the consumer's key questions and address good practices, such as layering of information stylistic and visual tools for paper and digital means.

2.2.2 Investment Strategy

The investment strategy should be developed and implemented in such a manner that contributions are invested in assets solely in the best interest of savers, taking into account their retirement income objectives and following the prudent person rule to ensure the security, quality, diversification, liquidity and profitability of the portfolio as a whole. Further, a long-term view on investments to encourage investing in appropriate asset classes, i.e. sustainable, long-term assets including the potential long-term impact of investment decisions on economic, social and governance factors is necessary.

Providing pensions is a long-term business, consequently the asset management has to follow a long-term objective. The long-term view on investments should encourage investing in appropriate, i.e. sustainable, long-term assets, taking good note of investment-specific factors and ratings in relation to economic, social and governance aspects. Alternative investments, green bonds and investments in infrastructure should be enabled, where appropriate. Assets traded on regulated markets, with the benefit of a certain level of liquidity and relying on market valuations are expected to remain the predominant asset class for private pensions. Similarly, passive investment strategies and investments linked to virtual or real indices may also provide for appropriate risk/return patterns.

Derivatives are complex financial instruments, which can be effective hedging tools and support market and credit risk management. If done in a prudent fashion, derivatives are a useful tool to reduce the investment risk or to facilitate efficient

---

[22]See EIOPA (2018c), pp. 6–7.

portfolio management. But, derivatives used for other purposes, for example trading, can exacerbate the risk exposure and create concentration risk in relation to one single counterparty. Generally, the investment pool for private pensions should be efficiently managed, diversified and well balanced to enable good outcomes at an appropriate level of investment risk.

The investment strategy of private pensions, in particular for the default or core investment option, will typically include risk mitigation techniques seeking to ensure the protection of pension savers against extreme negative outcomes. This is especially relevant because more pension savers bear investment risks, due to the shift from defined benefit and guarantees to defined contribution and unit-linked products. Further, as a consequence of the behavioural biases, consumers tend to follow loss avoidance strategies and prefer certainty and tend to have a naïve notion of diversification.

One approach to implement the retirement objective of private pension scheme and products in investment strategies is to apply life-cycling techniques. Life cycling means that younger generations' contributions will be invested in higher risk/ rewards-profiled investments and the older the generations grow, the lower the riskiness/rewards profile of the investments will be chosen. Life cycling should be done in a principle-based, adaptive manner, as the current, persistently low interest rate environment teaches to remain adaptable to the economic environment and not to blindly follow rules, which made perfect sense in 'normal' circumstances.

Another possible asset management strategy, and one example for a relevant risk mitigation technique, is to build up buffers in a way that the upturns in investment returns could help to balance future downturns. In the purest sense, this is similar to an equity investment that provides for dividends in good times, which do not fully match the realised profits, due to the company setting aside some reserves, and continues to pay dividends in bad times, funded by the company's reserves. Setting reserves is conducive to the long-term objective of private pensions. Reserves could be fed by a share of the contributions or of the asset returns—or both—and could be complemented by capital maintenance guarantees, so that the consumer participates in the upturn, yet is fully protected against potential downturns, shortly before or, at the time of retirement.

The design of such an investment strategy has to specify the pattern of the reserves' allocation to the individual consumer—or possibly to simplify to a higher granularity, for example, to cohorts. Therefore, simple, transparent and enforceable allocation rules are of paramount importance to make pension products and schemes safe, transparent and fair towards the consumer. This also entails that the corresponding investment portfolio needs to be legally and economically separated from the rest of the provider's assets or its scope of control (e.g. investments in shares of the provider or associated entities should be limited), without any possibility of recourse or interfering, also not in the event of bankruptcy of the provider. Again, the organisation of the investment framework has to ensure a transparent and enforceable reconciliation of the assets within the investment pool to the individual share or unit in that pool.

Private pensions should have a long-term perspective when it comes to establishing and implementing their investment strategy. Investment strategies should meet the objective of saving for retirement income. Alongside the use of default investment option and limiting the choice of alternative investment options, investment governance, defined as taking decisions collectively on behalf of pension savers and acting in their best interest, is commonly used to support effective investment decisions.[23] The provider's governance system, and in particular the risk management function, needs to be capable of running the investment pool with the consumers' interests in mind. This should be reflected in the cost structures of the provider. The incentives provided by asset manager's bonuses should be set in line to serving the interests of the consumers. Performance related charges should reconcile to the long-term objective of the savings. Clearly, any charges should be transparent to the consumer and presented in a fair manner.

Due to the principal importance of the one default option or the one single investment pool, the design of those have to be fully aligned with the consumer's needs. Because most consumers find it difficult—or are not prepared—to monitor the actual investment decisions made on their behalf, investment policies, investment restrictions and actual transactions have to be in line with the an appropriate governance policy. Investment governance committees may enforce an independent view on investment policies and can audit their actual application. Such committees have to be 'fit and proper' and consumers should have a decisive role in them.

Setting the investment governance should entail the monitoring of the ongoing suitability of the default investment option and the level of fees and charges are regularly reviewed with prompt actions to act in the sole and best interest of pension savers in the event of unsuitability.

The provision of a default or core investment option and reduced choice for alternative investment options also facilitate the standardisation of information disclosure to pension savers by improving both transparency and comparability of pension information, for instance through the use of benchmarks to measure performance between investment options or between providers. Pension savers should receive clear, fair and non-misleading communication explaining how the investment strategy is designed and how the downside of investment risk is being managed; and pre-contractual or pre-enrolment information clearly setting out the conditions and consequences of the life cycling and other risk mitigation techniques.

2.2.3   Linking Accumulation to Decumulation

Designing private pensions as 'default' products or schemes and a limited number of alternative options can help achieve economies of scale and cost efficiencies as well as help overcome behavioural, 'human' shortcomings. Addressing individuals' general inertia also by designing one default option within a product or scheme,

---

[23]EIOPA (2015).

helps to steer consumers to suitable solutions and enables scalable investment portfolios. At the same time, one single investment option safeguards fair outcomes for all savers, as the minority of individuals who actually switch funds regularly do create better outcomes for themselves—yet often at the expense of the remainder of the savers in terms of performance of the portfolio.[24] In terms of economies of scales and consequently cost effectiveness, sufficiently sizable investment portfolio are needed. In order to allow for time-consistent solutions—and neither to favour nor to discriminate consumers changing the provider or the product—the allocation of the consumers' savings to cohort portfolios may be beneficial.

A default or core option should be determined by an approach to investments that meets a range of needs regarding future retirement income and is suitable to a significantly large group of consumers. The number of available, alternative investment options should be limited and set in such a way that it prevents consumer choice overload and confusion. This can be done by following the principles of guided choice architecture and clear, meaningful labelling of investment options. The approach to the accumulation—the investment—phase must be driven by the view of ensuring superior pension outcomes and therewith link the accumulation to the decumulation phase.

In the area of decumulation and the design of the retirement phase, there is still ample room for financial innovation and to set out relevant patterns of the retirement phase's payments to equally invest the accumulated capital efficiently and to cover for the risk of outliving one's pension savings. Considering the potentially widely diverse personal circumstances and savings levels of consumers in different European countries, it is hard to imagine a 'one size fits all' solution that can address and match all individual specificities. Probably neither a full lump sum payment nor a full annuitisation at retirement can cater for consumers' needs and the objective to design a long-term retirement solution that can make a difference to individuals' lives as well as that can help to protect against old age poverty.

The decumulation phase has to be designed in a manner that is fair towards the consumer and is tailored to its personal circumstances and demands. It seems crucial to offer advice on a number of different options in a neutral and objective fashion. Longevity covers and annuities naturally play an important role in the decumulation phase, as protecting against the risk of outliving one's savings is an appropriate objective of any pension solution. The provider should be required to present the competitive offers of a number of annuity providers and should be able to explain them. Further, the consumer should be enabled to further benefit from the active asset management, if that corresponds to the consumer's financial planning in retirement, and which may be supplemented by programmed or flexible draw-downs or partly by lump sum payments.

Ideally, one target pension should be designed, taking into account future income from state pensions and other sources. Realistically this would bring up issues like

---

[24]See Dahlquist et al. (2016).

setting relevant assumptions for the forecasts and projections, as well as enforce-ability, considering the different legal bases of state and private pensions.

Making pensions more attractive and sufficiently flexible to adapt to individuals' personal circumstances and needs also necessitates designing pensions that facilitate a smooth transition between the accumulation and decumulation phases. Such transition from accumulation to decumulation is becoming more complex as the boundary between accumulation and decumulation has become less rigid and increasingly blurred. With the low-interest rate environment making annuitisation less attractive, some jurisdictions have abolished compulsory annuitisation. This trend may continue as a result of the persistently low interest rates.

Life-long annuities are not necessarily sufficiently tailored to individuals' vari-able spending, which tends to be J- or U-shaped over the retirement period. A J-shaped profile would mean more income at the end of retirement to pay for social and health care costs. A U-shaped profile would allow for higher income at the beginning of retirement when retirees are more active in addition to more income for social and health care costs at the end of retirement. Further, annuitising relatively small savings may lead to very low regular payments and relatively low value for the consumer. The use of deferred annuities, which become effective only at a later stage in the retirement phase, can help to tailor the retirement planning to facilitate a more active retirement and to cater for a phase that potentially requires higher expenses for providing health care in old age.

Variable career paths, spells of inactivity and improved life expectancy mean that increasingly people may need to work longer or retain a part-time activity for part of their retirement. Combined with the shift to DC pensions and personal pension products without guarantees or annuities, retirees are likely to continue investing part of their pensions in retirement, albeit with a different investment strategy seeking to maintain sustainable income streams and hence avoid outliving their savings.

Auto-enrolment and other initiatives seeking to harness people's inertia during the accumulation phase (e.g. default investment option) potentially nurture savers' disengagement with pension decisions including during pre-retirement and pay-out phase. Facilitating the transition from accumulation to decumulation requires devel-oping solutions to help overcome cognitive and behavioural biases for instance by designing default retirement income solutions and guided choice architecture.

2.2.4 Enforcing Quality Features

Private pensions are often regarded as an inefficient market, where consumers' demand is not matched by adequate supply of suitable solutions. Regulation has to address agency conflicts and information asymmetry as shortcomings of an ineffi-cient market. Conflicts of interests need to be acknowledged and the right incentives need to be put in place to facilitate optimised results for consumers. The main tools for enforcing these considerations are a robust regulatory framework, including authorisation regimes, governance, distribution rules and corresponding supervisory powers. To promote safe products also mean implementing relevant controls and limits on product design, including through product oversight and governance measures. By simplifying the characteristics of private pensions, standardisation seeks to overcome information asymmetries as well as help savers overcome cognitive and behavioural biases, which often lead them to sub-optimal retirement saving outcomes.

Regulating and authorising private pension products and schemes facilitate consistent designs and a framework for standardised and default solutions. Such a regulatory and supervisory framework can endorse a 'quality label' for private pensions and enables consumer trust, which allows for further efficiency gains and prevents potentially divergent practices. Through the authorisation and supervision, national competent authorities can set clear expectations on the products and schemes to be marketed throughout their legislation. A successful quality label, setting out qualifying product or scheme features, surely requires a strong and efficient authorisation process as well as certifying the appropriateness of the key quality features of the private pension product or scheme.

Access to all relevant and comparable information regarding marketed products and schemes should be centrally provided to the consumer and so promote consumer engagement, building trust and facilitate the individual's pension planning.

Further, to enforce the quality features of a pension product, the market has to be monitored and verified that only actually compliant products are marketed as such. Depending on the regulatory framework of the jurisdiction, that may require close collaboration and sharing of information with different national competent authorities and, in Europe, of the European supervisory authority. Further, the competent authorities must ensure that they receive all relevant information to exert effectively their supervision powers and enrich their supervisory review processes.

Efficient and effective product intervention powers are necessary to take actions against deficient pension products or schemes in a timely manner, as poorly designed or marketed products can raise significant concerns regarding consumer protection or pose a threat to the orderly functioning of the financial markets. And surely, any such event will further impair consumer trust in this already challenged financial services sector.

That is why national competent authorities should be enabled to act swiftly and to—temporarily—restrict or prohibit the marketing, distribution or sale of deficient pension products or schemes. That is particularly sensitive—yet essential—in the financial sector, and specifically in the pension sector, that is challenged by low consumer trust and high risk of significant negative effects on individuals and their standard of living in retirement—and eventually the financial stability of the sector.

3 Conclusion

The need to save—more—privately to ensure adequate retirement income is a conclusion reached by many policymakers globally. However, that need comes at a time of a persistently challenging economic situation for both consumers and providers of long-term occupational or personal pension scheme arrangements. That creates two challenges for policymakers: making consumer aware of the need and providing for an appropriate framework for valuable and effective private pension products and schemes.

To address those challenges, a number of policy ideas have been developed: first and foremost, the need to design transparent, well governed and cost efficient products and schemes. Transparency about features, cost and charges and sustainability of the private pension solution and its provider, is necessary to build up consumer trust and allowing consumers making informed decisions.

Private pension products and schemes also have to be cost efficient, which can be achieved by reaching economies of scale. Here, both consumer behavioural biases and providers' commercial interests can be attended to at the same time by providing smart 'default solutions', where a set of high quality standardised features can be complemented by flexible components. Leaving room for innovation and flexibility is needed to help consumers making beneficial—life—choices and for providers finding superior solutions.

Policy and prudential frameworks have be capable of enforcing such high quality private pension solutions, be they occupational or personal, building on the effective regulation and the provider's strong governance structures, enabling sustainable private pensions.

References

Benartzi S, Thaler RH (2004) Save more tomorrow: using behavioral economics to increase employee saving. J Polit Econ 112:S164–S187

Dahlquist M, Martinez JC, Soederlind P (2016) Individual investor activity and performance, September 2016

EIOPA (2015) Report on investment options for occupational DC scheme members

EIOPA (2016) EIOPA's advice on the development of an EU single market for personal pension products (PPP), 6 July 2016

EIOPA (2017) 2017 IORP stress test report

EIOPA (2018a) Seventh consumer trends report

EIOPA (2018b) 2017 Market development report on occupational pensions and cross-border IORPs

EIOPA (2018c) Implementation of IORP II: report on the pension benefit statement: guidance and principles based on current practices, November 2018

European Commission (2017) Pan-European Personal Pension Product (PEPP) – frequently asked questions, MEMO17–1798

European Commission (2018a) Action plan: financing sustainable growth; COM (2018) 97 final, March 2018

European Commission (2018b) Consumer markets scoreboard 2018

Eurostat (2019a) Unemployment rate of active population aged 18–25. https://ec.europa.eu/eurostat/tgm/table.do?tab=table&plugin=1&language=en&pcode=tipslm80

Eurostat (2019b) Gender differences in aggregate replacement ratio. https://ec.europa.eu/eurostat/web/products-datasets/-/tespn260

Eurostat (2019c) Adjusted gross disposable income of households per capita in purchasing power parities. https://ec.europa.eu/eurostat/web/products-datasets/-/tec00113

Financial Times (2019) Securing pensions needs more than jail threats. Prison time for CEOs grabs headlines but a broader review is required, February 2019
Kahneman D, Tversky A (1979) Prospect theory: an analysis of decisions under risk. Econometrica 47:263–292
Kahneman D, Slovic P, Tversky A (1982) Judgment under uncertainty: heuristics and biases. Cambridge University Press, New York
Rutkowski M (2018) Reimagining social protection. New systems that do not rely on standard employment contracts are needed. In: Worldbank (2018): Finance & Development, December 2018
Thaler RH, Sunstein C (2008) Nudge: improving decisions about health, wealth, and happiness. Yale University Press, New Haven, CT
World Economic Forum (2018) Howe we can save (for) our future, June 2018

Gabriel Bernardino Chairman of the European Insurance and Occupational Pensions Authority (EIOPA). He is responsible for the strategic direction of EIOPA and represents the Authority at the Council of the European Union, the European Commission and the European Parliament. Mr. Bernardino prepares the work of EIOPA's Board of Supervisors and also chairs the meetings of the Board of Supervisors and the Management Board.

Mr. Bernardino is the first Chairperson of EIOPA. He was elected by the Board of Supervisors of EIOPA on 10 January, 2011. His nomination followed a pre-selection of the European Commission and was confirmed by the European Parliament after a public hearing held on 1 February, 2011. Mr. Bernardino assumed his responsibilities on 1 March, 2011 for a first 5-year term. On 16 December 2015 the European Parliament confirmed the re-appointment of Mr Bernardino for a second 5-year term, which started on 1 March 2016. Prior to his current role, Mr. Bernardino was the Director General of the Directorate for Developments and Institutional Relations at the Instituto de Seguros de Portugal (ISP). He has served in several positions of increasing responsibility since he joint the ISP in 1989 and represented EIOPA's preceding organisation, CEIOPS, as Chairman between October 2009 and December 2010.

Welfare Gains from a Capital Market Union with Capital-Funded Pensions

Thomas Davoine and Susanne Forstner

Abstract We analyze and compare the long-run effects for a country introducing a capital-funded pension pillar in two scenarios: The case of separate capital markets, on the one hand, and the case of integrated capital markets (a capital market union), on the other hand. Our analysis is based on simulations with a large-scale overlapping-generations model. We find that, in the long run, the introduction of capital-funded pensions is more attractive in integrated capital markets than in separated capital markets, if other countries in the integrated capital market have pay-as-you-go pension systems.

1 Introduction

The design of pension systems varies significantly across European countries. Some countries, such as Austria, France, Italy, and Spain, rely almost exclusively on public pay-as-you-go pension schemes. In other countries, such as Denmark, the Netherlands, Slovakia and Sweden, a substantial part of the pension system consists of mandatory savings in capital-funded pensions. In still other countries, such as Ireland or the United Kingdom, the public pension system is complemented substantially by voluntary private pension schemes.[1] However, differences in pension systems can have large economic and welfare consequences. In a pay-as-you-go system, contributions from salaries are transferred to retirees for immediate consumption. In contrast, in a capital-funded pension system, contributions from salaries are invested and earn a return on the capital market. They are used for the

---

[1]See OECD (2018) for detailed information on the composition of the pension system across EU and OECD countries.

T. Davoine · S. Forstner (✉)
Institute for Advanced Studies (IHS), Vienna, Austria
e-mail: davoine@ihs.ac.at; forstner@ihs.ac.at

© Springer Nature Switzerland AG 2019
N. da Costa Cabral, N. Cunha Rodrigues (eds.), *The Future of Pension Plans in the EU Internal Market*, Financial and Monetary Policy Studies 48,
https://doi.org/10.1007/978-3-030-29497-7_9

contributor's own consumption after retirement, based on the value of the assets accumulated in the pension fund.

The different components of a pension system all have their benefits and drawbacks. The scientific debate on the merits of capital-funded pensions relative to pay-as-you-go pensions remains open. For instance, Feldstein (2005) finds that the benefits from capital-funded pensions are higher than from pay-as-you-go pensions, while Diamond (2004) finds the opposite and argues for a pay-as-you-go scheme. A more nuanced review of arguments on both sides can be found in Lindbeck and Persson (2003). Among frequently mentioned benefits of capital-funded pensions are their financial robustness to population aging and the labor market incentive effects stemming from the returns to contributions. Under conditions which are debated, capital-funded pensions may also increase national savings and thereby promote output growth. Among the frequently mentioned drawbacks of capital-funded pensions are the exposure of pension savings to return risk, with potentially negative returns, and the absence of a social insurance function, in particular against old-age poverty among low-educated households. Hybrid pension systems with a pay-as-you-go pillar and a capital-funded pillar seek to maximize benefits and minimize drawbacks.

We contribute to this ongoing debate by showing that the benefits of introducing a capital-funded pension pillar in a country are, ceteris paribus, larger in integrated capital markets than in separate capital markets, if other countries in the capital market union have pay-as-you-go systems. Our methodological contribution is the use of a multi-country general equilibrium model with explicit modelling of capital-funded pensions. By contrast, existing multi-country studies do not explicitly model capital-funded pensions (e.g. Börsch-Supan et al. 2006, or Attanasio et al. 2007), while existing studies with explicit modelling of capital-funded pensions are single-country analyses (e.g. Lassila and Valkonen 2001, or Fehr and Habermann 2010).

We find that households in a country introducing capital-funded pensions would enjoy long-run welfare gains amounting to between 0.3% and 0.5% of lifetime consumption if the country is in a capital market union, compared to separated capital markets. The main mechanism behind this finding is that the introduction of capital-funded pensions increases national savings, since contributions are saved for future consumption (instead of being immediately consumed by retirees in a pay-as-you-go system). Higher savings then decrease the interest rate, and therefore also decrease the returns on savings in the capital-funded pension pillar. If capital markets are separated, all savings have to be invested domestically, leading to a large drop in the interest rate. In contrast, if capital markets are integrated, households can invest part of their savings in the other countries that have pay-as-you-go pension systems and benefit from the relatively higher interest rate there. As a result, households' returns on savings are higher under integrated than under separated capital markets. This allows for higher lifetime consumption and therefore constitutes a welfare gain.

The rest of the chapter continues as follows: In the next section, we describe the model used in the analysis and the basis for its calibration. In the following section, we describe the simulation scenarios and present and discuss long-run simulation results. The last section summarizes our findings and concludes.

2 Model

In this section, we provide an overview of the model used for the simulation analyses. We focus on presenting and describing central features of the model that are crucial to understanding and interpreting subsequent results and the mechanisms at work behind them. In the following, we present the model in its pre-reform state where there are no capital-funded pensions and, where relevant, add the post-reform model features related to the capital-funded pillar of the pension system. A difference will be made between two scenarios: a closed economy scenario with separated capital markets, and a two-country scenario with integrated capital markets.

The model we use is a large-scale overlapping-generations (OLG) model of the Auerbach and Kotlikoff (1987) family. Households differ in age and in skill (or education) level. Age groups differ in their productivities to mimic the life-cycle income profiles as well as in their mortality probabilities, delivering realistic demographic dynamics. Skill groups differ in their productivities to reproduce observed income differentials.

The life cycle is divided into periods of education, working age and retirement.[2] Working age households take labor supply decisions along a number of margins: labor force participation, number of hours worked and search effort while unemployed. While working, they accumulate pension rights in a publicly financed pay-as-you-go system. When retired, they consume out of their pension benefits and their private savings. Firms decide how much to invest in physical capital and how intensely to search for workers on a frictional labor market. The government collects taxes and social security contributions to finance general government expenditure, firm subsidies, and social security benefits of various kinds. The institutional framework of both tax and social security systems is modeled in detail. A comprehensive description of the model can be found in Berger et al. (2009). In order to analyze the effects of introducing a capital-funded pension pillar, we use the extension of the model to a three-pillar pension system developed in Keuschnigg et al. (2015).

2.1 Demographics

Households go through eight life-cycle stages $a \in \{1, \ldots, 8\}$ in their lives. Each stage a lasts several time periods. Moreover, households belong to one of three skill groups $i \in \{1, \ldots, 3\}$. The skill level of a household is determined exogenously at birth and remains fixed over their lifetime. After birth, households acquire education (depending on their skill level), then enter the labor market, and finally retire. Education has no monetary cost, but delays entry into the labor market for medium and high skilled households. Several stages a of the life-cycle cover labor market

---

[2]Education decisions are assumed to be exogenous.

activity, reflecting different productivity levels and labor market conditions. Retirement is defined exogenously and happens at age a^r. Each period, a fixed number of households of different skill level enter the economy. Households in age group a face an age-dependent probability $(1 - \gamma^a)$ of dying at the end of each period, replicating the empirical age structure of the population.[3] Since households do not switch between skill groups during their life time, household optimization problems can be regarded separately by skill level. To save notation, we therefore drop the skill index i when describing the household sector below.[4]

2.2 Households

Households are risk-neutral and maximize expected lifetime utility according to the following Epstein-Zin preferences

$$V_t^a = max \left[(Q_t^a)^\rho + \gamma^a \beta (GV_{t+1}^a)^\rho \right]^{1/\rho}$$

where V_t^a is the expected remaining lifetime utility of a household in age group a at time t, ρ defines the intertemporal elasticity of substitution $1/(1 - \rho)$, β is the discount factor, Q_t^a denotes effort-adjusted consumption, and $G = 1 + g$ is an exogenous productivity growth factor.

There is a threshold age level a^r at which households move from working life to retirement. Households in retirement $(a \geq a^r)$ just decide about optimal consumption, that is, $Q_t^a = C_t^a$. Households of working age $(a < a^r)$ decide about optimal consumption C_t^a, participation in the labor market δ_t^a, hours worked l_t^a when employed, and search effort s_t^a when unemployed. Their effort-adjusted consumption is given by $Q_t^a = C_t^a - \overline{\varphi}_t^a$, where the term $\overline{\varphi}_t^a$ incorporates disutility from participation $\varphi^P(\delta_t^a)$, from working $\varphi^L(l_t^a)$, and from searching for a job $\varphi^S(s_t^a)$, weighted by the respective probabilities of being in the relevant labor market state.[5]

The per-period net income of households of working age $(a < a^r)$ is given by

$$y_t^a = \delta_t^a \left[(1 - u_t^a)\theta_t^a l_t^a w_{t,net}^a + u_t^a \theta_t^a b_{t,net}^a \right] + (1 - \delta_t^a) y_{t,npar}^a$$

---

[3]In the implementation, households also differ in the speed at which they go through the stages of the life cycle, which reflects differences in appetite for effort, luck or other unobserved attributes, a generalization of Gertler (1999) used in Jaag et al. (2010). For ease of presentation, we ignore this model feature.

[4]Interaction between the household problems of different skill groups only occurs through prices and general equilibrium effects, and differences in the household problems only arise from differences in parametrization.

[5]All disutility functions $\varphi^j(\cdot)$ are assumed to be increasing and convex.

Here, θ_t^a is the age-group specific labor productivity, $w_{t,net}^a$ is the net wage rate per effective hour of labor supply, and $b_{t,net}^a$ are net unemployment benefits. The net value of not participating in the labor market, $y_{t,npar}^a$, captures basic welfare benefits and home production.[6]

The per-period net income of retired households ($a \geq a^r$) before the reform consists of after-tax pension payouts from two sources, both part of the public pension system, and are given by

$$y_t^a = \left(1 - \tau_t^a\right)\left[P_0 + \nu^a P_t^{E,a}\right]$$

where P_0 is an exogenous flat part and $\nu^a P_t^{E,a}$ is the entitlement to a pay-as-you-go pension payment, where the conversion factor ν^a translates accumulated pension points $P_\alpha^{E,a}$ into actual payments. Households accumulate pension points $P_t^{E,a}$ during their working life through contributions based on their labor market income.

The reform we consider introduces a third, capital-funded, pillar into the pension system. The per-period net income of retired households then becomes

$$y_t^a = \left(1 - \tau_t^a\right)\left[P_0 + \nu^a P_t^{E,a} + P_t^{F,a}\right]$$

where $P_t^{F,a}$ is the annuity payment that stems from mandatory savings in the capital-funded pension pillar. Households accumulate their asset stock in this third pillar, $A_t^{F,a}$, through mandatory contributions based on their labor market income during their working life. When the household retires, the asset stock is converted into an annuity plan based on life expectancy.[7]

The intertemporal budget constraint of households (or law of motion for regular assets A_t^a) is given by

$$G\gamma^a A_{t+1}^a = R_{t+1}\left(A_t^a + y_t^a - C_t^a\right)$$

where y_t^a denotes the period income flow, C_t^a denotes household consumption, and $R = 1 + r > 1$ is the interest rate factor. Households maximize their expected lifetime utility subject to this intertemporal budget constraint and the laws of motion for pension rights and pension payments in the different pillars of the pension system.

2.3   Production and Labor Market Matching

There is a representative firm that produces a single composite good using capital and three types of labor corresponding to the three skill levels of workers. Due to

---

[6]The full model also incorporates non-participation due to disability and income from disability benefits.

[7]See Keuschnigg et al. (2015) for details on both the pay-as-you-go and the capital-funded pension pillars.

perfect competition, it takes input prices (wage rates and the interest rate) and the price of the output good (which serves as numeraire) as given. The production of aggregate output Y_t is represented by a linear homogeneous production function

$$Y_t = F^Y\left(K_t, L_t^{D,\,i=1}, L_t^{D,\,i=2}, L_t^{D,\,i=3}\right)$$

where K_t denotes physical capital and $L_t^{D,\,i}$ labor input from the respective skill group. We assume that the different types of labor are imperfect substitutes, and, in particular, that high skill labor and capital are more complementary than low skill labor and capital.[8]

The labor market is characterized by search frictions, that is, the probability that a match between a worker and the firm is made depends on the search effort of unemployed workers and on the amount of vacancies created by the firm. Once a match is formed, the worker and the firm bargain over the wage, splitting rents that arise from search frictions.[9]

Each period, the representative firm decides how much to invest (I_t) and how many vacancies to post $\left(v_t^{a,\,i}\right)$ in order to maximize its end-of-period firm value (that is, the discounted value of future dividends)

$$V^F(K_t) = \max\left[\chi_t + \frac{GV^F(K_{t+1})}{R_{t+1}}\right]^{1/\rho}$$

subject to the law of motion for physical capital $GK_{t+1} = (1 - \delta^K)K_t + I_t$. Period dividends χ_t are defined as firm output minus total investment costs, minus total labor costs, minus total vacancy creation costs, and minus total tax payments (net of subsidies).

2.4 Government Budget and Asset Market Clearing

The government collects taxes on labor income, capital income, firm profits and consumption, as well as social security contributions from both workers and firms.[10] With these revenues, it finances general government expenditures, firm subsidies, and social security benefits (including welfare benefits, unemployment benefits, public pension payments, public health insurance payments and lump sum transfers to households). Government debt DG_t evolves according to

---

[8]The production function is specified as a nested CES-function, following Jaag (2009).

[9]The modelling of the labor market is based on a static search-and-matching framework as in Boone and Bovenberg (2002). We assume that there are separate labor markets for each age and skill group.

[10]Labor income taxes and social security contributions also apply to unemployment benefits and pension payments.

$$G \cdot DG_{t+1} = R_{t+1}(DG_t - PB_t)$$

where PB_t is the government's primary balance in period t (revenues minus expenditures).

The asset market is central to understanding the results of the simulations presented later on. Asset market clearing, however, differs between the scenarios we will investigate. In the pre-reform scenario of the closed economy, total private assets (A_t) are invested in the domestic representative firm $\left(V_t^F\right)$ and government debt (DG_t), so that asset market clearing requires

$$A_t = V_t^F + DG_t$$

When the capital-funded pension pillar is introduced, total household assets in pension funds $\left(A_t^F\right)$ have to be added to the left hand side of the above equation. Finally, when we consider a two-country scenario, the countries can trade in goods, and domestic households can invest abroad and vice versa. The net foreign asset position DF_t then evolves according to

$$G \cdot DF_{t+1} = R_{t+1}(DF_t - TB_t)$$

where TB_t denotes the trade balance in period t. The trade balances of the two countries have to add up to zero in each period. The asset market clearing condition for the country introducing the capital-funded pension pillar then becomes

$$A_t + A_t^F = V_t^F + DG_t + DF_t$$

2.5 Calibration

The calibration of the model is standard for large-scale overlapping-generations models, based on both macro and micro data sources as well as parameter estimates from the literature. Details on the calibration strategy can be found in Berger et al. (2009). We use the model calibrated to the Austrian economy and current institutional settings. Population aging is calibrated by changing mortality probabilities of households over time in order to match demographic projections from Eurostat (2015). The results and conclusions, however, also apply for other European countries with large welfare states.

3 Simulations

In our simulation analyses, we compare the outcomes from two different scenarios, one with a closed economy and one with two countries in a capital markets union. In this section, we first describe the two scenarios. We then present and discuss differences in long-run effects between the two scenarios from the perspective of the country implementing a pension reform that introduces a third, capital-funded, pension pillar.

3.1 Description of the Simulation Scenarios

In the first scenario, we consider a single country as a closed economy ("CE"). The country starts out with a two-pillar public pension system (flat pension payments and earnings-related pension payments from a pay-as-you-go system). Then a pension reform is implemented, introducing a third, capital-funded, pension pillar. Contribution rates to the public pension system and the capital-funded pillar are changed immediately. In particular, contribution rates to the pay-as-you-go pillar are reduced, and pension payouts from this pillar are reduced too. At the same time, mandatory contribution rates to the capital-funded pillar are introduced, and the capital-funded pension pillar then slowly builds up over time. In parallel, the demographic composition of the country changes due to population aging.

In the second scenario, we consider two countries in a capital market union ("CMU"). That is, the countries can trade in goods and there is free movement of capital between them. The two countries are of the same size and initially have the same economic and institutional environment, starting out with a two-pillar public pension system. Then, in country A, the same pension reform is implemented as in the single country of the closed-economy scenario, introducing a capital-funded pension pillar with immediate change in contribution rates. Country B implements no reform and sticks to its two-pillar public pension system. The populations of both countries age at the same speed similar to the demographic change in the closed-economy scenario.

The parameters of the pension reform in both scenarios are set as follows: Employees' contribution rates to the second, pay-as-you-go, pension pillar are reduced by 5% points, while employers' contribution rates are reduced by 7.5% points. Both employees' and employers' contribution rates to the third, capital-funded, pension pillar are then set to values so that households would on average receive the same total pension payments, ceteris paribus (in particular, keeping total population and its demographic composition constant). Since there are returns to contributions in the third pension pillar, the increase in contribution rates to the third pillar is lower than the decrease in contribution rates to the second pillar, so that both employees' and employers' total contribution rates decline: the employees' contribution rate into the capital-funded pillar only needs to be increased 1.5% points and that of the employers 2.25% points.

When calculating the effects under population aging, pension payments from the third, capital-funded pension pillar do not fully compensate for the reductions in the payments from the second, pay-as-you-go pension pillar. The reason is that the third pension pillar pays an annuity which depends on remaining life expectancy, and as this life expectancy increases, the annuity payments from the third pillar decrease.

Such a mechanism ensures that the capital-funded pillar is financially balanced, even with population aging. In contrast, the pay-as-you-go pension pillars are financially unbalanced and lead to social security deficits when the pillars are not reformed and the population is aging.[11]

In both scenarios, the effective retirement age of households remains unchanged over time. General government consumption and public health expenditures per capita are kept constant, but their total value increases over time due to population aging. It is also assumed that the government does not issue new debt, but balances its budget every period by adjusting lump-sum transfers to households.

3.2   Simulation Results

In the following, we present and discuss long-run simulation results for the country introducing a third, capital-funded, pension pillar. In particular, we compare outcomes between the two simulation scenarios, the closed-economy (CE) case on the one hand, and the two-country capital market union (CMU) case on the other hand. The reported results correspond to the effects observed 100 years after the reform.[12]

Population aging is the same in both scenarios and leads to an increase in the dependency ratio, the fraction of the population older than 65 years over the population aged 15–64 years, from 26.28 to 48.39%. The population (of age 15 and above) increases by 12.59%. The fraction of retirees in the population increases from 25.22% to 37.09%.

Table 1 presents long-run macroeconomic outcomes for the country implementing the pension policy reform under the two scenarios.[13] As expected,

Table 1 Macroeconomic variables

	Closed-economy (CE)	Capital market union (CMU)
GDP ($\Delta\%$)	3.26	3.12
Capital stock ($\Delta\%$)	10.33	9.87
Aggregate effective labor input ($\Delta\%$)	1.58	1.52
Capital/labor ratio ($\Delta\%$)	8.61	8.23
Interest rate ($\Delta\%$)	−16.78	−15.98
Average labor costs ($\Delta\%$)	0.88	0.76
Foreign assets (% of GPD)	0.00	12.40

$\Delta\%$: change in percent relative to pre-reform value
Source: IHS (TaxLab simulations)

[11]In our simulations, the deficit is covered by a reduction in lump-sum transfers to households.

[12]We consider the effects 100 years after the reform because it takes considerable time for the capital-funded pension pillar to grow to its final steady-state level.

[13]Note that, in all tables in this section, changes in output, production inputs, income, consumption and pension payments are reported as deviations from the aggregate growth trend.

the capital stock increases in both scenarios, as the introduction of mandatory savings for the third, capital funded, pension pillar increases national savings. However, the capital stock increases by less in the capital market union (+9.87%) than in the closed economy (+10.33%). Accordingly, the interest rate decreases by less, too (−15.98% in the CMU versus −16.78% in the CE). The lower increase in the capital stock in the capital market union is due to the fact that households can invest parts of their mandatory savings for the capital-funded pension pillar in the other country that does not implement the pension reform. Indeed, in the capital markets union, net foreign asset holdings of domestic households 100 years after the reform amount to 12.40% of GDP.

Since labor and capital are complementary in production, the increase in the capital stock also leads to an increase in labor demand in both scenarios. As a consequence, aggregate effective labor input (hours worked times labor productivity summed over all age and skill groups) increases too. Due to the lower increase in the capital stock in the capital markets union, this increase in aggregate effective labor input is slightly lower, too (+1.52% in the CMU versus +1.58% in the CE). The increase in capital and labor inputs leads to an increase in GDP in both scenarios. However, since inputs increase by less in the capital market union, GDP also increases by less (+3.12% in the CMU versus +3.26% in the CE).

In both scenarios, the capital-labor ratio increases, as the increase in the capital stock outweighs the increase in aggregate effective labor input. This, in turn, leads to higher average labor costs per hour (average gross wage rate) in both the capital market union and the closed economy. However, since the capital-labor ratio increases by less in the capital market union (+8.23% in the CMU versus +8.61% in the CE), average labor costs increase by less in the capital market union (+0.78% in the CMU versus +0.88% in the CE).

Given that population aging leads to an increase in the population, it is informative to look at several economic indicators in per capita terms, as presented in Table 2. First of all, population aging with constant retirement age leads to a drop in labor supply per capita. As a consequence, GDP per capita decreases in both cases, with a slightly stronger decrease in the capital market union (−8.42% in the CMU versus −8.29% in the CE).

Increased private savings lead to a significant increase in assets per capita (and assets plus pension funds per capita) in both the capital market union and the closed economy. However, the rate of return on assets (the interest rate) is higher in the

Table 2 Per capita variables

	Closed-economy (CE)	Capital market union (CMU)
GPD/capita (Δ%)	−8.29	−8.42
Assets/capita (Δ%)	13.96	14.05
Assets and pension funds/capita (Δ%)	22.32	22.42
Consumption/capita (Δ%)	−12.51	−12.44

Δ%: change in percent relative to pre-reform value
Source: IHS (TaxLab simulations)

capital market union than in the closed economy. Therefore, assets per capita (and assets plus pension funds per capita) increase by slightly more in the capital market union (+14.05% in the CMU versus +13.96% in the CE for assets per capita, and +22.42% in the CMU versus +22.32% in the CE for assets plus pension funds per capita).

Finally, consumption per capita decreases in both scenarios, as population growth outweighs output growth. However, it is noteworthy that the decrease in consumption per capita is less pronounced in the capital market union than in the closed economy (-12.44% in the CMU versus -12.51% in the CE). This already provides an indication that households in the country introducing the third, capital-funded, pension pillar benefit from the capital markets union. The main reason behind this is that households in the capital market union benefit from a higher interest rate by investing in the foreign country, as evidenced by the larger increase in financial assets per capita.

Table 3 presents changes in the pension system for the country implementing the pension policy reform under the two scenarios. The level of aggregate pension expenditures (measured in percent of pre-reform GDP) rises in both the capital market union and the closed economy relative to the pre-reform value of 12.26%. Part of this increase is simply due to the increasing number of retirees in the population. Aggregate pension fund assets 100 years after the pension reform amount to 85.76% of pre-reform GDP in the capital markets union, whereas they only amount to 85.60% in the closed economy. As a result, in the capital markets union, pension payouts from the third, capital-funded, pillar have a slightly larger weight in aggregate pension expenditures, too. As fraction of aggregate pension expenditures, payouts from the third pillar reach a level of 14.40% in the capital markets union, but only 14.36% in the closed economy.

Pension payments per retiree decline in both scenarios. This is mainly due to the fact that the size of the second, pay-as-you-go, pension pillar is significantly reduced through the reform, and, as discussed in the previous section, the third, capital-funded, pillar does not fully compensate for this reduction with an aging population.

Table 3 Pension system variables

	Closed-economy (CE)	Capital market union (CMU)
Aggregate pension expenditures (% of pre-reform GDP)	18.66	18.67
Aggregate assets in pillar 3 pension funds (% of pre-reform GDP)	85.60	85.76
Pension expenditures per pillar		
Pillar 1 (% of aggregate expenditures)	25.85	25.83
Pillar 2 (% of aggregate expenditures)	59.79	59.77
Pillar 3 (% of aggregate expenditures)	14.36	14.40
Pension payments per retiree, all pillars ($\Delta\%$)	-8.13	-8.07

$\Delta\%$: change in percent relative to pre-reform value
Source: IHS (TaxLab simulations)

156   T. Davoine and S. Forstner

Table 4 Labor market variables

	Closed-economy (CE)	Capital market union (CMU)
Gross wage rate (Δ%)	0.88	0.76
Net wage rate (Δ%)	9.45	9.33
Hours per worker (Δ%)	0.84	0.83
Hours per capita (Δ%)	−10.40	−10.46
Participation rate (Δpp)	−0.07	−0.08
Unemployment rate (Δpp)	−2.85	−2.83

Δ%: change in percent relative to pre-reform value; Δpp.: change in percentage points relative to pre-reform value
Source: IHS (TaxLab simulations)

The decline is slightly larger in the closed economy than in the capital market union (−8.07% in the CMU versus −8.13% in the CE), for the following reasons. In both scenarios, average pension payments per retiree from the second, pay-as-you-go, pillar decline by roughly 28% relative to their pre-reform level. However, as discussed above, the level of assets accumulated in the third, capital-funded, pension pillar is slightly higher in the capital markets union. The third, capital-funded, pillar can therefore compensate slightly more for the reduction in the second, pay-as-you-go, pillar, so that average total pension payments per retiree decline slightly less in the capital market union than in the closed economy.

Table 4 reports effects on the labor market for the country implementing the pension reform, again under the two scenarios. As discussed above, the increase in the capital stock triggers an increase in labor demand, and therefore leads to an increase in the average gross wage rate (average labor costs) in both the capital union and the closed economy, with a slightly higher increase in the closed economy. The average net wage rate, however, increases by much more, namely by 9.45% in the closed economy and by 9.33% in the capital markets union. A small part of this large increase is of course due to the increase in gross wages. The larger part, however, stems from the fact that households' total contribution rates to both the pay-as-you-go and to the capital-funded pension pillars after the pension reform are lower than the contribution rates to the pay-as-you-go pension pillar in the pre-reform situation.[14] The net wage rate increases slightly more in the closed economy than in the capital market union, because the gross wage increases slightly more, too.

This increase in the net wage rate creates incentives for households to work more hours, therefore the average number of annual hours per worker increases, again with a slightly lower increase in the capital market union than in the closed economy (+0.83% in the CMU versus +0.84% in the CE). However, due to population aging, the ratio of retired to working households increases so much that annual work hours per capita decrease significantly (−10.46% in the CMU versus −10.40% in the CE),

---

[14]See the discussion on the parametrization of the pension reform in the previous section.

demonstrating the relative drop in labor supply per capita that comes with population aging and constant retirement age.

Regarding changes in labor market participation, there are counteracting forces at play. On the one hand, workers increase their labor market participation due to the higher wage rates. On the other hand, population aging also leads to an aging of the labor force, that is, the average age of workers increases. Since the labor market participation rate declines over the life cycle,[15] the aging of the labor force leads to a decrease in the average participation rate. The net effect on the participation rate turns out to be negative, but very small, in both the capital market union and in the closed economy (-0.07% points in the CMU versus -0.08% points in the CE).

Finally, the unemployment rate drops significantly in both scenarios, with a slightly stronger effect in the closed economy (-2.85% points in the CMU versus -2.83% points in the CE). Given that labor market participation remains roughly constant, this significant decline in unemployment stems from the relatively strong increase in labor demand by firms and the increased incentives for unemployed workers to search for a job due to higher net wages.

Table 5 finally presents a welfare comparison between the capital market union and the closed economy scenarios from the perspective of the country introducing the third, capital-funded, pension pillar. The welfare measure applied is that of consumption-equivalent variation (CEV) for households born 100 years after the reform. The thought experiment behind this measure is the following: Take the consumption of a newborn household in the closed economy over the whole life-cycle; By how much (in percent) would this household's consumption in each life period have to be increased (or decreased) so that its expected lifetime utility would be the same as that of a newborn household in the capital markets union?

Table 5 reports this measure for newborn households for each of the three skill groups. The result shows that, for all groups, consumption would have to be increased in the closed economy in order to attain the same lifetime utility as in the capital markets union. That is, in welfare terms, all types of newborn households 100 years after the reform benefit from the capital market union relative to the closed economy. The main reason is that returns to their mandatory savings in the capital-

Table 5 Welfare gains, newborn households

	Capital market union (CMU) relative to Closed-economy (CE)
Welfare gains	
Low-skilled (CEV)	0.49
Medium-skilled (CEV)	0.38
High-skilled (CEV)	0.28

CEV: Consumption-equivalent variation
Source: IHS (TaxLab simulations)

---

[15]This is in particular the case when non-participation due to disability is taken into account, as it is in our full model.

funded pension pillar are higher in the capital markets union, increasing their retirement income from this pillar.[16]

What is also noteworthy is that the welfare gains are highest for low-skilled households: Their consumption would have to be increased by 0.49% each period in the closed economy scenario to reach the utility of the capital markets scenario. For medium-skilled households, consumption would have to be increased by 0.38%, and for high-skilled households it would have to be increased only by 0.28%. This variation arises from the different savings reactions of households of different skill levels. The per-capita assets of low-skilled households increase by roughly 16% due to the pension reform, while those of high-skilled households increase only by roughly 12%. The main mechanism behind this is the following: The pension reform leads to an increase in the capital stock, and, because of capital-skill complementarity, this leads to a higher wage increase for high-skilled than for low-skilled households. Low-skilled households therefore have to increase their savings more in order to finance consumption in old age. As a result, low-skilled households benefit more from the higher returns in the capital market union relative to high-skilled households.

4   Summary and Concluding Remarks

In this chapter, we analyzed the long-run effects for a country introducing a capital-funded pension pillar under two scenarios: On the one hand, we considered the situation of separate capital markets, where all additional savings have to be invested domestically. On the other hand, we considered the situation of integrated capital markets with another country that does not introduce capital-funded pensions, where part of the additional savings can be invested.

We find that households in a country introducing capital-funded pensions would enjoy long-run welfare gains amounting to between 0.3% and 0.5% of lifetime consumption if the country is in a capital market union, compared to separated capital markets. This result is mainly due to the fact that returns to savings in the capital-funded pension pillar are higher under integrated capital markets than under separated ones, as households can invest abroad and benefit from the relatively higher interest rate there.

In order to put our main quantitative results into perspective, three remarks are in place. First, the capital-funded pension pillar in our simulations remains relatively small, amounting to less than 15% of aggregate pension expenditures in the long run. If a larger-scale introduction of capital-funded pensions were considered, the welfare

---

[16]It is important to keep in mind that the welfare gains for the country introducing the capital-funded pensions brought about by the capital market union hinge on the fact that the other country in the union remains with its original pay-as-you-go system. If both countries introduced capital-funded pensions in the same fashion, outcomes in the closed economy and in the capital market union would be identical.

gains from integrated capital markets could be larger, too. Second, the welfare gains we find are comparable to other results in the literature. For instance, Krusell et al. (2009) find that average welfare gains of U.S. households from eliminating business cycles range from 0.1% of lifetime consumption (in the benchmark economy) to 1% of lifetime consumption (when long- and short-term unemployment are distinguished). Third, because it takes time for pension funds to accumulate, the welfare benefits from introducing a capital-funded pension pillar in a capital market union require time to materialize. As a consequence, only future generations will enjoy benefits from the capital market union, while generations living at the time of the pension reform do not see any of the benefits.

Finally, our results relate to current debates on policy design. The introduction of a capital-funded pension pillar is indeed debated in several European countries. At the same time, European capital markets are becoming more and more integrated, but are not fully integrated yet (e.g. Morelli 2010). To prevent sovereign debt crises in the future, as the Eurozone experienced in 2010, there are calls to further support the integration of capital markets through the creation of a capital market union (European Commission 2017). With this background, countries considering the introduction of capital-funded pensions might be more willing to do so if a capital market union (CMU) is indeed implemented.

References

Attanasio O, Kitao S, Violante GL (2007) Global demographic trends and social security reform. J Monet Econ 54(1):144–198

Auerbach AJ, Kotlikoff LJ (1987) Dynamic fiscal policy. Cambridge University Press, Cambridge

Berger J, Keuschnigg C, Keuschnigg M, Miess M, Strohner L, Winter-Ebmer R (2009) Modelling of labour markets in the European Union. Final Report for DG EMPL of the European Commission

Boone J, Bovenberg L (2002) Optimal labour taxation and search. J Public Econ 85:53–97

Börsch-Supan A, Ludwig A, Winter J (2006) Ageing, pension reform and capital flows: a multi-country simulation model. Economica 73(292):625–658

Diamond P (2004) Social Security. Am Econ Rev 94:1–24

European Commission (2017) Reflection paper on the deepening of the economic and monetary union. European Commission, Brussels

Eurostat (2015) Population projections, Europop 2013. European Commission, Brussels

Fehr H, Habermann C (2010) Private retirement savings and mandatory annuitization. Int Tax Public Financ 17(6):640–661

Feldstein M (2005) Rethinking social insurance. Am Econ Rev 95:1–24

Gertler M (1999) Government debt and social security in a life-cycle economy. Carn-Roch Conf Ser Public Policy 50:61–110

Jaag C (2009) Education, demographics, and the economy. J Pension Econ Finance 8:189–223

Jaag C, Keuschnigg C, Keuschnigg M (2010) Pension reform, retirement, and life-cycle unemployment. Int Tax Public Financ 17:556–585

Keuschnigg C, Davoine T, Schuster P (2015) Aging, pension reform and the current account. Research report for the Jubiläumsfonds of the ÖNB. Institute for Advanced Studies, Vienna

Krusell P, Mukoyama T, Şahin A, Smith AA (2009) Revisiting the welfare effects of eliminating business cycles. Rev Econ Dyn 12(3):393–404

Lassila J, Valkonen T (2001) Pension prefunding, ageing, and demographic uncertainty. Int Tax Public Financ 8(4):573–593
Lindbeck A, Persson M (2003) The gains from pension reform. J Econ Lit 41:74–112
Morelli D (2010) European capital market integration: an empirical study based on a European asset pricing model. J Int Financ Mark Inst Money 20:363–375
OECD (2018) OECD pensions outlook 2018. OECD Publishing, Paris. https://doi.org/10.1787/pens_outlook-2018-en

Thomas Davoine Affiliation: Institute for Advanced Studies, Josefstaedter Strasse 39, 1080 Vienna, Austria

Education:

2013   PhD in Economics, University of St.Gallen, Switzerland.
2000   Master of Science in Operations Research, Rutgers University, USA.
1997   MSc. in Mathematics, EPFL, Lausanne, Switzerland.

Employment:

Since 2012   Applied Research, Institute for Advanced Studies, Vienna, Austria.
2009–2011   Research assistance, University of St.Gallen, Switzerland.
2001–2009   Management consulting, France, Switzerland.

Research focus: Public Finance, Macroeconomics, Computable General Equilibrium

Selected publications:

Berger, J., Davoine, T., Schuster, P. and Strohner, L. (2016): "Cross-country differences in the contribution of future migration to old-age financing", International Tax and Public Finance, vol.23 (6), 1160–1184.

Susanne Forstner Affiliation: Institute for Advanced Studies, Josefstaedter Strasse 39, 1080 Vienna, Austria

Education:

2013   PhD in Economics, European University Institute, Florence, Italy
2008   MRes in Economics, European University Institute, Florence, Italy
2006   MA in Economics, University of Vienna, Austria

Employment:

Since 2016   Applied Research, Institute for Advanced Studies, Vienna, Austria
2014–2016   Post-doc in Economics, RWTH Aachen University, Germany
2012–2014   Post-doc in Economics, Stockholm University, Sweden

Research focus: Quantitative Macroeconomics, Public Finance, Labor Economics

SeLFIES for Portugal: An Innovative Pan European Retirement Solution

Robert C. Merton, Arun Muralidhar, and Rui Seybert Pinto Ferreira

Abstract With a rapidly aging population, Portugal faces some serious pension challenges including a Social Security system which is under pressure, and pension benefits gradually approaching levels that will require individuals to supplement Social Security with private savings. In addition, Portugal has a low rate of financial literacy and hence transferring the responsibility of retirement planning to the general population runs a major risk of many individuals retiring poor. While some attempts have been made to create private pension plans, they have not had the level of acceptance as has been the case in some of the Anglo-Saxon countries. This paper argues that the government of Portugal could issue a new form of Sovereign Contingent Debt Instrument (SCDI) that can address the growing retirement challenge and achieve other goals as well. SeLFIES (Standard-of-Living indexed, Forward-starting Income-only Securities) are a new type of bond that greatly simplify retirement planning to the level of basic financial literacy and can not only address retirement security, but also improve the government's debt financing and funding for infrastructure. Finally, since Portugal is part of the EU, the demand for these new bond instruments could be Euro-wide thereby providing additional benefits to the government in reducing its overall financing cost.

R. C. Merton
Sloan School of Management, Massachusetts Institute of Technology, Cambridge, MA, USA
e-mail: rmerton@mit.edu

A. Muralidhar (✉)
AlphaEngine Global Investment Solutions LLC, Great Falls, VA, USA
e-mail: asmuralidhar@mcubeit.com

R. S. P. Ferreira
Lisbon, Portugal

© Springer Nature Switzerland AG 2019
N. da Costa Cabral, N. Cunha Rodrigues (eds.), *The Future of Pension Plans in the EU Internal Market*, Financial and Monetary Policy Studies 48,
https://doi.org/10.1007/978-3-030-29497-7_10

1 Introduction

There is a looming retirement crisis globally as countries have to deal with aging populations, low savings, insufficient pension coverage, and poor investment choices. In this chapter we specifically address the challenges faced by Portugal and, using finance science, recommend an innovative financial instrument that the Portuguese government can introduce that can greatly improve retirement security, while also benefitting the government (and potentially individuals in other European countries). It is critical that countries implement these innovations immediately as the longer the governments delay the higher will be the cost borne by future generations to ensure retirement security (Merton 2010).

Interestingly, the OECD has released a new report focused solely on the pension system in Portugal (OECD 2019). Our chapter anticipates many of the OECD's recommendations including, seek alternative indexation baskets to inflation pegging, improve survivor pension levels and access conditions, incentivise individual and group pension plan saving, make voluntary pension plans true long term saving plans by limiting withdrawal options, make pension plan costs more transparent, link savings for voluntary pension plans to actual saving outcomes, and simplify turning lump sum payments of matured pension plans into regular installments during the retirement period. The chapter goes a step further in providing a unique solution to the challenges that the OECD identifies including, promote and improve financial literacy, ensure adequate funding of voluntary individual and group pension plans, ensure pension plans are invested to earn the required returns to cover pension obligations, and delink the impact of changing labour market dynamics from state pension eligibility and obligations.

The chapter is structured as follows: Section 2 provides some background on Portugal and the challenge of pension security that it will face in the coming years; Section 3 discusses attempts by Portugal to introduce defined contribution (DC) plans; Section 4 reviews Portugal's current debt structure to highlight some of the challenges faced by Portugal; Section 5 introduces the new financial innovation—SeLFIES (Standard-of-Living indexed, Forward-starting, Income-only Securities)—as a possible solution to the many challenges faced by Portugal; Section 6 describes SeLFIES' innovative design aspects; Section 7 describes how SeLFIES foster self-reliance among Portuguese (and other European investors), especially in countries where financial literacy is low; Section 8 demonstrates how there could be demand for SeLFIES from investors other than retail investors; Section 9 discusses why SeLFIES are advantageous to governments; Section 10 discusses additional issues related to SeLFIES and Sect. 11 concludes.

2 Background on Portugal and the Challenge of Pension Security

As is the case in most EU countries, and even globally, the pension component of the Social Security defined benefit (DB) system in Portugal is financially unsustainable in the long term (OECD 2019). The same applies to the often overlooked separate pension system for public servants, a further contingent liability of the nation.

The chosen financing method is the widely adopted *pay-as-you-go* (PAYGO) system which is based on a solidarity contract between generations. Under pure PAYGO, current payments into the social security system are used to pay current expenditures. Under this system, unlike say the United States which has built up reserves from previous contributions in a Trust Fund, pension expenditures can only be met by taxing the working population. As a result, the stability of this system is highly susceptible to small changes in demographics (e.g., life expectancy and population growth) and productivity growth (Modigliani and Muralidhar 2004).

For many years now, Portugal has struggled with the PAYGO system (Cabral 2017). As a result, Portugal has had to make some difficult adjustments. One the one hand, general tax receipts have been used and national debt issued to make up for the shortfall. However, the government has also tried to correct the benefits side of the equation with reductions in pension and early retirement entitlements, extending the retirement age gradually, and furthermore, lengthening the period for calculation of benefits (from 10 to 15 years to the full contributory period). For spouse or survivor pensions in particular, the impact has been dramatic.

The Portuguese retirement savings system is based on three pillars:

1. The Citizenry Social Protection System ("Sistema de Protecção Social de Cidadania");
2. The Providential System ("Sistema Previdencial") and
3. The Complementary System ("Sistema Complementar").

This proposal does not address the first two, both managed by the state, but instead tries to increase the effectiveness and reach of the third, as well as make the third pillar a real and viable alternative to currently offered savings products for retirement. As is the case in the rest of the world, with PAYGO DB systems struggling from low economic growth and worsening demographics (Modigliani and Muralidhar 2004), there is increasing pressure to transfer the responsibility of saving for retirement onto the individual by encouraging them to contribute to DC systems—either voluntarily (as in the United States) or mandatorily (as in many Latin American countries). Essentially, these DC systems will need to be robust to complement the declining benefits that will be earned from struggling PAYGO DB systems. If these DC systems are not appropriately designed, and assets invested poorly, the government will have to bail out poor retirees, leading to higher costs to future governments.

The Portuguese PAYGO DB and overall pension challenge is best understood by examining some key facts noted in two European Commission reports (2018a, b):

1. By 2070, Portugal's population will decrease by 2.3 mln, a reduction of 22%. More importantly, the population aged 65 years or more, will increase by 27% and will be 3 times the young population, while the population aged 80 year or more, will increase by 165%. Over the 2016–2070 period, the dependency ratio (the ratio of 65 and more year olds to 15–64 year olds) will double from 32.1% to 67.2%. For the 80 year olds and more to 15–64 year olds, the total dependancy ratio rises from 53.6% to 89.7%, the highest in the EU!
2. The same report predicts a pension substitution ratio (average starting pension to average salary) of 55.9%. It was 68.3% in 2016 and is only likely to decline further given worsening demographics. Survivors/spouses currently get 50% of the original benefit.

Clearly, pension entitlements are going to be further limited by (a) the requirement that the calculation of benefits will be based on 40 years of contributions; (b) the impact of part time work; (c) volatility in earnings; (d) career interruptions due to unemployment (the unemployment rate has declined to 6.7% as of Q4 of 2018 from 16.2% in for 2013); and (e) other aspects such as illness, stays abroad, training etc.

For 2017, the Pordata database by FFSS Foundation (Pordata N/A) highlights the following additional challenges:

1. both public servants and private sector pensioners already comprise 41% of the country's population;
2. there are 153.2 seniors for 100 youths and there are only 1.5 social security contributors for each pensioner;
3. the average annual pension is €5131.4, for spouses it's €2732.9. By contrast, Portugal's minimum annual wage stands at approximately €8400.
4. pensions paid by the social security system alone amount to 7.2% of GDP.
5. national debt per capita amounts to €23,593.8 in 2017, an increase of 277% from 2000 (€6257.1).

3   Portugal: Attempts to Create a DC System

In 1989, the Portuguese government saw the writing on the wall and launched legislation for the commonly denominated *private PPR* pension savings plans. These pension plans would fall under the third pillar, the Complementary System.

The complementary system comprises three DC sub-systems:

1. The savings that are capitalised and managed by the "Instituto de Gestão de Fundos de Capitalização da Segurança Social", a state entity. These are publicly managed *state PPRs,* initially funded voluntarily by employees. From Nov 2018, employers can also contribute to the individual's PPR.
2. Collective complementary pension systems promoted by corporates or self organised professional groups; and

3. Complementary savings products sought by individuals such as *private PPRs* offered by the finance industry, term life insurance and savings plans offered by mutualist associations.

The success of all three of these DC sub-systems of the Complementary system has been limited at best.[1] The initial and generous tax incentives granted to *private PPRs* have been whittled down to be immaterial over the years. Furthermore, subsequent changes to legislation have made early redemptions more flexible to the point where PPRs lost their clear long term savings character. By the end of 2018, *state PPRs* had €44 mln under management and 7619 policy holders (in a country with a population in excess of 10 mln).[2] By 2017, only €540 mln were managed under PPRs.[3] Closed end pension funds by corporates (mainly banks and insurers) make up the bulk of pension assets. PPRs as such, intitiated and funded voluntarily by (only) individuals are negligible.

Total private pension assets make up only approximately 10% of Portugal's GDP and have remained constant at approximately €20 bln for some years now. Contributions for these three sub-systems amount to 0.3% of GDP and only to 2% of Portugal's total pension outlays. In contrast and by way of example, for Spain and Sweden these ratios were 0.7% and 5.3% and 2.5% and 21.7%, respectively (OECD 2019).

Also in 2017, only 6.4% of the active population had savings in a pension plan of any kind. Roughly half each had corporate and individual plans. Among 30 year olds, the ones most likely to, and in need to save for the long term, the ratio was only 2%.

Only 2.3% of corporates (less than 1000) with 10 employees or more offered independently managed pension plans to their employees[4] and only 2.5% of the active population were beneficiaries of matured pension plans.[5]

This is fascinating given the fact that the current average pension is below the current minimum wage suggesting that without additional savings and private pensions, many will retire with a low standard-of-living.

Even more worrisome is the composition of pension portfolios. The annual report of Autoridade de Supervisão de Seguros e Fundos de Pensões ASF (1) for 2017

---

[1]"O Sector dos Serviços e os Desafios da Segurança Social" by Confederação do Comércio e Serviços de Portugal, "Segurança Social: Modelos e Desafios" by Conselho Económico e Social and "Estatísticas Anuais e Trimestrais" by Autoridade de Supervisão de Seguros e Fundos de Pensões (ASF).

[2]IGFCSS Annual Report 2017 and "Fundo dos Certificados de Reforma – Folheto Informativo, Dec 312,018 by Segurança Social Portugal, http://www.seg-social.pt/documents/10152/16069308/ Newsletter_2018/2cbc6b0a-c93b-4f96-9a9b-491ae0da2c96

[3]"O Sector dos Serviços e os Desafios da Segurança Social" by Confederação do Comércio e Serviços de Portugal, "Segurança Social: Modelos e Desafios" by Conselho Económico e Social and "Estatísticas Anuais e Trimestrais" by Autoridade de Supervisão de Seguros e Fundos de Pensões (ASF).

[4]"Segurança Social: Modelos e Desafios" by Conselho Económico e Social and "Estatísticas Anuais e Trimestrais" by Autoridade de Supervisão de Seguros e Fundos de Pensões (ASF).

[5]Authors' calculation from ASF Annual Report and the active population from PORDATA.

shows equities making up only 8.4% of total assets with Portuguese public and private debt making up another 30% and 16.5%, respectively. None of these bonds have the requisite long duration needed by pension funds (as demonstrated later), suggesting that these pension funds are bearing meaningful asset-liability risk.

All three sub-systems share similar attributes which may explain to a large extent their limited reach.

1. They are all voluntary and on an "opt-in" basis. As a result, participation in these plans depends on the financial wisdom and literacy of the saver. Opting-in means that mostly young savers must make an informed choice to defer current consumption *in lieu* of future income during retirement. Savers not only need to calculate how much money they will need at retirement but also rely on professional help to choose the right product at the right time (Bodie et al. 2008). Asset allocation happens over the working life and is not a one-off affair (Merton 2010 and Levitan and Merton 2015). It so happens that Portuguese financial literacy is among the lowest in the EU. According to Klapper et al. (2015) only 26% of adults are financially literate, and Portugal is not an outlier as many countries suffer from adult financial illiteracy. As Merton (2012a) notes, financial illiteracy may be better addressed by using finance science to create financial innovations than to try to educate a vast population on appropriate financial planning techniques.
2. Savers, especially unsophisticated savers, are likely to rely on financial and real estate market professionals to achieve their financial goals for retirement. However, this increases costs as management, trading and administration costs accrue over time, even during market downturns. More importantly, with current market instruments, market volatility may also hit the pensioner at the wrong time, and leave them with a relatively poor pension. Long term returns from investing are far from assured and depend on the point of entry and exit. Long periods of low interest rates, as has been experienced in Europe, including negative interest rates, especially post the Great Financial Crisis (GFC), force money managers into increasingly risky investments, to obtain competitive returns. More importantly, standard-of-living changes and inflation can erode the true value to an individual of a nominal pension.
3. Current products in the market are not ideally designed for stable pension payments. As private pensions fall due, most pay out the capital upfront (i.e., "lump-sum" payments), but typically pensioners ideally would like their accumulated wealth in these DC plans to be paid out over the rest of his/her life time. Annuity usage in Portugal is limited.

4   Background on Portugal's Current Debt Issuance

Clearly, there are a number of challenges that must be addressed in Portugal. While financial literacy can be increased through financial education programs (OECD 2019), there is clearly scope for financial innovation and the use of finance science to improve DC pension outcomes (Muralidhar 2019). The government will need to play a key role in addressing this looming crisis and hence we examine the government's current debt situation as our proposal requires the Portuguese government to issue an innovative new debt instrument. A similar proposal has already been made for EU countries in general (Merton and Muralidhar 2017a) and even for France (Merton et al. 2017), the United States (Merton and Muralidhar 2017b), Korea (Merton 2018) and India (Merton and Muralidhar 2018).

Portugal's current debt to GDP ratio is approximately 122% and approximately Euro 247 bln.[6] As of February 2019, the average maturity of the outstanding national debt was 7.9 years and 6.4 years if EU and IMF debt is included (IGCP Monthly Bulletin, February 2019). By nominal amount, while 38% of Portuguese debt is held by residents in Portugal, only 12% are instruments tailored to and held by retail investors.[7] One of the challenges for Portugal, now that it is a part of the EU and issues bonds in Euros, is that it is competing in the issuance market with other issuers as well. As a result, Portugal's ability to extend maturity and issue more debt is impacted by the availability of other issuers with potentially higher credit standing (e.g., Germany).

At a very high level, the typical asset allocation model for pension saving portfolios should require a very long duration asset to hedge pension liabilities (Sharpe and Tint 1990). Therefore, the relatively low duration of current Portuguese debt relative to instruments ideally held in pension portfolios or used by insurance companies to offer annuities will lead to either enormous retirement risk in retail portfolios or an absence of annuity offerings by private pension or insurance companies. These investors may need to consider other Euro issuers to achieve this higher duration, but one of the other challenges that has plagued Euro-debt has been the existence of negative interest rates at the medium end of the maturity spectrum. For example, as of September 2019, the German 10 year bund yield was -0.69%.

The state's interest in obtaining the longest possible maturity for its bonds is demonstrated by Fig. 1.

Interestingly, Portugal's Instituto de Gestão de Crédito Público (IGCP) has issued GDP-linked securities for retail investors and they were (initially) successful. From 2013 to Oct 2017, IGCP issued €12 bln of 5-year maturity, retail-driven securities called "Certificados do Tesouro Poupança Mais (CTPM)". For CTPM, the fourth and fifth annual coupons were linked to 80% of Portugal's GDP's growth rate. From Oct 2017, a new type of GDP growth rate indexed securities was issued, but its terms were far less attractive and the general consensus is that these securities were not a success. One of the challenges of GDP-linked securities is that they are not a natural hedge against any particular type of investment goal that investors may have (Merton and Muralidhar 2017a). They are attractive from the point of view of the issuer because the coupon payments are reduced in periods of low economic activity,

---

[6]https://tradingeconomics.com/portugal/government-debt-to-gdp
[7]https://www.igcp.pt/fotos/editor2/2019/Boletim_Mensal/02_BM_fev.pdf

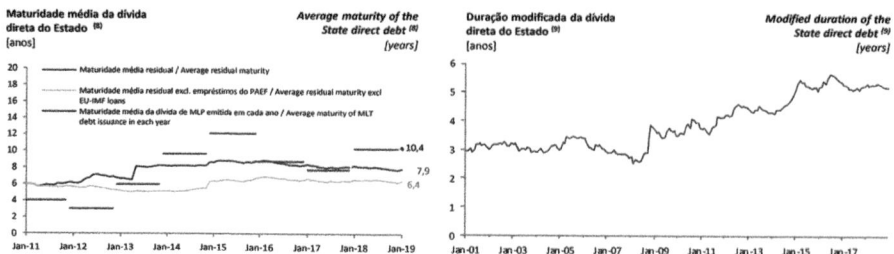

Fig. 1 Average maturity and modified duration of Portugal's direct debt (Source: IGCP 2019). https://www.igcp.pt/fotos/editor2/2019/Boletim_Mensal/02_BM_fev.pdf

when the issuer of the bond might be struggling with their own revenue challenges. As a result, GDP-linked securities offer good asset-liability management opportunities to the issuer (i.e., typically the government), but since they do not meet the needs of investors, especially the growing segment of retirement investors, the demand is likely to be limited and a possible explanation for the performance of the 2017 CTPM.

5 SeLFIES as a Potential Solution

Given the unique circumstances of Portugal, as a member country of the EU, but also one facing severe challenges of aging and a high debt/GDP ratio (and limited duration of the debt), the need for reform and innovation is critical and could be addressed through a single innovation. As noted earlier, the risk for retirement will need to be transferred to individuals as DB pension plans cannot be offered by governments or companies given the high current cost and probably the inability to expand DB coverage. Therefore, individuals will need to be increasingly moved into DC pension plans, where they will be responsible for an increasing share of their retirement resources. Even if individuals are not (mandatorily) enrolled in DC plans, given the low and declining levels of payments from Social Security DB systems relative to a reasonable standard-of-living, individuals will need to save in personal accounts to complement current benefits.

For optimal portfolio management, members of DC plans should focus on maximising funded status or retirement income (not wealth, as in traditional investment approaches) as noted in Merton (2013). Further, unlike multigenerational DB plans, DC plans must achieve their objectives in a single lifetime, and the decisions are extremely complex for the average individual (see Bodie et al. 2008; Bodie et al. 2010). Further, it is hard to pool DC risks across multiple individuals and cohorts because these plans are inherently flexible: (a) participation is often voluntary; (b) participants may require liquidity; (c) retirement ambitions, risk tolerance and life expectancy vary; and (d) employment patterns change over time (i.e., the gig

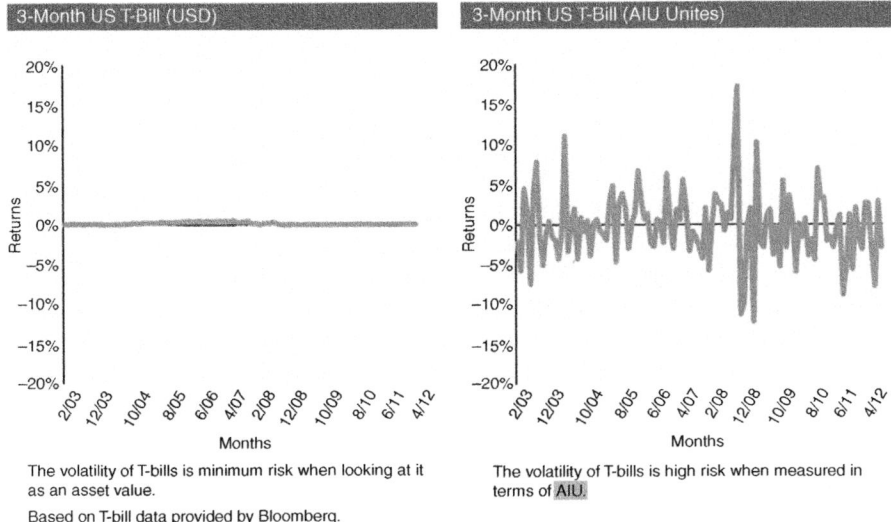

Fig. 2 Measuring the risk of T-Bills from an absolute and relative volatility perspective (Source: Merton 2012a, 2013, 2014)

economy does not tether an individual to a single company).[8] A new financial instrument is needed to enable financial security for retirees in the current environment (Muralidhar 2015; Muralidhar et al. 2016). DC investors seek to ensure a guaranteed, real income, ideally from retirement to death (Merton 2007, 2012a, b, 2013, 2014). It is also reasonable to assume they would want to lead a lifestyle comparable to pre-retirement. Investing in existing assets (stocks, bonds, or real estate) is risky because these do not provide a simple cash flow hedge against desired retirement income. For example, viewed through the retirement income lens, a portfolio of traditional, 'safe' government securities, unless heavily financially engineered, would be risky because of the cash flow (and potential maturity) mismatch between traditional bonds and the desired income stream. Figure 2 shows that T-bills, the traditional "safe asset" from the perspective of volatility as the measure of risk (or capital preservation) is actually a risky instrument when measured in terms of annuity income units (or the annuity income such a bond would buy on different dates).

One might assume that an annuity might be the "safe" investment in DC retirement portfolios but there is an annuity puzzle (Modigliani 1986); namely, that despite the attractive cash flow profile an annuity provides to a retiree, their utilization in retirement portfolios is extremely low. Many have attributed this to the fact that annuities can be complex, costly, illiquid, and potentially do not allow for bequests. More recently, research has shown that individuals do not buy annuities

---

[8]Muralidhar (2018).

because they perceive them as being unfair[9] in that individuals who die early (i.e., below the average life expectancy) run the risk of not enjoying a long stream of payments for which they believe they may have contributed. What is interesting is that investors do not object to DB pensions, which are no different from private "annuities" in terms of payments, complexity, illiquidity and inability to bequeath, but there seems to be an aversion to "annuities."

There is thus a need for governments to issue a new 'safe' bond instrument, which we call SeLFIES (Standard-of-Living indexed, Forward-starting, Income-only Securities). These will ensure retirement security and the government is a natural issuer (Merton and Muralidhar 2017a, b).

6   The Innovative SeLFIES Design

A default-free bond offers certainty about two characteristics critical for DC retirement portfolios: (i) a commitment to pay over a particular time horizon (how/when one is paid); and (ii) a specific cash flow (what is paid). DC investors require a guaranteed cash flow that protects their real purchasing power in retirement. Two simple innovations could create the 'perfect' instrument.

The first innovation addresses (i) 'how/when one is paid' by creating forward-starting, income-only bonds. These would start paying investors upon retirement, paying coupons-only for a period equal to the average life expectancy at retirement (e.g., Portuguese bonds would pay for 20 years).[10] Investors saving for retirement do not need coupon payments while still employed (which have to be re-invested and thereby engender interest rate risk), or a stub principal payment at the end, but rather a smooth stream of real cash flows (as in Fig. 3). SeLFIES are designed to pay people when and how they need it. SeLFIES blend accumulation and decumulation by incorporating the retiree's desired annuity-like cash flow profile in the payout phase.

The second innovation addresses (ii) 'what' is paid, by indexation to per-capita consumption (Merton 1983). Preserving standard of living requires inflation-protected payments. With increasing longevity, a fixed standard of living may not be adequate, because cumulative increases in the standard of living can leave a retiree feeling 'left behind', much like inflation causes nominal fixed income retirees to experience a decline in standard of living (see Fig. 3).

So, instead of a Treasury inflation protected securities (TIPS)-like adjustment, solely focused on inflation, SeLFIES would cover both the risk of inflation and the risk of standard of living improvements. This coupon would be ideal for people who assess their economic well-being on the basis of their standard of living relative to those around them. Figure 3 provides a simple chart of a SeLFIES bond targeted to a

---

[9]https://www.anderson.ucla.edu/faculty-and-research/anderson-review/annuities-fairness

[10]https://www.europeandatajournalism.eu/News/Data-news/Life-expectancy-after-retirement-a-very-unbalanced-Europe

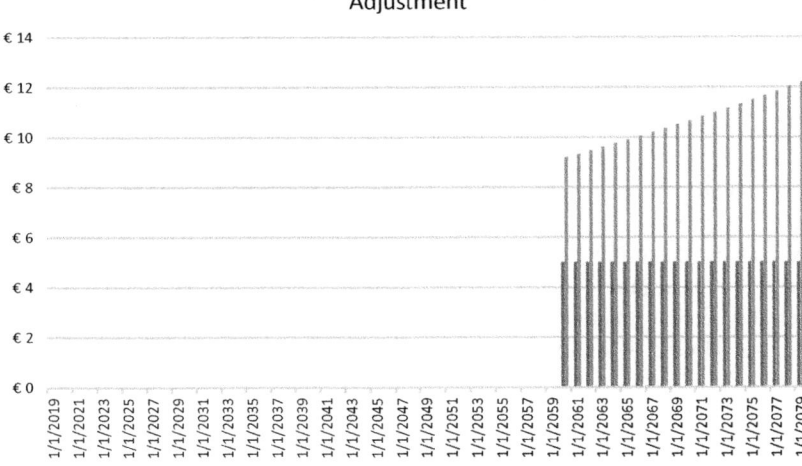

Fig. 3 Example of real and nominal cash flow from SeLFIES (Source: Authors 2019)

25 year old in 2019, who retires at the age of 66 (2060), and then seeks a steady stream of real Euro 5/per year till 2080. The set of columns fixed at euro 5 reflect the real coupon and the set of columns rising from 2060 to 2080 reflect the nominal coupon assuming a standard-of-living indexation of 2% p.a.

7 How SeLFIES Foster Self-Reliance and Work for Those not Financially Literate

In effect, SeLFIES would pay the holder annually for 20 years, starting at a fixed future date, a fixed amount (say €5), indexed to aggregate per capita consumption. So, 56-year-olds in 2019 would buy the 2029 bond, which would start paying SeLFIES coupons upon retirement at 66 in 2030, and keep paying for 20 years, through 2050. In this case, unlike Fig. 3, the positive columns will start at year 2030, for just 20 years, so each SeLFIES bond will have its own unique cash flow profile that caters to the individual cohort.

These innovations ensure even the most financially illiterate individual can be self-reliant with respect to retirement planning (without requiring a forecast of expected returns, optimisers/retirement calculators, or even intermediaries). For example, if investors want to guarantee €3000 annually in supplementary pensions, risk-free for 20 years in retirement, to maintain their standard of living, they would need to buy 600 SeLFIES (3000 divided by 5) over their working life.

The complex decisions of how much to save, how to invest, and how to draw down as in Bodie et al. (2008) are simply folded into a calculation of how many SeLFIES to buy. In addition to being simple, liquid, easily traded, and with low credit risk, SeLFIES can be bequeathed to heirs (spouses and children), unlike current pensions for surviving spouses or high-cost, inflexible and illiquid annuities (which are not common in the context of continental EU). The inheritability of SeLFIES overcomes investor fears that premature death means leaving money on the table. Buying SeLFIES would be similar to creating an individual DB scheme, with the guaranteed pay-out determined simply by the number purchased.

SeLFIES greatly simplify retirement investing by allowing participants to be self-reliant in managing their portfolios. It is easy to see why these bonds would be preferable to inflation-linked or GDP-linked bonds which Portugal has issued,[11] or even the current practice of investing in target-date/lifecycle funds in the United States and United Kingdom (which rotate into traditional bonds, or annuities with age). Asset pricing models greatly simplify when the numeraire for measuring returns is consumption (versus either wealth or real wealth).[12] So bonds denominated in consumption units are a natural asset for investors.

Moreover, SeLFIES could become the safe asset in any pension portfolio and even in these target-date strategies. They could also be used as safe, liability-hedging assets in dynamically managed target-income strategies (Levitan and Merton 2015)—allowing investors to target a higher retirement standard of living/income by investing in risky assets early in their life cycle, but dynamically locking in gains by investing in SeLFIES later in life when gains have been made in the portfolio. Further, simple account statements would illustrate the level of real, locked-in retirement standard of living, based on the number of bonds purchased. In today's DC plans, account statements focused on wealth accumulated give investors no sense of retirement standard of living, or what to do to achieve their retirement objectives. Locking in a wealth level, does not automatically translate into stable and reliable retirement cash-flows and SeLFIES address this problem by focusing entirely on ensuring stable and reliable cash flows.

8   Demand from Other Investors

Additionally, there is a substantial and natural buyer for SeLFIES within the State itself. This would be under the social security system, the "Fundo de Estabilização Financeira da Segurança Social (FEFSS)". This Social Security Financial Stabilization Fund was created in 1989 with the purpose of contributing to the financial

---

[11] Admittedly, this is not a fair comparison as proponents of GDP-linked bonds have tried to use this bond to create PAYGO like pension plans, and ensure counter-cyclical payments (ie, high returns when market rates of interest are low or negative). See Frijns et al. (2016).

[12] Breeden (1979).

stabilisation of the social security system through a security cushion that could be activated to pay pensions in the event of a breakdown of the current resources in the *PAYGO* system. This has not happened yet, but only because the system gets an annual injection from the State's general budget. FEFSS currently holds assets equivalent to 1.3 years of pensions paid out by the social security system, still less than the 2 years required by law. 72.4% of FEFSS' assets are Portuguese state bonds and guarantees. In 2013, the law was amended instructing FEFSS to replace OECD countries' debt with Portuguese sovereign debt. SeLFIES could be included in such holdings and would provide a much better hedge against potential pension payments as noted in Figs. 2 and 3. Given that life insurance companies and pension funds also have to match the duration of long-term obligations potentially with short term assets, they too would find the ultra long maturity of SeLFIES an attractive alternative to traditional long term assets.

9 Advantages for Governments

SeLFIES would be advantageous for the Portuguese government, making them efficient issuers. Given the volume of current debt issuance, some of the current bonds could easily be replaced by SeLFIES. First, SeLFIES will give Portugal (or any other EU government) a natural hedge of revenues against the bonds, as revenues earned from value-added-taxes (VAT) are essentially proportionate to consumption. This means less risk, more control, and perhaps higher ratings for EU governments to issue consumption-linked rather than inflation-linked or GDP-linked bonds. Investors from all parts of the lifecycle would find them attractive. Interestingly, Uruguay has issued a wage-indexed bond targeted to pension funds and insurance companies to allow them to offer wage-indexed pensions and the initial indications are that this bond was well received by the market (i.e., oversubscribed) and has led the government to issue additional bonds as well.

Second, as governments struggle to finance infrastructure, bonds with steady payments and forward-starting payment dates offer an effective mechanism to finance such needs. Cash flows from SeLFIES offer governments an effective way to collect monies today for upfront capital expenditures for infrastructure projects, and pay these back in the future, once the projects generate revenues.

Third, Portugal has benefitted from low rates post the GFC as shown in Fig. 4. With SeLFIES, there is the potential to tap a new investor segment, not just in Portugal but also across the entire EU as DC pension plan participants in other countries can easily purchase Portuguese SeLFIES for their DC plans. This then adds the potential for lower funding costs—especially with the first few governments that issue SeLFIES before they become mainstream. The fact that Portugal is a member of the EU makes SeLFIES a Pan-European solution to the EU pension crisis (and may lead other countries to issue such debt). There is clearly some credit risk to lending to a foreign government, but at least there would be no currency risk for EU

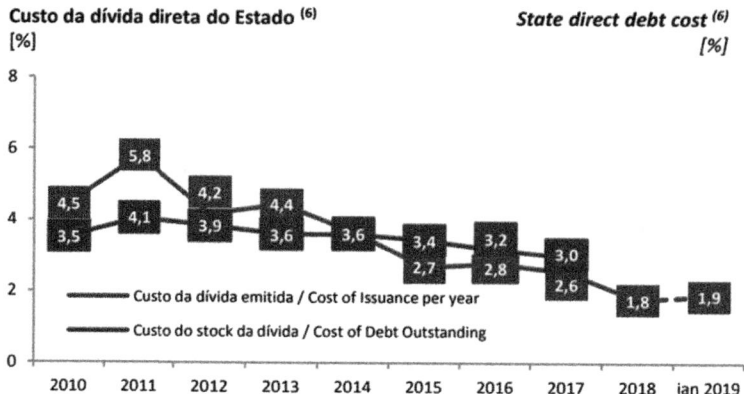

Fig. 4 State direct debt cost (Source: IGCP 2019). https://www.igcp.pt/fotos/editor2/2019/ Boletim_Mensal/02_BM_fev.pdf

investors. However, the foreign holders of Portuguese SeLFIES might benefit from the fact that it is highly unlikely that the Portuguese government would default on a bond that provides the livelihood for its aging population. In effect, one could argue that there is a pecking order of default that might be created by SeLFIES, with governments more likely to default on bonds held by foreign (speculative) investors than to default on retirees in the EU.

Fourth, if DC plan investments do not facilitate safe and adequate outcomes, the Portuguese government will be forced to bail out participants, thereby privatising gains but socialising risks. SeLFIES potentially reduce those additional costs and risks to the Portuguese government.

Furthermore, SeLFIES could be valuable to the insurance industry, since it allows them to offer new low-cost annuities, with an improved ability to hedge liabilities.

In this fashion, the government can not only help to complete financial markets, but also improve their overall sovereign debt management operations (through better hedging of revenues and bond payments and potentially extending duration), while also lowering the future cost of many retirees which under the current set up will retire poor.

10 Additional Issues

Simple or dynamic investments in SeLFIES will not solve issues like insufficient savings (resulting in low retirement income), insufficient income growth (which locks in a low standard of living in retirement), or hedging longevity risk. Longevity risk is potentially handled through complex measures, such as trading longevity swaps or bonds. Alternatively, Muralidhar (2018) suggests the creation by governments of a new LIVE (Longevity Indexed Variable Expiration) bond that addresses longevity risk by cohort. However, since longevity for cohorts changes slowly (low-frequency), it may be adequate to periodically review the change in longevity and adjust the portfolio goal. SeLFIES hedge the relatively rapidly changing (high frequency) interest rate, inflation, and standard of living growth risks, which are important as one nears retirement, until the retiree chooses to purchase a life annuity, providing longevity risk protection. For longevity risk protection, participants could purchase long-deferred annuities that pay out beyond the age of 85 (and hopefully these markets develop in Portugal with the introduction of SeLFIES). The deferred annuity approach combined with SeLFIES, would be an efficient way to hedge individual longevity risk while preserving financial flexibility and control, and can be incorporated into a well-designed target income product. However, annuities are not very popular in the non-Anglo Saxon world, and hence it will be interesting to see what innovations such a new instrument might foster. Fabián et al. (2018) have argued that social security systems are better suited to handle longevity risk, with DC arrangements handling retirement income through average life expectancy (and hence SeLFIES would be well suited to this approach proposed for Spain). As a result, there are multiple approaches to handling the residual micro longevity risk (Merton and Muralidhar 2019).

SeLFIES would require an appropriate measure of consumption to be articulated for the index; specifically, how consumer-durable purchases are treated and whether or not to include leisure time, not normally included in consumption. If a simple per-capita consumption index is hard to calculate, another alternative might be to use nominal VAT receipts divided by the population and VAT tax rate. In another variation, a wage index, as in Uruguay, may be considered for this bond. Many of these same challenges are embedded in TIPS or GDP-linked bonds. In any case, SeLFIES are materially closer to covering inflation and standard of living changes than nominal bonds. Of course, further work is needed to establish other technical design details of SeLFIES (eg, are they paid semi-annually or annually? Are bonds re-opened monthly, quarterly or less frequently when DC contributions are collected? Is €5 an optimal size of real coupon or should it be double that to make calculations simpler and require fewer purchases?). These are not insurmountable, given the potential benefits of the bonds to the concerned parties. As an initial solution, the current technical approach used in TIPS or the GDP-linked bonds can be adopted.

11 Conclusion

The looming retirement crisis in Portugal needs to be addressed by timely innovation, because the longer governments wait, the higher the cost will be. SeLFIES are a safe and sound solution for governments, especially for Portugal given worsening demographics and a declining monthly payout from the PAYGO DB system. As Portuguese citizens will increasingly feel the need to join a Complementary DC system, they will bear increasing risk unless there is innovation in the financial markets that allows them to achieve their goals at relatively low cost and with relative ease given the levels of financial literacy. We have shown that SeLFIES give investors more control over their retirement planning and lower costs, complexity, risks, and illiquidity of retirement outcomes relative to existing or other conceived options. It is critical to ensure effective retirement outcomes as the population ages. To quote the famous Portuguese saying, "*Mais vale prevenir do que remediar*" ("*Better to plan ahead than to improvise*"). Unless the Portuguese government is willing to plan ahead and innovate to complete the markets, it will run the risk that many will not receive safe and reasonable pension benefits and have to bail them out.

Acknowledgements Thanks to Adam Kobor and Herman Kamil for help and feedback. All errors are our own. These are the personal views of the authors.

References

Bodie Z, Treussard J, Willen P (2008) The theory of optimal life-cycle saving and investing. CFA Research Foundation Publications 2008, no. 1 (February). CFA Institute

Bodie Z, Fullmer R, Treussard J (2010) Unsafe at any speed? The designed-in risks of target-date glide paths. J Financ Plan 23(3):42–48

Breeden DT (1979) An intertemporal asset pricing model with stochastic consumption and investment opportunities. J Financ Econ 7:265–296. North-Holland Publishing Company

Cabral N (2017) A Sustentabilidade da Segurança Social. In: da Silva JP, Ribeiro G de A (coord) Justiça entre Gerações: perspectivas interdisciplinares. Universidade Católica, Lisboa, pp 352–260

European Commission (2018a) The 2018 Ageing Report, Underlying Assumptions & Projection Methodologies, Institutional Paper 065, November 2018, Brussels. https://ec.europa.eu/info/sites/info/files/economy-finance/ip065_en.pdf

European Commission (2018b) Pension Adequacy Report 2018 – Current and future income adequacy in old age in the EU, vol 1. European Commission, Directorate-General for Employment, Social Affairs and Inclusion, Brussels. https://ec.europa.eu/social/main.jsp?catId=738&langId=pt&pubId=8084&furtherPubs=yes

Fabián ID, Devolder P, del Olmo García F, Herce JA (2018) A two-step mixed pension system: how to reinvent social security with the help of notional accounts and term annuities. Retire Manage J 7(1):31–40

Frijns J, van der Klundert T, van Nunen A (2016) Why the Netherlands should issue retirement bonds. Investment & Pensions Europe, August 2016

IGCP Monthly Bulletin, Instituto de Gestão da Tesouraria e da Dívida Pública, Lisbon, February 2019. https://www.igcp.pt/fotos/editor2/2019/Boletim_Mensal/02_BM_fev.pdf

Klapper L, Lusardi A, van Oudheusden P (2015) Financial literacy around the world: insights from the standard & poor's ratings services global financial literacy survey. World Bank Development Research Group (November), Washington DC

Levitan SM, Merton RC (2015) Defined-contribution retirement fund investment strategies: an appropriate default? Presented at the Actuarial Society of South Africa's 2015 Convention, November 17–18, 2015, Johannesburg, South Africa. http://www.colourfield.co.za/defined-contribution-retirement-fund-investment-strategies-an-appropriate-default

Merton RC (1983) On consumption-indexed public pension plans. In: Bodie Z, Shoven JB (eds) Financial aspects of the U.S. pension system. University of Chicago Press, Chicago

Merton RC (2007) The future of retirement planning. In: Bodie Z, McLeavey D, Siegel LB (eds) The future of life-cycle saving & investing. Research Foundation of the CFA Institute, Charlottesville, VA

Merton RC (2010) Observations on individually funded pension system design: advances for the future. In: Developing the potential of the individually funded pension systems. International Federation of Pension Fund Administrators, Santiago, pp 61–76

Merton RC (2012a) Observations on financial education and consumer financial protection. In: Bodie Z, Siegel LB, Stanton L (eds) Life-cycle investing: financial education and consumer protection. The Research Foundation of the CFA Institute, Charlottesville, VA, pp 1–20

Merton RC (2012b) Funding retirement: next generation design. JASSA Finsia J Appl Financ 2012 (4):6–11

Merton RC (2013) Applying life-cycle economics: an income-oriented DC retirement solution that integrates accumulation and payout phases. UK NEST Conference on Retirement, London, pp 64–70

Merton RC (2014) The Crisis in retirement planning. Harv Bus Rev 92(7/8):43–50. July-August. https://hbr.org/2014/07/the-crisis-in-retirement-planning

Merton RC (2018) SeLFIES – A globally applicable bond innovation to improve retirement funding and lower government financing cost. Presentation at the World Knowledge Forum, Seoul, Korea. October 18, 2018. https://jinrong.swufe.edu.cn/info/1127/3901.htm

Merton RC, Muralidhar A (2017a) Time for retirement SeLFIES. Investment & Pensions Europe. April 3–4

Merton RC, Muralidhar A (2017b) Selfies can improve the nation's retirement security. Plan Sponsor Magazine, November 20, 2017

Merton RC, Muralidhar A (2018) SeLFIES for India: these long-term bonds can fund India's infrastructure needs and improve retirement security. The Times of India (February 5). https://blogs.timesofindia.indiatimes.com/toi-edit-page/selfies-for-india-these-long-term-bonds-can-fund-indias-infrastructure-needs-and-improve-retirement-security/

Merton RC, Muralidhar A (2019) Taking a closer look at SeLFIES: added thoughts and clarifications. Pensions & Investments, June 21, 2019

Merton RC, Muralidhar A, Martellini L (2017) Pour la création "d'obligations retraite". Le Monde, April 4, 2018. https://www.lemonde.fr/idees/article/2018/04/06/pour-la-creation-d-obligations-retraite_5281686_3232.html

Modigliani F (1986) Life cycle, individual thrift and the wealth of nations. Economic Sciences (based on Lecture on receiving Nobel Prize in Economics), pp 150–170

Modigliani F, Muralidhar A (2004) Rethinking pension reform. Cambridge University Press, London

Muralidhar A (2015) New bond would offer a better way to secure DC plans. Pensions & Investments (December 14). http://www.pionline.com/article/20151214/PRINT/312149974/new-bond-would-offer-a-better-way-to-secure-dc-plans

Muralidhar A (2018) Managing longevity risk – The case for Longevity-Indexed Variable Expiration (LIVE) bonds (October 10, 2018). Available at SSRN: https://ssrn.com/abstract=3224236. https://doi.org/10.2139/ssrn.3224236

Muralidhar A (2019) Can (financial) ignorance be bliss? Financ Anal J 75(1):8–15

Muralidhar A, Ohashi K, Shin SH (2016) The most basic missing instrument in financial markets: the case for forward-starting bonds. J Invest Consult 16(2):34–47

OECD (2019) OECD reviews of pension systems: Portugal. OECD Publishing, Paris

PORDATA (N/A) Base de Dados Portugal Contemporâneo by Fundação Francisco Manuel dos Santos, Lisbon. https://www.pordata.pt/en/About+Pordata by https://www.ffms.pt/en

Sharpe W, Tint L (1990) Liabilities – a new approach. J Portf Manag 16(2):5–10. Winter 1990

Robert C. Merton PhD Recipient of the 1997 Alfred Nobel Memorial Prize in Economic Sciences, is the School of Management Distinguished Professor of Finance at the MIT Sloan School of Management. He is also Resident Scientist at Dimensional Fund Advisors, a global asset management firm headquartered in Texas, and John and Natty McArthur University Professor Emeritus at Harvard University.

Arun Muralidhar is Founder of Mcube Investment Technologies LLC and Founder and Client CIO of AlphaEngine Global Investment Solutions. He is the author of Fifty States of Gray: An Innovative Solution to the Defined Contribution Retirement Crisis, Investments and Wealth Institute, 2018. His primary focus is on dynamic (intelligent) beta and currency management and how clients can get paid to manage risk. Arun has written extensively on pension reform, asset allocation and currency management. He is serving as an Expert Advisor to the World Economic Forum's Retirement Investment Systems Improvement Project, and the Strategic Retirement Advisory Council for the Investments & Wealth Institute (formerly IMCA) for their Retirement Management Advisor (RMA) designation.

He is also adjunct professor of Finance at George Washington University and was Academic Scholar at Georgetown University's Center for Retirement Initiatives. He holds a PhD in Managerial Economics from the MIT Sloan School of Management, and a B.S. from Wabash College.

Rui Seybert Pinto Ferreira Independent Senior Consultant, Lisbon.

Extensive experience at West Deutsche Landesbank, Dresdner and Banco Finantia.

The Pan-European Pension Product and the Capital Markets Union: A Way to Enhance and Complete the Economic and Monetary Union?

Nuno Cunha Rodrigues

Abstract The article provides a general framework for the proposal for the Pan-European Personal Pension Product (PEPP) and details some particular aspects that will be discussed in the context of its application such as "national compartments" and the problem of PEPP taxation.

The PEPP is analysed as an instrument of the Capital Markets Union (CMU). It is concluded that it represents an opportunity for the EU to obtain long-term investment liquidity but also that, in the end, it is just a small palliative measure to alleviate the structural deficiencies of the EMU that remain to be solved.

1 The Pan-European Personal Pension Product (PEPP)

The European Union (EU) is nowadays facing new challenges.

From a political point of view, the fragmentation of the European project caused by Brexit[1] and, at the same time, the emergence of populism in several EU member states, along with problems caused by the deficient pursuit of democratic principles are still to be solved.

From an economic perspective, the rise of protectionism measures taken by world countries or economic regions has caused the European Union to shift its traditional neutral position towards international trade to a more aggressive one.[2]

---

[1] See Rodrigues (2018), pp. 65–82.

[2] See Regulation (EU) 2019/452 of the European Parliament and of the Council of 19 March 2019 establishing a framework for the screening of foreign direct investments into the Union, OJ L 79I, 21.3.2019. On the new approach of the EU to international trade, see Rodrigues (2017).

N. Cunha Rodrigues (✉)
CIDEEFF - Center for European, Economic, Financial and Tax Law Research, University of Lisbon, Faculdade de Direito de Lisboa, Alameda da Universidade, Lisbon, Portugal
e-mail: nunorodrigues@fd.ulisboa.pt

© Springer Nature Switzerland AG 2019
N. da Costa Cabral, N. Cunha Rodrigues (eds.), *The Future of Pension Plans in the EU Internal Market*, Financial and Monetary Policy Studies 48,
https://doi.org/10.1007/978-3-030-29497-7_11

Finally, the European Union is still recovering from the major economic crisis that affected some EU Member States since 2008.[3]

Meanwhile, demographic changes have been happening mainly because of the ageing of the EU population. This is gradually causing pressure on social service systems and public finances across the EU.[4,5]

The solutions to tackle these problems come from various levels.

In many areas, Member States still have the power to take decisions since EU-level competence on pension systems is limited.[6]

Against the ageing demographic backdrop, many EU-countries started reforms in national pension systems to make them more sustainable.

Furthermore, one of the main aspects of EU Member-States pension systems is that they are not portable across the EU for their users. This does not fit within the concept of the internal market nor, specifically, within the functioning of the freedoms of movement of people and workers, something that was already recognized in the past by the European Commission (EC).[7]

Given this, the EC saw the possibility of creating a product that would enhance the positive effects of the internal market and, at the same time, the function of the Capital Markets Union (CMU).

---

[3]See Rodrigues and Gonçalves (2017).

[4]It is known that in the next 50 years, the share of the retirement age population compared to the share of working age will double (to four to one, from two to one, i.e. two working-age people for each retired person). See Calu and Stanciu (2018), p. 102.

[5]The working age population (aged 15 to 64) shrank for the first time in 2010 and is expected to decline every year to 2060. In contrast, the proportion of people aged 80 or over in the EU-28 population is expected to more than double by 2050, reaching 11.4%. For more in-depth information see Nieminen and Eatock (2018), p. 5.

See also the Study on the feasibility of a European Personal Pension Framework, FISMA/2015/146(02)/D, European Commission, 2017, available at https://ec.europa.eu/info/sites/info/files/170629-personal-pensions-study_en.pdf (last accessed April 2019), p. 260: "In the context of a challenging economic environment with low rates and different trends in government budgets, anticipating the evolution of pensions only within the framework of the first and second pillars does not appear to be sufficient to fill the pension gap. Hence, the development of supplementary pillar 3 products has become a major issue for Member States and European institutions that is likely to continue in the next decade."

[6]The Treaty on the Functioning of the European Union (TFEU) does not provide powers other than those of Article 308 to take appropriate measures within the field of social security for persons other than employed persons. See recital 2 of Regulation (EC) No. 883/2004 of the European Parliament and of the Council of 29 April 2004 on the coordination of social security systems. Limits also arise from the subsidiarity principle. See Article 5 of the Treaty of the European Union.

Nevertheless, according to Article 114 of the TFEU, the EU has competence when dealing with the internal market, which was used as the legal base for the proposal for the PEPP.

[7]See the communication of the European Commission issued on 19 April 2001, "Communication on the elimination of tax obstacles to the cross-border provision of occupational pensions", COM (2001) 214 – 2001/2212 (COS): "A fully functioning single market for occupational pensions is essential to ensure that citizens are able to exercise their rights to free movement enshrined in the EC Treaty and thus to enhance labour mobility".

The creation of the Pan-European Personal Pension (PEPP) proposed in June 2017 by the EC[8] aimed to give EU citizens a new option for good value and safe voluntary supplementary pension saving. The PEPP introduced an EU-wide voluntary pension product that can complement national statutory and occupational pensions for citizens that so wish to do so. EU citizens will have more choice when saving for retirement—knowing that, for the moment, most pension income for EU citizens comes from public pensions (qualified as 'pillar I')—helping to address the demographic challenges of ageing populations by complementing state-based and occupational pensions.[9] The product tries to replicate, in the EU, similar ones that are offered in the USA.[10] By creating the PEPP, the EC has also tried to consolidate incentives for more financial market integration and for an equity culture to serve old age security. Doing so it has tried to solve two problems: reduce government's obligation to secure living standards in old age and diversify longevity risks concerning pension savings.[11]

The PEPP is a standardized product to be sold within the so-called "third pillar" of the European pension market, as it allows EU citizens with some economic capacity to save money in addition to their state and occupational pensions. To a certain point, this makes the PEPP almost inaccessible to the majority of the population in the poorest countries in the EU and makes it directed only at rich EU Member States and citizens leaving to the side a possible European social dimension of the measure.[12]

The appearance of the PEPP as a strict saving product aims to replace traditional ones that guarantee payment of capital at the end, such as term deposits. In order to guarantee some safety, the PEPP will supply funds for institutional investors that will be allocated in long-term investments into the real economy.[13]

As recognized by the EC, the PEPP will help meet the needs of people wishing to enhance the adequacy of their retirement savings; address the demographical challenge; complement existing pension products and schemes, and support the cost-efficiency of personal pensions by offering good opportunities for long-term investment of personal pensions.

Consequently, the proposal tries to limit the application of PEPP in speculative products. It starts from the core principle of the *prudent person rule*,[14] demanding

---

[8]See the Proposal for the Regulation of the European Parliament and of the Council on a pan-European Personal Pension Product (PEPP), Brussels, 29.6.2017, COM (2017) 343 final.

[9]According to the EC, currently only 27% of Europeans between 25 and 59 years old have enrolled themselves in a pension product. See EC - Capital Markets Union: Pan-European Personal Pension Product (PEPP), Brussels, 4 April 2019 available at http://europa.eu/rapid/press-release_MEMO-19-1993_en.htm (last accessed April 2019).

[10]See, in the USA, the Employee Retirement Income Security Act of 1974 (ERISA).

[11]See Schelkle (2019), p. 600 and Van Meerten and Van Zanden (2018).

[12]See Articles 4, 2, b) and 153, 1, c) and k) do the TFEU. See also Vila (2018), p. 82.

[13]See recital number 1 and 2 of the proposal.

[14]See the definition in footnote 26 of the proposal: "The requirement that a trustee, an investment manager of pension funds, or any fiduciary (a trusted agent) must invest funds with discretion, care, and intelligence. Investments that are generally within the prudent person rule include solid "blue

PEPP providers are prevented from investing in high-risk and non-cooperative jurisdictions.[15]

The proposal establishes that PEPP providers shall offer up to five investment options to PEPP savers (see Article 34/1) and that the default investment option should let the PEPP saver recoup the invested capital (see recital 39 and Article 37/2). Additionally, PEPP providers can offer alternative investment options to PEPP savers, allowing them to make an investment decision. At least one shall offer a cost-effective investment option to PEPP savers (see Article 38/1).

The proposal defines the concept of "instruments with a long-term economic profile" (see recital 35). Under the scope of the CMU this notion is broad involving non-transferable securities that are not transmissible in secondary markets. Consequently, the proposal tries to restrict it calling on PEPP providers—financial undertakings authorised to create a PEPP and distribute it—to contribute to the development of the CMU by investing in non-liquid assets such as shares and in other instruments that have a long-term economic profile and are not traded on regulated markets, multilateral trading facilities (MTFs) or organised trading facilities (OTFs), within prudent limits (see recitals 34 and 35).

In addition, PEPP providers are encouraged to allocate a sufficient part of their asset portfolio to sustainable investments in the real economy with long-term economic benefits, in particular to infrastructure and corporate projects (see recital number 35).

Here, the proposal can be criticized for the lack of provision of a safety net for failing pension providers.[16] As is recognized by some authors,[17] the PEPP proposal shares this blind spot with the CMU initiative that assumes stock market investors can bear their losses.

At this point, one can say that the PEPP was designed to be another tool for financing long-term investment in the real economy, in the context of the CMU.

2 The Portability of the PEPP and the Tax Obstacles

One of the main goals of the PEPP is to enhance the functioning of the internal market and cross-border mobility by providing a simpler pension product for people who have worked or who plan to work in several Member States.

Any EU citizens who decide to have a PEPP can pay contributions to the existing provider independently of the country where they live during their professional and retired life.

---

chip" securities, secured loans, federally guaranteed mortgages, treasury certificates, and other conservative investments providing a reasonable return."

[15]See recital number 37 and article 33 of the proposal.

[16]There is only one reference in Article 49 of the proposal concerning the protection of savers in the event of financial losses below the PEPP provider's default.

[17]See Schelkle (2019), p. 610 and Vila (2018), p. 83.

Furthermore, the European dimension of the PEPP will help to provide economic consequences allowing supranational operations to deliver greater benefits to Member States (increased voluntary pension savings), savers (better and cheaper products, larger variety of products) and service providers (larger customer base, simplified legislation, fewer cross-border transaction costs).[18]

To enable this, provisions on portability were created that will allow PEPP savers who change their domicile to continue paying into a PEPP that they have already taken out with a provider in the original Member State.

The idea of portability within the EU, which lies behind the PEPP, is new.[19] In order to ensure this, the concept of "national compartments" was established to guarantee PEPPs could be designed in a way so as to be compliant with (different) national rules.

This mechanism envisages opening a new compartment within each individual PEPP account that corresponds to the legal requirements and conditions for using tax incentives fixed at a national level for the PEPP by the Member State to which the saver moves.

According to Articles 12–17 of the proposal, the mechanism follows a staggered approach. During the first 3 years of application of the Regulation, PEPP providers will have to provide information on the available compartments. Afterwards, PEPP savers will be entitled to open national compartments that cover all Member States' regimes.

The existence of "national compartments" leads to another problem that is known, for some, as "the elephant in the room" of the proposal: the taxation of the PEPP.

The elimination of tax obstacles to pan-European pension funds has been a historical worry for the EC.[20] Taxation is not an EU competence and EU-level action regarding taxation needs a unanimous decision in the European Council. Knowing this limitation, the EC has been limited to promoting studies and issuing recommendations on the subject.

For national products similar to the PEPP, it is known that taxation usually can occur during two occasions (i) the accumulation phase (see Articles 33 to 40) and (ii) the decumulation phase (see Articles 51 and 52).

For the first phase, accumulation features are generally flexible.[21] Here, access to national tax incentives concerning in-payments[22] is decisive for the success of the PEPP.

---

[18]See Nieminen and Eatock (2018) p. 4.

[19]Portability is not allowed, at present, for any other third pillar product. Even for pillar I and II there is no legal framework for the transfer of pension contributions within the EU. For pillar I, see Regulation (EC) No. 883/2004 of the European Parliament and of the Council of 29 April 2004 on the coordination of social security systems. For pillar II, see Directive EC/2014/50 that requires the preservation and fair treatment of occupational pension rights for workers moving across borders.

[20]See the European Commission communication issued in April 2001, *"Communication on the elimination of tax obstacles to the cross-border provision of occupational pensions"*, COM (2001) 214 - C5-0533/2001.

[21]E.g., no mandatory holding period or possibility of changing the level of in-payments.

[22]Tax incentives may take the form of a tax reduction, reduced tax base, tax credit or other (e.g. financial incentives).

In the second phase—decumulation—the most significant parameters of the definition of a national PPP are retirement age and outpayments—which, according to the proposal, should take the form of (a) annuities; (b) lump sum; (c) drawdown payments; (d) combinations of the above forms (see Article 52/1)—that differ from one Member State to another.

Here, national legislation generally ensures limitations on early out-payments, such as retirement age, that are more difficult to harmonise. Consequently, there is a very high number of possible combinations to tax both the accumulation and the decumulation phase of national products similar to the PEPP across all Member States.

In fact, until now taxation of national products similar to the PEPP is conceived by each Member State that has selected a tax-treatment based on national preferences.[23] One of the key problems concerns the withholding tax (WHT) which poses a major barrier to cross-border investments in the EU and, eventually, to the future functioning of the PEPP.[24,25]

In a study carried out in 2017, the EC concluded that there were 49 different retirement voluntary and non-state based (excluding first and second pillar pensions) financial products identified among the EU Member States.[26] Each of these 49 products could be taxed differently based on the specificities of each Member State's pension system.[27]

Following the identification of the tax problems concerning pensions plans in the 2017 EC study, the EC in the same year issued a recommendation that accompanied

---

[23]There are different ways to tax such as the ETE system or the EET system. See the Study on the feasibility of a European Personal Pension Framework, FISMA/2015/146(02)/D, European Commission, 2017 available at https://ec.europa.eu/info/sites/info/files/170629-personal-pensions-study_en.pdf (last accessed April 2019), p. 18.

[24]There are many cases from the ECJ that have shown that withholding tax practices in many EU Member States is discriminatory with respect to dividends earned by foreign funds. See, for example, *Denkavit*, C-170/05, 14 December 2006, ECLI:EU:C:2006:783; *Amurta*, C-379/05, 8 November 2007, ECLI:EU:C:2007:655; *Aberdeen*, C-303/07, 18 June 2009, ECLI:EU:C:2009:377; *Santander*, joined cases C-338/11 to C-347/11, 10 May 2012, ECLI:EU:C:2012:286. Also, from the EFTA court, see *Fokus Bank*, case E-1/04, 23 November 2004.

[25]The EC starts from the national treatment principle, stemming from Articles 21, 45, 49, 56 and 63 of the TFEU and interpreted by the Court of Justice of the European Union, to consider this applicable to PEPP savers. See, for example, several ECJ cases such as *De Groot*, C-385/00, 12 December 2002, ECLI:EU:C-2002:750 (paragraph 94); *Turpeinen*, C-520/04, 9 November 2006, ECLI:EU:C:2006:703 (paragraph 20) and *Renneberg*, C-527/06, 16 October 2008, ECLI:EU:C:2008:566 (paragraph 51).

[26]See the Study on the feasibility of a European Personal Pension Framework, FISMA/2015/146 (02)/D, European Commission, 2017, available at https://ec.europa.eu/info/sites/info/files/170629-personal-pensions-study_en.pdf (last accessed April 2019). According to the study, 37 out of 49 PPPs in 22 out of 28 Member States benefit from incentives on in-payments and are subject to taxation during the decumulation phase. The study concludes (p. 262) stating the need for the PEPP to benefit from tax incentives on in-payments has driven the analysis of features that should be harmonised at the EU level so that PEPP holders can have access to local tax incentives.
Discussing the effectiveness of the PEPP Tax Recommendation see Hooghiemstra (2018).

[27]See Nieminen and Eatock (2018), p. 15.

the proposal for a PEPP Regulation, concerning Member States' application of tax rules to individuals who qualify as PEPP savers.[28]

In the 2017 recommendation, the EC encouraged Member States to grant PEPPs the same tax treatment as that granted to national personal pension products (PPPs).[29]

In the event that Member States have more than one type of tax regime for national PPPs (e.g. a Member State could grant beneficial tax treatment at the accumulation phase and/or during the decumulation phase), they were encouraged to give PEPPs the most favourable tax treatment available to their national PPPs.[30]

Since taxation of the PEPP is expected to be one of the biggest obstacles to its implementation in the future, one can expect that the definition of certain characteristics of a "PEPP case" used to create a level playing field for Member States taxation purposes will be based on common denominators from all the national laws applicable to similar pension products in the EU Member States, particularly during the decumulation phase,[31] such as the highest pensionable age.[32]

If not, the lack of harmonization of EU Member States pension products will represent, in the end, an enormous obstacle to the possible success of the PEPP.

3 The Capital Markets Union and the PEPP

The EU has been struggling for a number of years to catch up with the financial crisis that began in 2008 and which severely affected some of the EU Member States. This is due to the fact that the EMU had—and still has—several structural problems that

---

[28] See the European Commission Recommendation of 29.6.2017 on the Tax Treatment of Personal Pension Products, including the Pan-European Personal Pension Product. C (2017) 4393 Final.

[29] See recital 9 of the European Commission Recommendation of 29.6.2017 on the Tax Treatment of Personal Pension Products, including the Pan-European Personal Pension Product. C (2017) 4393 Final: "Member States are encouraged to extend the benefits of the tax advantages they grant to national PPPs also to the PEPP, so that a future PEPP can fall within the scope of existing national tax incentives for PPPs even when it does not fulfil all the national criteria for tax relief."

According to the EC, the volumes for PPPs combined with the PEPP could reach EUR 2.1 trillion by 2030 in the most favourable scenario whereby the PEPP would be granted a favourable tax treatment in all Member States. See Commission Staff Working Document Impact Assessment Accompanying the document Proposal, Brussels, 29.6.2017 SWD (2017) 243 final, p. 34.

[30] See *Skandia Ramstedt*, C-422/01, 26 June 2003, ECLI:EU:C:2003:380, paragraph 62: "Article 49 EC precludes an insurance policy issued by an insurance company established in another Member State which meets the conditions laid down in national law for occupational pension insurance, apart from the condition that the policy must be issued by an insurance company operating in the national territory, from being treated differently in terms of taxation, with income tax effects which, depending on the circumstances in the individual case, may be less favourable."

[31] See Lannoo (2018), p. 2.

[32] See Nieminen and Eatock (2018), p. 18. Also, considering several critical tax elements defining pension products see Nieminen and Eatock (2018), pp. 17–19.

find their roots in the fact that it was built as being a (fake) optimum currency area (OCA).[33] Consequently, the existence of a single monetary policy in the EMU and, in particular, in the euro area, was unable to react to the asymmetric shocks that happened.

Under the current circumstances, and without political will, little can be done in the field of monetary policies in order to appease all the EU Member States.

Specifically in financial markets, the existence of a strongly fragmented layered structure did not make it possible to provide a concrete and structured approach to the financial crisis. Some of the deficiencies have been identified such as (a) a high level of segmentation in market agents; (b) the lack of mechanisms to consolidate information on transactions at a European level with accounting and auditing standards that are harmonized and comparable within the EU; (c) difficulties around the creation of a single tax regime for capital movements, both for borrowers and issuers; (d) difficulties in harmonising national supervision level practices and (e) the need for centralised infrastructures to disclose financial information, relevant facts for investors and also conflicts of interest that might exist.[34]

Furthermore, there were several obstacles to the creation of a real mechanism of risk-sharing within the EU.

Working mobility is possible but made harder since the EU is not an optimum currency area (OCA) due to linguistic and cultural barriers. Furthermore, the EU budget is still insufficient to deal with economic asymmetric shocks similar to those that happened in the past.

A tax system at the supranational level is also unrealistic and limits on fiscal deficits also harm Member-States in their attempts to smooth large economic shocks.[35]

Several steps have been taken towards greater coordination of national economic and monetary policies trying to ensure more risk-sharing inside the EU that mitigates the effects of country-specific shocks in the EMU.

The focus has been placed on deepening structural reforms that can overhaul the functioning of the internal market, especially concerning freedom of movement of capitals.[36]

One relates to the improvement of the integration of capital markets, together with more connected banking systems, that can help to maintain cross-border capital flows and sustain investment in Member States suffering large asymmetric macro-economic shocks.[37]

---

[33]See Rodrigues and Gonçalves (2017).

[34]See Henriques (2018), p. E-118.

[35]See Henriques (2018), p. E-112.

[36]See Henriques (2018), p. E-105.

[37]See the Communication from the Commission to the European Parliament, the European Council, the Council, the European Central Bank, the European Economic and Social Committee and the Committee of the Regions, "*Capital markets union: progress on building a single market for capital for a strong economic and monetary union*", 15 March 2019, Brussels, COM (2019) 136 final.

As is recognized by several authors, the attention given to capital markets[38] is an important development in the internal market which has not been addressed and has been delayed when compared to other processes of European economic integration. After all, market integration happens by harmonising national legislation and regulation that ensures the freedom of capital and financial services.[39]

As such, building a Capital Markets Union (CMU) has been a key priority for the Juncker Commission,[40] as was recognized by the European Commission in the Communication entitled *"Capital markets union: progress on building a single market for capital for a strong economic and monetary union"*, issued on 15th March 2019.[41]

The CMU aims to anchor the enabling conditions for reforming the EU financial system, which involves rebalancing the mix between bank and non-bank finance; enhancing capital markets integration; increasing firms' and citizens' access to capital markets and boosting the competitiveness of European financial centres.[42]

The expression Capital Markets Union was chosen by the EC to indicate that this is complementary to the Banking Union and necessary for the completion of the EMU, which has been the focus of considerable intergovernmental debate and EU legislative activity from 2012.[43] The word "union" connects the CMU to the previous EMU and the Banking Union as it refers to 'an incremental improvement of the existing regulatory framework governing the integration' of different EU Member State capital markets.[44]

However, the CMU is different from the Banking Union and the EMU.

---

[38]Capital markets are financial market segments not involved in bank intermediation.

They include corporate bond issuance, corporate debt securitization, private equity investment, public equity issuance and initial public offerings, venture capital, the direct purchase of loans by insurers and investment funds from banks and credit intermediation by specialized non-bank financial firms, including leasing companies and consumer finance companies.

[39]See Schelkle (2019), p. 599.

[40]In fact, the Communication from the Commission to the European Parliament, the Council, the European Economic and Social Committee and the Committee of the Regions on the Mid-Term Review of the Capital Markets Union Action Plan, Brussels, 8.6.2017, COM (2017) 292 final recognized the importance of the CMU in the context of the EMU. It stated that "CMU reinforces the third pillar of the Investment Plan for Europe. It will offer benefits for all Member States, while also strengthening Economic and Monetary Union (EMU) by supporting economic and social convergence and helping absorb economic shocks in the euro area."

[41]See Communication from the Commission to the European Parliament, the European Council, the Council, the European Central Bank, the European Economic and Social Committee and the Committee of the Regions, *"Capital markets union: progress on building a single market for capital for a strong economic and monetary union"*, 15 March 2019, Brussels, COM (2019) 136 final.

[42]See Communication from the Commission to the European Parliament, the Council, the European Economic and Social Committee and the Committee of the Regions on the Mid-Term Review of the Capital Markets Union Action Plan, Brussels, 8.6.2017, COM (2017) 292 final.

[43]See Quaglia et al. (2016), p. 185.

[44]See Quaglia et al. (2016), p. 197.

Unlike the EMU and the Banking Union, the concept of the CMU is broader and less defined, considered by some as an umbrella term for regulatory changes directed at the overall development of European capital markets.[45] As European Commissioner Lord Jonathan Hill said, the CMU involved building "a single market for capital from the bottom up, identifying barriers and knocking them down one by one." He concluded that the "CMU is about unlocking liquidity that is abundant, but currently frozen, and putting it to work in support of Europe's businesses, and particularly SMEs".[46]

The CMU will be applicable in all EU Member States differently to the Banking Union that applies only to EMU Member States and others that decided to opt in.

Furthermore, the Banking Union centralized banking supervision and resolution for euro area Member States—with the creation of the SSM and the SRM-, with a top-down structure coming from Frankfurt, which is different from the CMU that does not involve the same level of regulatory integration for EU capital markets.

According to the EC, the main priorities for the CMU are the following[47]:

(i) Strengthening the effectiveness of supervision to accelerate market integration;
(ii) Enhancing the proportionality of rules to support initial public offerings and investment firms;
(iii) Harnessing the potential of fintech;
(iv) Using capital markets to strengthen bank lending and stability;
(v) Strengthening the EU's leadership in sustainable investment and cross-border investment;
(vi) Supporting the development of local capital market ecosystems.

In the end, the CMU represents a *softer* union imposed by the EU when compared to the Banking Union and the EMU where all the rules are defined *top-down*. For some, the CMU is mostly 'market-making' differently from EU financial reforms over the last decade considered to be primarily as 'market-shaping'.[48]

The CMU aims to harmonize and create more efficient rules with the wish to establish foundations for the development of EU capital markets and the diversification of the sources of financing available to EU companies.[49] For this, the EC considers that securitisation will be central within the CMU, allowing more investors to purchase shares of assets, thereby increasing liquidity and freeing up capital for economic growth.

---

[45] See Henriques (2018), p. E-105.

[46] See Unlocking Funding for Europe's Growth - European Commission consults on Capital Markets Union, available at http://uepc.org/news/article/117/Unlocking-Funding-for-Europes-Growth-European-Commission-consults-on-Capital-Markets-Union (last accessed April 2019).

[47] See Communication from the Commission to the European Parliament, the Council, the European Economic and Social Committee and the Committee of the Regions on the Mid-Term Review of the Capital Markets Union Action Plan, Brussels, 8.6.2017, COM (2017) 292 final.

[48] See Quaglia and Howarth (2018), p. 991.

[49] See Henriques (2018), p. E-106.

As such, and differently to the Banking Union, the CMU will not involve a profound change to financial markets in the short-term.

The CMU Action Plan establishes moving forward with three legislative proposals[50]:

(i) The Pan-European Personal Pension Product (PEPP) which was recently approved;
(ii) A legislative proposal for an EU-framework on covered bonds to help banks finance their lending activity;
(iii) A legislative proposal on securities law to increase legal certainty on securities ownership in the cross-border context.

If these priorities are accomplished, new forms of funding will be developed in order to facilitate access to financial markets by SMEs, decreasing the EU's economic reliance on bank lending. This is, in the end, one of the narratives of the EC in order to mobilize the political support of the Member States, the financial industry and the non-financial sector to the CMU.[51]

Departing from these goals, the proposal of the PEPP aims to create another source of long-term investment funds.

For citizens, the PEPP and the measures to improve the EU's investment fund market will provide new saving and investment opportunities, which is aligned with the main CMU objectives. By diversifying sources of finance for EU businesses, the CMU can support investment in innovation and technological developments, thereby promoting the EU's global competitiveness.

In the end, the EU is trying to instrumentalise financial market integration for pension provision which does not necessarily lead to the financialization of old age security.[52]

However, this can be considered as but a small palliative to attenuate some of the structural problems of the EMU such as the need for a real EU budget; the completion of the Banking Union and the approval of mechanisms to prevent asymmetric economic shocks happening in the EU.

The main structural problems of the EMU, which have been identified,[53] remain to be solved.

---

[50]See Communication from the Commission to the European Parliament, the Council, the European Economic and Social Committee and the Committee of the Regions - *action plan on building a Capital Markets Union*, Brussels, 30.9.2015 com (2015) 468 final and "*Completing the Capital Markets Union: Building on the first round of achievements*", Brussels, 8 June 2017, p. 2.

[51]The second narrative was to boost the size and internal and external competitiveness of EU capital markets. See Quaglia and Howarth (2018), pp. 991; 998–1003.

[52]See Schelkle (2019), p. 612. See also Hassel et al. (2019), pp. 483–500.

[53]See Rodrigues and Gonçalves (2017), pp. 284–285: "(. . .) the EMU theoretical framework is not yet closed, since the following have yet to be achieved: (i) political union, (ii) a true union of capital, (iii) an institutional regulation model for the financial system which is uniform and consistent between the Member States, (iv) an institution which, effectively, ensures the functions of lender of last resort (LOLR) and, finally, ensuring effective forms of (iv) accountability and liability within the actual Banking Union."

A final remark should be made on the supervision of the PEPP. It is clear this product was built as a tool to enhance the CMU, which is at the epicentre of the work developed by the ESMA, the authority for securities and markets. Nevertheless, being a pension product, the PEPP will naturally be supervised by EIOPA. This is because, differently from the Banking Union, the goals of the CMU are spread throughout different supervising bodies, both at an EU and at a national level.

As such coordination, cooperation and convergence among the EU supervisors (including the ECB and EBA) will be crucial not only to ensure that CMU provisions are properly enacted and applied by the agents of a united and multilevel EU financial system[54] but also to specifically ensure the success of the PEPP.[55]

Guidance through soft law will also be necessary both for the national supervisors and for the PEPP providers and users.[56] Here, special attention to the implementation of the "national compartments" is crucial and must be considered, especially during the transitional period established in Article 13/3.[57]

After overcoming the obstacles, there is no doubt that, in the future, the PEPP will help to improve the functioning of the internal market; to enhance working mobility within the EU; reinforce trust in the EU institutions among EU citizens and provide liquidity to long-term investments. The first results will be analysed in the report on the main findings that will be made 5 years after the entry into force of the Regulation that should indicate the pros and cons of it and how the Commission will address the problems concerning the implementation of the PEPP.[58]

References

Calu M, Stanciu C (2018) An insight of the future - Pan European pension product. Global Economic Observer, "Nicolae Titulescu" University of Bucharest, Faculty of Economic Sciences, Institute for World Economy of the Romanian Academy, June 6(1):102. Available at https://ideas.repec.org/a/ntu/ntugeo/vol6-iss1-18-101.html (last accessed April 2019)

Hassel A, Naczyk M, Wiß T (2019) The political economy of pension financialisation: public policy responses to the crisis. J Eur Publ Policy 26(4):483–500

Henriques SC (2018) The role of the Capital Markets Union: towards regulatory harmonisation and supervisory convergence. Perspect Federalism 10(1):201, E-103–E-125

Hooghiemstra SN (2018) European Union - Pan-European personal pension products – will the proposed European tax recommendation work? Eur Tax 58(10):453–462

---

[54]See Iglesias-Rodriguez (2018), pp. 645–651 and Henriques (2018), p. E-114. See Article 23/4.

[55]See Articles 5/4; 6/2 and 6 and 10. Also Article 55, referring to cooperation between competent authorities and EIOPA.

[56]See Article 56, referring to the settlement of disagreements between competent authorities in cross-border situations.

[57]According to this number, 3 years at the latest after the entry into application of the Regulation, each PEPP shall offer national compartments for all Member States upon request addressed to the PEPP provider.

[58]See Article 63 of the proposal.

Iglesias-Rodriguez P (2018) Supervisory cooperation in the single market for financial services: united in diversity? Fordham Int Law J 41(3):589–667 (specially 645–651). Available at https://ir.lawnet.fordham.edu/cgi/viewcontent.cgi?article=2699&context=ilj (last accessed April 2019)

Lannoo K (2018) The PEPP could become the new UCITS. ECMI Commentary No 57, September 2018. Available at http://aei.pitt.edu/94493/1/The_PEPP_could_become_the_new_UCITS.pdf (last accessed April 2019)

Nieminen R, Eatock D (2018) Pan-European pension product. European Parliament, March 2018, PE 615.656, p 5. Available at http://www.europarl.europa.eu/RegData/etudes/IDAN/2018/615656/EPRS_IDA%282018%29615656_EN.pdf (last accessed April 2019)

Quaglia L, Howarth D (2018) The policy narratives of European capital markets union. J Eur Publ Policy 25(7):990–1009. https://doi.org/10.1080/13501763.2018.1433707

Quaglia L, Howarth D, Lieb M (2016) The political economy of European capital markets union. J Common Mark Stud 54:185–203

Rodrigues NC (2017) The use of public procurement as a non-tariff barrier: relations between the EU and the BRICS in the context of the new EU trade and investment strategy. Public Procure Law Rev 3:135–149

Rodrigues NC (2018) Brexit and the future of EU: move back or move forward? In: Rodrigues NC, Gonçalves JR, Cabral NC (eds) After Brexit - Consequences for the European Union. Palgrave, London, pp 65–82

Rodrigues NC, Gonçalves R (2017) The European Banking Union and the Economic And Monetary Union: the puzzle is yet to be completed. In: Rodrigues NC, Gonçalves JR, Cabral NC (eds) The Euro and the crisis - Perspectives for the Eurozone as a monetary and Budgetary Union, Financial and monetary policy studies, vol 43. Springer, Bern, pp 271–288

Schelkle W (2019) EU pension policy and financialisation: purpose without power? J Eur Publ Policy 26(4):599–616. https://doi.org/10.1080/13501763.2019.1574871

Van Meerten H, Van Zanden JJ (2018) Pensions and the PEPP: the necessity of an EU approach. Eur Co Law 15(3):66–72

Vila ML (2018) El futuro reglamento sobre un producto paneuropeo de pensiones individuales (PEPP): Europa, quo vadis? Lex Soc 8(2):76–103

Nuno Cunha Rodrigues is Bachelor (1995); Master in Laws (2003) and PhD (2012) in Law by the Faculty of Law of the University of Lisbon.

Associate Professor of the Faculty of Law of the University of Lisbon (FDL).

Non-executive member of the Board of Directors of Caixa Geral de Depósitos. Lawyer.

Vice-President of the European Institute of the FDL. Lawyer.

Investigator and Deputy Director of CIDEEFF (Center for Research in European Law, Economic, Financial and Fiscal).

Editor and member of the Advisory Board of the Journal of Competition and Regulation.

Member of the Editorial Committee of the Journal of Public Finance and Tax Law.

Member of the Scientific Council of the Faculty of Law of the University of Lisbon.

Coordinator of the Jean Monnet (Erasmus +) module on Public Procurement, conferred by the European Commission (2015-2018).

Member of the Advisory Board of the Journal of Regulation and Competition.

Member Editorial Committee of the Journal of Public Finance and Tax Law.

Member of the Procurement Law Network.

Head of a Jean Monnet Chair, awarded by the European Commission (since 2018).

Author of several books, articles and papers in the field of EU Law; Competition Law; Public Procurement; Economic Regulation and Public Finance.

The Final PEPP or How to Kill an Important EU Commission Proposal

Karel Lannoo

Abstract Not much is left of the Personal European Pension Product (PEPP) as intended by the European Commission in June 2017. Proposed as a core element of the Capital Markets Union (CMU), the text as agreed between the European Parliament (EP) and the EU Council has become unclear, unattractive and unsuitable. The EP should not have rushed into signing off on an inadequate measure, or the EU Commission would have done well to withdraw the text. Key elements of the proposal were watered down or replaced in response to heavy pressure from member states and certain organisations. It is a classic example of how not to create the capital markets union: protecting national idiosyncrasies and vested interests, and losing out globally at the same time.

1   The Need for a Long Term EU Savings Product

The PEPP was intended to generate large-scale portable, cost-efficient and simple long-term savings products that would be on offer alongside national pension product regimes throughout the EU. Over time, this first buy-side initiative from the EU under the CMU programme was supposed to become a significant investment vehicle in support of the EU economy, similar to the UCITS fund product, first adopted in 1985. An interesting novelty of the original Commission proposal was that authorisation would be in the hands of the European Insurance and Occupational Pensions Authority (EIOPA), but prudential supervision of product providers would reside with the national authorities. A default investment option would be structured as an insurance product with capital protection, whereas four other options would be long-term savings products.

Comments from Cosmina Amariei and Ole Stahr are gratefully acknowledged.

K. Lannoo (✉)
CEPS, Bruxelles, Belgium
e-mail: klannoo@ceps.eu

© Springer Nature Switzerland AG 2019   193
N. da Costa Cabral, N. Cunha Rodrigues (eds.), *The Future of Pension Plans in the EU Internal Market*, Financial and Monetary Policy Studies 48,
https://doi.org/10.1007/978-3-030-29497-7_12

The generally limited savings of European households for retirement alongside the high costs of investment funds, and even higher costs for life insurance products, underscore the need for a well-structured PEPP. Currently, European households are overweight in deposits, which may also be caused by the inefficiency of investment fund markets. European fund markets, which function partially as a private savings vehicle for retirement (third pillar), are very fragmented with a low average size per fund, and high charges. A recent study for the Commission found that the average first-year cost for an investment product was 4%. ESMA revealed that performance charges of funds reduce returns by up to one third, and that countries with unbundling requirements, now part of MiFID II, clearly have lower costs.[1]

Against this background, the PEPP was designed to encounter a huge latent demand and go a long way to tackle the inefficiencies in current investment fund markets. According to the Commission, with PEPPs receiving the same tax treatment as national products, the personal pension funds market could reach €2.1 trillion by 2030. The first report by the EP, published in September 2018, made the proposal clearer and more attractive, by subdividing PEPPs into two different products, an insurance and a long-term savings product, and limiting the number of elements where delegated provisions can apply to three. The EP also proposed a maximum limit for charges of 1%.

2 The Final PEPP Text

However, the final text is a messy compromise.

- To start with, it has become two thirds longer, with a higher number of articles subject to delegated acts and technical standards. The simple initial proposal has become much more complex, and devolves more elements to member states, with all this implies for the attractiveness of the product. And this is not a directive but a regulation, an EU legal instrument that is directly applicable in the member states.
- The investment options have been multiplied to six, with one 'basic PEPP' or default option with a capital guarantee, while the others provide a guarantee or risk-mitigation technique (i.e. life-cycling) intended to ensure sufficient capital protection for PEPP savers (Art. 42.3). But it is unclear what is the precise difference between a capital guarantee and a simple guarantee. It could lead to the perception that also under the other options, the capital is guaranteed, which is not the case.[2] For the basic PEPP with a guarantee, providers will have a legal obligation to ensure that PEPP savers recoup at least the capital invested. For the

---

[1]See Lannoo, K. (2018), "Funds, fees and performance", ECMI Commentary No. 54, July.

[2]See Better Finance press release https://betterfinance.eu/publication/better-finance-is-happy-that-the-ep-adopted-the-pepp-regulation-but-hopes-that-the-major-guarantee-issue-for-european-savers-can-be-adequately-addressed-in-the-near-future/

basic PEPP with other risk mitigation techniques, it has to be consistent with the objective of allowing PEPP savers to recoup their capital, but without any legal obligation (see Art. 34.3). This is extremely confusing. As with the very fragmented UCITS market, it is hard to see efficient competition emerging for guaranteed solutions due to their complexity, which may unduly motivate advice or selection preferences. Here again, the EP option of only two basic PEPP products was much clearer.

- The limitation of costs and fees has been kept at 1%, but it is subject to review: "Every 2 years from the date of application of this Regulation, the Commission shall (. . .) review the adequacy of the percentage value referred to in paragraph 2. The Commission shall, in particular take into account the actual level and changes in the actual level of costs and fees and the impact on the availability of PEPPs. The Commission is empowered to adopt delegated acts (. . .) to amend the percentage value referred to in paragraph 2 of this Article in the light of its reviews with a view to allowing appropriate market access for PEPP providers" (Art. 45.4).
- The text has become applicable exclusively to individual pension savings in the third pillar, not for any form of occupational pension. This is made clear throughout the text, indicating that the latter are subject to the IORP (Institutions for occupational retirement provision) directive. This excludes the possibility of using the PEPP as a form of occupational pension for SMEs (see Art. 1(c): where it is defined as "neither a statutory nor an occupational pension product"). This is based on an illusion that a clear distinction can be made in Europe between second and third pillar pensions, or that countries with labour rights-related pay-as-you-go pension schemes could not have a form of second pillar funded pension scheme. IORPs that already provide personal pension products would be able to offer PEPPs while ring-fencing the corresponding assets.
- EIOPA's function has been relegated to simply that of maintaining a registry of all the PEPPs available in the EU and their providers. This is a long way from its initial authorisation role as proposed by the Commission and retained by the EP. EIOPA could refuse to register a PEPP, but this would be a frontal attack against a member state who had just authorised it, and would have to pass through the board of supervisors of EIOPA, where EIOPA management has no say. EIOPA also has PEPP market monitoring and intervention powers, but again under the control of its board.
- The conditions related to the accumulation phase as well as decumulation phase and the out-payment of the national sub-accounts will be determined by member states unless they are specified in the regulation.
- The national compartments, in between which mobile workers can switch, have become national sub-accounts, which providers can offer in other member states. The sub-account should be used to keep a record of the contributions made during the accumulation phase and the out-payments made during the decumulation phase in compliance with the law of the member state for which the sub-account has been opened. This is in order to qualify for the tax incentives in that member state. Switching between providers is possible, but at a cost of a maximum 0.5%.

In that case, the contributions made to and withdrawals from the sub-account may be subject to separate contract terms.

- The final agreement reached by the EP and the Council did not preserve the Commission's much more ambitious approach on portability. PEPP providers are now only obliged to provide PEPPs comprising sub-accounts for at least two member states within 3 years of the entry into force of this regulation. However, partnerships between potential providers in different member states might ease the burden of entering the PEPP market.
- The fragmented nature of the account construction across countries will have an impact on the diversification of the assets. PEPP providers are required to invest assets in accordance with the 'prudent person' rule (Art. 41). The assets are to be invested in such a manner as to ensure the security, quality, liquidity and profitability of the portfolio as a whole, but will this be possible if funds cannot achieve a minimum scale?
- PEPP savers will be able to choose the form of out-payments for the decumulation phase (annuities, lump sum, regular drawdown payments or a combination of these) both at the conclusion of a contract and when opening a new sub-account.
- PEPPs can be offered by all EU-authorised forms of financial services providers, including IORPs and Alternative Investment Fund Managers (AIFM), which sits oddly with the narrowed scope of the regulation.

Where the PEPP was designed initially as an insurance or savings product, it has become an insurance product only, as there is always a guarantee element involved. This is possibly what made the text so much more onerous, as this is the first EU-wide insurance product regulation. But this also means that it cannot become a UCITS or achieve their success, as we discussed in a previous piece. This is a missed opportunity. The EU is not only in need of a large-scale portable private pension product, but also of a long-term savings product, with lower liquidity requirements than a UCITS and more limited withdrawal options. The PEPP text as adopted leaves the impression that it is impossible to construct a truly EU-wide long-term savings product.

3 Conclusion and Implications for the CMU Agenda

The poor outcome of PEPPs leaves a poor scoreboard for CMU, 5 years after the start. The first two measures, the STS and the prospectus regulation, were not seen to be very far-reaching, and the ESA review achieved not even half of what the EU Commission intended. EMIR 2.0 puts in place a very sketchy structure of supervision of CCPs, in a way that the ECB distanced itself from the entire process, and withdrew its proposal for a EU Treaty change on the subject. The new European Commission will thus need to make a big splash if she wants to maintain CMU as a credible project.

Karel Lannoo Chief executive of CEPS since 2000, one of the leading independent European think tanks. Published some books and numerous articles in newspapers, specialised magazines and journals on general European public policy, and specific financial regulation and supervision matters. Latest book: *'The Great Financial Plumbing, From Northern Rock to Banking Union'*, Rowman and Littlefield, 2015;

Karel Lannoo holds a baccalaureate in philosophy (1984) and an MA in modern history (1985) from the University of Leuven, Belgium and obtained a postgraduate in European studies (Centre d'Etudes européennes, CEE) from the University of Nancy, France (1986).

Deepening Financialization Within the EU: Consequences for Pension Regimes

José Castro Caldas

Abstract This chapter deals with the deepening of financialization in the EU which is intended with the Capital Markets Union (CMU) and its consequences for pension regimes. It departs from a brief overview of financialization and its meaning. It focuses next on deciphering the CMU as an institutional reconfiguration aimed at removing impediments to the circulation of capital and reviving the role of financial markets in the EU. The revival of finance-friendly views and policies in the EU institutions, after the traumatizing experience of the Global Financial Crisis, is interpreted as the outcome of a political stalemate on 'fiscal unification' which opened the path for the advance of the idea of *private* risk-sharing through finance as a substitute for *public* risk-sharing in a Fiscal Union. The pan-European personal pension product (PEPP), which is part of the CMU, is then addressed as a plan to speed up the shift of pensions schemes in the EU from Pay As You Go (PAYG) to funded pensions. Finally, the consequences of the possible development of an EU 'third pillar' of funded pensions with respect to the future of member states pension systems are highlighted.

1 Introduction

In February 2019 the European Parliament and Member States reached a political agreement on the proposal for a pan-European personal pension product (PEPP) which is publicized by the Commission as a voluntary personal pension product,

The research for this chapter has been partially funded by FCT—the Portuguese Foundation for Science and Technology—in the framework of the project "Social security rights and the crisis: Social retrenchment as the normality for the financial state of exception", Ref: PTDC/DIR-OUT/32096/2017.

J. C. Caldas (✉)
Collaborative Laboratory for Work, Employment and Social Protection (CoLABOR), Lisbon, Portugal

Centre for Social Studies of Coimbra University, Coimbra, Portugal
e-mail: josecaldas@ces.uc.pt

complementary to existing national products, allowing for (a) more choice and mobility for citizen's retirement savings, (b) cheaper options for pension providers offering services across the EU, (c) abundant capital supply to long-term investments, and (d) better retirement income for all EU citizens.[1]

Greeted by the Commission as an important milestone for the Capital Markets Union (CMU)[2] PEPP is in fact not a new product, but a "regulatory template... that pension providers [insurance companies, occupational pension funds, investment firms, asset managers and banks] could elect to use when offering products across the EU". This 'pension plan' was part and parcel of the 2015 Commission's Action Plan on the Capital Markets Union (European Commission 2015: 19). The basic concern in this action plan was directed against the obstacles "in the way of the full development of a large and competitive market for personal pensions" resulting from diverse and conflicting rules at the EU and national levels. The stated goal was "incentivizing and removing obstacles to the development of individual ('third pillar') [funded] pension plans in Europe" (European Commission 2015: 19).

Given the recent traumatic experience with funded pension schemes resulting from the adverse effects of the financial markets crises in 2001/2002 and 2007/2008 (Wiß 2015, 2019)—given moreover, the participation of market-based finance in setting up the conditions that triggered the 2007–2008 crisis—setting the expansion of funded pensions as a priority goal of the EU in the framework of the CMU constitutes a puzzle (Braun et al. 2018).

Drawing on previous contributions that have addressed this puzzle, this chapter deals with the deepening of financialization which is intended with the CMU and its consequences for pension regimes. For readers less familiar with the concept of financialization, Sect. 2 offers a brief overview of its meaning as a feature of contemporary capitalism and an analytical construct meant to address it. The section pinpoints the key aspects of financialized capitalism and highlights the conceptual development of financialization as the outcome of a process of theoretical hybridization in political economy encompassing, Keynesian, Marxian and institutionalist contributions. Section 3 deciphers the Capital Markets Union as a major institutional reconfiguration aimed at removing impediments to the circulation of capital and reviving the role of financial markets in the EU. Drawing mostly on Braun and Hübner's (2018) interpretation of 'post-crisis' events and policy debates within EU institutions, it argues that the revival of finance-friendly views and policies in the EU institutions, after the traumatizing experience of the Global Financial Crisis, can be interpreted as the outcome of (a) a political stalemate on 'fiscal unification' which opened the path for the advance of the idea of *private* risk-sharing through finance as a substitute for *public* risk-sharing in a Fiscal Union, and (b) a convergence of the world-views and interest of prominent financial actors. It further argues in light of the in-depth documental analysis of Engelen and Glasmacher (2018) that: (a) the

[1]European Commission Fact-sheet: "A pan-European personal pension product", 13/02/2019.
[2]"Capital Markets Union: Commission welcomes political agreement on new rules to help consumers save for retirement", European Commission—Press release, Brussels, 13 February 2019.

same financial instruments which triggered the Global Financial Crisis are being resurrected as low risk assets by European regulators, (b) rather than an additional source of finance for SME, those instruments tend to fuel mortgage lending, real estate inflation, and possibly housing bubbles; and that (c) they are primarily meant to allow banks to transfer risk from their balance sheets possibly resulting in increased systemic risks. Section 4 highlights the origins of PEPP even before the inception of the CMU, its motivation as a bypass to the 'joint decision trap' inscribed in the diversity of pension regimes in member states, and surveys arguments challenging the shift from Pay As You Go (PAYG) to funded schemes. Section 5 evokes the conceptual frame of Hirschman's (1980) *Exit, Voice and Loyalty* to address the consequences of the possible development of the EU 'third pillar' of funded pensions with respect to the future of member states pension systems. Section 6 states the main conclusions.

2 Financialization and its Key Features

Financialization is a theoretical construct that emerged in political economy across diverse theoretical traditions to denote and analyse ongoing transformations of contemporary capitalism. This section intends to firstly clarify, its meaning as a feature of capitalism, and secondly its articulations as an analytical device.

2.1 Financialization as a Feature of Contemporary Capitalism

Financialization denotes a structural transformation of contemporary capitalism initiated in the late 1970s, marked by a rapid expansion of financial activities and growth of financial profits, permeating the economy and society and subordinating public policies to the concerns of the financial sector (Lapavitsas 2013).

This transformation of capitalism is structural in the sense that it represents a shift from production (and consumption) to finance with respect to the drivers of accumulation prevailing in the post-II World War world. The post-war regime was marked by mass production and consumption, increasing productivity and rising real wages in the developed capitalist countries and an international monetary system (Bretton Woods) with fixed exchange rates and strict capital controls which severely limited cross border capital flows, and regulated national capital markets and banking with interest rates and bank lending rules mandated by law.

Coinciding with the collapse of the Bretton Wood Agreement in 1973, such post-war accumulation regimes manifested signs of exhaustion. Concomitant with rising unemployment and inflation, the emergence of alternative international monetary arrangements based on the dollar as a quasi-world-currency fuelled a considerable instability in exchange and interest rates. This spurred international capital flows and financial markets, the expansion of which was also enhanced by innovations in information and communication technologies and academic developments in financial mathematics. However, the steady rise of finance since the late 1970s was only made possible by institutional reconfigurations driven by political decisions taken at the national, European and global levels, that liberated international capital flows, deregulated (or rather reregulated) capital markets and banking at the national level, and opened up new spheres of investment to financial capital (Lapavitsas 2013; Nölke 2017).

The main features of financialization, as highlighted by Lapavitsas (2013) are (a) the increasing engagement of non-financial enterprises in financial processes, (b) the shift of banking from borrowing and lending to transacting and profiting in open financial markets, (c) the increasing reliance of individuals on the formal financial system as a means to access vital goods and services.

The increasing engagement of non-financial enterprises in financial processes is manifest in the focus on 'shareholder value' as the main driver of management, involving share options, and exorbitant bonus payments indexed on dividends, as a means to align the incentives of 'agents' (management) and 'principals' (shareholders), share buyback programmes intended to inflate the market value of equity, and also the restructuring of companies via take-overs. It is furthermore patent in activities conducted by non-financial corporations in the financial sector through specialized financial service companies or departments.

The shift of banking from borrowing and lending to transacting and profiting in open financial markets is apparent in the increased focus on investment banking and in trading in securities via 'shadow-banking'. Particularly relevant is the role played by the banking sector in the expansion of derivative markets since the 1980.[3] As signalled by Lapavitsas (2013: 13) "Banks function as market-makers, that is, as agents that stand ready to buy and sell in the over-the-counter market; they are the dealers that are integral to market functioning. Banks also provide the necessary market infrastructure through vital market institutions such as the International Swaps and Derivatives Association (ISDA)."

Finally, increasing reliance and engagement of individuals and households in finance is noticeable in the expansion of credit for housing, consumption and education, private funded pensions and health insurance, concomitant with the retrenchment of public provision in those domains.

---

[3]"[A] derivative is a contract that establishes a claim on an underlying asset—or on the cash value of that asset—which must be executed at some definite point in the future. The underlying asset could be a commodity, such as wheat; or another financial asset, such as a bond; or a financial price, for example the value of a currency; or even an entirely non-economic entity like the weather." (Lapavitsas 2013: 11)

2.2 *Financialization as an Analytical Device in Political Economy*

Financialization emerged as a concept and a domain of empirical research in political economy and spread to other subjects such as sociology, geography and political science. In political economy the concept is employed in a large spectrum of traditions encompassing Marxism, post-Keynesianism and Institutionalism. The following paragraphs illustrate the diversity of approaches by selecting four variants within political economy.

In reviewing the literature on financialization, Lapavitsas (2013) spots the origin of this concept in the works of Paul Baran and Paul Sweezy published in the mid-1970s. In *Monopoly Capital,* first published in 1966, Baran and Sweezy highlighted monopoly and expanding surplus as features of mature capitalism. With the absorption of surplus clashing against saturated consumption and productive investment, business interests were forced to continuously search for new consumer markets and investment opportunities, and pushed to increase advertising and other wasteful activities, like armaments (Wrenn 2016). Impediments to the absorption of surplus would moreover invite capital to search for refuge in the sphere of circulation, including the speculative sphere of finance. Financialization thus emerged in Baran and Sweezy's accounts as the outcome of channelling to the sphere of finance surpluses created in production which could neither be consumed nor invested in new means of production.

A second strand of literature on financialization stems from the work of Giovanni Arrighi, with antecedents being the research of historian Fernand Braudel, in which financialization figures as a recurrent feature of capitalism. Braudel's and Arrighi's approaches build on the notion of hegemony within world systems. Hegemonic powers, implied in the overall development of capitalist world systems, tend to shift, replacing each other cyclically through time and space, as their power in production and trade declines and they seek refuge in finance. Since finance detached from production and trade is unable to sustain accumulation throughout time, a new hegemony tends to emerge taking advantage of the financial resources of the declining financialized hegemon (Lapavitsas 2013). From this perspective, the present global crises would be a manifestation of the decline of the hegemony of the US in the twentieth century.

A third approach to financialization was initiated by the regulation school in France. This school elaborated the concept of accumulation regime to denote models of long-term growth of capitalism or, more precisely, to account for the influence of institutions regarding the distribution of income between wages and profits and the compatibility of, on the one hand, production and, on the other hand, consumption and productive investment. Both from a theoretical and a historic point of view, accumulation regimes feature as multiple across time and space (Boyer 2004).

The post-war model of advanced capitalism is described and analysed by the regulation school as a "Fordist accumulation regime" characterized by a coherent articulation of mass production and consumption achieved by a particular type of 'wage relation' allowing for a balanced distribution of productivity gains between capital and labour, a feeble international integration, and the management of money and credit by the government.

According to the regulation school, a crisis of 'Fordism' resurfaced in the 1970s caused by productivity slow-down, rejection of Taylorism by salaried workers, saturation of standardized consumption goods and the collapse of the Bretton Woods international regime. This for regulationists meant that a new post-Fordist capitalist accumulation regime was to take shape.

Among several candidates for the succession to Fordism, the possibility of a finance-led accumulation regime emerged in regulationist circles in the 1990s. In one of several contributions discussing the features of such a regime, Boyer (2000: 121, 142) inquired after the conditions under which this new system would be viable, to presciently conclude that "[t]he more extended the impact of finance over corporate governance, household behavior, labor-market management and economic policy, the more likely is an equity-based regime to cross the zone of structural stability".

A fourth approach to financialization is post-Keynesian. The post-Keynesian elaboration of financialization draws on Keynes' work, particularly his famous Chap. 12 of the *General Theory* (Keynes 1936).

Writing during a period of financial expansion—the inter war years—Keynes introduced in this chapter the suggestive distinction between *speculation* and *enterprise* and outlined the risks of the predominance of speculation over enterprise (Caldas 2009). Keynes highlighted this prospect against a historical background in which enterprises "were mainly owned by those who undertook them or by their friends and associates" and "investment depended on a sufficient supply of individuals of sanguine temperament and constructive impulses who embarked upon business as a way of life" (Keynes 1936: 150). In these cases, investment decisions were irrevocable, "indissoluble, like marriage" (Keynes 1936: 160) and 'productive' investment was solid.

However, with the development of organized 'investment markets', Keynes noted, this era had come to an end. Characterized by liquidity, 'investment markets' now undertook a daily reassessment of investment—something which did not make sense in the previous context—and as they reassessed, they gave the individual the opportunity "to revise his commitments" (Keynes 1936: 151), i.e. to get rid of his assets in order to acquire—or not—others available on the market.

For Keynes, liquidity was ambiguous, involving what he considered to be a dilemma: it "often facilitates, though it sometimes impedes, the course of new investment" (Keynes 1936: 160). The reason why liquidity may facilitate investment was obvious to Keynes. In a context of uncertainty, liquidity is the emergency exit that the investor needs to know exists, before daring to enter a poorly-lit tunnel whose end is out of sight. It is the escape route, in the event of an emergency: Liquidity "calms [the investor's] nerves and makes him much more willing to run a risk" (Keynes 1936: 149).

However, if, on the one hand, liquidity might facilitate investment, on the other hand it could hinder it, or channel it into wrong-headed directions since investment decisions in the context of developed and liquid 'investment markets' tend to be determined not by long-term expectation on the yield of the investment rooted in knowledge of the concrete business, but on volatile daily market valuations.

The market valuations, Keynes thought, can be "mistaken"—indeed they tend to be mistaken—because individual decisions in markets made in a context of uncertainty are not rooted in genuine long-term expectations. The market value of assets is *conventional* in nature; it results from a multiplicity of decentralized, but not independent, decisions in which all individuals are trying to guess others' guesses when making their own decisions. In fact, their gains and losses depend upon their capacity to predict the choices made by the others. As Keynes wrote, in liquid markets the question is not only one of predicting which assets are going to go up or down, or which the others think are going to go up or down; rather, there is a third, fourth and even higher degree of recursivity involved, in "anticipating what the average opinion expects the average opinion to be." (Keynes 1936: 156). Keynes termed this activity of second-, third- or higher-degree prediction *speculation*, which he considers a form of game-playing, contrasting it with *enterprise*, i.e. "the activity of forecasting the prospective yield of assets over their whole life" (Keynes 1936: 158).

To the extent that market valuations tend to be biased, *speculation*—the activity of anticipating the conventional valuations of markets—may hinder or mislead investment from its most productive placements to short-term alluring applications. It may also induce volatility leading to crashes and crises. As highlighted by Orléan (1999: 60), in certain circumstances, self-referential groups "manage to stabilise through the endogenous production of a belief recognised by all"—a convention. But such conventions are fragile in that they may collapse unexpectedly when they are challenged by 'the news' or come under the attack of speculators seeking advantages by 'playing' against them.

The final conclusion of Keynes with respect to the rise of speculation in liquid 'investment markets' was clear cut (Keynes 1936: 160):

> Speculators may do no harm as bubbles on a steady stream of enterprise. But the position is serious when enterprise becomes the bubble on a whirlpool of speculation. When the capital development of a country becomes a by-product of the activities of a casino, the job is likely to be ill-done.

Drawing on Keynes' insights, post-Keynesian political economists developed their concept of financialization in connection with its effects on investment, savings, distribution, growth and instability potential (Hein 2009).

Post-Keynesians tend to interpret financialization as an outcome of national and international liberalization and the development of new communication technologies. Their main focus is the identification of the main channels of influence of the expanded financial sphere on the 'real' economy.

One of those channels originates in the increasing shareholder orientation in the management of large non-financial corporations. The ascendancy of stockholders with a 'liquid' relationship with particular corporations would translate into increasing concerns with dividends and stock market valuation to the detriment of long-term performance or survival. Since shareholder orientation involves the setting up of mechanisms that align management incentives with shareholders' objectives, the managerial orientation for 'retain and invest' would tend to be replaced by the shareholder strategy of 'downsize and distribute'.

A second channel is the financialization of households and household consumption. Easier access to consumer credit facilitated by deregulation would stimulate effective demand and growth. However, as the burden of servicing debt on low income households increased, the same households would have to save a larger share of their income at the expense of consumption, thus depressing demand. In the process, income would be regressively redistributed from low income (debtors) to high income individuals (creditors).

The third channel relates more specifically to functional distribution. In this respect the expectation is that higher distributed profits to shareholders will result in a decline of wages in the national income. In fact, increasing risk of unemployment caused by the 'downsize and distribute' strategies, combined with the deregulation of labor markets, would weaken the bargaining power of workers and favour redistribution at the expense of labor.

As a consequence of the combined operation of those mechanisms financialization would in most post-Keynesian accounts turn into a 'contractive' regime in which interest and dividend payments to 'rentiers' would result in the decline of capacity utilization and capital accumulation. Due to the low propensity of rentiers to consume, rising rentier income and wealth would not compensate for the reduction in the consumption demand of workers. Insufficient aggregate demand combined with the loss of financial resources internal to the corporations due to generous dividend distribution would account for a reduction of (real) investment and a slowdown of accumulation. Moreover, this regime would be liable to systemic instability stemming from divergent trends in the financial and goods and services markets.

In short, financialization is an analytic construct meant to address features of contemporary capitalism which resurfaced, or which have become salient in the last four decades. As an analytical construct it is—more than political economists who praise allegiance to a particular tradition in political economy, be it Marxian, Keynesian or Institutionalist, tend to acknowledge—a product of cross fertilization of several theoretical traditions. As a feature of contemporary capitalism, it is a regime which has arisen since the 1970s from a shift of the drivers of accumulation from production to finance which has engulfed in financial processes on an unprecedented scale since World War II (a) non-financial enterprises, (b) banks, (c) individuals and households. In contrast to post-war welfare capitalism, financialized capitalism is an accumulation regime delivering low levels of productive investment, slow productivity growth, stagnated or declining average real wages, more precarious jobs, increasing intra-national (income and wealth) inequalities, and financial instability.

3 The Capital Markets Union: Turning a Problem into a Solution

In November 2014, the European Commission announced the goal of setting up a Capital Markets Union (CMU) as part of its 'post-crisis' plans to boost growth and make the Eurozone resilient. In September 2015, it adopted an action plan to establish an integrated capital market in the EU by 2019 (European Commission 2015). Meanwhile, surrounded by the inattention of politicians and public opinion, and in spite of EU political deadlocks in other domains, the setting up of the CMU has been moving forward quietly but at a steady pace (Epstein and Rhodes 2018).

3.1 The CMU as a Resurrection of Finance

The CMU represents a large scale institutional reconfiguration project, encompassing all EU member states, aimed at removing national impediments to the circulation of capital, namely jurisdictional differences, to obtain an expansion of the role of capital markets—bonds, equity, venture capital, and securitization markets—in the financing of the 'real' economy and the absorption of personal and corporate savings (Epstein and Rhodes 2018; Braun and Hübner 2018).

The thirty measures of the CMU blueprint (European Commission 2015) cover a wide range including, at its core, the lowering of information requirements for companies to access equity financing, a new market for securitizations ('simple, transparent and standardized securitizations')[4] allowing for banks to alleviate capital requirements by selling asset-backed securities in capital markets, and enhanced household participation in those markets, namely through the setting up of the above mentioned pension product PEPP (Braun and Hübner 2018; Engelen and Glasmacher 2018).

To a great extent the CMU does not represent an innovation or a departure from tradition in the EU. Attributions of 'Eurosclerosis' to European companies' over reliance on bank-lending for investment, in contrast to the situation in the US, reach back to the 1960s (Braun and Hübner 2018). The Lisbon agenda advocated the emulation of the US venture capital-model for innovation. The Single Market was set up as a replica of north-American federation. The services directive drew on US shareholder ideology (Engelen and Glasmacher 2018).

Unsurprisingly, the Global Financial Crisis, with its origin in the US financial markets, delegitimized EU narratives based on the mimicking of the USA. Given the wide consensus in the wake of the Global Financial Crisis attributing the crisis to market finance, namely to the securitization of mortgage-loans and to shadow-

---

[4]Securitization is a transformation of non-tradable loans (or other non-debt assets which generate returns) into assets which are sold on financial markets to investors who are repaid from the principal and remunerated with interest collected from the underlying debt.

banking in general, and its contribution to excessive leveraging, systemic contagion, and financial instability; given also, the subsequent retrenchment of securitization, pension funds, and other financial products; many expected as an outcome of the crisis an institutional reconfiguration, both in the US and EU, allowing not for financial expansion, but rather 'financial repression'.

In this sense, the adoption by the EU of an agenda for the deepening of financialization as part of a 'post-crisis' plan to boost growth and make the Eurozone resilient may indeed appear as a puzzle calling for an explanation (Braun et al. 2018). How can a problem, turn into a solution?

Such an explanation for the puzzling resurrection of financialization in EU policies may be searched, as shown by Braun and Hübner (2018), by reconstructing the 'post-crisis' events and policy debates within EU institutions, and between EU institutions and the main players of the financial markets.

The Global Financial Crisis was first addressed by the EU with a combination of measures targeted at containing the banking crisis and supporting aggregate demand through public spending. In the first quarter of 2010, with the crisis of the euro, these measures were suddenly reversed and replaced by 'fiscal consolidation' and 'internal devaluation', especially in the peripheral southern European countries and Ireland under 'adjustment programmes'.

Over the course of 2012, as the consequences of the approach adopted in 2010 materialized in recession, deflation, explosive unemployment, political unrest and disruption, especially in southern Europe, pressure mounted for a new shift that might deliver growth, employment and stabilize instability. Political agents—including the French and Italian governments—then translated that pressure into the proposal of complementing the austerity enshrined in the Fiscal Compact with a growth agenda—the *Compact for Growth and Jobs*—adopted by the Council in June 2012 and pushed for the expansion of the fiscal space at the EU level.

While refraining from reversing austerity, resorting instead to the rhetorical shift of rebranding it as 'differentiated growth-friendly fiscal consolidation', the 'Growth Pact' increased the capital base of the European Investment Bank, opening up the way for the so-called Junker Plan and advocated the reduction of the regulatory 'burden' at the EU and national level, the deepening of the European Single Market, and the restructuring of the banking sector aimed at restoring its lending capacity.

In the same Council summit (June 2012) that adopted the 'Growth Pact', Council President Van Rompuy was invited to prepare, in collaboration with the Presidents of the Commission, the Eurogroup and the ECB, a road map for the achievement of a 'genuine' Economic and Monetary Union. This resulted in the 'Four President Report' also delivered in 2012, which anticipated a slow move towards a fiscal union and a fiscal capacity meant to improve shock-absorption in member states.

Viewed in retrospect, both initiatives were largely inconsequential. While the fiscal union, due in 2014, was post-postponed, now re-emerging occasionally in the EU agenda as an issue to be dealt with in the future, the Compact for Growth and Jobs, with its reinstatement of austerity and modest supply side advocacy of bank-lending led investment resulted in little more than a small concession that the French president might offer as a trophy to his constituency.

The fact is that, since 2012, proposals aiming at a European fiscal union and other 'public risk-sharing' initiatives were blocked. Those proposals translated for the German government and public into a 'Union of Transferences' and thus elicited the exercise of veto power. Nonetheless, the notion implicit in the 'Growth Pact' that the main bottleneck in the EU economy was the lack of financing geared toward investment in firms, first and foremost small and medium firms (SME), remained and became influential in the EU narrative.

From this diagnosis attributing stagnation to a prolonged credit crunch affecting SME, to the notion that (given the imperative of bank deleveraging) capital market-financing was the only available alternative, was only a small step. Already in April 2012 the *OECD Financial Roundtable* gathered policymakers and private sector representatives in advocating securitization as a means both to support bank deleveraging and lending to firms.

In the summer of 2012, the ECB rejoined the OECD and extended the financial narrative by combining the advocacy of securitization as a solution both to banking deleveraging and SME investment financing with the notion that it was also a remedy for the malfunctioning of the 'transmission' mechanisms of its monetary policy.

In March, 2013 the Commission's *Green Paper on Long Term Financing of the European Economy*, subscribing similar arguments, became the catalyst for further contributions and initiatives of private and public actors: a report of the Association for Financial Markets in Europe on 'Unlocking funding for European investment and growth', and the appointment of a public-private 'High level group' by the ECOFIN on 'SME and Infrastructure Financing', both advocated securitization (Braun and Hübner 2018).

Meanwhile, beyond securitization as a potential solution to bank deleveraging, SME access to capital and obstructed transmission mechanisms of monetary policy, financial market solutions also emerged as an instrument for 'risk sharing' and 'shock absorption' in the European Monetary Union (EMU), that is, as an insurance mechanism allowing countries in the monetary union affected by an asymmetric shock to mitigate its impact on growth, and avoid deflationary 'adjustments'.

Conceptually, risk sharing in a monetary union may operate either through the public budget or through debt and equity markets. The operation of risk sharing through the public budget in a monetary union requires a fiscal capacity at the Union level. Risk sharing through debt and equity requires instead a high level of financial integration allowing for portfolios containing claims on output produced in different countries, through which losses in a country or region may be compensated by gains in parts of the portfolio related to other geographies (Braun and Hübner 2018).

European policy-makers, who had triggered austerity and internal devaluation in 2010, now attributed the euro-crisis to a lack of risk-sharing instruments within the EMU. Having flattered shortly with proposals for a Fiscal Union, they soon accommodated the policy stalemate blocking developments in this direction and turned to the idea of private risk-sharing through finance as the only viable substitute to public risk-sharing.

In short, the closing of one door—the stalemate on the setting up of a fiscal capacity at the Union level that might finance investment, employment and growth and perform a risk-sharing function—opened up another door for the deepening of financialization—at the core of which is further financial integration, securitization, further reliance of firms and households on financial markets, namely through funded pension schemes.

The open door was then seized by the key financial players in the EU. All of them had reasons to converge on the path to revive financial markets. Engelen and Glasmacher (2018) relate the CMU to an interest coalition involving European policy makers, national banking associations, central bankers, regulators, and asset managers and insurers. European policy makers (the European Commission and its staff) envision the CMU as a 'solution' from the stalemate of the fiscal union; national banking associations, in particular those of European countries with developed securitization markets, picture the CMU as a resuscitation of a market on which banks became dependent; central bankers face it as a means for the reestablishment of a 'normal' monetary policy (for banks now kept afloat through ECB funding, securitization would provide an alternative source of funding); regulators take securitization within the CMU as a reassurance of the bank's ability to access 'independent' sources; and asset managers and insurers anticipate it as an opportunity, in a low yield conjuncture, to reap yield above sovereign bonds.

Such is the logic of the Capital Markets Union. Obviously for the EU decision makers 'this time is different': "[C]loser integration of capital markets and gradual removal of remaining national barriers could create new risks to financial stability, [but] we will support actions to increase supervisory convergence, so that capital markets regulators act in a unified way and strengthen the available tools to manage systemic risks prudently" (European Commission 2015: 4).

3.2 This Time Is Different?

Nonetheless, critics of the CMU, especially of its drive towards reviving securitization, are sceptical with respect to the ability of the tools devised to prudently manage systemic risks. Analysing legal details in CMU documentation, Engelen and Glasmacher (2018: 168) warn that "the securitizations endorsed by the Commission are the spitting image of pre-crisis industry practices and as such are anything but 'simple', 'transparent' and 'standardized'". They found, that the CMU 'simple, transparent and standardized securitizations' (STS) criteria "only address the quality of the securitization process (structuring, tranching, rating and distribution) and have nothing to say about the 'quality' of the 'raw material' (the mortgage contract)..." (Engelen and Glasmacher 2018: 171), which is strange given that, as events of the sub-prime crisis have shown, the 'quality' of the securitized assets depends on the 'quality' of the mortgage contracts. They also found the labels 'simple', 'transparent' and 'standardized' misleading. STS, as all securitizations, are intrinsically complex—for professional investors only. They require the inclusion of swaps that complicate their risk-return profile and admit the possibility of giving the STS stamp to particularly risky securitizations—credit default swaps (CDS) and collateralized debt obligations (CDO). Finally, they found in the documentation provisions meant to reduce the regulatory capital charges for securitization established in Basel 3.

The authors (Engelen and Glasmacher 2018: 180) found, in short, that: (a) "the very same financial instruments which stood at the cradle of the crisis are again in the process of being treated as low risk assets by European regulators"; (b) rather than an additional source of finance for SME, securitization tends to fuel mortgage lending, real estate inflation, and possibly housing bubbles[5]; (c) securitization is primarily meant to allow banks to transfer risk from their balance sheets possibly resulting, as revealed by the sub-prime episode, in increased systemic risks.

4 Funding European Pensions

Although the proposal for a pan-European personal (funded) pension product (PEPP) arose in the EU and gained traction within the framework of the CMU, its antecedents reach back into the 1990s. In spite of the fact that the EU has no mandate over pension policies, the European Commission relied on the Open Method of Coordination to initiate, at the beginning of the new millennium, an effort to enhance funded pensions purportedly as a means to address the 'unsustainability' of PAYG schemes. The EU was in this effort influenced by the World Bank's advocacy of 'multipillar systems' combining PAYG with both a mandatory and voluntary funded pension—an approach which was formally adopted by the EU in 2003 when a Directive (2003/41/EC) was approved laying out the framework for pension regulation (Bonizzi and Churchill 2016).

Efforts by the EU were met in most member states by reforms in PAYG that reduced their benefits and promoted prefunded forms of private pensions. Despite marked differences in the point of departure, and market crises in 2001 and 2008 with adverse effects on funded pensions, life insurance and pension funds have since then been growing steadily in most EU countries. Nevertheless, the landscape of pension provision in the EU remains variegated with each national system involving particular mixes of State, employer-workers, and individual arrangements ranging from non-contributory universal social assistance to individual prefunded pension plans and including PAYG and occupational pension plans (defined benefit or defined contribution) among others (Rodrigues et al. 2018; Wiß 2019).

---

[5]"There is a functional reason for this. The riskiness of mortgage contracts is much easier to assess than that of SME-loans, while the risk assessments of the latter are much more difficult, time-consuming and hence costly. Since the difficulty of assessing SME-loans is not addressed in the proposal (there is no regulatory attempt to standardize SME-loans for instance), mortgage lending will again be the main beneficiary of the sanitized market for securitized assets the Commission aims to set up. This implies that most of the extra funding generated by securitization will again finance already existing assets (real estate)" (Engelen and Glasmacher 2018: 170).

The variegation in pension regimes poses difficult policy challenges for the EU project for the expansion of funded pensions and the integration of financial markets. Those challenges might be addressed either by harmonizing the national legislation of all member states or by creating an EU-wide pension scheme complementing (or competing) with national regimes.

In October 2000 the Commission launched an initiative aimed at harmonization of occupational pensions—a proposal for a directive for Institutions for Occupational Retirement Provisions (IORP)—according to which pension funds should enjoy the same market freedoms in the single market as banks, insurance companies and investment funds. Following convoluted negotiations in the European Parliament and the Council, the directive was adopted reflecting a narrow limited least common denominator (Haverland 2007).

Stemming from disappointment with the limited outcome of this process, the temptation of breaking out of the 'joint decision trap' on pension policy inherent in disappointing outcomes of attempts at harmonization, by erecting a European "third pillar" parallel to national arrangements gained traction. Moves in this direction, preceding the CMU, would come to fruition.

4.1 The History of PEPP in a Nutshell

According to Waltraud (2019), the origin of PEPP may be traced back to an initiative taken in the mid-2000s by the European Financial Services Round Table (EFR),[6] advancing a plan to create a standardized EU-wide personal pension scheme parallel to the national legal regimes of the member countries. The approach of the EFR, as straightforwardly stated by a global head of pensions at ING Group in an online journal of the pension industry, was clear (Waltraud 2019: 605):

> [A]rranging pan-European pensions by harmonising the national legislation of 25 EU countries is virtually a mission impossible. So why not take a short cut by having an EU-wide "26th regime" framework with only a limited number of basic principles that are acceptable to all member states?

In May 2007 the Economic and Finance Affairs Council (Ecofin) invited the EFR to specify their proposal. The EFR responded in a new report that dropped references to 'short cutting' and instead evoked other justifications that might be more appropriate for the EU to better advance the proposal. The new EU-wide pension was now presented by the EFR as responding to the 'demographic challenge' that inevitably would reduce the entitlements of tomorrow's pensioners creating a 'pensions gap' that only personal (and occupational) pensions could fill, thus coining the expression 'pension gap' that still remains in EU lingo.

In 2012, against the background of both the euro crisis and the predicaments of pension funds due to their losses in the stock market crash, the Commission

---

[6]EFR is an organization bringing together CEOs from the biggest banks and insurers in Europe.

launched a *White Paper* on 'safe, sustainable and adequate pensions'. By now the motivation for a new EU-wide pension scheme was framed in terms of: (a) care for the old age security of migrants; (b) the need to adapt regulation in line with the general shift towards individual responsibility for securing retirement income; (c) addressing market failures and improving governance and risk management in all member states; (d) compensating for low or declining replacement rates of public and occupational schemes (the 'pension's gap'). The best way to reach these goals, the commission advocated, in line with the EFR proposal, was the setting up of a common "standards for a scheme with a European 'kitemark' that would be acceptable in all member states and fully transferable across borders ... instead of a Directive harmonising European standards ..." (Waltraud 2019: 605). After long consultations with associations representing funded pension providers, the Commission published the final proposal for a PEPP in June 2017, shifting the emphasis to the contribution that such a pension product could make to the CMU. Finally, in February 2019 the European Parliament and Member States reached a political agreement on the proposal for PEPP.

4.2   Extending Funded Pensions in the EU: Puzzling

Given that arguments in defence of the extension of 'third' pillars in pension regimes were not as compelling at the outset as is generally believed, and tended to become weaker in the light of experience exposing the vulnerability of funded pensions to financial crises, the EU push for the setting up of PEPP is indeed at least as puzzling as the overall CMU project.

Consider first arguments for funding pensions. The rationale for 'multipillar' pension regimes has drawn, since its inception in the World Bank, on the one hand, on demographic projections anticipating worsening dependency ratios afflicting the financial sustainability of PAYG regimes, and, on the other hand, on the assumption that funded regimes were immune to demographic stress.

The demographic argument anticipated an impossible trilemma: either reduce PAYG systems' benefits, or increase labour costs for firms damaging their competitiveness in world markets, or increase fiscal transfers leading to a fiscal crisis of the state. The World Bank offered capitalization instead of PAYG as a way out of this conundrum: capitalization would provide a mechanism for transferring present savings into the future, inducing parsimony in the present generation, and alleviating future generations of the burden of the elderly. As spelled out by Engelen (2003) long before others, both lines of reasoning are ill founded.

Arguably (Engelen 2003), demographic projections are limited as a knowledge foundation for pension policies. Predictions in general presuppose closed systems and deterministic laws. They are unable to accommodate agency and reflexivity. They are necessarily based on *ceteris paribus* conditions, and yet highly sensitive to even small differences in those conditions. More importantly, the projections are dependent on assumptions regarding employment, productivity, wage growth and distribution and even the feedback of pension restructuring on those variables, which most studies fail to address. A proper examination of the impact of those neglected variables on pension regimes widens the scope of possible solutions, beyond the retrenchment of PAYG systems and the enhancement of funded ones, encompassing reforms in other policy domains—industrial relations, migration, education and, first and foremost, employment, wages and the functional distribution of income.

Arguably also, and more importantly (Engelen 2003), funded regimes are at least as vulnerable to demographic stress as PAYG regimes. Pension funds are indeed affected by the ratio between contributors and beneficiaries. The life cycle of a pension fund involves an 'expansion phase' engaging more contributors than beneficiaries—during which the fund is a net buyer of assets with limited liquidity requirements—, a 'maturation phase' of equilibrium, and finally, depending on demographic and economic trends, a 'retirement phase'—in which the fund becomes a net seller of assets due to growing liquidity imperatives, implying also a more 'speculative orientation' towards high yield liquid assets.

Finally, differently from PAYG regimes, funded regimes not only tend to feed the instability of financial markets in their drive for yield and liquidity in the maturation phase but are highly vulnerable to that instability. As shown by Wiß (2015, 2019), pension funds suffered heavy losses during the financial crises of 2001/02 and 2007/08. In the UK and the Netherlands, countries with highly financialized pension regimes, those losses were particularly damaging.

As a consequence, while reversals of pension financialization have taken place in some countries, namely Portugal (Rodrigues et al. 2018), what prevails in more financialized contexts as pensions funds recovered after each crisis, was a reinforced reliance of pensions on market solutions, increasing individual responsibility and risks. Revealing the vulnerability of funded pensions to demographic trends and financial market vagaries, in response to the crisis, Dutch occupational pension funds increased contributions to defined benefit (DB) schemes, switched from DB to defined contribution (DC), and final-salary to average-salary, linked benefits to financial market developments and life expectancy, extended individualized pension contracts, relaxed regulatory requirements, and increased the power of external technocrats in fund management at the expense of employee representatives. In the UK a shift of defined benefit (DB) to DC schemes also took place and member-nominated trustees were disempowered (Wiß 2019).

5   Private Funded and Pay-as-you-go Public Regimes: Complementary or Substitutes?

Presented as a voluntary regime complementary to other pillars, the EU-wide PEPP may seem an innocuous small increment to existing pension regimes providing reduced transaction costs for firms operating in various member states and safe pensions for mobile workers.

However, it may instead represent a disruptive innovation leading to a regime change. Such a paradigmatic regime change—especially from PAYG to a funded regime—involving high transition costs and often facing popular resistance can be implemented only incrementally.

The potential for disruption inscribed in the new EU-wide PEPP may be analysed with conceptual instruments drawn up by Hirschman (1970, 1980). In *Exit, Voice and Loyalty*, Hirschman dealt with the deterioration of the performance of organizations (*quality* of output) and mechanisms that may (or may not) repair the deterioration of performance and avoid collapse. The author highlighted two mechanisms: *exit* and *voice*.

Exit denoted the option by customers or organization members of switching from one provider to the next impelling management to correct whatever faults had led to exit. *Voice* refers to the option of customers or organization members that express their dissatisfaction directly to management, to any authority to which management is subordinated, or through open protest in the public space, possibly leading to the reparation of the faults causing dissatisfaction.

Exit is obviously related to markets, and voice to politics, and Hirshman's concern was with the tendency of economists (and with the actual general trend in society) towards extending exit to domains of social life which in principle are not, or should not be, marketized, underrating voice. His was an "essay in persuasion on behalf of voice" Hirschman (1980: 431).

Hirschman illustrated the economists' bias towards exit to the detriment of voice with Milton Friedman's proposal for the introduction of market mechanisms in public education systems. Friedman advocated the distribution of vouchers to parents which might be used to purchase educational services in the (competitive) market from private schools. In Friedman's view the extended 'freedom to choose' of parent-consumers substituted for their participation in political processes which he labelled as 'cumbrous' and dismissed as non-effective.

While admitting that market and non-market (political) mechanisms might operate in harmony and provide mutual support in some instances, Hirschman warned against the possibility of one getting in the other's way undercutting its effectiveness and producing unanticipated undesired outcomes. Friedman's voucher proposal might turn out to be one of those cases.

As explained by Hirschman, even without Friedman's vouchers, in any educational system where public and private schools compete side by side and parents are not locked into either one of the systems, exit is a viable option for parents. In such a case, if for instance the public-school system is perceived to be deteriorating, a tendency will arise among quality-education-conscious (or simply more affluent, informed or educated) parents to send their children to private schools. While this may trigger a positive response by managers of public schools toward quality improvement, it may also deprive the public schools of those members more motivated and equipped to fight deterioration. The outcome may be the cumulative decay of public schools, and the production of a segregated system of education, even if such an outcome was not intended. Friedman's voucher probably facilitates and speeds up such an outcome.

Following the publication of *Exit, Voice and Loyalty*, numerous researchers applied the exit and voice categories to analyse processes of decay and regeneration in various contexts. As illustrative as the school example are cases related to urban contexts (Hirschman 1980). In urban contexts, the response to the decay of particular neighbourhoods may also be either exit (the mute search for a new location) or voice (civic demand and engagement in the regeneration of the neighbourhoods). Assuming that quality-conscious (or simply more affluent) persons are prone to exit rather than voice, which may not be always the case, the preponderance of exit would deprive the neighbourhood of those better equipped to contribute to its regeneration. The outcome would be, as in the school example, the cumulative degradation of the decaying neighbourhood, and, as illustrated by Schelling's (1971) model of segregation, at a macro level the segregation of the urban space into affluent and poor, black and white, white-collar and blue-collar, neighbourhoods.

Hirschman's analytical framework may obviously also be applied to study the dynamics (disruptive or otherwise) induced by the setting up of a new funded pillar parallel to PAYG in a in a PAYG dominated system.[7] Such an application will be broadly outlined in the following paragraphs. Before that however, two remarks are in order.

In many instances in which the possibility of exit would preclude the provision of a vital public good, exit is blocked by law—possibly even "branded as criminal, ... labelled desertion, defection and treason" (Hirschman 1970: 17)—*loyalty* coercively imposed, and voice enacted as the legitimate option for attempting to repair decay. Moreover, as suggested by Hirschman, the interplay of voice and action is often more complex than implied in the previous illustrations. In the event of blocked exit, as in the case of participation in the funding of public spending through the fiscal system, exit, or partial exit, may be sought and achieved by dubious (even if legal) means, and voice can be mobilized to protest against compulsory loyalty, that is to achieve 'freedom to choose'.

5.1 Voice and Exit in the Pensions' Arena

PAYG systems are in most cases instances of institutions where participation is mandatory, and exit precluded. This obstructs transitions from PAYG to funded systems. Transition from PAYG to funded regimes involves the so-called 'double burden problem', meaning that in transition workers pay twice: for the funded pension and for the PAYG system (World Bank 2005). Understandably, in this frame the individual motivation to engage in funded pension schemes may be scarce. However, the reduction of benefits of PAYG, possibly combined with incentives for funded schemes, may shift the balance of motivations.

---

[7]Surprisingly, the author was unable to find any reference to such an application.

Under the pretext of the financial dire straits of PAYG this process has for a long time been taking place with so-called parametric reforms of PAYG meant to reduce their cost through (a) the reduction of the value of the pension with respect to the wage at the time of retirement, (b) increasing early retirement penalizations, (c) postponing the age of retirement, and (d) changing indexation procedures, namely uprating benefits in line with prices. In parallel, fiscal incentives for private retirement plans and life insurance are also resorted to as a means of shifting individual allegiances from PAYG to funded schemes. Additionally, employers may provide means for a partial exit from PAYG by offering pay rises under the form of a fringe benefit of different types, all of them exempt from contribution into the PAYG system, including employer's contributions to private (or public) funded pensions. Other partial exit mechanisms include the introduction of ceilings allowing wages to be exempted above a certain threshold to contribute to the system, with the correspondent adjustment of future benefits.

In short, even in pension systems dominated by PAYG, a number of policy measures may induce contributors—first and foremost more affluent contributors—to shift their preferences from PAYG to funded schemes, that is to prefer exit instead of voice.

Once preferences start to shift, the voices—first and louder those of more affluent contributors—will tend to express not discontent with the decay of PAYG and willingness to repair it, but discontent with PAYG and willingness to extend exit opportunities. A process of cumulative decay of PAYG is now under way which will reach a tipping point where it becomes very hard to revert this—financialized pension regimes create their own political support once they have reached a certain threshold—unless a major financial crisis erupts disrupting the private funded scheme. Deemed too big to fail the state then comes in, either reinstating the 'old' system or, most likely in the current environment, bailing out the 'new' one.

In spite of the claim that 'third pillars' are mere complements to PAYG, the real purpose of their creation is a replacement of all-encompassing PAYG systems by multipillar systems with PAYG as a "publicly managed system with mandatory participation and the limited goal of reducing poverty among the old" (World Bank 2005: 1). There is no ambiguity in the World Bank stance. The goal is "moving from pay-as-you-go to funded finance of retirement incomes" (World Bank 2005: 1). EU officials may shy away from such blunt statements, but surely, under the influence of the World Bank, most would secretly agree.

The trend for segregation of pension regimes inscribed in multipillar systems may, however, be counter-acted, especially in countries with dominant PAYG pillars, through the operation of other forces. The case of Portugal, as highlighted by Rodrigues et al. (2018), is instructive. In spite of major 'parametric' reforms reducing the benefits of PAYG, the growth of private pension schemes has been very limited and slow. In fact, in recent years major firms have even closed their pension funds and delivered them to the state. Private pension schemes play a minor role in the overall system engaging only a small and wealthy segment of households. This may be partly explained by the youthfulness of the Portuguese PAYG system, the immature securities markets, and above all the low levels of average disposable income. This suggests that transitions, and obstruction to transitions, operate differently in variegated pension regimes.

6 Conclusion

This chapter addressed attempts at setting up an EU-wide 'third pillar' pension scheme in the frame of the CMU. The endorsement by the EU of funded pensions in the aftermath of a financial crisis that greatly damaged pension funds (which incidentally contributed to triggering the crisis) was taken as a puzzling development calling for an explanation.

The expansion of private funded pension schemes as an alternative to public PAYG systems, and the CMU of which the new EU 'pension product' is part and parcel, may be interpreted and analysed as part of a deepening process of financialization. The explanation for the puzzling resurrection of financialization in the CMU in the aftermath of a crisis of financialization was searched for in the post-crisis events and policy debates within EU institutions and between those institutions and the main players in financial markets.

This search suggested that financialization emerged as a solution to the problems created by financialization as an outcome of the deadlock on proposals for the creation of a Fiscal Union and a fiscal capacity at the Union level that might perform a risk sharing function. In the face of suck a deadlock, the notion of private risk-sharing through deepening financial integration, securitization and the further reliance of firms and households on financial markets, namely through funded pension schemes, gained traction.

The CMU thus emerged spurred on by an interest coalition of European policy makers, national banking associations, central bankers, regulators, and asset managers and insurers, as an agenda that might deliver (for EU decision-makers) risk-sharing without a 'Union of Transferences', (for banks) security markets allowing for a reduction of capital requirements, (for central bankers) a means for the reestablishment of a 'normal' monetary policy, (for regulators) reassurance of the banks' ability to access 'independent' sources, and (for asset managers and insurers) opportunities to reap yield above sovereign bonds.

EU authorities claim that increased supervisory convergence will avert risks to financial stability stemming from closer integration of capital markets. However, a careful analysis of the technical documentation of the CMU strongly suggests that what is now being treated as low risk assets by the European regulator is very similar to the financial instruments which triggered the financial crisis. It also suggests that rather than an additional source of finance for SMEs, as claimed by EU authorities, securitization is primarily meant to allow banks to transfer risk from their balance sheets possibly resulting in enhanced mortgage lending, real estate inflation, housing bubbles and increased systemic risks.

Although presented within the framework of the CMU, the origin of PEPP may be traced back to the mid-2000s. Since the results of attempts at harmonizing the legislation of pension regimes in the member countries as a means to set up an integrated market for pensions had disappointed the actors concerned, the same actors conceived and advanced an alternative route consisting in the setting up of a framework for an EU-wide 'third pillar' that might complement, or rather compete, with other pillars at the member-state level.

In light of experience exposing the vulnerability of funded pensions to financial crises and increasing awareness of the weakness of arguments for the extension of 'third' pillars in pension regimes, the EU push for the setting up of PEPP is indeed at least as puzzling as the overall CMU project.

The World Bank advocacy of 'multipillar' pension regimes drew on demographic projections anticipating worsening dependency ratios, and the assumption that funded regimes were immune to demographic stress. Both are weak arguments.

Demographic projections are based on *ceteris paribus* clauses, and yet sensitive to even small differences in those clauses. They are dependent on unreliable assumptions concerning employment, productivity, wage growth and distribution. They neglect the feedback of pension restructuring on income, employment and growth. Removing the *ceteris paribus* clauses from those projections invariably exposes the importance of employment, wages and functional distribution of income, thus widening the scope of possible solutions beyond the retrenchment of PAYG systems.

Moreover, funded regimes are at least as vulnerable to demographic stress as PAYG regimes. However, differently from PAYG regimes, funded regimes tend to feed the instability of financial markets and are highly vulnerable to that instability. Such a lesson should have been learned from past financial crises.

Although presented as a voluntary regime complementary to other pillars, the EU-wide PEPP may indeed be intended as a substitute for PAYG. In spite of mandatory participation, PAYG schemes are not immune to exit-propelled cumulative dynamics that may transform them, as desired by the World Bank, into a residual pillar meant merely to counter old age poverty.

The creation of an EU-wide 'third pillar' may therefore trigger a disruptive process leading to dual (segregated) pension regimes. Once triggered, exit is hard to contain or reverse, especially if the fiscal constraints on the recovery of PAYG regimes are tight. Consequently, individuals wishing to preserve their pensions may be dragged even against their will and their civic commitments into a path that they neither chose nor are able to control.

Such a trend may be counteracted, especially in countries where PAYG is still dominant or a low level of average disposable income obstructs the 'transition'. However, if not, most, even those who were led to engage in funded pension schemes, may come to regret the substitution of an all-encompassing PAYG pension system, anchored on last-resource public guaranties, by a dual system consisting of a 'poverty pillar' and funded pillars, in which the responsibilities and risks are shifted to individuals, producing as an 'external' effect increased collective risks of social segregation and/or financial collapse.

References

Bonizzi B, Churchill J (2016) Pension funds and financialization in the European Union. Revista de Economia Mundial 46:71–90

Boyer R (2000) Is a finance-led growth regime a viable alternative to Fordism? A preliminary analysis. Econ Soc 29(1):111–145

Boyer R (2004) Théorie de la Régulation: 1. Les fondamentaux. la Decouverte, Paris

Braun B, Hübner M (2018) Fiscal fault, financial fix? Capital markets union and the quest for macroeconomic stabilization in the euro area. Compet Chang 22(2):117–138

Braun B, Gabor D, Hübner M (2018) Governing through financial markets: towards a critical political economy of capital markets union. Compet Chang 22(2):101–116

Caldas JC (2009) The art of escape: liquidity mechanisms. RCCS Annual Review #1, Available at https://journals.openedition.org/rccsar/180?lang=pt

Engelen E (2003) The logic of funding European pension restructuring and the dangers of financialization. Environ Plan A 35(8):1357–1372

Engelen E, Glasmacher A (2018) The waiting game: how securitization became the solution for the growth problem of the Eurozone. Compet Chang 22(2):165–183

Epstein R, Rhodes M (2018) From governance to government: banking union, capital markets union and the new EU. Compet Chang 22(2):205–224

European Commission (2015) Action plan on building a capital markets union. https://ec.europa.eu/info/publications/action-plan-building-capital-markets-union_en

Haverland M (2007) When the welfare state meets the regulatory state: EU occupational pension policy. J Eur Pub Policy 14(6):886–904

Hein E (2009) A (post-)Keynesian perspective on 'financialization'. IMK Studies, 1/2009. Available at https://ideas.repec.org/p/imk/studie/01-2009.html

Hirschman AO (1970) Exit, voice and loyalty: responses to decline in firms, organizations, and states. Harvard University Press, Cambridge, MA

Hirschman AO (1980) 'Exit, voice and loyalty': further reflections and a survey of recent contributions. Milbank Mem Fund Q Health Soc 58(3):430–453

Keynes JM (1936) The general theory of employment, interest and money. Macmillan, London

Lapavitsas C (2013) Profiting without producing: how finance exploits us all. Verso, London

Nölke A (2017) Financialisation as the core problem for a 'Social Europe'. Revista de Economia Mundial 46:27–48

Orléan A (1999) Le pouvoir de la finance. Odile Jacob, Paris

Rodrigues J, Santos AC, Teles N (2018) Financialisation of pensions in semi-peripheral Portugal. Glob Soc Policy 18(2):189–209

Schelling T (1971) Dynamic models of segregation. J Math Sociol 1:143–186

Waltraud S (2019) EU pension policy and financialisation: purpose without power? J Eur Publ Policy 26(4):599–616

Wiß T (2015) Pension fund vulnerability to the financial market crisis: the role of trade unions. Eur J Ind Relat 21(2):1–17

Wiß T (2019) Reinforcement of pension financialization as a response to financial crises in Germany, the Netherlands and the United Kingdom. J Eur Publ Policy 26(4):1–20

World Bank (2005) Transition: paying for a shift from pay-as-you-go financing to funded pensions. World Bank Pension Reform Primer Series. Available at https://openknowledge.worldbank.org/handle/10986/11242

Wrenn MV (2016) Surplus absorption and waste in neoliberal monopoly capitalism. The Monthly Review, July 1, 2016

José Castro Caldas is a researcher at the Collaborative Laboratory for Work, Employment and Social Protection and the Centre for Social Studies, Coimbra University, Portugal and a member of its Observatory on Crises and Alternatives. He received a PhD in Economics at ISCTE-Lisbon University Institute where he has been a professor. His main research interests are on the history and methodology of economics and the political economy of labour. His recent publications include Economia(s) (Porto: 2009), and the edited books Facts, Values and Objectivity in Economics (London: 2012), Valores em conflito Megaprojetos, Ambiente e Território (Coimbra: 2016), and Trabalho e Políticas de Emprego: um retrocesso evitável (Lisbon: 2017).

Part III
Pension Plans and the European Pillar of Social Rights: A New Scope for the EU Social Policy?

Pensions at a Crossroad Between Social Rights and Financial Markets: Which Way to Be Chosen?

Nazaré da Costa Cabral

Abstract Departing from the two basic historical models of social protection, the Bismarckian or labour model and the Beveridgean or universal model, the author proceeds with analysing two contrasting alternatives for the future design of pension systems: (i) The individual insurance model; (ii) The universal tax-financed model. Although motivated by common drivers—an ageing society and technological revolution—the responses and incentives are substantially (philosophically) different. Ultimately, there is a tension between social rights and financial markets that may end up with the predominance of one over the other. In the current (liberalizing) environment and considering past and recent EU policy guidance on this matter— the timidity of the social-rights centred strategy (contained in the European Pillar of Social Rights) in contrast with the impulse given to the development of the Capital Markets Union—may after all mean the triumph of a financial market-driven approach.

1 Introduction

Welfare states in the developed world, although presenting idiosyncratic features in each country, can be comprehended and eventually associated with two basic historical models of social protection: the Bismarckian or labour model and the Beveridgean or universal model.[1]

---

[1] An expanded taxonomy of social protection models was conceived by Esping-Andersen (1991), to include: *i)* Social assistance-type models; *ii)* Insurance-type (or Bismarckian) models; and *iii)* Universal (or Beveridgean) models. I will restrict the analysis to the two latter models, as prevalent in the developed world.

N. da Costa Cabral (✉)
CIDEEFF - Center for European, Economic, Financial and Tax Law Research, University of Lisbon, Faculdade de Direito de Lisboa, Alameda da Universidade, Lisbon, Portugal
e-mail: nazarecabral@fd.ulisboa.pt

© Springer Nature Switzerland AG 2019
N. da Costa Cabral, N. Cunha Rodrigues (eds.), *The Future of Pension Plans in the EU Internal Market*, Financial and Monetary Policy Studies 48,
https://doi.org/10.1007/978-3-030-29497-7_14

The basic features of the Bismarckian models (coming from the primary social risks created by the German chancellor Otto von Bismarck in the 1880s)[2] are: (i) Risk collectivization through the creation of social insurances that allowed for risk sharing within groups of workers belonging to the same company or industry; (ii) Financed through an insurance premium paid, on a mandatory basis, both by the employer and the employee as a proportion of the employees' wages; (iii) Aiming to ensure a replacement income as a proportion of the amount paid.

The two main functions of the social insurance model as it evolved most notably in most European countries over the twentieth century was to ensure risk provision on a collective basis and the replacement of income whenever the occurrence of a certain social risk prevented workers from obtaining work-related incomes.

Simultaneously, and due to the favourable demographic and economic conditions found in the second half of the twentieth century, public insurance-type systems evolved from typically funded schemes to schemes based on the financing principle of 'pay-as-you-go (PAYGO)'.[3] Musgrave (1981, p. 99) notes that PAYGO systems benefit from an expanding population and rapid productivity growth. Under the reserve (funded) system the rate of return equals the rate of interest. Under PAYGO, the rate of return from a constant tax rate equals the rate of population and productivity growth. Therefore, if rates of population and productivity growth exceed the interest rate, the rate of return of PAYGO is higher than that of a funded system.[4]

In turn, the universal model of social protection, although related to the publication of the Report *Social Insurance and Allied Services*—whose leading author was the British Minister William Beveridge (Beveridge 1942)—is embedded in the New Zealand and the United States (U.S.) *Social Security Acts*, enacted respectively in 1932 and 1935. The latter, in particular, was a major policy action promoted by President Roosevelt—in the course of the 'New Deal' programme—to fight the harmful social consequences of the Great Depression of the 1930s.

The main features of this model are: (i) Social protection is conceived as a citizenship right, to which all residents in the country are entitled regardless of their labour or professional status; (ii) It is based on a tax financing principle; (iii) It aims at ensuring not only income replacement but also social assistance in the event of need or poverty relief.

Considering the way the universal model evolved in the second half of the twentieth century and the way it was implemented in the Scandinavian welfare world (its extreme version), the basic functions of the model were to create, through

---

[2]Initially the case with health (1883), accident (1885), and disability and old-age insurances (1889).

[3]As explained by Musgrave (1981, pp. 97-98), the transition from funded to PAYGO systems (particularly in the case of the U.S.) was due to two main reasons. Firstly, it seemed unacceptable to exclude the then older generation from benefits, the more so their plight had been accentuated by the Great Depression. Secondly, the 1937 recession, which followed rapidly upon the introduction of the system, rendered a substantial system surplus undesirable on the grounds of stabilization policy.

[4]With a vice-versa situation occurring in the opposite scenario.

social rights, a safety net against poverty and social exclusion and to promote a higher degree of economic redistribution amongst individuals.

2 The Multi-Pillar Approach: Mining the Origins and Contextualizing the Current Situation

2.1 Bismarckian Models as Implicit Inheritors of Ancient Occupational Plans

Recalling the basic features of the Bismarckian model, it can be stated that these first mandatory social insurances were implicit inheritors of former occupational plans, established in several parts of the world, even if, by then, there was a prevailing voluntary aspect to them. In the U.S., for example, such occupational plans were introduced in colonial times and were promoted after independence. Early programmes included the Plymouth Colony settlers' military retirement programme in 1636, the Gallatin Glassworks' profit-sharing plan in 1797, and the American Express Company's private employer pension plan in 1875 (EBRI 1990, p. 3).

Social insurance of an occupational nature, sponsored by employers on behalf of their employees, thus preceded the creation of government sponsored and managed pension plans, as these would be generalized after the Bismarckian political initiative (to circumvent social and labour tensions and the risk of a socialist solution) and then throughout the twentieth century.

The main differences between seminal occupational plans and Bismarckian social insurance can be explained by the different characteristics of the latter: (i) Its mandatory nature; (ii) The underlying idea of collective-shared risk and collective management (with the involvement of labour unions); (iii) The progressive autonomisation of a new source of risk financing—that of the social contribution with distinctive features via-à-vis conventional private and individual insurance (a premium) and; (iv) The novel consideration of social risk provision not as a simple insurance device but actually as an employee social right.

The generalization of public pension plans (notably in labour-type models), with the increasing extension and generosity of social security systems throughout the twentieth century established in many countries (in particular, in European countries) a conceptual division between public mandatory plans (the core of the social protection system) and occupational or professional plans (*tout court*), either mandatory or voluntary, that were assigned to the role of supplementary pensions.

2.2   The World Bank Report of 1994

However, in the 1990s, the new economic (economic slowdown), demographic (ageing population) and political environment (the 'Washington consensus') favoured a new debate involving the so-called 'social security privatization'. This debate was to a large extent fostered by the publication of the important and controversial World Bank Report, *Averting the Old-Age Crisis* (The World Bank 1994).

In this Report, where a multi-pillar approach to the pension system was proposed,[5] the World Bank argued strongly against a single pillar model (relying predominantly on public pension plans) due to alleged 'government failures' that could be now be superimposed to traditional market failures in social risk markets.[6]

Amongst these government failures, The World Bank (1994) highlighted: (i) The incapacity of the public pay-as-you-go systems to deal with population ageing and productivity decline; (ii) The resulting negative incentives in labour markets, as a public pension scheme reduces the hiring of labour, promotes from the withdrawal of workers towards the informal sector and induces early retirement; (iii) The negative consequences on economic growth, notably by negatively affecting savings and investment and jeopardizing the well-functioning of capital markets; (iv) The heavy fiscal costs of public pension systems, causing increasing tax effort, budget deficits and public debt (both explicit and implicit debt).

The main assumptions and conclusions of the Report were not made out of criticism. The most disseminated idea in the Report was that funded regimes were in a better position to cope with the effects of the ageing population than PAYGO plans. Some authors consider this argument is wrong because a fully funded system is also affected by demographic change (Barr and Diamond 2010, p. 68). Indeed, unless a decline in the number of workers has no effects on output, output will be less than if the workforce had not shrunk. In this case, lower rates of return and higher prices would deny pensioners the income and consumption they expected. Barr and Diamond (2010, p. 70) then advocate that "PAYG and funding are both mechanisms for organizing claims on future output; since demographic change generally affects

---

[5]The first pillar—a mandatory publicly managed pillar—would have the limited object of alleviating old age poverty and co-insuring against a multitude of risks, preferably tax-financed (therefore relying on a pay-as-you-go principle). The second pillar—a mandatory privately managed pillar—would link benefits actuarially to costs and carry out income-smoothing or saving functions for all income groups of the population and this would be financed on a fully-funded basis. Finally, the third pillar—a voluntary pillar—would include occupational and personal saving plans, providing additional protection for people who wanted more income and insurance in their old age, and would also be fully-funded (The World Bank 1994, pp. 17–19).

[6]Typical market failures in this field are information asymmetry and adverse selection, positive externalities, and consumer myopia and procrastination. To these market failures should be added the inability of private plans to address poverty issues, and to ensure both intra-generational and inter-generational redistribution. Public plans had better (proper) conditions, notably due to government involvement in addressing these problems.

that output, it generally causes problems for pension systems however they are organized".

More recently, and using a different set of arguments, the International Labour Organization (ILO 2018, p. 13) considers that in practice pension privatization did not deliver the expected results, because: (i) Coverage rates stagnated or decreased, pension benefits deteriorated and gender inequalities were compounded; (ii) The risk of financial market fluctuations was shifted to individuals; (iii) Administrative costs increased, reducing pension benefits; (iv) The high costs of transition—often underestimated—created considerable fiscal pressures; (v) Governance was weakened; (vi) Worker participation in management was eliminated; (vii) Regulatory and supervisory functions were 'captured' by the same economic groups responsible for managing the pension funds, creating a serious conflict of interest; (viii) The private insurance industry—which ultimately benefits from people's savings—moved towards concentration; (ix) Pension reforms had limited effects on capital markets and growth.

2.3   The Reforming Movement in Pension Systems from 1990s Onwards[7]

In fact, reforms in the pension systems of several OECD countries have been undertaken since the end of the 1990s, marked by certain common features. As noted by Gern (2002, p. 445), these reforms, made to adjust to the pressures of the changing economic and demographic environment, have essentially proceeded along three routes: (1) redressing public pension systems; (2) strengthening the role of funded occupational pension schemes; and (3) increasing incentives for voluntary retirement saving.

I will detail each of these routes, analysing separately, on the one hand, route (1) and, on the other hand, routes (2) and (3).

2.3.1   Redressing Public Pension Systems

Regarding the first route, many OECD countries have adopted the so-called 'parametric reforms' aiming at simultaneously enhancing sustainability and adequacy in PAYGO public systems. Amongst such reforms, the following can be highlighted: (i) Increase in the retirement age and limits or penalties to early retirement; (ii) Restricting entitlement conditions (e.g. vesting periods); (iii) From a final pay formula to a career average formula in determining the reference wage or remuneration; (iv) Changes in the calculation of pensions aiming to reduce the replacement rate; (v) Using means-testing in certain types of pensions or pension supplements;

---

[7]See, for a broad picture of pension systems reforms, Modigliani and Muralidhar (2005).

(vi) Linking pensions in formation or in payment to life expectancy; (vii) Changing indexation rules (inflation, wages or economic growth), etc.

In this regard, Fall and Bloch (2014) distinguish between reforms related either to the sustainability or to the adequacy of pension systems. With respect to the former—sustainability[8] -, the authors highlight the type of policy measures aiming at ensuring actuarial neutrality (by strictly linking pension benefits to contributions), the automatic adjustment of pension parameters (contribution rates and periods, retirement age, valorisation and indexation) to demographic and economic trends, and the creation of buffer or reserve funds (e.g. the case with the Norwegian Government Pension Fund).

With respect to the latter—adequacy of pension systems[9]—Fall and Bloch (2014, p. 24) disentangle three dimensions: (i) *Earnings-related adequacy*: this is assessed by the pension replacement rate calculated as the share of either life-time earnings or final earnings that the pension benefit replaces; (ii) *Poverty related adequacy*: this is based on the comparison of the pension level with the poverty threshold (proportion of the median income); (iii) *Safety net related adequacy*: a low pension level, in particular for retirees with low earnings during their career, implies that people will need to rely on safety-net benefits.

In a similar vein, more recently, the European Commission (2018, p. 23) has presented its 'triangle of pension adequacy', the three vertices of which are: poverty protection (i.e. the risk and depth of income poverty and severe material deprivation), income maintenance (i.e. the capacity of the system to replace earned income before retirement) and pension duration (i.e. the length of retirement).

Some countries have introduced more structural changes in their pension system. The Swedish reform of the late 1990s is presented as a paramount example, because it has replaced typical defined-benefit (DB) schemes (under the context of PAYGO systems) with an adapted version of the defined-contribution (DC) scheme—the so-called 'notional-defined contribution accounts (NDC)'. As explained by Barr and Diamond (2010, p. 161), in this innovative model, a significant part of the contribution rate is used in the NDC component, where a notional interest rate (the rate of return) equals the rate of growth of average wages. Moreover, if at any time the calculated financial balance of the system is unsatisfactory, that rate is lowered automatically. When required by the beneficiary, the initial benefit is set by a quasi-actuarial calculation based on the mortality of the worker's birth cohort, the age she/he claims the benefits, and the anticipated rate of increase in benefits. Afterwards, benefits increase is based on the difference between the notional interest rate (normally the rate of wage growth) and the (set percentage of) anticipated annual increase.

---

[8]Defined as "the ability of pension systems to meet their liabilities in the medium to long term. This can be measured by the long-term actuarial balance of the system. Sustainability implies that the discounted present value of the stream of contributions and other revenues over a long horizon is sufficient to cover projected benefits" (Fall and Bloch 2014, p. 14).

[9]Allowing for consumption smoothing over the life-cycle (Fall and Bloch 2014, p. 23).

The capacity of adjustment of this model to economic and demographic conditions is clear. At the same time, the system allows the balancing of benefits and costs across different generations (e.g. workers and retired persons), in particular the benefits and costs related to the economic business cycle and demography trends.

This very idea of risk sharing between generations drives us now to the influential contribution of Musgrave (1981). The author identified, within PAYGO systems, four basic models: (i) Fixed-replacement rate (in fact, corresponding to the DB model); (ii) Fixed-contribution rate (corresponding to the DC model); (iii) Fixed-replacement rate adjusted (DB model, with automatic adjustment mechanisms for demographic changes and economic growth, respectively through contributions and benefits); (iv) Fixed relative position (the new model proposed by Musgrave himself).

As in the fixed–replacement rate (FRR), changes in productivity and population growth leave the replacement rate unaffected, as such changes are felt in the tax or contribution rate (it falls with population and productivity growth and rises in the opposite situation). In the fixed-contribution rate (FCR), in contrast, where the tax rate is fixed, benefits and the replacement rate will rise with population and productivity growth and fall with population and productivity decline. In a fixed replacement rate adjustment (FRRA), the tax rate is invariant to productivity changes but causes it to change inversely to population. Benefits and the replacement rate, in turn, are invariant to population changes but rise and fall with productivity (Musgrave 1981, p. 100).

In periods of rapid productivity and economic growth, those that are about to retire (or already retired) will benefit more with an FRRA and with an FCR than with an FRR. Young workers will in contrast benefit more from FRR than from FRRA and FCR. In the event of economic and demographic decline, the reverse happens: those about to retire or retired persons will benefit more from an FRR than from an FCR and from an FRRA; those entering the labour force will conversely benefit more from an FCR than from an FRR and from an FRRA (*Idem*, pp. 100–101).[10]

Since there is no clear evidence as to which of the models provides a more equitable solution, the question that arises is how risks from uncertain development should be distributed (Musgrave 1981, p. 103). Musgrave's proposal (*Idem*, p. 104) is of a 'fixed relative position': this model implies maintaining the PAYGO system and the intergenerational contract which it stands for, by setting a fixed ratio of *per capita* benefits to retirees to *per capita* earnings (net of social security tax) of workers. Assuming a ratio of 0.33, the tax rate would then be adjusted as needed in response to population and productivity changes to maintain the contractual ratio.

---

[10]More recently, Fall (2014) investigated the impact of (negative) productivity, migration and longevity shocks on both DB and DC (point) schemes. None of these schemes is exempted from suffering the consequences of these shocks. For example, in the event of a negative productivity shock, unlike DB schemes that enter immediately into deficit, the DC scheme—that is balanced by nature—will project the impact of the shock in future cohorts—these will be entitled to lower pension rights. In fact, the average pension of the DC point scheme will be considerably affected as it decreases in line with the contributions received by the scheme.

Tax and benefits could hence be set each year (or eventually adjusted every 5 years) as a function of the number of retirees, the number of workers, and the fixed relative position ratio. In sum, this new model would provide for fair risk sharing between generations with regard to both population and productivity changes.[11]

2.3.2 Strengthening the Role of Funded Occupational Pension Schemes and Increasing Incentives for Voluntary Retirement Saving

The role of supplementary pensions, starting with occupational pension plans has, with few exceptions (e.g. the United Kingdom, UK) increased in Europe since the 1990s, both within Beveridgean and Bismarckian pension systems.

In the former, they were designed as a complement to the different-nature first pillar, a universal, income related and tax financed pillar (e.g. as is the case with Scandinavian countries). In the latter, they were conceived as a natural extension to the first insurance-type pillar financed by social contributions (mostly qualified as payroll taxes) and based either on the 'pay-as-you-go' principle or on a funded-type financing scheme (e.g. Belgium, Germany, and France).[12]

Despite the general trend for an increasing role for supplementary pensions (in particular for occupational plans), the development of these pensions in the EU displays a clear regional pattern (European Commission 2018, p. 80). With respect to occupational pensions, the highest level of coverage can be observed in Northern European countries, where occupational plans fulfil the key income-replacement functions in old-age and are quasi-mandatory (not imposed by law but required by industry and nation-wide collective agreements) (European Commission 2018, pp. 80–81).

As for personal pension plans, the European Commission (2018, p. 83) denotes an increasing trend and explains that "while the rise of occupational pensions is rooted in industrial relations, personal pensions have been crafted as a financial product, targeted at individuals willing and able to make additional savings for their old-age".

The main factors that have positively favoured the growth both of the coverage and the amount of the assets associated with supplementary plans (mostly held by pension funds)[13] are:

---

[11]Schokkaert and Van Parijs (2003, p. 254) entering the debate on the European pension systems' reform subscribed to Musgrave's rule qualifying it as an 'automatic stabilizer' of the PAYGO system.

[12]In this this regard, Pavolini and Seeleib-Kaiser (2016, p. 7) identify three groups of countries in terms of employees' coverage of occupational pensions: high coverage countries (Sweden and the Netherlands); medium coverage countries (the UK, Germany and Belgium); and low coverage countries (Italy, Spain and Austria).

[13]In the OECD Report *Pension Markets in Focus* (OECD 2018a, p. 5), it is mentioned that in OECD countries "the overall amount of assets has grown every year since the financial crisis (except in 2015) and is well above the 2007 precrisis level. A majority of these assets are held in pension funds

(a) *The increase in mandatory supplementary pension plans (vis-à-vis voluntary plans)*

In OECD (2018a, p. 13), it is shown that the increase in funded and private plans was higher where participation in a plan was mandatory. As an alternative to the mandatory (or quasi-mandatory) nature, the promotion of automatic enrolment (e.g. the United Kingdom, U.K. and the New Zealand) has successfully led to higher coverage rates in these countries.

(b) *The involvement and driving-role played, in some countries, by social partners, providing these plans with an additional source of legitimacy, credibility and trust*

In contrast, the erosion of the '*partneriat social*' intervention in some other EU countries (e.g. Portugal), notably with the reduction of the celebration of labour collective agreements, may add to the resistance of many workers to accept the enhancement of supplementary pension plans, through not being covered by such agreements.

(c) *Links to the first pillar, in particular, the extension of the coverage, degree of sufficiency and generosity ensured by public pension plans notably for high-income beneficiaries.*

As noted by Gern (2002, p. 444), "the relative role of occupational pensions as a source of retirement income is found to be dependent on the scale of public pension provision, especially if there is generous provision for individuals with higher income levels." Indeed, when the public pension system ensures high replacement rates notably to higher income pensioners, the use of supplementary pensions— either occupational or personal—is not taken up. "By contrast, the role for additional pillars is likely to increase, when the replacement rate of public pensions decreases strongly with rising income so that the pensions are more like flat benefits, which is the case, for example, in the Netherlands or in Switzerland" (*Idem*, p. 445). On the other hand, as regards personal pension plans (the third pillar), much of its development depends on the amount of saving that is 'forced' by the first and second pillars (*Ibidem*, p. 445).

It should also be noted that the recent reforms (notably parametric reforms) in the public pay-as-you–go systems implying either the hardening of pension entitlement

---

(USD 28.5 trillion)". The two exceptions in this period were Hungary, where average real annual growth rate was −7.5% over the last decade and Portugal, where real growth was −2.4%. In the former case, this outcome was due to the 2011 pension reform, according to which new entrants to the labour market started being enrolled in the public pay-as-you-go system and no longer in a funded pension plan, while members of the previously mandatory funded pension plans were given the choice of keeping their accounts or transferring their assets into the pay-as-you-go system. Most of the participants chose to switch back to the pay-as-you-go system, leading to a large drop in pension assets in 2011. In the latter case, the decline in pension assets can be attributed to the transfer of assets in pension funds of some of the largest banks to the public pension system in 2011 (OECD 2018a, p. 12).

conditions or the reduction of the replacement rate have provided incentives for the development of supplementary pension plans (OECD 2018b).

One can say, in fact, that generous and self-sufficient public pensions crowd out the development of private pensions plans, in a similar way to the reinforcement of private plans tending to skim public pension plans, eventually depriving them not only of ensuring concurrent goals that can also be ensured by private plans (e.g. income replacement), but also the other typical goals a public system has managed to ensure over time—e.g. income redistribution and poverty adequacy.

In contrast, certain other factors have had and can in the future have opposite effects, all depending on the sense and intensity of the driver in question. Such factors are:

(a) *The amount of disposable income, where the coverage of supplementary plans depends on the beneficiaries' incomes*

Note that low-income households do not have the capacity and willingness to pay towards pension contributions even when fiscal incentives are provided (European Commission 2018, p. 80).

(b) *The type of work or employment, considering that non-conventional forms of employment can lead to job insecurity and therefore to income variability with consequences for pension coverage and the formation of a pension claim*

Between standard situations of employment and self-employment there are the so-called 'non-standard forms of employment' (*lato sensu*), that can in turn be either 'non-standard forms of employment *stricto sensu*' (e.g. part-time work, agency work, domestic work, casual work, voucher-based work, telework and crowd-work) or 'non-standard self-employment' (e.g. bogus self-employment). Two major shifts can be foreseen in this regard: (i) Conventional employment gives way to conventional self-employment; (ii) Conventional employment gives way to non-conventional employment and self-employment.

In public pension systems this shift has consequences both concerning the entitlement conditions for benefits and the calculation of pension amounts. Non-conventional forms of employment are marked, in general terms, by contributory gaps that affect the definition of vesting periods and the formation of rights. This is obviously a major challenge (already faced by public social security systems in most EU countries) but which should be addressed within supplementary pension schemes (see *infra*).

(c) *The functioning and performance of financial markets (e.g. risk and rate of returns) and the trust or distrust people have in the behaviour of these markets*

Barr and Diamond (2010, p. 43) note that both PAYGO and funded systems face large risks that are hard to predict: economic risks, demographic risks and; political risks. Besides these common risks, the presence of funds creates additional risks (*Idem,* p. 44): (i) Management risk that can arise through incompetence or fraud and that imperfectly informed consumers cannot monitor adequately; (ii) Investment risk, meaning that pension accumulations held in stock markets until retirement are vulnerable to market fluctuations and pension accumulations held in nominal bonds are vulnerable in addition to unanticipated inflation; (iii) Longevity risk, notably in case holding assets that are not in the form of an annuity leaves the individual facing the risk of outliving his or her assets; (iv) Annuities market risk, that depends both on the person's life expectancy and on the rate of return the insurance company can expect over those years.

(d) *Policy measures, both from the fiscal side and the monetary side*

Fiscal policy side incentives can be given first and foremost through tax exemptions. In the recent study conducted by the OECD (OECD 2018b), it has been shown that half of the OECD countries apply the so-called 'Exempt-Exempt-Tax Model (EET)" to retirement savings, according to which both contributions and returns on investment are exempt from taxation, while benefits are treated as taxable income upon withdrawal.

Alternatively to this special tax treatment, non-tax incentives can also be given, which is the case with matching contributions and fixed nominal subsidies. In both cases, the government makes direct payments to the pension account of eligible individuals, thus increasing the assets accumulated to finance retirement (OECD 2018b, p. 154). Matching contributions are usually conditional on the individual contributing and correspond to a proportion of the individual's own contributions, up to a nominal ceiling (e.g. Austria). Fixed nominal subsidies are designed to attract low-income individuals as the fixed amount paid into the pension account by the government represents a higher share of their income (e.g. Germany and Lithuania) (OECD 2018b, p. 155).

As for the impact of monetary policy, it should be mentioned that the impact on pension plans and funds of the (ultra) low interest rate environment and the effects of the expansionist (conventional and non-conventional) monetary policy adopted by the central banks in the aftermath of the great financial crisis has been discussed.

The European Central Bank has engaged into a 'quantitative easing—QE' policy with the 'expanded asset purchase programme', a programme launched in 2014 and which ended in December 2018. One should be aware that the effects of QE (or in general of a monetary policy favouring low interest rates) are double-edged (through the transmission mechanism of monetary policy): on the one hand, it affects interest rates; on the other hand, it affects asset prices. In principle, low interest rates negatively affect the performance of the portfolio, but at the same time they produce a positive effect by increasing the price of assets.

To assess which of these opposite-sign effects prevail depends either on the composition of the portfolio (equities versus bills and bonds including sovereign bonds) or on the type of the plan, that is, whether the pension plan is of defined benefit (DB) or of defined contribution (DC) and, in the former case, whether it is fully or only partially funded (on this matter, for further developments, see Bank of England 2012 and Pensions Europe 2015). When the interest rate effect prevails, and in order to prevent the bankruptcy and closure of these plans, some funds may be tempted to adopt more risky investment strategies, notably to engage in a 'search-for yield' policy (OECD 2015, p. 15).

This risk, however, is minor today due to the considerable regulatory restrictions imposed on these funds. In fact, "pension funds' investments are guided by the prudent person principle and therefore have limited options to move into other, riskier, asset classes" (Pensions Europe 2015, p. 7).

(d) *The regulatory framework*

Since the great financial crisis, pension fund investment strategies have indeed become more regulated. Some investment limits on the different asset classes have been put in place (Fall and Bloch 2014, p. 20). One important condition is that private occupational plans be well-funded: DC plans should be fully funded, whereas DB plans should be submitted to minimum funding rules or other mechanisms to ensure adequate funding of pension liabilities. As also noted by Fall and Bloch (*Idem*, p. 20), the funding standard, in particular rules to avoid the underestimation of liabilities, are crucial in non-fully funded plans. In DB occupational plans, prudential ratios require the sponsors to adjust the funding in line with liabilities and the performance of the plans.

In this regard, the new role of the European Insurance and Occupational Pensions Authority (EIOPA) on prudential supervision should be mentioned, in particular with respect to the implementation of the IORPs II Directive (*Institutions for Occupational Retirement Provision*).[14]

The effects of the new regulatory framework and supervision adopted in the aftermath of the great financial crisis are two-fold: on the one hand, this new framework increases transparency in the management of pension plans and trust from beneficiaries on the good performance of the funds; on the other hand, strict demanding prudential rules can jeopardize profitable long-term investment decisions, negatively affecting the provision of these same pension plans.

2.3.3 Paradigmatic Changes in the Current Pension Plans Environment: Risk Shifting; from Social Rights to Individual Savings

In the same way a transition in PAYGO systems—the first pillar—can be perceived from typical DB plans (with fixed replacement rates) either to DC plans (with fixed-contribution rates) or to DB adjusted (fixed-replacement rates adjusted), a similar pattern occurs with occupational plans—the second pillar.

---

[14]Directive (IORP II) was adopted in 2016 (Directive (EU) 2016/2341, of the European Parliament and of the Council, of 14 December 2016), aiming to replace the IORPs I Directive (approved in 2003), and was to be transposed to national legislations by January 2019. The IORPs II Directive sets common standards ensuring the soundness of occupational pensions and better protects pension scheme members and beneficiaries, by means of among others: (i) new governance requirements, (ii) new rules on IORPs' own risk assessment, (iii) new requirements to use a depositary, and (iv) enhanced powers for supervisors.

In fact, a tendency can be denoted to favour the establishment of DC over DB plans in several OECD countries (e.g. Australia, Denmark, Switzerland, the U.K and the U.S.). This is so, allegedly, in order to make occupational pension schemes more attractive, especially for smaller firms, and to reduce the problem of portability (Gern 2002, p. 446).

This tendency has been accelerating in recent years. Indeed, traditional DB plans are losing ground in some countries (OECD 2018a, p. 21) and this is mostly linked to DB pension plan underfunding.[15] The shortfall related to the difference between assets and liabilities occurs because while contributions to DB plans have risen the fact is that liabilities have grown even more, due to changes in parameters affecting DB plans, e.g. wages, tenure and accrual rates. In particular, as regards this last issue, it can be argued that the lower the discount rates,[16] the higher the present value of future benefit payments (OECD 2018a, p. 33). Therefore, this shortfall can be seen as a form of long-term debt for employers held by employees. Consequently, "as this shortfall grows, the probability of default of plan sponsors also increases as it may be more expensive for plan sponsors to finance themselves and roll over their other debts" (OECD, *Idem*, p. 22). Moreover, apart from the risk of bankruptcy, members of the plans can suffer benefit cuts while the plan is underfunded.

Note that a shift from DB to DC pensions plans involves shifting most risks that otherwise would be borne by employers or the sponsors of the plans to employees or beneficiaries. This is so notably in the case of investment and longevity risks (on this issue, see Stevens 2017). Additionally, as noted by Boeri et al. (2006, p. 8), "the reconsideration of traditional DB plans has also led to the development of hybrid pension schemes (. . .) Such hybrid plans incorporate elements of both DB (as the sponsor makes matching contributions and often bears at least some investment or guaranteed return risk) and DC plans (as benefits are often expressed in terms of an account balance). In principle, these hybrid solutions may allow to combine the advantages of both DB and DC schemes."

Moreover, the shift from DB to DC plans is also accompanied by a shift away from occupational to personal plans (the third pillar), and to the dilution of the boundaries between these two types of plans. This might also mean the erosion of industrial/labour type of plans—based on an idea of collective risk sharing and managing—to the enhancement of personal non-professional type plans—based on the idea of individual risk provision. In this respect, the European Commission (*Idem*, p. 84) notes that in some countries the boundaries between occupational and personal plans have been lessened as employer payments to the personal plans of the

---

[15]Indeed, the aggregate funding position of DB plans has deteriorated in most reporting jurisdictions over recent years. This position was lower in 2017 (or the latest year available) than in 2007 (or the first year available) for 9 out of the 15 reporting jurisdictions. The biggest drop in the aggregate funding ratio of DB plans between 2007 and 2017 happened in the Netherlands (difference of 47 percentage points between 2007 and 2017) (OECD 2018a, p. 24).

[16]Recall the current low interest rate environment associated with the monetary policy stance that impacts short-term, but also long-term, interest rates.

respective employees are used as a component of the pay package and subject to special tax treatment (e.g. tax deduction).

In sum, in the design of pension plans in OECD countries (and in European countries in particular), one can denote the following main paradigmatic changes:

– Firstly, a shift from the idea that social protection (in the first pillar and complemented by the second pillar) is mostly made to ensure, on a collective basis, the provision of social risks and to promote social rights to an idea where the basic driver is to foster individual savings;
– Secondly, a shift from the conception of old-age benefits as pensions (that is, a right to social protection in old-age) to a 'simple' extension of wages;
– Thirdly, a shift from defined benefit to defined contribution models (also meaning a shifting of risk from employers—as sponsors of the plans—mostly to employees);
– Finally, the tendency for the erosion and eventual substitution of occupational by personal plans.

3 Two Plausible Alternatives for Pension Plan Evolution: The Individual Insurance Model Versus the Universal Tax Financed Model[17]

3.1 Two Different Alternatives, but the Same Drivers

Although the two alternatives presented below correspond to antagonistic views concerning the design of pension systems and also about the involvement of Government in social protection, the respective drivers are common and they both provide good arguments for each of these opposite paths.

The main drivers are related, on the one hand, to population ageing (a topic that entered the agenda at the end of the 1990s and remains even more vivid today) and, on the other hand, with the Fourth Industrial Revolution (the Digital and Artificial Intelligence Revolution), a new *leit motiv* that includes the debate about the future of employment and social security. One can say that, in this first quarter of century, workers feel haunted and daunted by two sides: on the one side, from senior people, on the other side, from robots.

In the influential Report of the World Economic Forum (WEF) at Davos, entitled *The Future of Jobs* (WEF 2016), the WEF warned that while technological changes are leading to the 'fourth industrial revolution' and are transforming labour markets in a completely new fashion, they will lead to a net loss of over five million jobs in

---

[17]Note that the two alternatives here now presented are hypothetical Manichaean outcomes of the evolution of current pension systems. Indeed, current systems are, in many ways, mixed solutions that could—according to this thought—evolve to become closer to one or the other of these two extreme and 'pure' models.

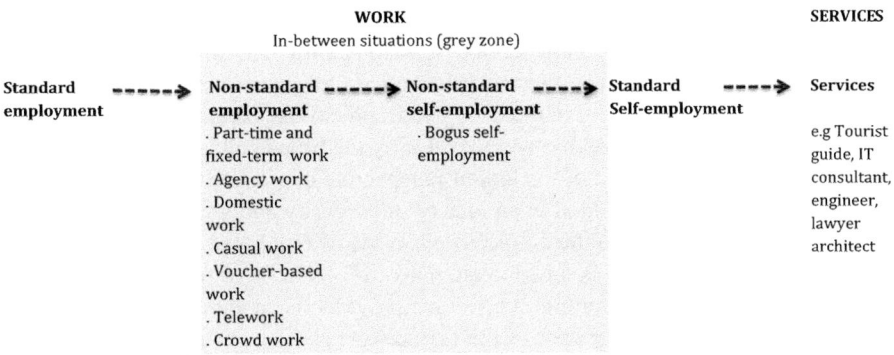

Fig. 1 A sequenced typology of forms of employment. Source: Author's own conception (2019)

15 major developed and emerging economies by 2020. Indeed, the WEF estimated that 7.1 million jobs could be lost through redundancy, automation, or disintermediation, while the creation of 2.1 million new jobs, mainly in more specialised areas such as computing, mathematics, architecture, and engineering, could partially offset some of the losses.

Moreover, this digital revolution may accentuate the on-going trend of replacement of conventional forms by non-conventional forms of employment, the main immediate consequences of which are job insecurity and the reduction of income or at least a higher variability in the achievement of work-related income.[18]

Figure 1 presents a typology of forms of employment, describing how conventional employment tends to lead the way to both non-conventional employment and eventually to self-employment (recall Sect. 2.3.2 line b). Note, in turn, that the boundaries between self-employment and services provision are quite thin, ultimately meaning that the concept of 'service' may end up encapsulating all (other) forms of work. In fact, the on-going erosion of work may lead most of the forms of employment (*lato sensu*) to be attracted (magnetized) by a new and more neutral notion of 'professional activity'. This movement may be reinforced by several factors. Firstly, the fact that labour and social security legislations become unable

---

[18]Abbott and Bogenschneider (2017) highlight the main good and bad consequences attached to the Digital (or Automation) Revolution. The good news is that automation increases productivity, which generates value and creates wealth. Moreover, automation will create jobs and replace unskilled jobs with more skilled ones. Finally, "automation may free up capital for investments in new enterprises, result in the creation of new products, or decrease production costs for existing products which may result in lower prices and thus greater consumer demand" (*Idem*, p. 10). The bad news is that automation can cause unemployment and under-employment. Furthermore, while automation generates wealth, it does so unevenly. Indeed, the gains coming from the increases in productivity may not be distributed fairly amongst groups of individuals. Moreover, automation tends to disproportionately affect lower-wage jobs and less educated workers, causing greater economic inequality. Increasing inequality can jeopardize social cohesion and foster social conflicts (*Ibidem*, pp. 11–12). For a more recent picture of the impacts of the Digital Revolution on employment and the welfare state, see Neufeind et al. (2018).

to accommodate the multiplication of these non-standard forms of employment or of self-employment. Secondly, these services tend to be provided to multiple categories of employers/clients. Thirdly, these work/services have, in many cases, a cross-border nature, therefore being marked by geographical displacement.

The replacement of 'work' by 'services' (or by the broad concept of 'professional activity') implies the erosion of the labour perspective of work, traditionally marked by protection devices embedded in an idea of job security and aiming to countervail the economic dependence of the employee vis-à-vis de employer. This new 'neutral' idea of professional activity is, in contrast, marked by a sense of functional volatility and territorial mobility, looking at the service provider as an economic independent individual vis-à-vis the contractor of the services.

For those that believe unconditionally in the benefits of a free market, this movement can be looked at as a positive shift, because it enables 'setting the work free'. In contrast, socialists and (neo)Marxists will presumably distrust the on-going movement, as it can involve the 're-commodification' of work,[19] that is, a process where work (*lato sensu*) is a precarious commodity exchanged in an unregulated market, undermining the work force.

Some possible consequences arising from the erosion of work can be anticipated: (i) Work (or better 'professional activity') conceived as intellectual property (e.g. software programmer, APP developer, technological consultant); (ii) Work considered as an intangible and highly mobile asset; (iii) The erosion and increasing volatility of the tax base, with consequences on the financing of tax systems and social security systems; (iv) The transformation of the tax and contributory base, where wages give way to a broad and diversified concept of income; (v) The increased risks of tax/contribution evasion and social dumping.

These final consequences—referring to the impact changes in work may cause on tax and social security systems (from the financing point of view)—are highlighted by Abbott and Bogenschneider (2017) when mentioning the impact of automation on work and, through it, on the obtaining of tax revenues by governments in the near future. In their opinion, this evolution may entail the significant reduction of tax revenues, and this is so because current tax systems mostly rely on incomes taxes including social security contributions. Indeed, as noted by the authors, "the bulk of taxes are currently remitted by workers either through wage withholding, income taxation of labor income, or indirect taxation of workers as consumers" (Abbott and Bogenschneider 2017, p. 6). Moreover, in the current scenario, tax systems are

---

[19]Esping-Andersen (1991, p. 21) qualifies 'de-commodifying welfare states' as those where "citizens can freely, and without potential loss of job, income, or general welfare, opt out of work when they themselves consider it necessary." In his opinion, "Beveridge-type citizens' benefit, may, at first glance, appear the most de-commodifying. It offers a basic, equal benefit to all, irrespective of prior earnings, contributions, or performance. It may indeed be a more solidaristic system, but not necessarily de-commodifying, since only rarely have such schemes been able to offer benefits of such a standard that they provide recipients with a genuine option to working" (*Idem,* pp. 19–20).

non-neutral when confronting labour taxation with capital taxation, including automation taxation—they tend to tax work more heavily than they tax capital.[20]

The substitution of labour-based employment—as we have known it so far—by a neutral concept of professional activity, volatile and uncertain, thus poses new challenges in the design of tax systems and of social security financing sources. In particular, the relevant tax base and the institution of new flexible forms of financing social protection, both from employees (service providers) and employers (service contractors) should be reconsidered.

3.2   First Alternative: The Individual Insurance Model and the Appeal of the Financial Markets

3.2.1   Characterization

In a liberalizing economic environment, the 'natural' outcome is that the second pillar (occupational pension plans) swallows the first pillar (public pension plans), and eventually that the second pillar is, in turn, also swallowed by the third pillar (personal plans).

In the context of Bismarckian countries, the first movement (the second pillar swallowing the first) is even more natural as pension plans in the first pillar also rely on an insurance approach, are labour-based and of a contributory nature, and assume income replacement as their primal goal. Recall that ancient voluntary occupational pension plans, sponsored by employers, can be seen as predecessors of Bismarckian-type social insurances, sponsored by the government. The ultimate step would hence consist of (re)transforming PAYGO public insurance schemes into funded private insurance schemes.

However, as we have seen, Beveridgean countries are also currently open to allowing an expansion of occupational pensions *pari passu* with parametric reforms implemented in the first pillar that make these less generous and self-sufficient. Recall that even in this case there is the possibility that the enlargement of such private plans be made at the cost of compression of the first pillar (a crowding out effect)—ultimately skimming this out of its fundamental resources to the extent that it is no longer able to pursue its basic functions (e.g. income redistribution and poverty adequacy).

The ultimate step of this 'individualizing movement' is that the third pillar (personal plans) swallows the second pillar. What is more, this is a tendency already verified in several countries: the shift from occupational to personal plans and the dilution of the boundaries between these two types of plans.

---

[20]In particular, as also noted, "automation allows firms to avoid employee and employer wage taxes levied by Federal, state, and local taxing authorities. It also permits firms to claim accelerated tax depreciation on capital costs for automated workers, and it creates a variety of indirect incentives for machine workers" (Abbott and Bogenschneider 2017, p. 5).

Following this, the individualizing and liberalizing path will be trodden until the end, being the right response to the sign of the times: setting work free amply justifies the substitution of industrial/labour type of plans (based on an idea of collective risk sharing and managing) by the enhancement of personal non-professional type plans (based on the idea of individual risk provision).

If the current trend involving population ageing and changes in the labour markets is accentuating this shift and leading to the prevalence of DC and fully funded occupational and personal plans, the design of the plans also faces new challenges in order to better adapt them to on-going demographic and employment changes.

In particular, the future design of such plans should consider the following issues: (i) The suppression of vesting periods (or allowing for the formation of vesting periods on the basis of intermittent working years); (ii) Different forms of contribution or insurance premia (e.g. different contribution rates or a different contribution basis) in order to adapt pensions plans to income variability during a working career; (iii) Generalization of the possibility of employers contributing to personal plans, thereby benefiting from tax incentives; (iv) The increasing coverage of low-income earners, either through the promotion of automatic enrolment or through incentives given by the government (e.g. matching contributions or fixed nominal subsidies).

In sum, the future evolution of private pensions plans may also involve the generalization of more 'tailor-made products' designed in accordance with specific life patterns and work profiles, which can eventually be redesigned as substantial changes in the beneficiary's career take place.

3.2.2   The Appeal of the Financial Markets Versus the Danger of 'Financialization'; Sustainable Finance as the Redemption of the Markets

The next question concerns which fundaments can make countries follow this individualizing and liberalizing solution. A significant part of the answer can be found in the 'appeal of the financial markets'. Efficiency arguments in favour of the deepening of the markets can also become sources of legitimacy: notably, and once again, the idea that private pension plans can foster savings, investment and economic growth (recall, in this regard, the main arguments used by The World Bank 1994).

However, the appeal of the financial markets is confronted by critics of the so-called 'financialization' of social protection. Indeed, delivering social protection to the moods of the market is gambling with a fundamental requisite of human dignity in the civilized world; moreover, 'financialization' means precisely the exacerbation of individual risk management putting at stake the basic cornerstones of the Welfare State (e.g. collective risk sharing) as it has evolved since Bismarck's foundation; eventually, 'financialization' implies skimming the welfare state, to an extent that it will no longer be able to address inequality and poverty. In short, 'financialization' means a return to untamed markets where social rights have no place.

The damaging effects of the recent financial crisis on the performance of pension plans and funds partially sustains this kind of criticism. As explained by Fall and Bloch (2014), private pension plans are exposed to investment risks as they seek to maximize investment returns. As noted, the recent crisis illustrated the considerable uncertainty and risks surrounding investment in stocks: pension funds lost 23% of their value in 2008, worth about USD 5.4 trillion.

From the point of view of the financial markets (and for all those that believe in the benefits of the markets in this field), the challenge is therefore to find new sources of justification and legitimacy for the role of the markets in pension provision. For example, in the eyes of the people, the reinforcement of regulation and supervision increases the perception of transparency, good management and accountability. More demanding regulation and supervision help to restore confidence in the markets. And in fact, since the crisis, pension fund investment strategies have become more regulated (Fall and Bloch 2014, p. 19).

Another option—probably more sophisticated and effective—consists in linking private pension plans to non-typical financing objectives, notably the promotion of environmental and human rights goals.

Departing from the UN[21] 2030 Agenda for Sustainable Development (adopted in January 2016),[22] *sustainable finance* (SF) has become fashionable. Rapidly, it has also entered the agenda of EU institutions.[23] The two main layers of SF are: (i) Environmental challenges[24] (ii) Social foundations: tackling poverty and promoting human rights.[25]

---

[21]United Nations.

[22]For further information on this, see: https://www.un.org/sustainabledevelopment/development-agenda/

[23]In the Action Plan on Financing Sustainable Growth, presented by the European Commission in March 2018, sustainable finance (SF) is defined as "the process of taking due account of environmental and social considerations in investment decision-making, leading to increased investments in longer-term and sustainable activities. More specifically, environmental considerations refer to climate change mitigation and adaptation, as well as the environment more broadly and related risks (e.g. natural disasters). Social considerations may refer to issues of inequality, inclusiveness, labour relations, investment in human capital and communities."

[24]As noted by Schoenmaker (2017, p. 12), by developing the concept of 'planet environmental boundaries' "a timely transformation towards an economy based on sustainable production and consumption, including use of renewable energy and reuse of materials, can mitigate these risks to the stability of the Earth system."

[25]Under this new approach, Schoenmaker (2017) confronts the so-called 'finance as usual', where $T = F$ (total value equal to financial value) and where only the 'shareholder value' matters, with steps towards a new approach for sustainable finance. In the first step (SF 01), associated with a 'refined shareholder value', $F > S$ and E (where F is financial value, S is social impact and E is environmental impact). In the second step (SF 02), $T = F + S + E$ and a shift from a simple shareholder value to a 'stakeholder value' occurs. Finally, in the last step, associated with a 'common good value', S and $E > F$.

SF represents a Copernican revolution in the conception of (corporate) finance that in turn begs for creativity, at least in the following areas: (i) The conception of new financial products (environmentally and human rights friendly); (ii) The definition of new portfolio composition; (iii) The development of new investment strategies.

Additionally, new challenges are posed at the policy level, in particular with respect to, on the one hand, the design of a new tax policy, favouring environmental, social and governance (ESG) goals with tax incentives and, on the other hand, new regulatory action targeted towards the pursuit of these same goals.[26]

Such policy action is supposed to be, furthermore, adequately sustained by market-driven incentives (e.g. peer pressure), involving either a new role for corporate governance, aiming to engage companies on ESG issues, or the development of new analytical tools, particularly the so-called 'societal cost-benefit analysis' (Schoenmaker 2017, pp. 42–44).

At the European Union (EU) level, the provisions regarding SF can be found in the Capital Markets Union Action Plan, and especially in the issue entitled "Investing for Long-term, Infrastructure, and Sustainable investment".

First and foremost, it should be noted that the creation of the Capital Markets Union (CMU) was one of the reform measures adopted after the great financial crisis, aiming to ensure the smooth functioning of the Economic and Monetary Union (EMU) and, in particular, the smooth functioning of the so-called private or market-driven risk-sharing mechanisms.[27] Indeed, one of the main goals of the CMU was to ensure the completion of the internal market with respect to capital mobility, allowing investors to share risks and consumers (of financial products) to experience smooth consumption. Furthermore, it was thought the CMU would address the so-called 'financial fragmentation' in the EMU allowing for the proper functioning of the transmission mechanism of the monetary policy. Moreover, it was intended to change the pattern regarding sources of financing of the economy that, in the EMU, mostly rely(ied) on banking debt instead of capital markets.

In the *Green Paper Building a Capital Markets Union* launched by the Commission in 2015, several alternatives to bank lending were suggested, notably through the development of equity or bond markets (e.g. improving access to finance, including to risk capital for small and medium enterprises, or the development of a more integrated European covered bond market for investment promotion). Ultimately, indeed, the CMU was seen as a fundamental pillar for enhancing investment and growth in the EMU.

The inclusion of SF goals was thus a subsequent step and a novel argument for the very existence of the CMU: SF goals give, indeed, a new legitimacy and a broader scope to the CMU.

---

[26]On-going regulatory actions take into account climate-related stress testing. In turn, the IORPs II Directive requires IORPs to include ESG issues as part of their governance and risk management.

[27]For a broad picture of the CMU, see Lannoo (2015)

Precisely with regard to this, in March 2018 the Commission presented its Action Plan on Financing Sustainable Growth. Key actions set out in the document include[28]: (i) EU classification system—or taxonomy—for sustainable activities; (ii) EU labels for green financial products (e.g. green bonds)[29]; (iii) Clarification of asset managers' and institutional investors' duties regarding sustainability; (iv) Strengthening the transparency of companies regarding their ESG policies; (v) A 'green supporting factor' in the EU prudential rules for banks and insurance companies.

The ultimate, while natural consequence of this development, is linking a particular segment of financial markets—pension funds and other managing institutions of pension plans—to the new ESG goals. The purpose is double-fold: (i) Firstly, to use (supplementary) pension plans and pension funds as instruments of the CMU, therefore meant to be linked to a strategy of savings promotion, investment and growth; (ii) Secondly, to give potential 'consumers' of these supplementary pension plans a new source of legitimacy and trust, by relating the respective investment strategy to 'good-will' and to new 'ethical ground', as this involves the promotion of ESG goals.

In sum, sustainable finance implies the redemption of the markets.

3.3 Second Alternative: The Universal Tax Financed Model

3.3.1 Characterization

Even if a universal tax financed model can coexist with private supplementary pensions, the question is rather which force prevails. As we have seen before, a universal tax financed system (in the context of typical Beveridgean countries) can also shrink at the cost of expansion of the second and third pillars. Alternatively, it can maintain its significant magnitude and then private schemes will keep their residual nature.

I will now analyse this second hypothesis. After all, the 'natural outcome' for Beveridgean type systems, in an environment of Government intervention, is to replace all insurance-type benefits (with a function of income replacement) by universal-type benefits, eventually delinking such benefits from the beneficiary's

---

[28]For information on this, see: https://ec.europa.eu/info/business-economy-euro/banking-and finance/sustainable-finance_en.

[29]See, in this regard, the European Commission *Study On the Potential of Green Bond Finance for Resource-Efficient Investments*. In this study, a green bond is considered "differentiated from a regular bond by its label, which signifies a commitment to exclusively use the funds raised to finance or re-finance 'green' projects, assets or business activities" (European Commission 2016, p. 8).

past registered incomes (or at least mitigating those links).[30] From the financing point of view, a universal type model primarily uses taxes instead of contributions.[31]

As noted by the European Commission (2015, p. 9), social protection system can be financed in two major ways: through social contributions or general government contributions. The latter can in turn be divided into earmarked taxes (the proceeds from taxes and levies which, by law, can be only used to finance social protection)[32] and general revenue (general government contributions from sources other than earmarked taxes).

Moreover, a tendency for shifting from contributions to taxes in social security financing has increased in recent years (European Commission 2015, p. 19), and the financial crisis may again have played a role in this change. Indeed, as also mentioned, "this overall shift from social contributions to general taxation especially in the crisis years 2007–2011 may, to a large extent, reflect the role of social protection systems as automatic stabilisers triggered by the economic downturn and decreasing employment (and hence social contributions), but could also reflect deliberate policy choices" (European Commission 2015, p. 21).

---

[30]The cases of the Netherlands and New Zealand (traditional Beveridgean countries) are illustrative in this matter (see Barr and Diamond 2010, p. 152 and p. 154, respectively). In the former case, a non-contributory pension is paid corresponding to 70% of the net minimum wage payable at age 65. This benefit is awarded on the basis of residence not past contributions, and depends on the number of years of residence in the country. In the latter, where the basis of the system is a non-contributory pension (New Zealand Superannuation) paid from general taxation to all persons over 65 who pass residency test and included in a person's taxable income. The pension is approx. 70% of the net average wage for a married couple, more per person for singles, and less if one of the couple is under 65.

[31]Social contributions designed in many countries as 'payroll taxes' (see the case of the U.S.) are based on a *principle of equivalence* (they are bilateral taxes), giving the beneficiary a legal right to a benefit that presents a link to the amounts paid throughout the entire contributory life. In contrast, 'general' taxes solely based on the *principle of ability to pay* do not present any link with a past tax record (they are unilateral taxes)—ultimately the benefits amount can be chosen by the government according to other criteria than past incomes/wages (recall the examples of the Netherlands and New Zealand). In redistributive programmes, those that pay more during their working life are not necessarily entitled to a higher amount; poor beneficiaries can receive more in relative terms. Therefore, the advantage of the contributory model is that it provides a legal entitlement to a pension and so pensions (and the respective amount) can ultimately be claimed before a judicial court. The same does not happen, in principle, with the tax model. The disadvantage of the contributory model happens on distributional grounds: payroll taxes typically have a regressive nature, because they do not have a relationship with ability to pay, there are no exemptions for low-income earners, there is no allowance for family size, and a flat rate is applied (Musgrave 1981, p. 110). In contrast, taxes allow for redistribution, as they rely on the ability to pay principle, provide for exemptions, and taken into consideration the size of the family and respective expenditures.

[32]Examples of earmarked taxes are certain excise or sales taxes (related for example with consumption of alcohol or tobacco), real estate taxes and taxes on high-valued assets (e.g. 'fortune taxes'), or even specific taxes made to be allocated to certain social benefits and that can have a narrower or a broader tax base (e.g. the French *contribution sociale généralisée*).

The same tendency is confirmed with respect to old-age pension schemes, where a shift occurred from social contributions (−6.5 percentage points—pp.) and in particular those paid by the employers (−5.5 pp.), towards general revenues (+6.7 pp.) (*Ibidem,* p. 22).

It can be stressed, in turn, that as contributory schemes are based on an equivalence principle (bilateralism) they also tend to attract—as a financing technique—the funding solution. Indeed, they involve a long-term commitment to a certain amount or at least to a quantitative benchmark that sustains that entitlement,[33] to which funding schemes—either DB or DC—are *naturally* more adapted.

In turn, in the same way that contributory-type systems tend to attract funding techniques, tax financed systems also attract pay-as-you-go. Indeed, an expenditure scheme financed by taxes is by nature a PAYGO scheme. In this case, the payment of expenditures (with old-age benefits) is no longer perceived as a long-term commitment but is rather viewed as a current expenditure to be paid, at any moment, by the current stream of tax revenues collected in each year. For this reason, the very concept of long-term commitment, and ultimately the concept of 'implicit' debt[34] becomes less interesting in a PAYGO tax system, simply because there is no legal commitment relating past contributions to the entitlement of benefits. Ultimately, the Government can legally modulate the amount of benefits (or to give and withdrew some of them), according to its own conditions, beginning with the existence of fiscal space or budget possibilities. For this reason, within a negative prospective, the (apparent) accounting relief that underlies a PAYGO tax system may be obtained at the cost of (future) less generous benefits.

It can be stressed, in turn, that the enhancement of the universal-redistributive perspective may after all imply, notably for high and medium incomes, less generous social benefits. Redistribution is in this case an argument for more moderate amounts of pensions. So, universal-type models, although relying on a social rights perspective, may be forced to compress those same social rights and to moderate the generosity of the system, notably to better address the costs of ageing.

Moreover, it can also be sustained that a purely financed tax model is even more adequate to a Musgravian type solution—the fixed relative position (*supra* Sect. 2.3.1)—whereby, in order to maintain a fixed ratio of *per capita* benefits to retirees to *per capita* earnings of workers, pensions can be, in each moment, modulated for example in function of the net average wage (recall the New Zealand Superannuation), which in turn should depend on economic growth and productivity. In this context of a universal-type model, this would be achieved by delinking pensions from each worker's past contributory record and adjusting, in each year, the amount

---

[33]As is, for example, the last wage or an average wage considering a certain period of time.

[34]The adjective 'implicit' was coined for this non-financial debt aiming at evaluating the long-term sustainability of first pillar PAYGO schemes: it involves an intergenerational accounting perspective, that implies estimating, in a given year, the current value of future taxes that, on average, each individual will have to pay less the current value of future transfers she/he will obtain.

of pensions paid by the system (with an upper limit by nature), in order to keep constant the ratio between different generations' incomes.

3.3.2 Universal Basic Income as an Exacerbation of the Universal Tax Financed Model

Although some Bismarckian countries have recently accentuated this shift from contributory financing to tax financing (e.g. France and Belgium), the deepening of tax financing is *naturally* more evident in Beveridgean countries (e.g. Denmark, the Netherlands and Sweden).[35]

Beveridgean countries are indeed the current, while mitigated, version of the universal tax financed model and a proper antechamber of the extreme version of the model, the so-called *Universal Basic Income* (UBI). This radical proposal—in the words of Van Parijs and Vanderborght (2017)—intents to be a step ahead of the existing Beveridgean world: benefits (including old-age beneficiaries) would be provided on a universal and unconditional basis, that is, not depending either on means testing or on activity testing. They would hence be universal (in the proper sense of the word), individual (not household targeted), and obligation free.

The proposal that has been criticised on the grounds of efficiency (e.g. negative incentives for work), equality (e.g. all citizens would be entitled to a fixed amount regardless of their economic status), adequacy (e.g. the risk of UBI being of an insufficient amount) and financial feasibility (e.g. how to sustain the scheme, through which taxes and under which tax effort)[36] is, however, justified by its defendants (in the first place by Van Parijs himself) with the main argument of setting society free by setting work free—free from the economic need that comes from wages. In fact, this is the ultimate version of an idea of the de-commoditization of work, that is, of delinking social rights from work. In an ageing digital society, where, as we have seen, non-conventional forms of employment (work leading to 'services' or 'professional activities') and job insecurity tend to prevail, the UBI would be a proper societal answer, also implying a major redesign of the welfare state.

Moreover, this model implies a complete cut with the contributory-financing scheme, because financing the UBI would not be dependent on wages and on past working life. It would be thus an exclusive tax-financed scheme. The available options within the menu of existing taxes in each country are of different types. The most referred to involve using the existing set of personal, corporate, and consumption taxes (including Value-Added Tax), but they also point to the creation of new types of taxes, including the taxation of natural resources, climate and energy, financial transactions (e.g. the Tobin tax) and fortune (e.g. the Piketty tax).[37]

---

[35]See European Commission (2015, p. 12).

[36]These criticisms are detailed and addressed by Van Parijs and Vanderborght (2017).

[37]Regarding these various proposals, see again Van Parijs and Vanderborght (2017).

Additionally, automation, digital operations and the virtual world can foster the definition of new tax principles, new tax bases and new taxpayers. Therefore, digital operations can lead to a shift from the origin principle in taxation to the destination principle (notably in corporate taxation) and to other measures to avoid the so-called Base Erosion and Profit Shifting (BEPS) (OECD 2013). Automation (especially when involving smart robots) can eventually lead to the rise of new taxes—the *Robot Tax*—where, in a pure version, the taxation is ascribed not directly (only indirectly) to the owner of the Robot.[38] This leads eventually to the conceiving of robots as a legal and autonomous centre of imputation of rights and liabilities, becoming therefore a new taxable 'person' (on the implications and design of this revolutionary solution, see Abbott and Bogenschneider 2017).[39]

In sum, in this exacerbated version of the tax-financed model—in the context of a *futuristic* digital world—taxing robots may definitely be used to finance human basic incomes.

4 The Redesign of the Welfare of State and the Role of the European Union: Which Path to Be Chosen?

As I have written elsewhere (da Costa Cabral 2017), the European project, unlike that which happened with respect to monetary and fiscal ingredients, has jeopardized the social dimension of the integration process—partially under the argument that it was a domain of the principle of subsidiarity.

As I noted then (*Idem, 2017*), since its inception (in the European treaties) social policy has always been considered a pretext either to accomplish or to prevent other economic or fiscal goals: firstly, social policy was considered a positive instrument for the creation of the internal market; secondly, it was implicitly deemed to have a negative impact on fiscal discipline and sustainability. Since the Maastricht Treaty, priority has been given to price stability and nominal convergence to the detriment of the pursuance of full employment and social inclusion.

Moreover, the effects of ageing, globalization and technological revolution on labour markets and on social rights were not sufficiently acknowledged by European institutions and legal frameworks. The Lisbon Strategy launched in 2000 was a first attempt to undertake that recognition, yet in an incomplete manner due to its restrictive scope and method—the open method of coordination, OMC—restricting social policy to soft law (Anderson 2015, 31).

---

[38]The immediate question is who is the owner of the Robot? The capital owner? The I.T. expert, the technical engineer with capacity to 'control and stop' the device? Who?

[39]An interesting technical issue regarding the design of this tax would be the choice of the tax base: Wage? Capital? Or a new tax base? If so, which measure to be used? Marginal or total robot productivity as a determinant measure? Or instead average wages or the wage of the replaced worker as a proxy for the robot wage?

The relative disregard of social policy has also favoured democratic erosion in the EU. In fact, the sense of belonging to a community and social inclusion has weakened (Anderson, *idem,* 215), and Europe has eventually become a landscape for a new social group, the 'globalization losers'—that the recent crisis has simply exposed.[40]

With the crisis, EU institutions showed themselves not prepared to support fragile countries facing increasing poverty and inequality, related to the rise in unemployment and to the retrenchment of national Welfare States due to the austerity measures. Besides this, it should be recalled that the fiscal framework imposed on Member Countries (e.g. the Stability and Growth Pact—SGP), while being cyclically adjusted, was/is not capable of capturing the social impact of macroeconomic shocks. Furthermore, notably for southern peripheral countries (with incomplete welfare states), the contradiction between different policy goals was reinforced during the adjustment process: on the one hand, the need to effectively enhance social rights; on the other hand, the need to accomplish fiscal objectives established in the aforementioned European framework—the latter possibly implying not just a temporary, but a permanent retrenchment of those same social rights (da Costa Cabral 2017).

The question is whether recent austerity can be seen as a radical break with the previous Europe tradition in social policies (the so-called 'European social model') or if it just meant the intensification of existing policy trends—the process of the disintegration of welfare states that had started at the end of the 1970s (see O'Cinneide 2014, p. 186). Indeed, for this same author, European social policy and the social model have become an increasingly faded dream (*Idem,* p. 200), a simple rhetorical feature entirely disconnected with reality (*Ibidem,* p. 170). And the reality is the increasing subservience of social policies to the imperatives of economic integration and macroeconomic stability that the crisis has only exacerbated (*Ibidem,* p. 186). In particular, it can be added, "the rhetorical commitment of European States to the concept of a 'social Europe' is not backed up by any firm legal standards at either national of the pan-European level" (O'Cinneide 2014, p. 193).[41]

The proclamation by President Juncker in November 2017 of the *European pillar of social rights* seemed to be an ambitious point of departure for a new strategy involving social protection in Europe—what I call a *social rights-centred strategy.* However, its contents are vague.[42] The 20 principles structured around three

---

[40]The Brexit decision has so far been the most significant political consequence of this ineffective integration, as a majority of people considered that the EU was no longer able to correspond to their prospects regarding well-being and safety (on the causes and consequences of Brexit, see da Costa Cabral et al. 2017).

[41]Also, regarding the impact of the crisis on social rights, see Hemerijck (2013) and Anderson (2015).

[42]Information available here: https://ec.europa.eu/commission/priorities/deeper-and-fairer-eco nomic-and-monetary-union/european-pillar-social-rights/european-pillar-social-rights-20-princi ples_en

categories (Equal opportunities and access to the labour market, Fair working conditions and Social protection and inclusion) appear as a mere 'letter of intent' with no prescriptions, timelines or effective measures added. What is more, no significant steps have been taken since then.

5 Concluding Remark

In sum, so far in the EU, there have not been significant developments towards a *social rights-centred strategy*.

In contrast, since the crisis significant steps were made—as we have seen above—in the development of a *(financial) markets-centred strategy*, as was the launching and immediate implementation of the Capital Markets Union. Major moves were made in this domain. An illustration, relevant for our purposes, is the recent creation of the *Pan-European Pension Product* (PEPP), the main goals of which are to improve cross-border access and strengthen the single market in personal private pensions, improving coverage and take-up with appropriate security of savings.[43]

In this recent political initiative, a social rights perspective is given a minor role. The emphasis is on the predominance of (financial) markets in regard to pension provision: after all, this seems to be the path to be chosen.

References

Abbott R, Bogenschneider BN (2017) Should robots pay taxes? Tax policy in the age of automation. Harv Law Policy Rev. Forthcoming. Available at SSRN: https://ssrn.com/abstract=2932483

Anderson KM (2015) Social policy in the European Union. Palgrave Macmillan, Basingstoke

Barr N, Diamond P (2010) Pension reform – a short guide. Oxford University Press, New York

Beveridge W (1942) Social insurance and allied services. http://news.bbc.co.uk/2/shared/bsp/hi/pdfs/19_07_05_beveridge.pdf

Boeri T et al (2006) Dealing with the new giants: rethinking the role of pension funds, Geneva Reports on the World Economy 8. International Center for Monetary and Banking Studies (ICMB), Geneva

da Costa Cabral N (2017) Europe will be (re)formed by social rights, or it will be not (re)formed at all. https://www.palgrave.com/gp/palgrave/campaigns/changing-europe/europe-will-be-reformed-by-social-rights

da Costa Cabral N et al (2017) After Brexit – consequences for the European Union. Palgrave Macmillan, Basingstoke

EBRI (1990) Fundamentals of employee benefit programs. Employee Benefit Research Institute, Washington, DC

---

[43]For further information, see: https://www.consilium.europa.eu/en/press/press-releases/2018/06/19/pensions-council-agrees-its-stance-on-pan-european-pension-product/pdf

Esping-Andersen G (1991) The three worlds of welfare capitalism. Princeton University Press, Princeton, NJ

European Commission (2015) Social protection systems in the EU: financing arrangements and the effectiveness and efficiency of resource allocation. EU, Luxembourg

European Commission (2016) Study on the potential of green bond finance for resource-efficient investments. http://ec.europa.eu/environment/enveco/pdf/potential-green-bond.pdf

European Commission (2018) Current and future income adequacy in old-age in the EU, Pension Adequacy Report 2018, volume I, Brussels

Fall F (2014) Comparing the robustness of PAYG pension schemes. OECD Department Working Papers, No. 1134

Fall F, Bloch D (2014) Overcoming vulnerabilities of pension systems. OECD Department Working Papers, No. 1133

Gern K-J (2002) Recent developments in old age pension systems – an international overview. In: Feldstein M, Siebert H (eds) Social security pension reform in Europe. University of Chicago Press, Chicago, IL, pp 439–478

Hemerijck A (2013) Changing welfare states. Oxford University Press, Oxford

ILO (2018) Reversing pensions privatization – rebuilding public systems in Eastern Europe and Latin America, International Labour Organization

Lannoo K (2015) Which union for Europe's capital markets? CEPS, ECMI Policy Brief No. 22/2015. https://www.ceps.eu/publications/which-union-europe%E2%80%99s-capital-markets

Modigliani F, Muralidhar A (2005) Rethinking pension reform. Cambridge University Press, New York

Musgrave RA (1981) A reappraisal of financing social security. In: Skidmore F (ed) Social security financing. The MIT Press, Cambridge, pp 89–120

Neufeind M et al (eds) (2018) Work in the digital era – challenges of the fourth industrial revolution. Rowman and Littlefield, London

O'Cinneide C (2014) Austerity and the faded dream of a 'social Europe. In: Nolan A (ed) Economic and social rights after the great financial crisis. Cambridge University Press, Cambridge, pp 169–201

OECD (2013) Action plan on base erosion and profit shifting. https://www.oecd.org/ctp/BEPSActionPlan.pdf

OECD (2015) Pension markets in focus. http://www.oecd.org/daf/fin/private-pensions/Pension-Markets-in-Focus-2015.pdf

OECD (2018a) Pension markets in focus. http://www.oecd.org/daf/fin/private-pensions/Pension-Markets-in-Focus-2018.pdf

OECD (2018b) Financial incentives and retirement savings. http://www.oecd.org/finance/financial-incentives-retirement-savings.htm

Pavolini E, Seeleib-Kaiser M (2016) Comparing occupational welfare in Europe: the case of occupational pensions, OSE Paper series, No. 30, October 2016

Pensions Europe (2015) Pensions Europe paper on the effects of quantitative easing on pension funds. https://www.pensionseurope.eu/system/files/PensionsEurope%20Paper%20on%20Quantitative%20Easing%20-%2024-04-2015_0.pdf

Schoenmaker D (2017) From risk to opportunity: a framework for sustainable finance. Rotterdam School of Management, Erasmus University, Rotterdam

Schokkaert E, Van Parijs P (2003) Social justice and the reform of Europe's pension systems. J Eur Soc Policy 13(3):245–279

Stevens Y (2017) The silent pension pillar implosion. Eur J Soc Secur 19(2):98–117

The Bank of England (2012) The distributional effects of asset purchases. https://www.bankofengland.co.uk/-/media/boe/files/news/2012/july/the-distributional-effects-of-asset-purchases-paper

The World Bank (1994) Averting the old-age crisis – policies to protect the old and promote growth. Washington, The World Bank

Van Parijs P, Vanderborght Y (2017) Basic income – a radical proposal for a free society and a sane economy. Harvard University Press, Cambridge

WEF (2016) The future of jobs employment, skills and workforce strategy for the fourth industrial revolution. http://www3.weforum.org/docs/WEF_Future_of_Jobs.pdf

Nazaré da Costa Cabral holds a license degree (1994), a Masters (1998), and a PhD (2007) in law, from Lisbon School of Law (Faculdade de Direito, Universidade de Lisboa), and she holds a license degree in economics (2015), from Nova SBE—School of Business and Economics (Universidade Nova de Lisboa).

Nazaré is Associate Professor in tenure, in Lisbon School of Law.

She also lectures in other Universities, either in Portugal or abroad.

Nazaré is principal researcher of the Center for European, Economic, Fiscal and Tax Law Research (CIDEFF) of Lisbon School of Law (Group IV on 'Crises, Public Policies, Fiscal Policy and the Euro'). She is also a member of the Board of 'Instituto de Direito Económico, Financeiro e Fiscal' (IDEFF), of the same School, in which she also lectures. Nazaré is vice-president of the journal Revista de Finanças Públicas e Direito Fiscal (Public Finances and Tax Law Journal), published by IDEFF and Almedina Editors. She is also a member of the Executive and Editorial Board of the journal Concorrência & Regulação (Competition & Regulation), published by The Portuguese Competition Authority, IDEFF and Almedina Editors, and a member of the Editorial Board of the journal Economia & Segurança Social (Economics & Social Security), published by Diário de Bordo Editores.

Nazaré is author of several books, articles and working papers, and her research areas are mainly on Public Finances, Economic and Monetary Union, and Social Security.

Professional experience:

2019—Appointed by the Portuguese Government as Chair of the Senior Board of the Portuguese Public Finance Council.

2018—Appointed as a member of High-level Group of Experts on Pensions, by the Director-General for Employment, Social Affairs and Inclusion and the Director-General for Financial Stability, Financial Services and Capital Markets Union (under Commission decision C(2017) 8523 of 18.12.2017 setting up a High-level group of experts on pensions).

2018—National expert at the EU project MoveS ('Network of independent experts in the fields of free movement of workers (FMW) and social security coordination").

2015–2017—National expert at the EU project FreSsco ('Network of Experts on Intra-EU Mobility—Free Movement of Workers and Social Security Coordination').

2015–2016—National expert at the EU project, developed by a scientific consortium led by CEPS (Centre for European Policy Studies) to the European Commission, and entitled 'National feasibility assessment of the different European unemployment benefit scheme options'.

2014—Appointed by the Ministry of State and Finance to integrate the Working Group charged with the reform of the Portuguese 'Budget Framework Law'.

1997–2002 and 2005–2007—Legal adviser in the Labor and Social Security Minister and Secretary of State Offices.

From Paris to Lisbon: The Ever-Changing European Social Policy Landscape

Pedro Adão e Silva and Patrícia Cadeiras

Abstract Since the early days of European integration, social policies have been a particularly contentious field. This was due, to an important extent, to the combined effect of the resilience of national welfare states and the idiosyncratic nature of the integration process. It was this context that led to the development of a specific pattern of social policies at the European level, characterised by the coexistence of different methods of governance. This chapter will reflect on the European repertoire of social policies, their distinctive features and how they have evolved over time. It will end with a discussion of how Europe, de facto, influences domestic social policies, as well as the challenges facing further developments in this policy field.

1 European Social Model(s)

For decades, social policies have been the monopoly of domestic institutions and have taken root deep within the borders of nation states. This trend resulted from the interconnection between the processes of State formation, democratisation and the development of the welfare state (Flora 1986; Baldwin 1990) and led to social policies being associated with demarcated territories and closed structures. Thus, during the twentieth century, the European nation state was transformed into a welfare state, albeit with different characteristics. However, a number of external factors have contributed to a slow but profound process of denationalisation of social policies, reducing domestic sovereignty over regulatory (more) and redistributive (less) policies. Among other factors, globalisation (Sykes et al. 2001) and European integration have been responsible for redesigning the conditions that shaped public policies and, consequently, the welfare state. In recent decades, European welfare

P. A. e. Silva (✉)
Department of Political Science and Public Policy, ISCTE-IUL, Lisbon, Portugal

P. Cadeiras
Ministry for Foreign Affairs, Lisbon, Portugal
e-mail: patricia.cadeiras@mne.pt

© Springer Nature Switzerland AG 2019
N. da Costa Cabral, N. Cunha Rodrigues (eds.), *The Future of Pension Plans in the EU Internal Market*, Financial and Monetary Policy Studies 48,
https://doi.org/10.1007/978-3-030-29497-7_15

states have witnessed an erosion of their borders and, simultaneously, have seen their capacity to prevent the intervention of external institutions in their policies diminished (Ferrera 2005).

The term 'European social model' is often used in public debate, albeit with different political meanings. While some see it as a positive and distinctive European feature when compared with other political and economic zones, there are also those who blame this model for the difficulties in adjusting European political economies. Beyond the political rhetoric, however, there is also the whole range of European social policies, which make up a much more complex reality.

Diversity is the strongest distinguishing feature of member states' social policies. Although there are common principles, shared by all member countries, the former manifest themselves in different ways, both institutionally and politically. This diversity has led several authors to identify important differences in European political economies, with consequences for the way in which well-being is produced (Esping-Andersen 1990; Ferrera 1996; Goodin et al. 1999; Adão e Silva 2002; Guillén and Palier 2004).

This diversity in the institutional organisation and political principles in which domestic social policies are embedded has, in itself, represented a major obstacle to the objectives of harmonisation and/or convergence of social policy at European level. After more than 60 years of integration, the essence of the social areas continues to be controlled by nation-states, to an important extent because the processes of state formation and the consolidation of democracies are intertwined with the development of social policies (Flora 1986; Baldwin 1990).

These national-based obstacles were, however, accentuated by the initial choices of the integration process. During the founding period of the Union, the objective was to build an economic community, tempered by some political integration, in order to guarantee peace. In addition to some timid attempts to respond to a threat of 'social dumping', the social dimensions present in the Treaties were limited to the removal of obstacles to the creation of the single market. Hence, the first social policy initiatives addressed the functional requirements arising from economic integration and the implementation of the four freedoms (Geyer 2000; Hantrais 1995; Kleinman 2002).

This side-lining of the social dimension in the integration process has, in fact, been reflected in the Treaties, making it possible to speak of a 'constitutional asymmetry' between, for example, the type of majorities needed for social integration, when compared with those on which economic integration rested.

Although most of the initial obstacles remain, preventing us from talking about a shared and integrated 'European model' (as in the case of monetary or agricultural policies) (see the volume edited by Wallace et al. (2014)), European social policy no longer occupies the status of 'Cinderella', where good intentions and great principles coexisted with little action.[1] Although social policy continues, in essential aspects,

---

[1] Lange has rightly defined European social policy as a history of "good intentions, high principles and little action" (Lange 2016).

to be the sovereign competence of member states, this domestic bond coexists today with a complex European system at various levels, that has progressively transformed the welfare states from sovereign entities into semi-sovereign entities (Leibfried and Pierson 2000). One of the decisive aspects of this new policy entity is that, contrary to what happened in domestic welfare states, the essential nature of its competences is regulatory and not redistributive (Majone 1996; Wincott 2003). Furthermore, its action focused on working conditions, gender equality and safety and health at the workplace, thus side-lining what were traditionally the central aspects of domestic social policies (e.g. income and employment replacement benefits).

2   From Paris to Rome

European social policy can be seen as an area where initial choices have placed significant constraints on subsequent developments. Since the beginning of the integration process, social policies have played a legitimising role in economic and political integration, showing little autonomy towards these policy fields. As it is recognised, the central objective of the founders was economic integration, with some mild political integration. This objective was based on the neoclassical economic principle, according to which the expansion of economic integration beyond the borders of the nation-state would necessarily lead to an improvement in economic efficiency (Geyer 2000: 21). The founding treaties reflected the pro-market inclination. Both the Treaty of Paris (1951)—which constituted the European Coal and Steel Community—and the Treaty of Rome (1957)—which constituted the European Economic Community—are paradigmatic of the low priority given to social dimensions. In general terms, the dominant tone rested on the idea that social policies would be a functional spill-over, resulting from the deepening of economic integration.

In the Treaty of Paris, the social dimensions were closely linked to the impact of structural changes on the industrial sectors that would be integrated. This led to the regulation of some aspects of labour in these sectors (Hantrais 1995: 1–3; Kleinman 2002: 84). Although the limited character of the first wave of integration and the secondary role attributed to social policies in this process, two political ambitions in the social field were part of the Treaty of Paris: 'social harmonisation' and 'social improvement'. The Treaty of Paris, although it did not grant extended competences or create adequate instruments in the social field, was an important step insofar as it settled the framework for the future European social policy (Geyer 2000: 24). In fact, a broad interpretation of the Treaty has made it possible to maintain that the Community had a significant mandate in the social field. However, the lack of material resources and policy instruments made social policy essentially dependent on intergovernmental cooperation.

The first few years of integration were characterised by an atmosphere of enthusiasm and satisfaction with the success of the initial steps in building an economic community. It was therefore unsurprising that after a short time member states began discussing plans to move from an integrated market for the coal and steel sectors towards deeper economic integration. This was the main ambition of the Treaty of Rome and although the harmonisation of social systems was explicitly mentioned in the Treaty, once again member states proved unable to specify either the objectives or the instruments to achieve the defined objective. Moreover, in some respects, it can even be said that the Treaty of Paris paid greater attention to social aspects than the Treaty of Rome (Hantrais 1995: 2). In any case, the foundations were laid for the development of a set of policies that, over a long period of time, would be based on a cautious and not very broad-spectrum platform.

3 The Seventies and the First Social Action Program

Considering the two decades between the Treaty of Paris (1951) and the first enlargement of the European Economic Community (1973) as the first period of European social policy, it is possible to identify some dominant themes, as well as the most used modes of governance and policy instruments.

First of all, this period coincided with a frank expansion of nationally based welfare states, based on a broad political consensus between social-democratic and Christian-democratic parties. This expansion took place in a context of economic growth, managed with Keynesian macroeconomic policies, focused on the expansion of aggregate demand, which would become known as the 'glorious 30 years'. Secondly, at the European level, within the framework of the transition to the common market, social policies aimed at dealing with problems posed by the free movement of workers (for example, the social protection mechanisms of migrant workers) and the harmonisation of working conditions (namely those related to health and safety at the workplace). Thirdly, policies were implemented through a process that was seen as automatic and that would inevitably lead to some form of institutional convergence—by virtue of the similarities between welfare states, all of which were part of the corporatist model. By that time, the European social fund was launched, and a set of policy instruments had acquired relevance.[2]

---

[2]Following articles 123-8 of the Treaty, the ESF was instituted in 1960. From the outset, the ESF had two main purposes: retraining and resettlement. On paper, the ESF created a common obligation to support and improve employment opportunities, encourage work force's mobility and develop vocational training. Hence, the linkage between European social policies and labour market functioning was reinforced, as the main areas of the fund were yet again labour-oriented. Nevertheless, contrary to its stated purposes, fighting unemployment was not a relevant aim of the fund. The fund's activity concentrated on promoting mobility to compensate for regional and sectoral labour shortages (e.g. from Southern Italy to Germany and France's industrial areas). However, financial resources allocated to the fund and, overall, to social dimensions were small, namely when compared with agricultural common policy.

The harmonization of policies—and even convergence—was seen as a goal that was at once achievable and that would tend to occur automatically.

However, from the end of the 1960s onwards, a period of scepticism about the integration of social policies began. This new context was not independent of the stage of European integration itself, in which a series of conflicts between the Commission and the Council culminated, in 1967, in the 'empty chair' period. For a year, France would refuse to take its place in the Council, blocking intergovernmental decisions. Also, at the domestic level, debates on the crisis of the welfare state gained ground, largely because of the signs of economic cooling that would culminate in the oil shock of the early 1970s.

Paradoxically, this context promoted the development of common social policies with a harmonizing tone. The pace of market integration, together with economic instability, forced the Community to pay greater attention to the social dimension, namely as a way to cushion the impact of economic integration.[3] In 1974, revealing a growing awareness of the importance of adopting common responses to the social question, the Council would stress that "economic expansion is not an end in itself, but should result in an improvement in quality, as well as in standards of living" (Council Resolution 1974).

The willingness to accommodate the impact of economic integration, combined with the need to answer some functional requirements created by that process, enabled some developments in European social policy. Even considering the difficulties caused by the 'joint decision trap' (Scharpf 1988), there was some supranational harmonisation. The option fell on legal instruments of a binding nature, in two areas where the Treaties conferred specific competences to the supranational level: coordination of social security systems and free movement of workers.

It was within this framework that the first 'social action programme' was approved (1974). Although its objectives have never been fully achieved, this programme established the guidelines that would shape European social policy for more than a decade. The 'social action programme' was designed with three fundamental aims: more and better employment; improved working conditions; and greater participation of workers in companies. The 'programme' was organised around 35 concrete proposals for action, which had to be discussed and approved individually by the Council. Even so, it was stressed that although the common social policy had a special role to play, it should not seek standardized solutions to all social problems or try to transfer to the community level responsibilities that would be more effectively assumed at other levels (Council Resolution 1974). Once again, the Council's vision of common competences in social areas was cautiously presented, announcing the principle of subsidiarity that would become prominent in European social policy over a long period (Geyer 2000: 36; Hantrais 1995: 4; Kleinman 2002: 85).

---

[3]In this respect, the role of the Council of Europe, which in 1961 adopted the "Social Charter", which put additional pressure on the Community to move forward in the social areas as well, should not be neglected.

The Council resolution expressed the political will to adopt the necessary measures, the problem was that, once again, neither the resources nor the instruments necessary for intervention were made available.[4] Consequently, further action depended on cooperation among member states and should be based on political commitments and not on legal instruments. This option would prove to be a very difficult task, which would become even more complex in the face of successive waves of enlargement.[5] The general tone of the programme was indicative of Europe's cautious stance on social issues, which continued to be seen as functional requirements of the process of economic integration. In this way, the programme emphasised principles such as the free movement of workers and competition between companies and social policies, which tended to be perceived as employment policies.

In conclusion, by the end of the 1970s, three decades since the start of integration, policy objectives remained relatively stable and unchanged. This was true for all European policies, and also for social policy. However, the next decade would represent a far-reaching change for European policy.

4 The Single European Act and the White Paper

The beginning of the eighties was marked by profound political changes, both at the domestic and European level. Firstly, there was a change of political power in many countries, with centre-left governments giving way to the centre-right (*maxime* with the election of Margaret Thatcher in the United Kingdom, which put at risk the unanimous votes in the Council); secondly, the abandonment of Keynesian solutions in many countries, particularly after the failure of economic policy during Mitterrand's first presidential term. The combination of these factors has brought European political economies to a more liberal path, which would lead to a process of reducing redistributive and regulatory mechanisms. On top of this, there was a growing fear that European welfare states would represent a competitive disadvantage for Europe in the global economy.

Paradoxically, and at a time when Euroscepticism was making its way, and when domestic constraints combined with the persistence of institutional blockages at the European level seemed to announce some European policy stagnation, there was a reversal of course. This would change the face of the integration process. Once

---

[4]Even though the resolution stated that the necessary resources would be provided, in particular by strengthening the ESF' and, further on, that it was intended to speed up the implementation of the European social budget'.

[5]By 1973, institutional diversity alone would begin to hinder the process of harmonisation, particularly as a result of the accession of countries with institutional cultures other than the founding fathers, the United Kingdom and Ireland (liberal model) and Denmark (social-democratic model).

again, after a long period of setbacks and hesitations, a common commitment was generated to accelerate the integration process.

Although belonging to different political families, the joint action of Thatcher, Kohl, Mitterrand and Delors contributed decisively to a new investment in European integration. To an important extent, because they all shared a growing perception of the interdependencies arising from economic globalisation. In fact, between 1983–1984, the member states with the greatest economic and political relevance had all abandoned protectionist economic policies and evolved into more liberal options. The traditional mechanisms of economic regulation had proved incapable of managing the crisis resulting from the oil shocks of the early 1970s and 1980s, which left the field open to those who advocated convergence in the choices surrounding macroeconomic policies and the creation of a true common market. In addition, a new European Commission was appointed in 1985, led by Jacques Delors, who would, as President of the Commission, become a new de facto political actor with enhanced powers, and which would decisively promote integration (Ross 1995).

It was in this context of transformations in the political landscape of the member states and of a new attitude towards desirable macroeconomic policies, as well as with new political actors that a new institutional architecture for Europe began to be designed.

The first task of the Delors Commission was to draw a project that would mobilise economic interests, in particular business associations and large European industrial groups, and at the same time give power to the Commission itself. The White Paper on completing the internal market fulfilled this objective (1985). As George Ross points out, the White Paper marks the beginning of the "renaissance of European integration" (1995: 362).

The main objective of the White Paper was to identify the set of obstacles to the free movement of goods, individuals, capital and services that persisted in the EEC. This document would end up listing 310 directives and regulations that should be adopted by the Council, as a way of completely abolishing the physical, technical and fiscal borders that persisted. This objective required a tight timeframe of about 7 years—1992 thus became, at the same time, a political objective and a slogan. However, most of the proposals could not be implemented without changes to both the institutional rules and the structure of Europe.

Consequently, there was a need to convene a European Council for revising and updating the Treaty of Rome in accordance with the objective of creating, in 1992, a single market.

After complex negotiations, the Single European Act was set in motion, making the creation of a common area feasible, with a strong emphasis on economic and market integration. The consequences would be profound, with changes at three levels: in the strategy for integration; in the decision-making process; and in the financial instruments (i.e. structural funds) (Young 2014). Consolidating an option that had already been put into practice since the 1984 Fontainebleau European Council, the decision-making process was now linked to the creation of the single market. Until then, the joint decision-making process was fully concentrated in the hands of the Council, with the Commission only having the right of initiative, without any legislative competence. What is more, decisions in the Council depended on unanimous voting. With the adoption of the Single European Act, qualified majority voting became applicable to all matters connected with the creation of the single market, helping to overcome the 'joint decision trap'. Even so, qualified majority voting was not extended to social areas, while at the same time some protective mechanisms—which in fact allowed the member states to veto more problematic legislation—were maintained.

Changes in the decision-making process were accompanied by transformations in the integration strategy. In the framework of a new enlargement (this time, Spain and Portugal), expressions such as 'mutual recognition' and 'subsidiarity' began to occupy in community's jargon the place previously occupied by 'convergence' and 'harmonisation'. Once again, institutional diversity increased and, consequently, the capacity to accommodate differences and promote a harmonising strategy decreased. Meanwhile, some decisions of the European Court of Justice have intensified the need for each Member State to recognise the standards of others (notably after the decision on the 'Cassis de Dijon' case). This change has led to a change in the level of policy formation, which has shifted from the European sphere to the intergovernmental one.

This move has had profound effects on European social policy. While the objective, though never explicitly stated, of the previous period was to 'harmonise' the social standards of member states, in the new phase, there was widespread fear that 'mutual recognition' would translate into a 'race to the bottom' process, in which, as a consequence of social dumping, social standards could be eroded. This fear stemmed, to an important extent, from the recent accession of three new member states from Southern Europe, with underdeveloped welfare states (Guillén and Matsaganis 2000).

Consequently, social policy played a secondary role in both the White Paper and the Single Act. In cases where there was some reference to the social dimension, the focus was invariably on removing barriers to free movement of workers. Nevertheless, the Single Act amended the Treaty in specific areas of social relevance, also giving new powers to the Commission. The new version of Article 118 stressed the importance of working conditions for the single market and provided for qualified majority voting in matters relating to health and safety at work (which previously depended on unanimity). However, what appeared to be an extension of European social policy and an open door that would ease decisions in areas where agreements had proved difficult to reach, was eventually contradicted by a provision of the same article, which stated that the Community "did not intend, by setting minimum requirements for safety and health at work, to discriminate unjustifiably against employers in small and medium-sized companies". What, at the time, no Government anticipated is that, in the following decade, what seemed a technical provision, with marginal impact, would become instrumental for integration in social areas, namely through the interpretation that the European Court of Justice has made of the Treaties (Leibfried and Pierson 2000; Falkner et al. 2005).

The second element of social policy in the Single Act referred to the idea of social dialogue between employers and labour at European level (Ross 1995). This theme has been subject to a lot of political investment at European level, but the practical results would be scarce.

More relevant was the reorganisation of the Community budget, which took place in the wake of Article 130 a–e. What would become known as the first 'Delors package' began to be designed on the basis of budgetary reforms and better coordination of structural funds. In this sense, the Single Act established that "the financial resources allocated to aid through the Funds (. . .) should be significantly increased in real terms, within the financing capacities" (Article 130d).

All in all, the social dimension of the Single Act was minimal. Even considering the changes described above, this revision of the Treaties left the issues of the 'social space' unresolved, and the social aspects of the Single Act were managed through a political spill-over, of a selective nature, closely linked to the creation of the common market (Kleinman 2002: 87).

However, social issues would not be abandoned. To an important extent because the Commission, much by Jacques Delors' action, kept the issue on the agenda, making the existence of a 'social space' a requirement for the creation of a common market. This political investment was based on what Delors' own office called the 'Matrioska strategy'. According to George Ross, Delors' strategy was to establish links between the various measures approved, so that one measure would imply the approval, later on, of other measures (1995: 363). In this way, each new step would lead to the Commission maximising its political resources and thus putting new issues on the agenda. It was within this framework that, at the Hanover Summit in 1988, the Commission invited the Economic and Social Council to become involved in the discussion on the content of a Charter of Social Rights, which would be presented as the social component of the Single Act.

Building on some of the principles set out in the preamble to the Single European Act in December 1989 at the Strasbourg Summit, the Council met to adopt the 'Charter of the Fundamental Social Rights of Workers', which would become known as the 'Social Charter'. In what would become a typical European approach, the Charter was not a binding document, but a solemn declaration reaffirming that responsibility for social policies lay with the member states. However, despite its non-binding nature, the Charter was the subject of deep political dissent and, after intense discussions, only 11 of the 12 member states would subscribe to it—with the United Kingdom falling outside the 'jurisdiction' of the document. Considering its content, the Charter maintained the traditional focus on workers rather than on citizens as a whole, reinforcing the bias in favour of the work that characterised European social policy during the first decades.

Nonetheless, the Social Charter proved less important because of what it actually proposed than for the debate it generated. So much so that, within the framework of the intensification of the integration process that would culminate in December 1991, with the approval of the Maastricht Treaty, with a view to creating Economic and Monetary Union, a discussion would take place with a view to integrating a social chapter into the Treaty. Despite the debate that took place during the Dutch Presidency, the British Government continued to show its opposition to further integration in the social fields. In the face of this blockade, the other 11 member states, instead of being trapped in the decision process, opted for an unprecedented institutional solution: the approval of a 'Protocol on Social Policy', annexed to the Maastricht Treaty. Although its legal status was frequently questioned,[6] this option proved to be an intelligent way of overcoming what was announced as yet another institutional blockade that seemed difficult to overcome (Kleinman 2002: 89).

The Protocol's priorities were: promoting employment; improving working conditions; appropriate social protection; social dialogue; investment in human resources as a means of promoting employment and combating exclusion (Article 1). The first article was particularly relevant in that it definitively replaces references to the objective of 'harmonisation' with expressions such as 'appropriate', which consolidated the principle of 'mutual recognition'. The second article of the Protocol, on the other hand, extended qualified majority voting to a wider range of issues—namely, health, safety and health at work; working conditions; workers' rights to information and consultation; equality between men and women in the labour market; and the integration of persons excluded from the labour market. Progress on these issues should be made through the adoption of hard-law instruments, including directives. However, in the same article (Article 1, §2), it was reiterated that "these directives should avoid imposing administrative, financial and legal constraints such as to jeopardize the development of small and medium-sized enterprises". Moreover, social objectives should be achieved through measures that "take into account the various national practices, in particular contractual relations and the need to maintain the competitiveness of the Community economy" (Article 1). Moreover, any activity was limited by the principle of subsidiarity, which was increasingly seen as central by the Commission, while member states could continue to introduce differentiated legal provisions compatible with the Treaties (Article 2, §5).

With the economic recession of the early nineties, employment, the fight against unemployment and social exclusion assumed a central position in the domestic political agendas. Although all member states converged around the priority to be assigned to these objectives, the understanding that was made about the role that Europe should assume was not shared. In the meantime, there was a new wave of enlargement, with the accession of three new member states (1994). With Austria, Finland and Sweden as member states, the institutional diversity intensified, which was, however, compensated by the fact that these were countries with developed welfare states that expressed clear preferences towards greater integration of social policy.

---

[6]Point 2 of the preamble noted "the United Kingdom of Great Britain and Northern Ireland shall not take part in the deliberations and the adoption by the Council of Commission proposals made on the basis of this Protocol and the abovementioned Agreement". "The opt-out procedure for the UK raised practical as well as legal questions. How realistic was it to assume that the UK representatives would not influence (whether deliberately or not) the decisions of the other 11 member states. The UK would continue to be involved in social policy decisions taken outside the Protocol." (Kleinman 2002: 89).

As a reflection of these changes, the Commission began to develop a more ambitious strategy for European social policy, which was seen not only as a corollary of the deepening of the Single Market and Economic and Monetary Union, but also of the concept of European citizenship.

In 1993, after a debate involving governments, social partners and experts, a Green Paper on European social policy was presented, which sought to map the constraints of integration in the social area, while identifying feasible lines of action. The Green Paper would be followed by a White Paper in 1994. These documents represented the first steps of a strategy designed to promote profound change. While the Social Charter, the successive action programmes and the Protocol contained a set of principles aimed at giving some coherence to European social policy, they did not represent a comprehensive and autonomous commitment to deepening integration in this area—namely because it was not possible to develop the necessary administrative structures and financial instruments.

The White Paper sought to address this weakness. In addition to stressing that social policy should play a vital role in the future of the integration process, it also advocated an extension of the themes that should be Europeanised. On the one hand, social policy could not be secondary to the development of the internal market; on the other, while employment should remain the priority, other areas should become more relevant (e.g. social services and combating exclusion).

Even if the White Paper continued to maintain the focus on social policy associated with the labour market and assumed that the European Union's main function was to promote cooperation and support the actions of the member states, new themes were introduced, namely in the area of social exclusion, paving the way for the dissemination of mechanisms of cognitive dissemination. These mechanisms would prove fundamental for the development of the common social policy, in the following years.[7]

If the White Paper can be seen as a defensive document, reflecting both the European moment (post-Maastricht) and the traditional blockages of common social policy, this did not prevent the Commission from taking the opportunity to present a new social action programme for the period 1995–1997, thereby trying to promote, once again, a common social policy agenda.

This programme stressed the idea that social policy should be seen as a productive factor, and not as an obstacle to economic competitiveness. In fact, the entire

---

[7]The document alleged that social policy was to play a 'vital part' in further integration. Accordingly, the scope of this policy field was to be widened, meaning that even though employment was to remain a top priority, other dimensions of the social question had to gain relevance. Hence, the foreword to the White Paper stressed that "the Union's social policy cannot be second string to economic development or to the functioning of the internal market. Growth in the numbers of the poor and of the unemployed, the possible emergence of an underclass, increasing pressures on social services (e.g., unemployment and health services) and increasing criminality all drain the resources available. The financing of social security now poses major challenges for all member states. In the Union, increased confidence can come only from a reconciliation between economic growth policies and their translation into higher social development with upgraded living standards for all" (Commission 1994).

document assumed that "social and economic progress should go from step to step", aiming at a more active role for European social policy, namely by proposing a multidimensional conception of social policy, less and less focused only on work.

5   From Amsterdam to Lisbon

From the mid-1990s onwards, the political context in major member states began to change once again. After the victory of the Socialist Party in France, with Lionel Jospin, and the defeat of the Conservatives in the United Kingdom (traditionally opposed to the deepening of European social policy), with the election of Tony Blair's New Labour, employment gained a new centrality and the conditions for the development of common social policies appeared to be met. Soon after the elections, the Labour Party promised to put an end to the British 'opt-out' of the 'social protocol', enabling its incorporation into the Treaty, thereby opening the door to a new phase of social integration.

This new phase was not limited to the inclusion of the 'social protocol' and the extension of qualified majority voting to other policy issues. What was the most striking feature of this period was the introduction of a chapter on employment in the Treaty, reflecting the growing concern with the rise in unemployment in Europe. The aim was, in a way, to emulate for employment policies the procedures that would lead to Economic and Monetary Union, establishing coordination mechanisms through medium-term objectives, comparable indicators and pressure for the convergence of national policies (Pochet 2005).

The 'social protocol' was to be incorporated as Chapter XI of the Treaty of Amsterdam with the title, 'social policy, education, vocational training and youth'. The new chapter recognised the commitment of member states to the development of the social dimension as an important component of the European integration process. At the same time, reflecting the political concern about rising unemployment, the reference to 'high levels of employment and social protection' became the second priority in the list of areas set out at the start of the Treaty revision.

The Treaty revision process was marked by deep political disputes. The United Kingdom, while agreeing to put an end to the opt-out, continued to oppose the existence of new mechanisms for regulating domestic labour markets, while also opposing the extension of European responsibilities in social issues. The British position would also be supported by the German Chancellor, Helmut Kohl. Hence, Blair seized the opportunity to oppose the harmonisation of employment policies, and also blocked further increases in the Community budget for employment programmes, which would remain limited to pilot experiments. At the end of the debate, the British perspectives would, in fact, emerge as dominant, contradicting the French Socialists' proposals for greater European intervention. Once again, Europe would seek to make progress through privileged cooperation mechanisms and coordinated action, rather than seeking harmonisation. Still, Article 130 of the Treaty created the 'Employment Committee', which would play a key role in subsequent developments in European social policy.

The priority assigned to employment would ultimately be reflected in the European agenda. During the Luxembourg presidency, still in 1997 and in anticipation of some of the Treaty provisions not yet in force, an extraordinary European Council was held entirely devoted to Employment. At this conference, an 'European employment strategy' was approved, together with its first pillars and guidelines. Moreover, for the first time, social partners took part in a Social Summit. This strategy, also known as the 'Luxembourg process', can be seen as a turning point for European social policy, as member states agreed on an approach—the open method of coordination—which was based on shared objectives, targets and means.[8]

6   From Lisbon Back to Lisbon

Three years later, during the Portuguese Presidency in 2000, a new agenda for European social policy was launched, consolidating the path initiated with the Luxembourg process. The March 2000 European Council launched the Lisbon Strategy, which aimed to "make the Union the most competitive and dynamic knowledge-based economy in the world, with sustainable economic growth, more and better jobs and greater social cohesion". A year later, meeting in Gothenburg, European leaders added the goal of sustainable development, thus completing the Strategy. It was Europe's response to the challenges of globalisation, the information society, increasing international competition and an ageing population. Policy adaptation was considered the way forward to maintain living standards and preserve the European social model in a knowledge society.

At the Laeken European Council in December of that year, five objectives, for which a set of indicators was defined to measure progress, were defined: (i) economic performance; (ii) employment; (iii) R&D, innovation, and education; (iv) economic reforms; and (v) social cohesion (and, after the Gothenburg Summit, (vi) sustainable development). The implementation of the Lisbon Strategy required not only concerted actions between the European and national levels of governance, but also increased cooperation and exchanges of good practices between member states, whose economies were becoming increasingly interconnected as a result of the internal market and the single currency.

This process was complementary to the existing processes of economic and social policy coordination: Luxembourg and the European Employment Strategy; Cardiff for structural reforms and Cologne for wage negotiations and monetary policies. At the same time, the open method of coordination, that was already being tested in the

---

[8]The resort to the OMC represented simultaneously a new commitment to address employment issues at the EU level and an attempt to redefine ESP governance method through a novel approach to regulation.

context of the European Employment Strategy, was institutionalised as a new method of governance, which could be transferred to policy areas other than employment.

Shortly afterwards, still under the influence of the 'Luxembourg process' and the 'Lisbon Agenda', during the French Presidency (second half of 2000), the Council adopted the 'Charter of Fundamental Rights', which codified social rights at European level ('solidarity rights', namely the right of workers to information and consultation, as well as the right to collective bargaining, fair and just working conditions, social security and social assistance), and which would later be incorporated into the failed Constitutional Treaty, finally enshrined in the Treaty of Lisbon.

In the meantime, the 'open method of coordination' would also be applied to policies to combat social exclusion, in a strategy that mimicked that which had been followed for employment. At the Nice Council, the 'Social Agenda for 2000/5' would be approved, reflecting a new role for common policies to combat social exclusion, as well as a shared approach to promote the sustainability of pension systems, in accordance with the provision of the Treaty of Nice (2001), which allowed the Community to adopt measures for cooperation between member states in social areas, but no longer restricted to employment, social exclusion and equal opportunities, as had been established in Amsterdam (Pochet 2005: 42). Still in Nice, the committee on social protection was created, following the example of what had already happened for employment.

In the sequence of the mid-term review of the Lisbon Strategy and in order to speed up progresses in the social field, the Commission launched a Social Agenda for the period 2006–2010. In 2006, the European Globalisation Adjustment Fund was set up to deal with the increased international competition that has led to bankruptcies and unemployment in some sectors, particularly those more exposed to global trade.

Almost 10 years after the adoption of the Lisbon Strategy, the Treaty of Lisbon, in force since December 2009, has enshrined the European social dimension in the Union's primary law. In addition to defining the EU's social objectives, in particular full employment and solidarity between the generations (Article 3), Article 6 of the Treaty gives the Charter of Fundamental Rights the same legal value as the Treaties.

Foremost, in the EU's Treaty on the Functioning of the European Union there is now a 'horizontal social clause', which states that: "In defining and implementing its policies and activities, the Union shall take into account requirements linked to the promotion of a high levels of employment, the guarantee of adequate social protection, the fight against social exclusion, and a high level of education, training and protection of health" (Article 9 TFEU). In the field of health, EU competence has been extended to "measures setting high standards of quality and safety of medicinal products and devices for medical use" (Article 168 TEU) and has introduced the objective of improving the complementarity of member states' health services in cross-border regions.

Aware of the limitations of the Lisbon Strategy, which fell far short of the objectives set, the European Commission launched in 2010, in the midst of the economic and financial crisis, the "Europe 2020 Strategy" for "smart, sustainable and inclusive growth". Organised around three axes—innovation, growth of employment rate and sustainability, the Europe 2020 Strategy set, among its five objectives, the commitment to rescue 20 million people from the risk of poverty and/or social exclusion and to increase the employment rate of workers aged between 20 and 64–75%. To meet these targets, seven legislative initiatives were launched: the Agenda for New Skills and Jobs, which proposed a review of flexicurity policies; Youth on the Move, to increase mobility and improve education and training; and the creation of a European Platform against Poverty and Social Exclusion. The achievement of the goals of the Europe 2020 Strategy is now part of the cycle of coordination of the economic policies of the member states, within the scope of the so-called "European Semester".

Already in 2017, the Commission, the Council and the European Parliament established the European Pillar of Social Rights, which identifies 20 principles, declined in social rights, which serve as a reference framework for social and employment policy at national and European level. With the aim of promoting convergence towards better living and working conditions in Europe, this pillar aims to create a more robust and fairer economic and monetary union. After a certain political stagnation in the run-up to the economic and financial crisis, this could open a new chapter in the development of the European social dimension. With the proclamation of the Social Pillar, social policy is gaining new impetus at European level, with the three institutions demonstrating their commitment to adopting the legislative acts necessary to implement the principles and rights enshrined in it.

The principles and rights of the Social Pillar are structured into three categories:

(i) Equal opportunities and access to the labour market: (1) education, training and lifelong learning; (2) gender equality; (3) equal opportunities; (4) active support for employment.

(ii) Fair working conditions: (5) Safe and adaptable employment; (6) Wages; (7) information on employment conditions and protection in the event of dismissal; (8) social dialogue and worker participation; (9) work-life balance; (10) Healthy, safe and well adapted work environment and data protection; (11) Reception and support for children.

(iii) Social protection and inclusion: (12) Social protection; (13) Unemployment benefits; (14) Minimum income; (15) Old-age benefits and pensions; (16) Health care; (17) Inclusion of people with disabilities; (18) Long-term care; (19) Housing and assistance for the homeless; (20) Access to essential services.

7 Different Forms of Governance

Along the process of integration of social policies, a specific pattern of governance has been consolidated, in which different modes of policy implementation coexist. The willingness to accommodate diversity, while common steps were taken, led to the development of decision-making processes that resulted from attempts to escape the blockages created by the interaction between mutual recognition and shared objectives at the European level.

This parallel development of different modes of governance has turned integration in social areas into a system of multilevel policy making, in which the central authority (i.e. the European Union) accepts and strengthens the authority of member states, rather than replacing or weakening it. This is largely due to the fact that member states, on the one hand, respect the central authority, and, on the other, strategically use the European Union as a mechanism to design and implement domestic social policies (Falkner et al. 2005). This perspective denotes an evolution from an initial harmonising objective towards less conflictive coordination mechanisms, which are even more shared. Stephen Leibfried and Paul Pierson classified this system as a 'multi-layered political community' (1995). According to these authors, although the member states retain many competences and a determining role in the development of policies, the European Union has been assuming institutional contours increasingly similar to the multi-layered systems, typical of federal states.

Although it is possible to identify links between the main developments in European social policy and the most mobilised forms of intervention, over time the dominant instruments of a given period were not fully replaced by those of a subsequent one. While it is true that binding legislative instruments ('hard law'), such as regulations and directives, correspond to the initial objectives of convergence or harmonization, and soft law instruments are typical of a more recent period in which mutual recognition gained relevance, when a certain type of regulatory mechanisms became predominant, this did not imply a total replacement of one type of instruments by another. On the contrary, what we have seen has been a cumulative process, which has led to a coexistence and sometimes an overlap of European social policies.

Accordingly, it is possible to distinguish three institutional pillars on which European social policy rests, and the use of instruments from each of the three pillars stems from a tension between the appropriate forms and levels of regulation, on the one hand, and the extension of supranational jurisdiction, on the other (Rhodes 2005).

The first pillar corresponds to the 'Community method' and is based on the legislative initiative of the Council, the Commission and the Parliament. It consists of legislated rights and was the dominant method in the first years of integration. The 'Community method' is identified with 'hard law' because it creates uniform rules, which member states have to adopt, incurring penalties if they have not done so. In case of non-compliance, the European Court of Justice is the body that directs conflicts and sets sanctions (Trubek and Trubek 2005). Over time, while the evolution from unanimity to qualified majority voting was essential to make the 'Community method' effective, the ECJ was central to ensuring compliance with legal provisions (Scott and Trubek 2002).

Two types of instruments can be distinguished in the context of the 'community method': regulations and directives.

According to Article 249 of the Treaty, regulations are legal instruments containing provisions which are automatically binding on the member states, so that no transposition into national law is necessary. The aim of regulations is not so much to promote harmonisation or convergence as to impose standardisation.

Directives are used when seeking to adapt or harmonize national regulations (Azzi 2000). They are unilateral acts that, contrary to the regulations, only impose objectives, leaving it to member states to choose both the form and the means for compliance (third paragraph of Article 249 of the Treaty). Thus, directives are binding as to the final result, leaving the competence as to the exact terms of the transposition to domestic institutions. When transposing directives, member states benefit from some margin of freedom or 'normative compliance', to the extent that they can accommodate the provisions of the directives in the legal, economic and social idiosyncrasies of the country. However, if a directive is not transposed within the legal timeframe, member states fall into non-compliance and are subject to ECJ sanctions. In social areas, directives have been used intensively in labour market issues, especially in areas subject to qualified majority voting (i.e., where the European decision is most facilitated), namely in safety and health at the workplace.

The second pillar is associated with the European social dialogue, intensively promoted by the Commission, namely during the Delors consulate (Ross 1995) and operates through legislation resulting from collective agreements. There are two dimensions to the European social dialogue: the tripartite macro-economic dialogue launched at the Cologne Council in 1994 and a bipartite and autonomous social dialogue created with the Single Act and strengthened at Maastricht with the 'social protocol'.

After several attempts by the Commission to put the European social dialogue on the agenda, the 'social protocol' made it possible for the social partners to sign agreements, which would be extended *erga omnes* by a Council directive or, alternatively, implemented voluntarily by their national affiliates. This possibility was based on a strategic objective: to replicate what was happening in some member states, in which social partners could autonomously regulate various matters related to the labour market, as well as social issues (Pochet 2005: 41). Thus, social dialogue became a distinct process of creating social legislation at European level, also translating into a different mode of governance (Johnson 2005: 61).

From the mid-nineties onwards, the role of the social partners at European level was in fact extended and the agreements between the European Trade Union Confederation (ETUC) and UNICE (now BusinessEurope) could be transformed into Council directives. This process differs from the first pillar not in terms of results, but in terms of the procedure leading to the adoption of a directive (Scott and Trubek 2002). This innovation in terms of mode of governance occurred in a context of renewed appreciation and vitality of corporatism, once again seen as a virtuous mechanism for overcoming the political and social blockages associated with the modernisation of European political economies. According to Martin Rhodes (2005: 288), three reasons led to political investment in European social dialogue: first, to give a new role to the social partners at European level, also as a way to rescue the role of trade unions in the member states; second, to overcome the traditional British blockade to social integration, promoting new actors, favourable to European social initiatives; third, the directives designed in Europe but implemented through negotiation were seen as being more able to accommodate the national diversity that characterised the domestic cultures of industrial relations and labour market regulation.

However, after an initial period of some legislative activity, the progress resulting from the European social dialogue would prove to be scarce, due to UNICE's reluctance to negotiate at the European level. Nevertheless, this approach had some importance, both in the context of the Essen strategy, for the approval of the chapter on employment in Amsterdam and later for the institutionalisation of the open method of coordination—which had as its distinctive element a greater participation and involvement of the social partners in the formation and implementation of the guidelines (de la Porte and Pochet 2005).

The third pillar refers to the 'soft law' mechanisms that the Commission has sought to promote since the beginning of integration, as a way of overcoming the most diverse institutional obstacles, particularly those resulting from the limitations placed by the Treaties on recourse to the first pillar. Even so, only recently have the modes of governance associated with soft law gained centrality, particularly after the approval of the Treaty of Amsterdam and the institutionalisation of the 'open method of coordination' with the Treaty of Lisbon.

The term 'soft law' is used to cover a wide range of European social policy instruments, which have in common the fact that they are not binding, contrasting with the 'Community method'. According to Senden (2004), soft law instruments share three distinctive features: (a) they focus on rules of conduct and commitments; (b) these rules and/or commitments have no legal force; (c) they seek to produce some kind of change in the behaviour of member states.

Four types of soft law instruments can be identified (O'Cinneide 2016): (a) preparatory and informative instruments, whose function is pre-legal (e.g., green and white papers, action programmes and informative communications); (b) interpretative and decision-making instruments—they play a post-legal role in supporting hard law instruments (e.g., Commission communications, some guidelines), (c) steering, which aims to set common objectives and define specific actions, performing a para-legal function based only on persuasion (e.g. recommendations); and (d) 'open method of coordination'.

The 'open method of coordination' is a more structured attempt to break with the 'community method' (Scott and Trubek 2002: 4), which however also differs from the other three types of 'soft law' (Borrás and Jacobsson 2004).[9] While the

---

[9]The OMC was first used with the EES (Goetschy 2016) and gained particular political relevance with the Lisbon Summit (Rodrigues 2000), where it consolidated its role as a leading governance method at the EU level—mainly as far as ESP is concerned. The OMC was then extended from employment to social exclusion (Nice Council in 2000) and, afterwards, to pensions (Stockholm in 2001), and health care (Gothenburg in 2001), not to mention other 'OMC-like' processes (de la Porte 2007). For a description of the various policy fields to which the OMC (or comparable processes) has been applied, see Susanna Borras and Kerstin Jacobsson (2004).

'Community method' creates uniform rules that member states have to adopt and provides sanctions for non-compliance, the OMC is based on open and generic guidelines rather than formal rules and does not presuppose formal sanctions (Trubek and Trubek 2005: 344). Hence it is seen as a 'third way', halfway between regulatory competition and harmonisation, on the one hand, and an alternative to intergovernmentalism and supra-nationalism, on the other. Hence, the objective of the OMC was to open a sustainable path between a fragmented Europe and a European "superstate" (Zeitlin 2005: 19).

In this sense, the OMC is usually described as a flexible means of working towards common European objectives, through national action plans, which are assessed according to shared criteria (e.g. monitoring indicators), following guidelines and benchmarks defined at the European Council. The method is not legally binding, but peer pressure and participation are seen as preferred ways of ensuring that governments meet European commitments (de la Porte and Pochet 2005). It is often argued that, in the context of the OMC, the exchange of good practices between member states promotes knowledge and enhances mutual learning processes, which strengthen national-based public policies, through cognitive mechanisms (López-Santana 2006; Pochet 2005: 41–42). Moreover, supporters of the virtues of the OMC underline that this method combines common objectives with freedom to achieve them through ways that are sensitive to domestic contexts (Scott and Trubek 2002: 5).

With the OMC, the EU has chosen to harmonise ideas and conceptions of policies and policy fields (promoting interactions between different levels of governance) rather than establishing binding rules, regulations and mechanisms. Diversity, until then often seen as an obstacle, would be mobilised as a resource, provided that best practices, which could be emulated by other member states, were amplified. Common objectives, respect for subsidiarity and the participation and involvement of different actors are central aspects of the OMC as a governance mechanism. These aspects have led, in a context of growing relevance of the OMC in social areas, namely when compared to some loss of relative importance of the 'Community method', to talk of an evolution of integration through laws towards a Europe driven by statistics (Bruno et al. 2006: 530).

The idea that obstacles to the Europeanisation of policies in social areas, both institutional and political, persisted as early as 2018. Hence, the President of the European Commission, following his speech on the State of the Union 2018, in which he defended the use of qualified majority voting in policy areas that currently require a unanimous decision, proposed the use of the so-called '*passerelle* clauses' (or bridging clauses). Article 48(7) of the Treaty on European Union (general *passerelle* clause) and Article 153(2) of the Treaty on the Functioning of the European Union (specific *passerelle* clause) in the social field.

The European Commission presented in April 2019 a Communication on the revision of these social clauses to ensure more efficient decision-making processes and faster outcomes through the flexibility of the legislative process. This also gives the European Parliament an equal role as co-legislator, although there is no change in the division of competences between the Union and the member states. Accordingly, the Commission also ensures full respect for the role of the Social Partners, who will continue to be consulted prior to the presentation of legislative proposals in these policy domains.

As mentioned, the vast majority of issues relating to social policy are already subject to qualified majority voting: gender equality, health and safety at work, labour mobility, the rights of posted workers, working conditions, and worker information and consultation. Nonetheless, some issues remain subject to the unanimity rule, namely, non-discrimination based on gender, racial or ethnic origin, religion or belief, age and sexual orientation; social security and protection of workers outside the cross-border context; protection of workers after termination of a contract of employment, collective representation and collective defence of the interests of workers and employers; and working conditions for third-country nationals residing legally on EU territory. According to the Commission's view, this dichotomy has resulted in an uneven development of the various social areas. The latter is expected to be corrected by the use of the *passerelle* clause (it should be noted that the activation of a *passerelle* clause always requires a unanimous decision by the Council or the European Council).

8   Different Policy Instruments, Different Domestic Impacts

Irrespective of the cyclical popularity of each of the pillars of European social policy and the extent to which they are used in each sub-area of social policy, each of them has, a priori, a different capacity for convergence of domestic policies. Citi and Rhodes (2006) have conceptualised the convergence capacity of the different governance mechanisms—establishing a continuum of greater to lesser convergence. Figure 1 defines the convergence capacity around five different types.

The first combination of instruments is the one that has the least convergence capacity and relies only on common benchmarks and/or recommendations. In the absence of political or peer pressure and/or media attention, its convergence capacity tends to be very low. The second combination is also based on common benchmarks

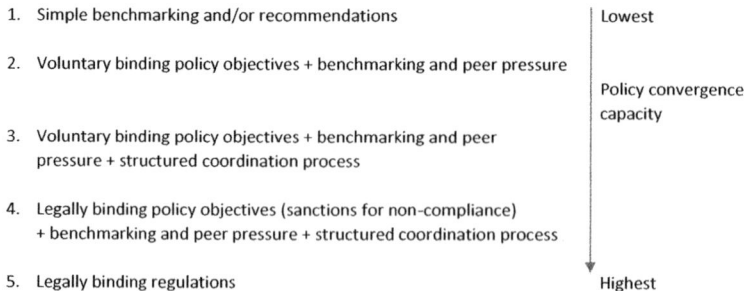

Fig. 1 Policy convergence capacity (adapted from Citi and Rhodes (2006))

but differs from the first because it has some degree, albeit weak, of peer pressure with explicit political commitments (for example, the OMC on pensions). The third combination reconciles voluntary commitments with common benchmarks and peer pressure within a structured coordination process. Even so, in these cases, the absence of sanctions for non-compliance leaves room for member states not to comply with the agreement (as is the case of the European Employment Strategy). The fourth combination differs from the third in that it has legally binding targets instead of voluntary commitments. It is the most powerful form of non-legislative governance, with non-compliance being punished with sanctions. Even so, this combination has not been adopted in social policies, having been limited to fiscal policy in the context of the Stability and Growth Pact. The fifth combination is based on binding forms of regulation, as typified by the 'Community method'. Although full harmonisation is not always achieved, considering the binding nature of this method, it tends to produce greater domestic impact and also greater convergence.

It is suggested that different policy instruments correspond to distinct processes of transformation of national policies. Thus, the transformations in the policy repertoires of member states operate differently according to the nature of European political pressure. This schematic definition of the potential for convergence of existing European social policy instruments can be seen as a useful starting point but must necessarily be complemented by explanations of how the pressures for change operate. In other words, if this type of analysis makes it possible to say something about results of specific pressures resulting from Europeanisation mechanisms, it is, however, incapable of unravelling the processes behind these results—i.e., by itself, it does not offer a model with explanatory capacity.

Advocates of soft coordination, as embodied in the OMC and consolidated with the Lisbon Strategy as a legitimate and effective form of governance, tend to affirm that, despite its weakly binding nature, this method of Europeanising domestic policies is effective and does bring about change. Essentially because it is a contextualised form of benchmarking (Visser and Hemerijck 1997), in which the development of "national action plans" is done through a complex method of permanent feedback during their elaboration and implementation process.

This method contrasts first and foremost with the traditional 'Community method', in which solutions were binding and uniform, not very sensitive to national diversity (recognised as one of the strongest obstacles to integration in social areas). It then facilitates policy development in areas where European competences are scarce and/or where regulation is impractical (because its nature is more flexible than traditional "co-decision processes" or "intergovernmental negotiations" (Hemerijck 2002). Thus, the OMC would aim to develop a European social model, but through a set of negotiated objectives, rather than being imposed or based on solemn but vague declarations, which traditionally result from European Summits.

According to several authors, the potential of this method lies in its ability to promote 'social learning'. The OMC would have created a consensus, whose nature was essentially cognitive, between the various member states around the common challenges, objectives and ways of addressing them. Through peer evaluation, benchmarks and the identification of good practices, smooth coordination would tend to produce material change, with an impact on domestic policy-making (Jacobsson 2004; López-Santana 2006; Bruno et al. 2006; for a review, see Zeitlin 2005).

However, one thing is normative approaches, another is what we do know today about how the OMC has transformed domestic social policies. In other words, what effect has it actually had?

Empirical evidence devalues the direct impact of social learning mechanisms (see the volume edited by Kvist and Saari 2007). In fact, the ability of soft Europeanisation to reformulate domestic cognitive frameworks, promoting certain ways to implement social policies, depends on the pre-existence of a prior European cognitive legacy. In areas where over the years Europe has indeed influenced national social policies (namely due to the presence of financial resources associated with the European Social Fund, which tend to bring about a priori soft pressure), soft-law mechanisms have tended to contribute more to the transformation of domestic policies—for example, by conferring legitimacy on the principles "exported" by the European Union (Silva 2009, 2011).

In this sense, it is possible to argue that the impact of soft coordination in the social areas was more focused on improving institutional and domestic policy conditions to reform public policies—redistributing power in favour of national actors with political preferences aligned with European priorities—than on soft learning mechanisms based on the sharing of good practices among peers.

9   Concluding Remarks

In the early days of European integration, social policy played a secondary role in the process of European union building. For institutional, political and economic reasons, social policy was mostly kept as a competence of domestic welfare states, and scarcely Europeanized. Nonetheless, a European social policy edifice was incrementally and slowly developed, assigning political salience to this policy realm. If in the initial stages of integration, social policy developments were a spill-over effect of economic and market integration, over the last three decades, social policy at the European level has evolved profoundly, surpassing the limitations posed by the absence of extensive competences in the Treaties. Hence, a combination of traditional communitarian mechanisms with innovative soft instruments has transformed the European social policy landscape, while producing significant impacts in domestic welfare states, which became semi-sovereign entities. Following the financial and economic crisis and its impact in the Euro project, European social policy suffered a backlash and lost political salience. It was (re)nationalized in its most relevant policy areas and devolved to its secondary role, with lack of autonomy vis-à-vis priorities defined at the Ecofin and Eurogroup.

In the last years, however, a new dynamic seems to be emerging with the proclamation of the European Pillar of Social Rights that sets out rights and principles to guarantee fair and well-functioning labour markets and welfare systems in the EU. Although the implementation of the Social Pillar remains the responsibility of member states, most of its success will also depend on the impetus from European institutions and Social Partners. Its potential in the context of the completion of Economic and Monetary Union should not be neglected.

In this chapter we argued that, following a brief period in which the European Union was decisive in boosting welfare policy innovations in member-states, while promoting some mild convergence, today, the development of European social policy faces dilemmas that are parallel to the ones that the European project is confronted with. The soft nature of European Social Policy might nevertheless prove to be a major asset to ensure the necessary flexibility in the response to the differentiated national impacts of major trends in European societies, from demography to the future of work.

One thing is to identify both the impacts and mechanisms that proved to be most effective in promoting domestic change, promoted by European level policy instruments, quite another is to recognize the constraints that persist and that objectively limit the deepening of common social integration.

In the past, as we argued in the first part of this chapter, the construction of a European social model, corresponding to a transfer of responsibilities and competences from the member states to the European sphere, has always been inhibited by a set of factors: e.g. the 'constitutional asymmetry' present since the founding moments; the priority assigned to the single market; the institutional and political diversity; and the lack of political consensus. When the Lisbon Strategy was adopted, and still benefiting from the political investment in social Europe that characterised the Delors Consulate (Ross 1995), many of the constraints of the past were apparently being overcome, or at least a virtuous way had been found to circumvent them, today not only do many of them seem to have returned, but we are also faced with new ones—the intensity of which is, moreover, greater.

Even after the most acute phase of the economic and financial crisis has been overcome, a context of permanent austerity persists, which constrains the available resources necessary for a common strategy at the social level, reinforcing the intergovernmental nature of the European Union and the difficulties in agreeing and converging political responses. As such, European policies tend to be more a repository of a set of national preferences, some of them in the opposite direction, than an integrated response. In fact, this means that all member states are selectively reviewing their European strategies in a 'cherry-picking' mechanism, mobilizing Europe to legitimise their domestic choices, many of them pre-existent.

If this diagnosis can be seen as a constraint, it also reveals some of the possible future paths of the integration process. Faced with the inability to find common and shared responses, member states seek to reflect their national preferences in Europe so as to subsequently strengthen their political and institutional capacity to implement these same policies, invoking the European legitimating element.

A second constraint, which is interlinked with the previous one, relates to the growing fragmentation of the European political landscape. The process of European construction, from the outset, but in a particularly intense way in the deepening of its social component, was based on a broad consensus between the two traditionally dominant political families—Christian-Democrats and Social-Democrats. This consensus no longer exists, and it has clearly been impossible to reinvent a political constellation favouring the construction of a social Europe. It is no coincidence that in the mechanisms where it is more difficult to make progress without the participation of the Council, social progress has been almost non-existent, as shown by the paralysis in the use of the Community method, which makes it difficult to recall which was the last relevant social directive to be adopted.

A third constraint refers to the successive waves of enlargement. While the six founding states all belonged to the same (corporatist) welfare state family, successive enlargements have increased institutional diversity in social issues, inhibiting integration in these areas. In fact, there seems to be a more or less implicit trade-off between widening and deepening integration beyond the single market (or at least the functional requirements necessary for the functioning of the single market). The choice to make the Union a much larger policy area—with all its associated advantages—objectively limits the ambition to deepen the integration in the social field. Moreover, this option has objectively strengthened coalitions between member states that have historically resisted progress in social integration, those that, due to the domestic political situation, defend the same position and those that have less demanding social standards and see it as a competitive advantage, making the threat of social dumping return (even if, in the past, it was never, in fact, proven (Guillén and Matsaganis 2000)).

This set of constraints has had several effects. The first of these is the strengthening of some of the traditional obstacles to the development of a common social policy. Then, it has led to a progressive degradation of political balances in social areas. Accordingly, in recent years the European Union has proved incapable of approving hard-law instruments through the 'community method' in social areas; what was the 'second pillar' of European social policy (i.e. the social dialogue at the European level) is, now, non-existent. Finally, in the context of the third pillar (i.e. Europeanisation through soft-law) we have witnessed a growing fragmentation of processes, to which has been associated a growing national invisibility of European strategies (e.g. the marginalisation in the context of public employment services of the European guidelines after an initial phase in which they were central axes for their action).

Primarily, from a substantive point of view, demographic developments in the European Union, with a general trend towards an ageing population, and changes in the world of work, with new patterns and forms of work, will require adjustments and new measures at European level. To this end, it will be necessary to create adequate social safety nets and new forms of protection, modernise education and training systems, and expand lifelong learning to enable skills to adapt to the new requirements of the digital society and increased occupational mobility. Maintaining flexible forms of coordination between systems will facilitate these future adaptations. However, it is not only the transformation of the nature of social risks that requires changes in the repertoire of European social policies. Substantive priorities need to be realistically based on modes of governance that are sensitive to the policy environment in the member states.

References

Azzi G (2000) The slow march of European legislation: the implementation of the directives. In: Azzi G (ed) European integration after Amsterdam. OUP, Oxford

Baldwin P (1990) The politics of social solidarity: class bases of the European welfare state, 1875–1975. Cambridge University Press, Cambridge

Borrás S, Jacobsson K (2004) The open method of coordination and new governance patterns in the EU. J Eur Publ Policy 11(2):185–208

Bruno I, Jacquot S, Mandin L (2006) Europeanization through its instrumentation: benchmarking, mainstreaming and the open method of co-ordination . . . toolbox or Pandora's box? J Eur Publ Policy 13(4):519–556

Citi M, Rhodes M (2006) New modes of governance in the EU: a critical survey and analysis. In: Jørgensen KE, Pollack M, Rosamond B (eds) Handbook of European Union politics. Sage, London, pp 463–482

de la Porte (2007) Good governance via the OMC? The cases of employment and social inclusion. Eur J Leg Stud 1(1):118–162

de la Porte, Pochet P (2005) Participation in the open method of coordination – the cases of employment and social inclusion. In: Zeitlin J, Pochet P (eds) The open method of coordination in action – the European employment and social inclusion strategies. P.I.E. – Peter Lang, Brussels

Esping-Andersen G (1990) The three worlds of welfare capitalism. Polity Press, Cambridge, p 1996

Falkner G, Treib O, Hartlapp M, Leiber S (2005) Complying with Europe: EU harmonisation and soft law in the member states. Cambridge University Press, Cambridge

Ferrera M (1996) The southern model of welfare in social Europe. J Eur Soc Policy 6(1):17–37

Ferrera M (2005) The boundaries of welfare: European integration and the new spatial politics of social protection. OUP, Oxford

Flora P (ed) (1986) Growth to limits: the Western European welfare states since World War II. Walter de Gruyter, Berlin

Geyer RR (2000) Exploring European social policy. Polity Press, Cambridge

Goetschy J (2016) The European employment strategy: genesis and development. Eur J Ind Relat 5 (2):117–137

Goodin RE, Headey B, Muffels R, Dirven H-J (1999) The real worlds of welfare capitalism. Cambridge University Press, Cambridge

Guillén AM, Matsaganis M (2000) Testing the 'social dumping' hypothesis in southern Europe: welfare policies in Greece and Spain during the last 20 years. J Eur Soc Policy 10(2):120–145

Guillén A, Palier B (2004) Does Europe matter? Accession to EU and social policy developments in recent and new member states. J Eur Soc Policy 14(3):203–209

Hantrais L (1995) Social policy in the European Union. Macmillan Press, London

Hemerijck A (2002) The self-transformation of the European social model(s). In: Esping-Andersen G et al (eds) Why we need a new welfare state. OUP, Oxford, pp 173–213

Jacobsson K (2004) Soft regulation and the subtle transformation of states: the case of EU employment policy. J Eur Soc Policy 14(4):355–370

Johnson A (2005) European welfare states and supranational governance of social policy. Palgrave, Oxford

Kleinman M (2002) A European welfare state? European Union social policy in context. Palgrave, Hampshire

Kvist J, Saari J (2007) The Europeanisation of social protection. Policy Press, Bristol

Lange P (2016) Maastricht and the social protocol: why did they do it? Polit Soc 21(1):5–36

Leibfried S, Pierson P (2000) Social policy. In: Wallace H, Wallace W (eds) Policy-making in the European Union. OUP, Oxford, pp 267–292

López-Santana M (2006) The domestic implications of European soft law: framing and transmitting change in employment policy. J Eur Publ Policy 13(4):481–499

Majone G (1996) Regulating Europe. Routledge, London

O'Cinneide C (2016) The European social charter and EU labour law. In: Bogg A, Costello C, Davies ACL (eds) Research handbook on EU labour law. Edward Elgar Publishing

Pochet P (2005) The open method of coordination and the construction of social Europe – a historical perspective. In: Zeitlin J, Pochet P (eds) The open method of coordination in action – the European employment and social inclusion strategies. P.I.E. – Peter Lang, Brussels

Rhodes M (2005) Employment policy: between efficacy and experimentation. In: Wallace H et al (eds) Policy-making in the European Union, 5th edn. Oxford University Press, Oxford, pp 279–304

Rodrigues MJ (coord.) (2000) Para uma Europa da inovação e do conhecimento – emprego, reformas económicas e coesão social. Celta Editora, Oeiras

Ross G (1995) Jacques Delors and European integration. Polity Press, Cambridge

Scharpf F (1988) The joint-decision trap. Lessons from German federalism and European integration. Public Adm 66(2):239–278

Scott J, Trubek DM (2002) Mind the gap: law and new approaches to governance in the European Union. European Law Journal 8(1):1–18

Senden L (2004) Soft law in the European community law. Hart Publishers, Oxford

Silva PA e (2002) O modelo de welfare da Europa do Sul: reflexões sobre a utilidade do conceito. In: Sociologia – Problemas e Práticas, n°38. Celta Editora, Oeiras

Silva PA e (2009) Waving the European flag in a Southern European welfare state: factors behind domestic compliance with European social policy in Portugal. Phd Dissertation presented at the EUI

Silva PA e (2011) The Europeanisation of social policies in Portugal. Port J Soc Sci 10(1):3–22

Sykes R, Bouget D, Prior P, Campling J (eds) (2001) Globalization and the welfare states: challenges and change. Macmillan, London

Trubek DM, Trubek LG (2005) Hard and soft law in the construction of social Europe: the role of the open method of coordination. European Law Journal 11(3):343–364

Visser J, Hemerijck A (1997) A Dutch miracle: job growth, welfare reform and corporatism in the Netherlands. Amsterdam University Press, Amsterdam

Wallace H, Pollock MA, Young AR (eds) (2014) Policy making in the European Union. Oxford University Press, Oxford

Wincott D (2003) Chapter 12. The idea of the European social model: limits and paradoxes of Europeanization. In: Featherstone K, Radaelli C (eds) The politics of Europeanization. OUP, Oxford, pp 279–302

Young AR (2014) The single market: from stagnation to renewal. In: Wallace H, Pollock MA, Young AR (eds) Policy making in the European Union. Oxford University Press, Oxford

Zeitlin J (2005) The open method of coordination in action – theoretical promise, empirical realities, reform strategies. In: Zeitlin J, Pochet P (eds) The open method of coordination in action – the European employment and social inclusion strategies. P.I.E. – Peter Lang, Brussels

Pedro Adão e Silva Assistant Professor, Department of Political Science and Public Policy at ISCTE-IUL. Director of the Ph.D. Program in Public Policy, he's been lecturing at ISCTE-IUL since 2007, where he graduated in Sociology in 1997. Completed his Ph.D. in Social and Political Sciences at the European University Institute in Florence in 2009, with a dissertation on the Europeanisation of social policies. Board member of CoLABOR (Collaborative Laboratory for Work, Employment and Social Protection) and vice-president of IPPS-IUL.

Patrícia Cadeiras Graduate of the Institut d'Études Politiques de Paris (Sciences Po Paris) and Master of Arts from the College of Europe (Bruges).
Diplomat.
From November 1999 to February 2002, as an Advisor to the Prime Minister's Office and in the framework of the Portuguese Presidency of the Council of the European Union in the 1st semester 2000, she worked as an Assistant to the Action Line "Employment, Economic Reform and Social Cohesion—towards a Europe of Innovation and Knowledge" that led to the Lisbon Agenda for Growth and Jobs.

From February to October 2002, she was an Advisor to the National Innovation Support Programme.

From November 2002 to March 2005, she assisted the "Advisory Group to the European Commission for Social Sciences and Humanities in the European Research Area".

From January 2009 to June 2010, she worked as Assistant to the President of the Reflection Group "Europe horizon 2020–2030", Felipe González.

From November 2015 to September 2017, she worked as an Advisor to the Portuguese Minister for Foreign Affairs.

She is currently Advisor for EU Affairs at the Portuguese Prime Minister's Office.

Pension Reforms After the Crisis: Bringing Adequacy Back in the Domestic and EU Policy Equation?

Slavina Spasova, Christos Louvaris Fasois, and Bart Vanhercke

Abstract This chapter analyses the intense reforms which have taken place in the European Union after the Great Recession (2014–2019) by looking at how Member States addressed the adequacy side of pensions schemes. It also assesses the discourse at EU level regarding pensions for the period 2011–2019, demonstrating an incremental but visible evolution towards a more socially oriented EU approach. Principle 15 of the European Pillar of Social Rights stresses that all workers have the right to an adequate income. Both the Member States and the EU have begun to bring adequacy back in the policy equation, but the shadow of previous austerity policies still looms large over pension reforms.

1 Introduction

Old-age pensions are among the main policy and politics' concerns when it comes to social protection. In the current context of population ageing and the baby boomers entering retirement, policy makers have been primarily trying to reform pensions schemes in order to ensure their financial sustainability. Indeed, expenditure on old-age pensions is the highest (40% in 2016) in overall social protection expenditure. However, policies focused on sustainability have been increasingly colliding

S. Spasova (✉)
European Social Observatory (OSE), Brussels, Belgium

Centre d'étude de la vie politique (CEVIPOL), Université Libre de Bruxelles, Brussels, Belgium
e-mail: spasova@ose.be

C. Louvaris Fasois
European Association of Paritarian Institutions (AEIP), Brussels, Belgium

B. Vanhercke
European Social Observatory (OSE), Brussels, Belgium

HIVA – Research Institute for Work and Society, University of Leuven, Leuven, Belgium
e-mail: vanhercke@ose.be

© Springer Nature Switzerland AG 2019
N. da Costa Cabral, N. Cunha Rodrigues (eds.), *The Future of Pension Plans in the EU Internal Market*, Financial and Monetary Policy Studies 48,
https://doi.org/10.1007/978-3-030-29497-7_16

with those aiming to ensure pension adequacy, the main purpose of which is to guarantee an adequate income after retirement.

The first part of the chapter aims to look at how the EU 28 Member States have been addressing the issues of adequacy of pensions in the aftermath of the 2008 economic and social crisis which also affected the social situation of pensioners. Section 1 analyses the main trends of pension adequacy reforms in the period of recovery of the European economies after the crisis (2014–2019). Pension systems have indeed been intensely reformed over many years, becoming increasingly complex as they serve a variety of adequacy goals, including ensuring income maintenance after retiring; redistribute income to reduce old-age poverty; fill the gender gaps; encourage longer working lives to address the needs of an ageing population; and interact fairly and efficiently with financial services (European Commission 2018b: 47). This first section also highlights which dimensions of adequacy national reforms have mostly focused on and demonstrates the difficulties to disentangle adequacy and sustainability goals. For the sake of this chapter, the focus is on three types of reforms: (a) prolonging working lives; (b) adequacy safeguards; and (c) income maintenance.

The second part of the chapter focuses on the discourse at EU level regarding pensions for the period 2011–2019. Although old-age social protection remains by and large a national competence, ideas and policy proposals on how to shape pension systems have been conveyed since the end of the 1980s by international organisations such as the World Bank and the International Monetary Fund (Barr 2002; Orenstein 2008a; Nooruddin and Simmons 2006). In more recent years (after 2000s), largely drawing on these international organisations' main ideational lines, the EU also became a part of influential pensions' policy and "epistemic" communities[1] (Orenstein 2008b; Spasova 2013). Its ideational influence in pension policies has been mostly channelled through the Open Method of Coordination and the European Semester, mostly in terms of enhancing the financial sustainability and promoting supplementary pension schemes. *But what about the adequacy of pensions in the specific crisis-driven context when the Semester cycle was created?*

Without looking for a direct "impact" on the national reforms described in Sect. 1, the remainder of the chapter traces the incremental but visible evolution of a more socially oriented EU discourse, notably in the European Semester. While pensions were seen primarily from a budgetary point of view during the first Semester cycles, the European Commission's narrative gradually became more socially balanced and nuanced.

More generally, Principle 15 of the European Pillar of Social Rights stresses that (a) workers and the self-employed have the right to a pension commensurate with contributions and ensuring an adequate income; (b) women and men shall have equal opportunities to acquire pension rights; and (c) everyone in old age has the right to resources that ensure living in dignity. In practice, these ambitions are promoted by the European Commission's Directorate General for Employment,

---

[1]Haas P.M. (1992), « Introduction: Epistemic Communities and International Policy Coordination », *International Organization*, vol. 46, n° 1, p. 1–35.

Social Affairs and Inclusion (DG EMPL) through the Pension Adequacy Report which analyses pension adequacy—i.e. maintaining the income of men and women for the duration of their retirement and preventing old-age poverty.

The Chapter is based on qualitative analysis of primary and secondary sources of data. Section 1 is mainly grounded on the analysis of the reforms described in the European Commission's Pension Adequacy Report (2018b, c) and on the European Social Policy Network (ESPN) Country reports on Financing Social Protection (forthcoming 2019). Section 2 draws on official European Commission documents as well as the Annual Growth Surveys (AGSs), since these provide a good basis which broadly reflects the development of the European Commission's approach to pensions. Moreover, it focuses on public discourse of officials in the media and relies on an original set of semi-directed interviews. Using process tracing in this section allows us to provide a comprehensive overview of the gradual shift in the approach taken to pension policies at EU level.

2   National Old-Age Pension Reforms Since the Great Recession: A Return to Adequacy or Damage Control?

This section analyses the main reforms which have taken place in the EU Member States since the Great Recession, over the period 2014–2019.

Among the social protection policies, pension policies have undergone the greatest socio-economic transformations over the past two decades. In the demanding context of population ageing, most of these reforms, and especially those enacted in the wake of the 2008 financial and economic crisis, have been put in place in an attempt to safeguard the financial sustainability of pensions (European Commission 2015c, 2018c; von Nordheim 2016). Although between 2009 and 2010, many countries implemented counter-cyclical measures to improve the adequacy of pension benefits, these were quickly followed by austerity measures in several countries (Natali 2017, 2018). Indeed, until around 2015, most pension reforms in the EU focused on safeguarding the financial sustainability of pension systems, at the expense of pension adequacy, mainly through cost-containment. This was done most notably by increasing pensionable ages and reducing pension benefits in payment, freezing indexation and making access conditions more stringent (e.g. with closer links between contributions and benefits) (European Commission 2015d; Natali 2018).

Certain of these crisis policy patterns are reflected in pension expenditure, both as a share of GDP and in terms of overall expenditure. Although pension expenditure as a share of GDP may not always tell a clear story—as a result, for example, of fluctuations in GDP related to the economic situation—Fig. 1 shows that, over the period 2005–2010, there was an almost universal trend for expenditure on old-age pensions to increase relative to GDP. Over the subsequent 6 years, 2010–2016, however, when a more widespread trend of this nature might have been expected as

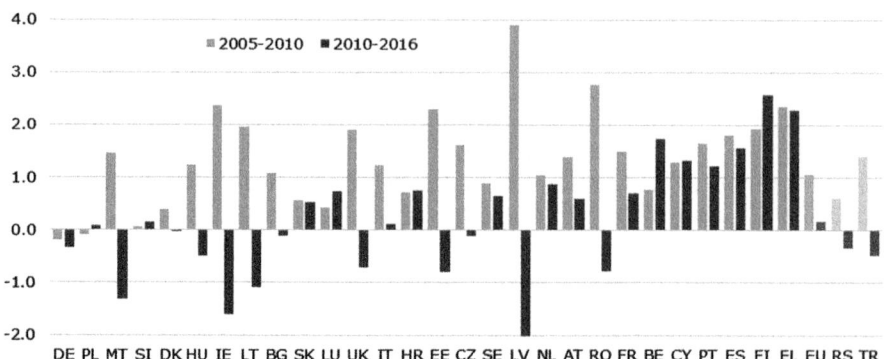

Fig. 1 Changes in expenditure on old-age pensions as a % of GDP, 2005–2016 (percentage point change). Source: Spasova and Ward (2019)

the baby-boom generation reached retirement age, in 11 EU Member States spending on old-age pensions fell relative to GDP. This was particularly the case in Latvia, Ireland, Malta and Lithuania: in these countries expenditure relative to GDP declined by no less than 1 p.p. (Spasova and Ward 2019).

The same trends can be seen with regard to pension expenditure as a share of overall social protection expenditure: this grew by on average 0.8 p.p. in the EU during the period 2005–2016. By contrast, if we look at the core years of the recession, the relative share of pension expenditure fell by 0.3 p.p. (2008–2010), followed by a slight increase (1.1 p.p. in 2010–2016) (Spasova and Ward 2019).

Since the crisis period, although cost-containment policies are still high on many Member States' pension agendas, these have been coupled with measures reorienting the pension mix with a view to increasing its adequacy. These developments are an attempt to respond to certain key labour market and pension system challenges (e.g. combining work with pensions, tailoring pensionable rights to specific categories of workers, etc.).

Pension adequacy is a concept which has been defined differently according to the policy and scientific contexts and purposes (Grech 2013). In general, research has mostly looked at the capacity of pensions to replace the income earned before retirement (mainly measured through replacement rate indicators). Nevertheless, several studies have argued that taking into account the poverty protection and the gender dimension are equally important in order to measure adequacy (Saunders and Wong 2011; Chybalski and Marcinkiewicz 2016; Alonso-Fernandez et al. 2018).

The new Pension Adequacy Report 2018 proposes a triangular concept of pension adequacy which builds on three aspects: *poverty protection, income maintenance* as well as on an innovative one which is the *pension duration* (European Commission 2018b, c). The aim of the latter is to create a link between adequacy and sustainability and to strike a balance between the duration of working life and the duration of retirement "for intergenerational fairness in a context of rising life expectancies" (European Commission 2018b: 89). The new pension duration aspect, proposed by the European Commission and the Social Protection Committee (SPC), seems to be in line with overall EU discourse and its recommendations on pensions (see Sect. 2). The Pension Adequacy report estimates this aspect through the ratio between average years spent in retirement and at work which varies from about 40% (meaning 10 years working for every 4 years in retirement) in Estonia to 60% and more in Belgium, Greece, France, Luxembourg and Slovenia (meaning 10 years of work for 6 plus years in retirement) (Ibid.:90).

Indeed, recent old-age pension reforms that have focused on promoting longer working lives through increases in pensionable ages and through restrictions in access to early retirement options are underpinned by the idea of a win-win scenarios and are expected to "offer the possibility of overcoming the adequacy and financial sustainability trade-off by lowering costs and developing extra revenues, thereby creating the basis for sustainable pension benefits that are higher" (von Nordheim 2016:). The rationale behind these reforms were linked to the rise in average educational achievement levels, as many older workers became employed under the less strenuous working conditions in the service sector (as opposed to manufacturing and primary sector occupations) and as the share of employed women increased significantly (Ibidem).

However, the aspect of pension duration is difficult to estimate as it is linked to several dimensions such as life expectancy, working-life duration and possible interruptions (especially for women) as well as healthy life years, especially for certain categories of workers (Pestieau and Racionero 2016; Cambois et al. 2011). In this chapter we consider reforms aimed at prolonging working lives which have an impact on the age at which people start receiving a pension. We do not consider this aspect as mainly relating to adequacy; rather we conceive it as an issue linked to financial sustainability which in turn impacts adequacy. In this sense, this section aims to critically revisit the main interpretations of the 2018 Pension Adequacy Report. The following analysis is based on the description of reforms[2] in the latter report as well as on the descriptions of reforms provided in the country reports on financing social protection by the European Commission-funded European Social Policy Network (Spasova and Ward 2019) (Table 1).

2.1 Prolonging Working Lives: Confirmation of the Long-Term Trend Towards Maintaining the Sustainability of Pensions

In line with the pattern of crisis and post-crisis reforms, the prolongation of working lives by postponing the date when people enter into retirement continued to be among the key focuses of pension reforms during the period 2014–2017. The main

---

[2]Slavina Spasova, on behalf of the Network Core Team (NCT) of the European Social Policy Network, was the main contributor to the chapter on reforms of the PAR 2018.

Table 1 Reforms affecting pensions in the Member States (2014–2018)

Pension duration						Income maintenance				Poverty reduction		
Increase in pensionable ages	Link to life expectancy	Reducing early retirement opportunities	Tightening eligibility conditions	Incentives for later retirement	Flexible retirement	Contributions	Favourable indexation rules	Favourable rules for certain categories of labour	Reinforcing supplementary pensions	Introducing/ improving minimum pensions	Introducing/ improving other min benefits	Introducing/ improving basic pensions
BG BE CZ EL FsI UK	BG CZ EL FR PT SK	AT BE BG DE DK FI EL LU MT RO	BE EL ES FI FR SK	AT BG HR DK FI FR	AT DE FI SI	AT BG DE EL FI HU RO SI SE	CZ HR EL FI FR LT PT RO SK	FI FR IT LV RO	BE CZ DK EE FR IE IT MT NL SI UK	AT BE BG CY IE MT PL RO SK SI	CZ EE IT SE	EL

Source: Authors own elaboration based on the Pension Adequacy Report 2018b, c (Volumes I and II). The table does not claim to be exhaustive

levers of these reforms were the increase in pensionable ages, tighter eligibility conditions and reductions in early retirement opportunities.

In the post-2014 reforms, the main measures addressing pension duration continued to relate to increasing pensionable ages, extending contributory periods and reducing early retirement opportunities. However, unlike in the previous reform period, these and other measures were less austerity-driven (i.e. fewer direct cuts in benefit payments) and were also expressed in more "positive" terms (e.g. greater "flexibility" in retirement regimes). Moreover, in order to enhance the poverty protection and income maintenance aspects, Member States enhanced the minimum guarantees given to low-income pensioners and removed freezes on pension indexation. Many European countries also tried to address certain key challenges by diversifying pension benefits and providing better coverage of certain categories of workers.

2.1.1 Increasing Pensionable Ages

Uncontestably, increasing pensionable ages has been the main instrument used to improve the sustainability of public pensions. This measure is usually justified by a reference to increasing life expectancy, although this link is the subject of wide scientific and political debate. Indeed, while in some countries life expectancy has been rapidly increasing, in others this has not been the case. Life expectancy also applies differently to different categories of labour and should ideally be linked to measurements of healthy life years (Pestieau and Racionero 2016; Cambois et al. 2011). The PAR's pension adequacy dimension of "pension duration" is therefore equally debatable, as prolonging working lives may lead to shorter pension duration if life expectancy indicators do not develop in line with projections on its increase.

During the period 2014–2019, several Member States (Belgium, Bulgaria, Czech republic, Finland, Netherlands, Portugal, UK) increased or implemented planned increases in, the pensionable age. Finland and Portugal adjusted some parameters of the mechanism linking life expectancy to pensionable age. In Finland, under the new reform implemented as of 2017, the lowest pensionable age will be gradually increased from 63 to 65 (between 2018 and 2027) and the difference between the lowest and highest pensionable ages is to be 5 years. The current increase in pensionable age is 3 months per cohort (starting with those born in 1955); as of 2030, it will be set at 1–2 months per cohort in line with increases in life expectancy (European Commission 2018b, c).

Other countries, such as Bulgaria and the Czech Republic, enacted reforms to link the pensionable age to life expectancy, although further legislation will be required. However, the process and the outcomes of these reforms in the medium-term are quite different in these two countries. In Bulgaria, the pensionable ages for men and women will both reach 65 in 2037, to be linked to life expectancy thereafter. By contrast, in the Czech Republic, the 2017 pension reform capped the ongoing increase in the pensionable age at 65, to be reached in 2030; afterwards the pensionable age is due to be reviewed in the light of life expectancy gains (European Commission 2018b, c).

Poland, quite remarkably, is the only country where the trend towards increasing the pensionable age has been reversed. The previously legislated increase in the pensionable age to 67 for both sexes was indeed annulled: according to the current rules, it will remain at 60 for women and 65 for men. The reform reducing the legislated pensionable age has had an immediate impact on pension claims. In October and November 2017 (i.e. the first two months after the lowering of the pensionable age), almost 350,000 new pensions were granted (compared to less than 230,000 in the whole of 2016), of which almost 60% were for women. The average amount of these newly granted pensions was almost twice as low for women as for men, i.e. PLN 1627.11 (€378) and PLN 2791.728 (€634) respectively (European commission 2018c).

In addition to raising the pensionable age, another key feature of reforms aimed at extending the time spent in work is an increase in career length requirements (e.g. Belgium, Bulgaria, Czech Republic, Finland, France, Italy, Lithuania, Malta, Spain, United Kingdom). The average increase amounts to 5 years of career over the next 15–20 years. In Lithuania, for example, the length of the contributory period will gradually increase, from 30 years in 2017 to 35 years by 2027. In Bulgaria, the required length of service will increase by 2 months each year until it reaches 40 years for men and 37 years for women (European commission 2018b).

Along with raising the pensionable age and extending the time spent in work, some countries have also increased contribution rates for pensions (e.g. Bulgaria, France, Hungary, Italy, Sweden) with a view to improving sustainability. The comprehensive pension reform in Greece imposed a freeze on pensions in payment and revised the calculation rules to improve pension sustainability (e.g. the average pension benefits paid over a working life are now taken into account instead of the years of best earnings; the contributory ceiling for pensions and the ceiling for the net amount of pensions have been lowered). Similarly, Belgium and Bulgaria adopted an overarching reform package, including not only a statutory pensionable age increase and longer career requirements, but also stricter conditions for access to early retirement (European Commission 2018b, c).

2.1.2 Early Retirement: Becoming a Remnant from Another Era?

Early retirement opportunities, which in the past constituted an important aspect of old-age pensions, especially in some sectors and for specific professions, have been reduced still further over the period under scrutiny (e.g. Austria, Belgium, Bulgaria, Denmark, Finland, Luxembourg, Portugal, Slovakia, Spain). The key leverages in these reforms have been to raise the minimum pensionable ages, increase contributory periods and establish penalties relating to early retirement schemes (e.g. Austria, Belgium, Bulgaria, Denmark, Greece), as well as phasing out such early retirement schemes (e.g. Austria, Luxembourg) or transforming them (e.g. Finland, Germany). Other countries applied changes regarding access to disability (e.g. Austria,

Bulgaria, Denmark) and unemployment (e.g. Belgium) benefits, in order to make it more difficult to use these as "proxy early retirement" schemes (European Commission 2018b, c).

An example of considerable changes to eligibility conditions is Portugal, where early retirement was suspended during the bailout assistance agreement, but was reintroduced in 2015. However, early retirement can now only be taken on meeting strict eligibility conditions: by workers with a contribution record of 48 years (compared to 40 years previously) and workers aged 60 or more with a contribution record of 46 years, who started their working life at the age of fourteen or younger.

A phasing out of early retirement schemes is currently taking place in Luxembourg. The early retirement scheme ("*pré-retraite solidarité*") will be phased out as of June 2018. This form of pre-retirement currently allows private sector employees aged 57 or older to leave the labour market three years prior to meeting the eligibility criteria for early retirement (European Commission 2018c).

Along with abolishing and applying stricter conditions to access to early retirement, flexible retirement rules aimed at facilitating longer working lives are becoming more widespread, and have been adopted in Austria, Finland, Germany and Slovenia. In Slovenia, the payment of pensions is no longer limited to the age of 65, and flexible forms of transition from employment to full retirement have been implemented: the minimum threshold is now two hours per day (compared with the previous minimum threshold of four hours a day), with a proportionate share of pension (European Commission 2018b, c).

Finland replaced the previous part-time pension and closed early exit routes, replacing them with more flexible possibilities to combine partial retirement with employment. In the context of the 2017 pension reform, a new type of pension, a *flexible partial old age* (FPOA) pension, was introduced as of 61 years of age, with no restrictions on work or earnings. 25% or 50% may be drawn from the pension entitlements. Whereas it is possible to later increase the take-up rate from 25% to 50%, the opposite move is forbidden. If the claimants take out a partial old-age pension early, the part they are taking out will be permanently reduced by 0.4% for each month until they reach the pensionable age. In Germany, the "Flexi-pension law" (2017) includes a statutory entitlement to participation benefits (prevention and rehabilitation) and promotes a more flexible transition from employment to retirement, and extension of an individual's working life (European Commission 2018b, c).

Probably one of the clearest examples of the link between "pension duration" and adequacy is encouraging retirement later than the pensionable age through bonuses. Several countries have indeed introduced measures of this type: this is for example the case in Austria, Bulgaria, Croatia, Denmark, Finland and France. In Austria, pension insurance contributions are reduced by half for a period of three years if a person chooses to work longer than the pensionable age. In Croatia, since 2014, full deferred retirement is being encouraged by an accrual bonus of 0.15% per month of later retirement, but for a maximum of five years (hence currently up to the age of 70). In Bulgaria, since 2017, indexation has been applied in a way which favours length of contribution over age, in order to reward longer participation in the labour market. (European Commission 2018b, c).

2.2 Adequacy Safeguards as the Main Dimension of Adequacy Policy Reforms

Unsurprisingly perhaps, since the financial crisis, reforms strengthening adequacy have mainly focused on *poverty reduction*. To some extent this reflects the easing of fiscal pressures and acknowledgement of poverty among pensioners, particularly those on a low income (European Commission 2015c, 2018b). Most reforms implemented have strengthened the minimum guarantees for low income pensioners.

After a period of reforms during the crisis—which have directly affected the level of current pensions, such as direct cuts in benefit payments—several Member States sought to improve the protection of low-income pensioners. They did so mainly by introducing basic pensions (Greece) or raising/improving minimum and/or basic pensions, such as in Austria, Belgium, Bulgaria, Cyprus, Ireland, Malta, Poland, Romania, Slovakia and Slovenia. Other countries targeted additional benefits (Czech Republic, Estonia, Italy, Sweden). Moreover, several countries removed the freeze on indexation or introduced new indexation mechanisms (e.g. Bulgaria, Cyprus, Lithuania, Portugal) (European Commission 2018b, c).

Greece introduced a state-funded (basic) national pension equivalent to the at-risk-of poverty threshold for a single person, which was set (for 2016) at €384 per month for a person with 20 years of contributions. This amount is reduced by 2% for every year which falls short of 20, down to 15 years of insurance (15 years being the minimum contributory period for pension entitlement). Moreover, a means-tested social solidarity allowance was established—€360 per month—for uninsured elderly persons (European Commission 2018c).

Malta and Romania have raised the non-taxable minima, which should benefit, in particular, recipients of lower pensions. Bulgaria and Poland increased minimum pensions. While indexation was frozen for several years during and after the economic crisis, in 2015 Romania increased the minimum pension benefit by 14%. Portugal enacted a rise of 10€ per month for low pensions (less than 631.98€ per month) to compensate for the loss of purchasing power caused by the suspension, from 2011 to 2015, of the indexation mechanism. Italy increased the amount of the 14th monthly pension instalment and extended the latter to ca. 1.2 million individuals on low pension benefits; it also increased the minimum non-taxable pension level to €8000 per year for pensioners below the age of 75. In Austria, since January 2017 the minimum pension has been increased from €883 to €1000 per month for people with at least 30 years of contributions. Spain introduced a supplement to contributory pensions for mothers with two or more children (European Commission 2018b, c).

Latvia has tried to make the design of their social contributions more progressive by introducing, in 2016, a "solidarity tax" on income above the social contribution ceilings. The purpose of this was to maintain the same level of total labour taxes for high earners as for low and middle earners. However, in 2017 there was a legal challenge to the tax in the Constitutional Court, which brought about significant changes in its design. It now has the opposite effect from what was originally intended: presently, high earners pay proportionally lower taxes, at the same time accumulating pension rights from income above the social contribution ceilings (Rajevska and Rajevska 2019).

2.3 Income Maintenance: The Neglected Dimension of Pension Adequacy Reforms?

The income maintenance dimension was mostly reflected in reforms aiming to (re-)introduce favourable indexation mechanisms and, to a lesser extent, in reforms reinforcing the role of supplementary pensions. In a few countries, reforms also targeted specific groups such as workers in arduous and hazardous jobs, the self-employed and non-standard workers.

2.3.1 Indexation Mechanisms

In many cases, these measures consisted in the lifting of crisis-induced temporary measures, such as indexation and early retirement freezes. Several countries used **indexation** to improve the real value of pensions (e.g. Bulgaria, Cyprus, Czech Republic, Latvia, Lithuania, Portugal, Romania and Slovenia). Latvia adjusted its pension accrual rules to protect entitlements during the economic downturn, while Lithuania revised its indexation rules and Portugal reintroduced indexation for low and medium-level pensions. Croatia introduced a new rotating indexation system, index-proofing pensions twice a year. Latvia applied a new annual indexation formula to all pensions[3] (European Commission 2018b, c).

2.3.2 Promoting Supplementary Pensions

Since 2015, partly reflecting the post-crisis period, reforms of supplementary pension schemes (occupational and personal pension schemes)[4] have been launched or envisaged in several countries, with the aim of market diversification, individualisation of old-age risk and improvement of income maintenance (e.g. Belgium, Denmark, Estonia, France, Germany, Ireland, Slovenia). Supplementary pensions and,

---

[3]However, the share of the benefit subject to indexation is only equivalent to 50% of the average insured wage for the previous year.

[4]This section does not refer to statutory funded pension schemes. These were subject to extensive reforms during the period 2009–2014 (see PAR 2015). Only some countries have proceeded to minor changes in these schemes (e.g. Bulgaria, Estonia, Lithuania, see European Commission 2018c, Vol. II).

especially, private funded pensions, have also, since the 1990s, become a fundamental component of the EU's programme (Natali 2015). In general, it should be noted that supplementary, and especially private pensions have low coverage, except for in some countries. In most cases, these schemes have undergone parametric reforms, to improve their coverage and adequacy as well as their regulatory structure (European Commission 2018b, c).

Attempts to improve the coverage of occupational pension plans have been made in several countries. Slovenia introduced changes to the occupational insurance system, reinforcing its solidarity element (increase in the lowest occupational pension, a ceiling on the highest pension and the introduction of solidarity reserves). In order to increase the employer's involvement in occupational pension plans, Estonia gave employers more rights to decide on a minimum age for pay-outs from occupational schemes. Belgium enacted a reduction in the legally-guaranteed minimum return from occupational pension funds. It is also considering additional incentives to further promote voluntarily contributions to these schemes. For instance, workers could ask their employers to contribute a further share of their wages to a second pillar. In France, the reform has significantly changed the rules applicable to occupational schemes in terms of the age of retirement. From January 2019, the reform establishes a 10% reduction in pensions for employees who do not continue to work for an extra year after reaching the pensionable age, which amounts to an inducement to extend the working life (European Commission 2018b, c).

Several countries with multiple retirement schemes for different categories of workers within the statutory pension scheme have also improved transferability between schemes. Italy and France now facilitate the cumulation of contributions paid into different first pillar pension regimes. In Greece, all main statutory (contributory) pension funds have been combined into the *Unified Agency for Social Insurance* (EFKA) and all the statutory auxiliary pension and lump sum benefit funds integrated into the *Unified Fund for Auxiliary Social Insurance and Lump Sum Benefits* (ETEAEP) (European Commission 2018b, c).

2.3.3 Extending and Improving Pension Rights to Specific Groups

Along with this more general measure, there were more targeted measures to improve access to old-age protection for specific categories of workers. There are no overall trends in this respect but some country-specific developments.

Such targeted measures took various forms: the granting of legal access to previously excluded categories or making statutory access compulsory for the self-employed (e.g. Greece, Poland, Lithuania, Romania); creating schemes for workers in arduous and hazardous jobs (e.g. Finland, France, Italy); improving effective access to old-age schemes by devising favourable eligibility conditions (e.g. Italy); and improving the transferability of entitlements between old-age schemes related to different categories of workers (e.g. France, Greece, Italy, Poland, Spain).

Lithuania granted access to the statutory pension scheme to "persons engaged in individual activities under business certificates": these statuses became fully integrated into the statutory scheme at the beginning of 2017. Romania extended eligibility for the statutory pension scheme to some categories such as notaries, clerics and lawyers who now can opt in voluntarily. In addition, in 2016 mandatory enrolment was extended to all the self-employed whose earnings are higher than a certain income threshold. As of 2015, Romania also restored the "special service schemes" (with more advantageous pension calculation algorithms, and lower overall contribution levels) for some public sector employees. Poland extended its social insurance coverage to workers on "civil contracts". Spain modified the eligibility conditions (e.g. career length requirements) of part-time workers in order to maintain proportionality with full-time workers (European Commission 2018b, c).

Germany, Italy, Romania and Slovakia enacted reforms which enhance opportunities for early retirement, though in some cases only for specific groups of workers. Thus, Italy has adopted measures facilitating early retirement for some selected categories of "disadvantaged" workers: the APE pension ("Anticipo finanziario a garanzia pensionistica") which provides two different options.[5] Finland has introduced easier access to early retirement for the unemployed. (European Commission 2018b, c).

During the past decade, the main trend has been towards stricter eligibility conditions and the phasing out of certain schemes (Natali et al. 2016) leading Spasova and Vanhercke (2018) to plea for a nuanced debate about the assumed "generosity" of pensions for workers in "hard jobs". However, in some rare cases, countries pushed through reforms creating more favourable conditions for these categories. Finland set up a new scheme for workers in arduous and hazardous jobs: the "years-of-service pension" (minimum pensionable age of 63). France established a "personal prevention account" (*Compte Professionnel de Prévention*), which allows workers to acquire points as a result of exposure to six risk factors—to be used for vocational training, part-time-work on the same pay and early retirement. However, it is worth noting that this account only includes six of the initial ten criteria relating to arduous conditions, and the financing will no longer be covered by specific employer contributions, but by the state. Italy modified special rules for workers in arduous and hazardous jobs, allowing them to retire prior to reaching the pensionable age, provided they have worked as employees in such jobs for at least seven out of the previous ten years before applying for retirement or, alternatively, if they have worked in such jobs for half their career. On-going policy discussions along these lines are currently taking place in Belgium, Croatia and Slovakia (European Commission 2018b, c).

The question is then how the domestic reforms described above are in line with— or may have even have been inspired by—the EU's "soft" policy coordination and overall discourse in the area of pensions, to which we turn in the next section.

---

[5]The financial APE consists of a loan allowing an individual to leave the labour market up to 3 years and 7 months earlier than the legal pensionable age (i.e. at 63 years) by means of a loan issued by a bank. The "social APE" is state-subsidised. It allows certain categories of disadvantaged workers, with at least 30 years of paid contributions, to exit early from the labour market (also up to 3 years and 7 months before the legal pensionable age) through the provision of an allowance of maximum €1500/month.

3   The Evolution of the EU Discourse on Pensions During the Period 2010–2019[6]

Overall, the evolution of the EU discourse on pension policies in the years during and since the EU crisis, from 2010 to 2019, can be categorized into three distinct—albeit interconnected—periods.

The *first* period coincides with the arrival of the "Barroso II" European Commission (November 2010–October 2014), which considered pension reform as an indispensable part of the—much needed—fiscal stabilisation of national budgets, and at the same time called for a wider reflection on the future sustainability of pension systems (primarily through the Green Paper and White Paper on Pensions). Nevertheless, the notion of pension adequacy was also present, and the initiatives which took place at the EU level during that time referred extensively to complementary pensions. The *second* period of EU discourse on pensions starts with the Juncker Commission (as from November 2014) and lasts until the official launch of the European Pillar of Social Rights in November 2017. During that period, the Commission still focused on the fiscal sustainability of pensions; nevertheless, clearer references were made to the trade-off between pension reforms and better budgetary projections, while the Commission made more forceful and socially-minded statements regarding pension adequacy. The novel approach of the Juncker Commission led to the European Pillar of Social Rights, which marks the beginning of the *third* and last period for the EU's discourse on pensions. The Pillar was announced as a renewed approach for social Europe, and the role of pension systems and old age income was referred to as a central element in the improvement of social inclusion and social protection. As reflected in the consecutive Annual Growth Surveys (AGS), these three periods should be understood as an incremental process inextricably linked to the economic, political and social circumstances, rather than as three distinct periods.

3.1   The Green and White Papers on Pensions

The European Commission's 2010 Green Paper on pensions was the starting point for EU policy discourse during the financial and economic crisis.[7] The Green Paper came in the midst of the sovereign debt crisis; it was a consultation aiming to identify common challenges within the various pension systems of Member States and suggest policy priorities for coping with long-standing problems, which had been

---

[6]Specific passages in this section have previously appeared as part of unpublished chapters in the PhD thesis of Louvaris Fasois (2018a).

[7]The EU's involvement largely predated the crisis: in the context of the Broad Economic Policy Guidelines (BEPG), the Member States were invited, since 1999, to "review pension and health care spending in order to be able to cope with the financial burden on welfare spending of the ageing population" (Council of the EU 1999).

aggravated substantially during the last years. To that end, the Paper adopted a broad approach, underlining the need to address the issue of pensions from multiple angles. In that regard, it stressed the need for "an integrated approach across economic, social and financial market policies" (European Commission 2010: 4) and gave a comprehensive overview of all existing soft governance and legal instruments that address pension policies. The notions of "sustainability", "adequacy" and "safety" of pension systems are central to the Green Paper; nevertheless, emphasis was put on policy coordination mechanisms, as a means to stabilize the EU's overall fiscal situation, mitigate any risks and contain spill-over effects between countries.

The European Commission's 2012b White Paper on Pensions adopted as a follow-up to the Green Paper consultation, adopts a similar approach and wording to its predecessor, adhering to the idea of "sustainable, safe and adequate pensions"—indicated in its title. Along the same lines, it also calls for "comprehensive strategies in order to adapt pension systems to changing economic and demographic circumstances" (European Commission 2012b: 3) and underlines the important role of structural reforms in facing the existing challenges. In this regard, it refers to the importance of policy coordination for adjusting the national pension systems and makes explicit reference to the Europe 2020 goals and the Annual Growth Surveys (AGS) as part of the European Semester.

3.2   The Creation of the European Semester

The creation of the European Semester (ES) came as a response to the sovereign debt crisis, as an all-encompassing framework which synchronised and integrated the existing fiscal, economic, employment as well as social coordination mechanisms. Pensions are among the most prominent policies addressed by the Semester, since they have budgetary, macroeconomic and social aspects. We have therefore chosen to analyse the development of EU pension discourse by also showing the changing perception of the role the European Semester, as an overarching coordinating mechanism in which pension policies play a central role.

In May and June 2010, the newly formed European Commission ("Barroso II") proposed the establishment of the Semester, and the Council of Finance Ministers gave its approval on 7 September 2010 (European Commission 2011a). The Semester brings together budgetary, economic, employment and social objectives in one set of recommendations. Putting together—or "yoking together" in the words of Armstrong (2013)—goals and instruments which refer to different policy areas was not something totally new in EU coordination processes: for example, in 2005, the employment guidelines were already incorporated in the Broad Economic Policy Guidelines. Nevertheless, the ES must be seen as a novel institutional arrangement, due to its wide scope, upgraded structure and enhanced degree of interconnectedness. As Bekker (2015: 16) remarks, within the Semester, its distinct coordination mechanisms have influenced each other with regard to their goals and recommendations.

The rationale behind its launch was to enhance ex-ante coordination by setting general policy goals at the beginning of the annual cycle, followed by feedback from each Member State (MS) and ending with country-specific guidance from the Commission and the Council of the EU. The Social Open Method of Coordination (Social OMC) was not officially included in the European Semester, but after 2010 it became clear that the Commission's Secretariat-General (SECGEN) wanted to simplify reporting procedures for the MS, and therefore streamlined social reporting in the Semester through the Europe 2020 procedures (Zeitlin and Vanhercke 2014: 29).

3.3 The Barroso II Commission

Faced with the financial and economic crisis, which required a decisive response, the EU institutions as well as the Member States were under pressure to swiftly adopt extensive regulatory reforms to mitigate the fiscal risks and prevent any spill-over effects inside the Eurozone. The unprecedented crisis called for better coordination within the EMU's decentralised economic pillar (Puetter 2012: 172) and enhanced the role of the European Council, the Economic and Financial Affairs (ECOFIN) Council formation and the Eurogroup, which found themselves at the epicentre of the crisis management (Dinan 2011).

In terms of content, the scope of the Semester has expanded significantly, to include a wide range of macroeconomic, employment and social issues. These existed within the Europe 2020 strategy and the Social OMCs before the launch of the Semester, as was also pointed out by the Commission (EUobserver 2011b: 15 June). However, in recent years employment and social inclusion issues—including pension reforms—have been referred to more frequently in the Country Specific Recommendations (CSRs), thus feeding into domestic political debates and enhancing their link with the growth situation in the EU and in the Eurozone particularly. The chapter does not analyse the CSRs in great detail, as this is a more elaborate exercise more closely related to economic policy and the interaction between the EU and national levels.[8]

With the creation of the European Semester, the momentum seemed right for adopting more reforms via the "fast-track" procedure (European Commission 2011a). On 29 September 2010, the Commission proposed six legislative measures for the creation of stricter rules on fiscal and macroeconomic issues. The so-called "Six-Pack", which is made up of five Regulations and one Directive, was backed in principle by all Member States. The Six-Pack introduced measures for better monitoring and closer surveillance, as well as rules for enhanced implementation. In addition, the two Regulations comprising the Pack were a further step towards

---

[8]Guidi and Guardiancich (2018) provide a comprehensive quantitative analysis of the CSRs specifically focusing on pensions, between 2011 and 2016.

budgetary and fiscal coordination: by 30 November of each year, the Commission must examine the draft budgetary plans of the MS, in order to assess their alignment with the Stability and Growth Pact (SGP) rules, before they are adopted in December.

Proper implementation of the new coordination framework tested the credibility of the capabilities and independence of the European Commission, which was under pressure to learn quickly how to act effectively under the new circumstances (L'Echo 2014: 5 May). As a result, in its first cycles it adopted a strict stance, with overly prescriptive and top-down recommendations together with harsh references to the complaints made by the MS. This caused many academics and members of the public to note that the EU "governs by rules and rules by numbers" in the Eurozone (Schmidt 2015). In fact, the Commission wanted to act quickly in order to avoid a prolonged economic recession as a result of low growth and growing public debt, as the statement of President Barroso shows: "We face a simple choice: a decade of debt or a generation of growth" (EUobserver 2011a: 12 January). For that reason, the CSRs in the first Semester cycles were overly prescriptive and focused explicitly on austerity measures, wage containment and greater flexibility of the labour market for better competitiveness. The pressure was considerable, as in December 2011, 23 out of 27 Member States were subject to an Excessive Deficit Procedure (EDP) (European Commission 2011b). Given this alarming context (which, some argue, was aggravated by the Commission's own austerity initiatives), pension sustainability became a central topic of discussion as a means to balance the dire fiscal and budgetary situation. The statement made by László Andor, who was at the time Commissioner for Employment, Social Affairs and Inclusion, shows that the sustainability of pension systems was perceived as an overarching priority from the very beginning of the European Semester, since the issue played a central role in regard to fiscal coordination: "The pension system will be less sustainable in the long run and the imbalances in the social security system can contribute to an overall problem of the public finances" (Euractiv 2011: 25 March).

In October 2010, nine Member States had tabled a proposal, which was eventually voted on by the national Ministers of Finance, stipulating that the cost of pension reforms should be taken into account in a favourable way when considering whether to open or abrogate an EDP for a Member State, in accordance with the SGP rules. As a 2013 European Commission memo clarifies, the criterion for deciding on abrogation of an EDP is based on its "durable correction". When the deficit is close to the reference value of 3% of GDP and the debt level stays below 60% of GDP—as stipulated in the SGP rules—the Commission "will also take into account the net cost of the implementation of pension reforms involving the setup of a mandatory, fully funded second pillar" (European Commission 2013a). More precisely, account should be taken of whether exceeding the 3% debt reference value is sufficiently explained "by the net cost of the implementation of the pension reforms" (ibidem).

In that sense, the European Semester established a trade-off mechanism between the national reforms that need to be taken and the fiscal space that Member States enjoy. The Ageing Working Group of the Economic Policy Committee (EPC), a (ECOFIN) Council advisory body, incorporates the national projections on age-related expenditure (including pensions) into the EU-level triennial Ageing

Reports. The projected estimates of age-related expenditure feed into the formula for the calculation of Medium-Term Budgetary Objectives (MTOs) of each individual Member State. So, in that regard, if a new pension reform leads to reduced projections of age-related government expenditure, this automatically decreases the MTO and leaves more fiscal leeway available to the Member State as prescribed in the SGP rules.[9]

The Annual Growth Surveys (AGS) can provide a good overview of the main policy principles set by the European Commission over the years in regard to pension system reform. The AGS are the Commission's planning documents for defining the EU's broader economic and social priorities for the year to come, and mark the start of each European Semester cycle, which finishes with the publication and endorsement of the Country Specific Recommendations. According to Guardianchich and Guidi (2017) the first AGS, published in January 2011, reflected the general direction of the European Semester which had "a three-pronged strategy, based on higher retirement age and restricted eligibility, efficient labour markets for elderly workers and enhanced complementary savings". Since the focus was primarily on the financial sustainability of pension systems, both the 2011 and 2012 AGS make no explicit reference to pension adequacy, but rather mention that the development of "complementary private savings" is important for strengthening retirement incomes (European Commission 2011c: 7; European Commission 2011d: 6). Likewise, the 2013 AGS addresses pension reforms with the clear aim of ensuring "cost-effectiveness and sustainability", thus mentioning them together with health care system reforms. At the same time, there is no real elaboration and further development of the notion of adequacy in the 2013 AGS.

Despite the central position of the sustainability of pensions in the AGS over the years, pension adequacy was an issue which was (somewhat) present during the Barroso Commission. Nevertheless, it was presented as a separate policy issue from sustainability, while the policy preparation and decision-making procedures for these topics were not closely linked. On the one hand, the financial sustainability of pensions is analysed in the triennial ageing reports prepared by the Economic Policy Committee (EPC)'s Working Group on Ageing Populations and Sustainability (AWG) and the Commission's Directorate General (DG) for Economic and Financial Affairs (ECFIN). On the other hand, the Commission's DG for Employment, Social Affairs and Inclusion (EMPL) and the Council's Social Protection Committee (SPC) jointly published their first Pension Adequacy Report in May 2012, which, among other things, mentions the importance of supplementary pensions for higher retirement income, as also seen from the statement of Commissioner Andor: "With a rapidly growing role for occupational pensions, the portability of second pillar pension rights is gaining importance" (European Commission 2012a).

As the risk of a default among the Eurozone states receded, the Barroso II Commission gradually softened its approach, building up trust with the MS and becoming more open to discussing its recommendations. With much fiscal effort, the

---

[9]For a more detailed analysis see: Louvaris Fasois (2018b).

number of Member States under an EDP dropped gradually to 17 in 2014 (The European Sting 2014: 6 June) and decreased further to 11 in the summer of 2015 (European Commission 2015b). The slightly softer stance of the European Commission is reflected in the 2014 AGS which, together with the fiscal sustainability of pension systems, explicitly mentions their role "in meeting social needs and ensuring essential social safety nets" (European Commission 2013b: 8). At the same time, although the notion of linking statutory retirement age to life expectancy has been mentioned steadily since 2012, it is more prominent in the AGS from 2014 onwards.

3.4   The Juncker Commission

The Juncker Commission adopted a new focus as well as a communication strategy on social policies (achieving a "social triple A" rating), by openly expressing the need to enhance the social dimension of policy-making at the EU level, in response to the effects of the EU crisis. Already as President-elect, Jean-Claude Juncker referred to the issue of pension adequacy and better social inclusion in his political guidelines for the new Commission: "I am a strong believer in the social market economy. It is not compatible with the social market economy that during the crisis, ship-owners and speculators become even richer, while pensioners can no longer support themselves" (Frazer et al. 2014: 5).

With the arrival of the Juncker Commission, the CSRs became more explicitly focused on structural reforms—in which pensions play a central role—while several MS, most notably Italy and France, hoped that the Semester's budgetary rules would be interpreted in a more lenient way (EUobserver 2014: 22 October). Ultimately, they were right (see: Reuters 2016: 3 June) as the discourse in the Five Presidents' Report also hints (Juncker 2015). On 13 January 2015, the Commission published a communication on interpreting the SGP rules in a more flexible way. This was a small breakthrough, since it made the link between fiscal discipline and structural reforms more explicit, by amending two clauses.

The "structural reforms clause", firstly, stipulates that when assessing the permitted deviation of a MS from its Medium-Term Budgetary Objectives, the Commission can take into consideration not only measures with direct growth impact, but also measures which can potentially lead to growth. Likewise, in its report on opening an EDP against a delinquent MS, the Commission shall take a broader view when considering domestic structural reforms. Such reforms referred primarily to pensions, since they could have direct and long-term budgetary effects (Angerer 2015). Conversely, if a MS fails to adopt the agreed reforms, this can be considered an "aggravating relevant factor" (European Commission 2015a:13) in the assessment of the effective action taken. On the other hand, the updated "investment clause" stipulates that when a country deviates temporarily from the MTO adjustment path, the Commission can allow investment provided that GDP growth is negative and that the country does not exceed its 3% of GDP deficit—leaving out the debt reduction criterion which was previously in place. As a result, the use of structural reforms and investment became more explicit, thereby officially opening the road to a more flexible interpretation of the fiscal consolidation rules.

The Juncker Commission explicitly recognized the existing trade-off mechanism embedded in the European Semester, thus making it easier for national politicians to understand the politics of pension reform and engage in bilateral bargaining with the European Commission. In the words of a Commission high official:

> We have issued a communication in January 2015, the flexibility document, in which we more or less explicitly said you can use it as a trade-off. If you ask me about the difference about the former Commission and this one on the Semester, I would say that's it. For the previous Commission, you had to pursue structural reforms, get your budget in order and this Commission sees it as dependent variables to some extent, like if you do this on this from you can do slightly less on this front and this flexibility communication is a symbol now. (COM01)

All in all, the Juncker Commission clarified the relationship between fiscal responsibility and structural reforms, through the politicization of the procedure and by expressing the existence of such a trade-off mechanism.

At the same time, the streamlining—or revamping—of the European Semester during the first year of the Juncker Commission came as a response to legitimacy concerns, aimed at greater national ownership and implementation of the reforms. In an effort to simplify the process and the recommendations of the European Semester, but also to prioritise its policy goals, the Commission reduced the number of CSRs and made them less prescriptive, while increasing the visibility of the social objectives. In addition, the Commission's Staff Working Documents (SWD) were merged with the Macroeconomic Imbalance Procedure's (MIP) "In-Depth Reviews" into a single document, and its publication was moved to February, in order to allow time for discussions with the national governments and social partners (Zeitlin and Vanhercke 2017). In a similar way, since 2014, the practice of bilateral meetings has gained ground within the European Semester, becoming a central factor of peer pressure and improving deliberations between the MS and the Commission. Although their number may vary between countries, there are a few important bilateral meetings within each cycle, according to Coman and Ponjaert (2016: 49). The Economic and Financial Committee (EFC) has recently taken stock of these positive developments, adding the streamlining of macroeconomic objectives and the more balanced presentation of structural reforms as a whole (EFC 2016).

The renewed approach of the Juncker Commission in regard to social policies is reflected in the respective AGS of that period. Looking at the 2015 AGS, pension adequacy is mentioned on a more equal footing, and more extensively than in the past: "the adequacy of pension systems needs to be preserved, so that a decent level of income after retirement is ensured" (European Commission 2014: 12). Even as the economic situation in most of the EU Member States began to normalize, the social and economic disparities between them were still much in evidence, as a legacy of the crisis. Consequently, the Commission's discourse focused on "strengthening the recovery and fostering convergence" through enhanced investment, structural reforms and responsible fiscal behaviour (European Commission 2015c). In the 2016 AGS, pension systems continue to be seen primarily as a means to responsible fiscal policies, but at the same time there is extensive mention made of pension adequacy and the use of complementary pension schemes with a view to achieving that goal. Along the same lines, the role of the social partners is mentioned for the first time.

The narrative on the need to promote economic recovery in the EU continued in 2017. In particular, the AGS of that year recognizes that multiple reforms have already taken place in various MS. At the same time, it adopts a broad approach by referring to the extension of working lives as the appropriate policy response to address both sustainability and adequacy of pensions (European Commission 2016: 16). Importantly, supplementary pension systems are also seen as an aid to pension income adequacy, while the Commission underlines that any measures in that direction should be designed "depending on the national context" (European Commission 2016: 12).

3.5 The European Pillar of Social Rights

The formal proclamation of the European Pillar of Social Rights (EPSR) marks the final period of EU discourse on pension policies. Although the Pillar initiative does not refer to pensions per se, it is a new symbol for the enhancement of the EU's social dimension, hence it should be considered as the beginning of a new period at the EU level, also relevant to pensions. Vanhercke et al. (2018: 157) stress that the Pillar could be seen first of all as a symbol that shows "the EU's renewed commitment to protecting the social rights of its citizens". As Vandenbroucke (2018) also observes, the EPSR must not be seen as an "isolated event", since it is included in the wider evolution of EU discourse and policy-making, which have gradually given more prominence and coverage to social issues and underlined even more the need for balance, together with fiscal and monetary policy coordination.

Several authors furthermore underline (Costamagna 2019; Ferrera 2018) that the European Pillar of Social Rights came as a policy response to "increasing criticism about the EU's social deficit" (Garben 2019). It is made up of twenty principles, of which two are linked to social protection and inclusion: principles 12 and 15 refer to social protection as well as to old age income and pensions respectively, while they both mention the right to adequate social protection and adequate pension income. In that sense, the Pillar introduces a "rights-based social investment approach" to these policies (Sabato and Corti 2018: 61), a fact which is very pertinent given the fiscal and macroeconomic character of pensions. Since the European Semester emphasises the financial sustainability of pension systems, the Pillar might be able to further enhance its social dimension, by channelling recommendations on pension adequacy in an even more consistent manner within the annual socio-economic coordination process. A similar point, which is relevant to the Pillar's capacity to promote the social dimension of pensions, has appeared in the European Commission's latest AGS, stating that the mainstreaming of the Pillar has supported the process of structural reforms (European Commission 2018a: 5).

As Sabato and Corti (2018: 56) point out, the European Semester has taken on board the European Pillar of Social Rights "to a fairly satisfactory degree". Overall, the focus of the Semester's discourse during the last couple of years has been on maintaining the momentum for reforms despite the favourable economic climate. The AGS for 2018 and 2019 adopt a holistic approach to pension policies, but recommendations are framed rather broadly. For example, the 2018 AGS refers to pension sustainability and adequacy, adding that "retirement incomes can be boosted by extending working lives… and supporting other complementary means of retirement incomes" (European Commission 2017:12). Likewise, the AGS of the following year underlines that pension reforms remain essential for the two aspects of pension systems and refers once again to the importance of complementary retirement savings. Importantly, the AGS of both years make reference to the European Pillar of Social Rights as an important EU initiative, clarifying that this "should be used as a compass" (ibidem: 3).

All in all, the discourse, process and content of the Semester's recommendations have gradually become more social, including on the issue of pensions. Even more so, during this last period of EU discourse initiated with the EPRS, there are signs that several actors in the Commission aim to continue the existing integrated approach in policy-making. The 2018 Pension Adequacy Report states that it "supports Member States in designing pension systems that are adequate while remaining financially sustainable, being mutually complementary with the Ageing Report" (European Commission 2018b: 17). Furthermore, the Social Protection Committee (SPC), an advisory body of the Employment, Social Policy, Health and Consumer Affairs Council (EPSCO) Council formation involved in the preparation of the Report together with DG EMPL, underlined the necessity "for a holistic reflection on the adequacy of old-age incomes and the financial sustainability of pension systems" while at the same time it invited the actors involved in the drafting of the triennial "Ageing Reports" prepared by DG ECFIN to "jointly promote the findings" of that year (ibidem:21).

The trend towards a more integrated approach in regard to the future development of complementary pensions can also be seen in the Commission's decision to form the High-Level Group on Pensions in the second half of 2018. Together with the adoption of a more holistic understanding of pension systems and the inclusion of stakeholders from various backgrounds, the initiative aims to enhance cooperation between DG EMPL and DG for Financial Stability, Financial Services and Capital Markets Union (FISMA), as lead and associate DG respectively. It remains to be seen to what degree the results of the group's workings will reflect a substantially global approach to pension policies, as well as how the cooperation of the Commission's Directorates will unroll for the dissemination of the group's final output.

4 Conclusions

This Chapter explored the main reform trends in the EU Member States in terms of pension adequacy during the period of recovery after the Great Recession 2014–2019 as well as the European Commission's discourse and policy orientation with regards to pensions since the start of the European Semester. In terms of adequacy concerns both the Member States and the EU have begun to bring adequacy back in the policy equation. However, the shadow of previous austerity policies still looms large over pension reforms. In many cases, national reforms seem to have been more about "damage control", softening the worst social outcomes of previous reforms, rather than reflecting a firm political choice to boost pension adequacy.

These national developments are also mirrored in the EU discourse on pensions which changed gradually, from a strict and primarily fiscally oriented approach at the peak of the EU crisis, to greater concern for social issues at the end of the Barroso Commission. The Juncker Commission went even further, explicitly adopting a more socially oriented discourse, culminating in the adoption of the European Pillar of Social Rights. Pension policies in the European Semester are still addressed primarily from a fiscal point of view; nevertheless, concerns related to their social dimension have been mainstreamed over the years, thus becoming more visible at the EU level, as part of the overarching socio-economic policy coordination process.

The development of the EU discourse on pensions is inextricably linked to the evolution of the European Semester, since the former has occupied a central place in the Commission's recommendations regarding structural reforms. The analysis of the AGS for the years 2011–2019, showed the Commission's policy orientation in relation to pensions. Despite the central position that fiscal sustainability of pensions has had over the years (in particular through the recommendations focusing on increasing the pensionable age and restricting early retirement), adequacy has gradually come to prominence, contributing to a more balanced approach to pension policies. The earlier strict approach was deemed necessary to cope with the effects of the Euro crisis, but waned later on, as economies started to recover and dissenting voices began to multiply. As the EU narrative gradually shifted from strict fiscal consolidation to the promotion of growth and structural reforms, the notion of "national ownership" increased in importance and the social dimension of various policies became more pronounced.

In this context, the chapter shows also that the Pension Adequacy report tries to reconcile sustainability and adequacy policies, in particular through the innovative triangular conception of pension adequacy: poverty reduction, income maintenance and the new dimension of *pension* duration. The latter is the bridging point to financial sustainability. However, drawing in the reforms described under the pension duration's aspect of pension adequacy in the 2018 PAR, we show that these reforms (e.g. increasing pensionable ages etc) have served mainly financial sustainability concerns rather than adequacy goals. Thus, the point of departure is clearly financial sustainability, the outcomes are still to be seen and indeed, whether could be interpreted in the light of adequacy achievements. The new Pension's adequacy Report 2018 puts also the accent—for the first time—on supplementary pensions, which have consistently been presented by the EU as a means for enhanced sustainability of social security systems and better pension adequacy.

At least from a communication perspective, the EU has incrementally adopted a more holistic approach to pensions, addressing both adequacy and sustainability on a progressively equal footing. The collaboration between EU level policy makers on the social and fiscal dimension of pensions, as seen after the publication of the 2018 Ageing Report and the 2018 Pension Adequacy Report, marks probably a first step towards better collaboration and a more integrated procedural approach in the years to come. As mentioned earlier, it also remains to be seen how the final report of the expert group on pensions will be communicated and how a broader range of stakeholders will participate in the ensuing debate.

List of Interviews
COM1: High Official in the European Commission Representation in Belgium [May 2016].

References

Alonso-Fernandez J-J, Meneu-Gaya R, Devesa-Carpio E, Devesa-Carpio M, Dominguez-Fabian I, Encinas-Goenechea B (2018) From the replacement rate to the synthetic indicator: a global and gender measure of pension adequacy in the European Union. Soc Indic Res 138:165–186

Angerer J (2015) Stability and growth pact – an overview of the rules, briefing, economic governance support unit. European Parliament, Brussels, 18 December

Armstrong KA (2013) The new governance of EU fiscal discipline. Eur Law Rev 38(5):601–617

Barr N (2002) Reforming pensions: myths, truths, and policy choices. Int Soc Secur Rev 55(2):3–36

Bekker S (2015) European socioeconomic governance in action: coordinating social policies in the third European Semester. OSE Research Paper No. 15, European Social Observatory, January

Cambois E, Laborde C, Romieu I, Robine J (2011) Occupational inequalities in health expectancies in France in the early 2000s: unequal chances of reaching and living retirement in good health. Demogr Res 25:407–436

Chybalski F, Marcinkiewicz E (2016) The replacement rate: an imperfect indicator of pension adequacy in cross-country analyses. Soc Indic Res 126(1):99–117

Coman R, Ponjaert F (2016) From one Semester to the next: towards the hybridization of new modes of governance in EU policy. Cahiers du CEVIPOL No. 5/2016, Issue on the Economic Governance, Université Libre de Bruxelles

Costamagna F (2019) The European Social Union as a "Union of national welfare states": a legal perspective, 5 January. http://www.euvisions.eu/the-european-social-union-as-a-union-of-national-welfare-states-a-legal-perspective/. Assessed 12 March 2019

Council of the EU (1999) Draft Report from the Council (ECOFIN) on the Broad Guidelines of the Economic Policies of the Member States and the Community, appended to the Presidency Conclusions of the Cologne European Council 3–4 June 1999. Doc 8586/99

Dinan D (2011) Governance and institutions: implementing the Lisbon treaty in the shadow of the Euro crisis. J Common Mark Stud 49(1):103–121

EFC (2016) 2016 European semester process: encouraging implementation. No. 12727/16, Brussels, 4 October

EUobserver (2011a) Brussels demands yet more austerity from member states, 12 January. https:// euobserver.com/economic/31632. Accessed 12 Mar 2019

EUobserver (2011b) Four states push back against 'EU Semester', 15 June. https://euobserver.com/ economic/32494. Accessed 12 Mar 2019

EUobserver (2014) EU fiscal rules won't be changed says Juncker, 22 October. https://euobserver. com/news/126197. Accessed 12 Mar 2019

Euractiv (2011) Andor: 'Make room for more social inclusion measures with ESF funding', 25 March. https://www.euractiv.com/section/social-europe-jobs/interview/andor-make-room-for-more-social-inclusion-measures-with-esf-funding/. Accessed 12 Mar 2019

European Commission (2010) Green Paper towards adequate, sustainable and safe European pension systems. COM (2010) 365 final, Brussels, July

European Commission (2011a) European semester: a new architecture for the new EU Economic governance. MEMO/11/14, Press Release, 12 January. http://europa.eu/rapid/pressrelease_ MEMO-11-14_en.htm. Accessed 12 Mar 2019

European Commission (2011b) EU Economic governance "Six-pack" enters into force. Press Release, 12 December. http://europa.eu/rapid/press-release_MEMO-11-898_en.htm#footnote1. Accessed 12 Mar 2019

European Commission (2011c) Annual growth survey: advancing the EU's comprehensive response to the crisis. COM (2011) 11 final, Brussels, 12 January

European Commission (2011d) Annual growth survey 2012. COM (2011) 815 final, Brussels, 23 November

European Commission (2012a) Sustainable pensions for Europe – the need for action. Press Release, 19 September. http://europa.eu/rapid/press-release_SPEECH-12-619_en.htm. Accessed 12 Mar 2019

European Commission (2012b) White paper. An agenda for adequate, safe and sustainable pensions. COM (2012) 55 final, Brussels, February

European Commission (2012c) Annual growth survey 2013. COM (2012) 750 final, Brussels, 28 November

European Commission (2013a) Commission takes steps under the excessive deficit procedure. Brussels, 29 May. http://europa.eu/rapid/press-release_MEMO-13-463_en.htm. Accessed 12 Mar 2019

European Commission (2013b) Annual growth survey 2014. COM (2013) 800 final, Brussels, 13 November

European Commission (2014) Annual growth survey 2015. COM (2014) 902 final, Brussels, 28 November

European Commission (2015a) Making the best use of the flexibility within the existing rules of the stability and growth pact. Communication, COM (2015) 12 final, 13 January

European Commission (2015b) Tax shift in Belgium: what impact on poverty? ESPN Flash report, 2015/36, July

European Commission (2015c) Annual growth survey 2016: strengthening the recovery and fostering convergence. Press Release, Brussels, 26 November. http://europa.eu/rapid/press-release_IP-15-6069_en.htm. Accessed 12 Mar 2019

European Commission (2015d) Pension adequacy report 2015 – current and future income adequacy in old age in the EU, vol 1. European Commission, Brussels

European Commission (2016) Annual growth survey 2017. COM (2016) 725 final, Brussels, 16 November

European Commission (2017) Annual growth survey 2018. COM (2017) 690 final, Brussels, 22 November

European Commission (2018a) Annual growth survey 2019: for a stronger Europe in the face of global uncertainty. COM (2018) 770 final, Brussels, 21 November

European Commission (2018b) Pension adequacy report 2018 – current and future income adequacy in old age in the EU, vol 1. European Commission, Brussels

European Commission (2018c) Pension adequacy report 2018 – current and future income adequacy in old age in the EU, vol II. European Commission, Brussels

Ferrera M (2018) Crafting the ESU – towards a roadmap for delivery. EuVisions, 3 December. http://www.euvisions.eu/crafting-the-european-social-union-ferrera/. Assessed 12 March 2019

Frazer H, Guio A-C, Marlier E, Vanhercke B, Ward T (2014) Putting the fight against poverty and social exclusion at the heart of the EU agenda: A contribution to the mid-term review of the Europe 2020 strategy. OSE Paper Series, No. 15, October

Garben S (2019) The European pillar of social rights: an assessment of its meaning and significance. Camb Yearb Eur Leg Stud:1–27

Grech A (2013) How best to measure pension adequacy. CASE/172, Centre for Analysis of Social Exclusion, London School of Economics, London, United Kingdom

Guardianchich I, Guidi M (2017) Pensions and the European Semester: from national to supranational policy domain? EuVisions, 22 May. http://www.euvisions.eu/archive/pensions-european-supranational/. Accessed 12 Mar 2019

Guidi M, Guardiancich I (2018) Intergovernmental or supranational integration? A quantitative analysis of pension recommendations in the European Semester. Eur Union Polit 19 (4):684–706

Juncker J-C, in close cooperation with Tusk D, Dijsselbloem J, Draghi M, Schulz M (2015) Completing Europe's Economic and Monetary Union, June 2015. https://ec.europa.eu/commission/sites/beta-political/files/5-presidents-report_en.pdf. Accessed 12 Mar 2019

L'Echo (2014) La Belgique devant les juges de Schuman, 5 May. http://www.lecho.be/dossier/europe/La-Belgique-devant-les-juges-de-Schuman/9497317. Accessed 12 Mar 2019

Louvaris Fasois C (2018a) The political economy of the social dimension of economic and monetary union: the effects of the European Semester on social and employment policies in Belgium, PhD thesis. University of Amsterdam, Amsterdam

Louvaris Fasois C (2018b) Mechanisms of policy learning in the European Semester: pension reforms in Belgium. In: Dunlop CA, Radaelli CM, Trein P (eds) Learning in public policy. Analysis, modes and outcomes. Palgrave Macmillan, Cham, pp 75–96

Natali D (2015) Pension reform in Europe: what has happened in the wake of the crisis? CESifo DICE Rep 13(2):31–35

Natali D (ed) (2017) The new pension mix in Europe. PIE Peter Lang, Brussels

Natali D, Spasova S, Vanhercke B (2016) Retirement regimes for workers in arduous or hazardous jobs in Europe. European Commission, Brussels

Natali D (2018) Recasting pensions in Europe: policy challenges and political strategies to pass reforms. Swiss Polit Sci Rev 24(1):53–59

Nooruddin I, Simmons J (2006) The politics of hard choices: IMF programs and government spending. Int Organ 60(4):1001–1033

Orenstein M (2008a) Privatizing pensions: the transnational campaign for social security reform. Princeton University Press, Princeton

Orenstein M (2008b) Out-liberalizing the EU: pension privatization in Central and Eastern Europe. J Eur Publ Policy 15(6):899–917

Pestieau P, Racionero M (2016) Harsh occupations, life expectancy and social security. Econ Model 58:194–202

Puetter U (2012) Europe's deliberative intergovernmentalism: the role of the council and European Council in EU economic governance. J Eur Publ Policy 19(2):161–178

Rajevska F, Rajevska O (2019) ESPN thematic report on financing social protection. European Commission, Latvia

Reuters (2016) Dijselbloem dénonce l'indulgence de la Commission pour France, 3 June. http://fr.reuters.com/article/frEuroRpt/idFRL8N18V0RB. Accessed 12 Mar 2019

Sabato S, Corti F (2018) 'The times they are a-chaning?' The European pillar of social rights from debates to reality check. In: Vanhercke B, Ghailani D, Sabato S (eds) Social policy in the European Union: state of play 2018. ETUI and OSE, Brussels

Saunders P, Wong M (2011) Pension adequacy and the pension review. Econ Labour Relat Rev 22 (3):7–26

Schmidt VA (2015) The Eurozone's crisis of democratic legitimacy: can the EU rebuild public trust and support for European Economic Integration? Discussion Paper 015, September, Directorate-General for Economic and Financial Affairs, European Commission, Brussels

Spasova S (2013) Les réformes des retraites dans les Pays d'Europe centrale et orientale: entre influences internationales et déterminants nationaux. La Revue de l'IRES 77(2):129–163

Spasova S, Vanhercke B (2018) The 'generosity' of pensions for workers in hard jobs: in need of a nuanced debate. ETUI Policy Brief N° 12/2018. European Trade Union Institute, Brussels

Spasova S, Ward T (2019) Social protection expenditure and its financing in Europe. A study of national policies 2019, European Social Policy Network (ESPN), European Commission, Brussels

The European Sting (2014) The EU slowly exits from "Excessive Deficit Procedure" and hopefully from 'Excessive Austerity Procedure' too, 6 June. https://europeansting.com/2014/06/06/the-euslowly-exits-from-excessive-deficit-procedure-and-hopefully-from-excessive-austerity-proceduretoo/. Accessed 12 Mar 2019

Vandenbroucke F (2018) The European pillar of social rights: from promise to delivery – Introduction to the "European Social Union (ESU) public forum debate", EuVisions, 3 December. http://www.euvisions.eu/europea-social-union-public-forum-debate-vandenbroucke/. Accessed 12 Mar 2019

Vanhercke B, Sabato S, Ghailani D (2018) The European pillar of social rights as a game changer. In: Vanhercke B, Ghailani D, Sabato S (eds) Social policy in the European Union: state of play 2018. ETUI and OSE, Brussels

von Nordheim F (2016) The 2015 pension adequacy report's examination of extended working lives as a route to future pension adequacy. Intereconomics 51(3):125–134

Zeitlin J, Vanhercke B (2014) Socializing the European Semester? Economic governance and social policy coordination in Europe 2020. SIEPS Report 2014:7. Swedish Institute for European Policy Studies, Stockholm, December

Zeitlin J, Vanhercke B (2017) 'Socializing the European Semester: EU economic and social policy coordination in crisis and beyond', Journal of European Public Policy. In: Zeitlin J, Verdun A (Guest eds) EU socio-economic governance since the crisis: the European Semester in theory and practice, pp 149–174

Slavina Spasova PhD in Political Science, has been a researcher in the area of social protection at the OSE since January 2016 and is a Research Associate at the Centre d'étude de la vie politique (CEVIPOL), Université Libre de Bruxelles. Her research agenda focuses on various social protection and employment related subjects, including systemic pension reforms in Central and Eastern European countries, labour market reforms and social dialogue. She worked on a variety of issues—including, work-life balance, long-term care, social protection for non-standard workers and the self-employed etc. She was the lead researcher for the European Social Policy Network (ESPN) input to the European Commission's 2018 Pensions Adequacy Report (PAR) and will provide a key contribution to the PAR 2020.

Christos Louvaris Fasois is policy advisor on pension & financial affairs at the European Association of Paritarian Institutions (AEIP). He holds a PhD (October 2018) jointly from the Institute for Social Science Research at the University of Amsterdam and from the Department of Social and Political Sciences of the University of Milan. His thesis focused on the influence of the European Semester on employment and social policies. In particular, it analysed the effects and mechanisms that lead political actors to adopt reforms in the field of pensions, tax-shift away from labour as well as inclusion of migrants in the labour market. In his current position, he researches on the role of occupational pension funds within the EU social security systems, primarily from the perspective of adequacy and financial sustainability.

Bart Vanhercke PhD in Social Science, has been Director at the Brussels-based European Social Observatory since 2010. He is therefore in charge of the broad research strategy, the internal organization of the team, managing the budget, and overseeing the OSE communication strategy. He was appointed as Policy Fellow at the Institute for the Study of Labour (IZA Berlin) in November 2015. His current research focuses on the European Pillar of Social Rights and the social dimension of the new European economic governance, topics on which he also works as associate academic staff at the Research Institute for Work and Society (HIVA), the University of Leuven. Earlier research experience dealt with the Europeanization of domestic social inclusion, health care and pensions policies through different EU policy instruments (law, governance and financial instruments) and the social challenges of EMU and EU enlargement. Bart Vanhercke was appointed, for the academic year 2013–2014, Associate Professor at the Institute for European Studies of the Saint-Louis University (FUSL). In March 2016 he obtained his PhD (cum laude) at the Amsterdam Institute for Social Science Research (AISSR) of the University of Amsterdam.

How to Best Address Pension Adequacy and Financial Sustainability in the Context of Population Ageing: The Labour Market as a Key Determinant

Josef Wöss and Erik Türk

> *Raising employment levels . . . is arguably the most effective strategy with which countries can prepare for population ageing*
>
> (European Commission 2008)

Abstract Against the background of population ageing pension debate has focussed for many years on the future increase of the so-called old-age dependency ratio, i.e. the number of older people against the number of people of working age. Incomprehensibly, this ratio is often misinterpreted as the ratio between workers and pensioners. Yet, wrongly equalizing the number of people of working age with the number of people in employment distorts the view of the most effective strategy with which countries can prepare for population ageing—which is improving the employment integration of those of working age.

Referring to a study recently carried out in Germany the authors show that improving employment integration across all ages would help to significantly contain the future increase of economic dependency ratios and, thus, significantly support pension adequacy and financial sustainability.

1 Introduction

Since the early 1990's, public debate on the long-term perspective of pension systems has been focused on demographic change, the increase of old-age dependency ratios and the resulting pressure on public budgets.

Yet, from an economic or budgetary point of view demographic data taken on its own is not as significant as often argued. In this respect, it is far more important to

---

J. Wöss (✉) · E. Türk
Chamber of Labour, Vienna, Austria
e-mail: josef.woess@akwien.at; erik.tuerk@akwien.at

© Springer Nature Switzerland AG 2019
N. da Costa Cabral, N. Cunha Rodrigues (eds.), *The Future of Pension Plans in the EU Internal Market*, Financial and Monetary Policy Studies 48,
https://doi.org/10.1007/978-3-030-29497-7_17

look at the economic status of people, especially at the level of employment integration of those of working age. What, besides productivity and income growth, ultimately counts much more than the numerical relationship between age groups is the ratio between benefit recipients and contributors.

In this article we show that in the context of massive population ageing making a clear distinction between demographic and economic 'dependency' is a basic condition for forward-looking pension policy. Good employment integration across all working ages shows up as a key determinant both of long-term adequacy and financial sustainability of pension systems.

The more our societies succeed in improving employment integration of those of working age, the less population ageing will translate into an increase in the economic dependency ratio. Unfortunately, this simple mechanism has been widely ignored even in key documents addressing pension perspectives in the context of ageing populations.

With an integrated strategy of pension and labour market policy, both sustainability and the adequacy challenge can be best addressed.

2 Demographic Change

Obviously, the ageing of populations is one of the key challenges our societies will have to face over the next few decades (Table 1).

The table clearly shows two defining demographic trends:

1. Shrinking number of people in the age group 15–64
2. Increase in the number of older people.

In 2016, in EU-27 there were 291 million in the age bracket 15–64, while predictions say in 2070 it will be only 246 million (−16%). Simultaneously, the number of older people is projected to increase from 87 million to 128 million (+48%). As a result of both developments the old-dependency ratio (65+/15–64) is expected to increase from the current level of about 30% to more than 50% by 2070.

It has to be noted that both the current age structure and demographic projections differ a lot from country to country and from region to region. In 2016, the old-age dependency ratio varied between 20.9% in Ireland and 34.5% in Italy. The

Table 1 Eurostat's demographic (baseline) projection 2016–2070 (EU-27)

	Age group 0–14	Age group 15–64	Age group 65+	Old-age dependency ratio (65+/15–64)
2016	68 m	291 m	87 m	29.9%
2030	66 m	275 m	111 m	40.3%
2050	66 m	253 m	132 m	52.3%
2070	65 m	246 m	128 m	52.2%

Source: EU Commission (2018a)

projections for 2070 show a variation between 41.2% in Ireland and 67.2% in Portugal.[1]

Naturally, there is much uncertainty in projections over such a long period of time. However, despite uncertainty about its extent, derived from the current age structure it is evident that massive population ageing will take place.

3 Pension Reforms

Against the background of forthcoming population ageing since the late 1980s containment of public pension expenditure has become the key goal of pension policy. Ensuring the long-term financial sustainability of pension systems became the main driver of pension reforms, jeopardizing pension adequacy.

Furthermore, key options for action were often obstructed by misleading analysis, namely by confusing demographic and economic dependency ratios.

Financial Sustainability

To put it in a nutshell, financial sustainability means that today's pension commitments can and will be met in the future. Actually, financial sustainability is a political concept; precise limits of unquestionable scientific merit do not exist.[2]

Mainly based on demographic projections, international organizations such as the World Bank, IMF and OECD have been pushing for wide-ranging reform of public pension systems since the early 1990's. The World Bank's report 'Averting the old age crisis'[3] became the most influential document; its 3-pillar-model served as a blueprint for many pension reforms around the globe. In line with its recommendations, in many countries the generosity of the pay-as-you-go financed public 1st pillar was significantly reduced and the expansion of pre-funded 2nd and 3rd pillar, occupational and private pensions, promoted.

In the period following the 2008 financial market crisis, measures targeted at reducing public pension expenditure continued, now mainly by raising the legal retirement age. In contrast to prior reforms, based on negative experience, many countries have now reversed the expansion of pre-funded schemes.[4]

Measures such as the tightening of the rules for the pension calculation and indexation, increasing legal retirement age and restricting access to early retirement have a major impact on public pension expenditure both now and, even more, in the future. "The pension reforms undertaken over the past decade are biting."[5] While assuming massive population ageing as a result of the reforms adopted the 2018

---

[1]European Commission (2018a), Table III.1.60.

[2]See Blank et al. (2018), pp. 194 f.

[3]World Bank (1994).

[4]See ILO (2018).

[5]OECD (2015), p. 9.

Ageing Report's long-term pension expenditure projections now even indicate that by 2070 the GDP share of public pension spending in EU-27 will be 0.5 percentage points below the 2016 level.[6]

Statements of the EU Commission, such as disputing the long-term financial sustainability of the Austrian public pension system because of a predicted 0.5% increase of the needed GDP share between 2016 and 2070,[7] show that the Commission tends to apply the current level of public spending as a benchmark for measuring long-term financial sustainability. However, not to accept at least moderate increase of the GDP share over the next few decades despite massive population ageing misses the intergenerational fairness target at the expense of today's youth.

Adequacy

"Providing people with income in old age that allows them a decent living standard and protect them from poverty is the very purpose of pension policy."[8]

The 2018 Pension Adequacy Report's findings disclose that in many countries the adequacy target is not met. Significant pension gaps especially exist among women and among people working in atypical and precarious types of employment. 18.2% of people aged 65 and over in the EU are at risk of poverty or social exclusion.[9]

Many pension reforms adopted almost exclusively focused on long-term containment of public pension expenditures at the expense of the generosity of pension schemes mainly towards today's youth. Calculations of the long-term evolution of theoretical replacement rates signal that in many EU Member States replacement rates will substantially decrease entailing increasing danger of poverty among older people.[10]

Longer working lives with good quality jobs will therefore be increasingly vital to enable men and women to acquire adequate pensions. Yet, while increasing employment integration of people of higher working ages clearly supports pension adequacy, raising the legal retirement age can entail additional risks especially for susceptible groups. "In most countries, under current projections there will be a rise in the pensionable age that will outpace the projected rise in the age of exit from the labour market . . . Since this difference grows in almost all countries, it is likely to leave more people with an income gap that will increase demand for early-retirement pathways or other bridging transfers, and an incomplete contribution record that will reduce pension adequacy."[11]

As in recent years many pension reforms focused on raising the legal retirement age, employment opportunities of those concerned will have to keep up, otherwise pension gaps will widen.

---

[6]European Commission (2018a), Table III.1.66.

[7]See European Commission (2018b).

[8]European Commission (2015a), p. 9.

[9]European Commission (2018c), p. 15.

[10]Ibid, Chap. 5.

[11]Ibid, p. 129.

Furthermore, it has to be noted, that both current and future replacement rates are not only affected by pension reforms, but also by labour market trends such as the proliferation of atypical and low paid jobs, continuing problems to reconcile employment and family life and persisting high levels of unemployment in vulnerable groups. These additional labour market-related risks to adequacy, particularly those affecting less-favored groups, becomes increasingly important when instruments of social balancing are weakened by gradual shifts from public to private pensions.

Furthermore, it has to be noted that shifting pension responsibility from pay-as-you-go financed public to pre-funded private schemes does not lead to cost reduction. At best it leads to cost shifting, in many cases pension costs (and risks) will increase.[12]

4   Economic Versus Demographic Dependency

The demographic old-age dependency ratio is a very important indicator to describe age structure and demographic change. Yet, only to look at demographic figures falls short of basic economic realities. Pure demographic figures do not capture the economic status, especially the fact that many people of working age are not actually working, but are often dependent on public benefits.

Even in key documents, future shifts in the age structure of the population are misinterpreted in terms of changes in the relationship between workers and pensioners.

A look at the figures the European Commission used in its info graphic to the publishing of the 2015 Ageing Report[13] can serve as example. Under the headline "The ratio of workers to pensioners will decrease" the Commission states that between 2013 and 2060 the ratio of workers to pensioners will change from 4:1 to 2:1. However, what is interpreted as being the ratio of workers to pensioners in reality is something very different: the ratio between the age groups 15–64 and 65+. Yet, it is obviously wrong to equalize the number of people of working age with the number of people in employment and the number of people aged 65+ with the number of pensioners. In 2013,[14] out of 335 million Europeans in the age group 15–64 only 215 million were in employment.[15] And among the remaining 120 million not in employment a big proportion were pensioners; among the total number of

---

[12]See ILO (2018), p 22 f / 32 f.

[13]http://ec.europa.eu/economy_finance/graphs/2015-05-12_ageing_report_en.htm

[14]2013 was the base year for the 2015 Ageing Report's analysis.

[15]Furthermore, among those earmarked by Eurostat's Labour Force Survey (LFS) as being in employment there are many millions only marginally integrated in employment (in LFS each person working at least 1 h for pay during the reference week is counted as employed).

pensioners the share of people younger than 65 ranged between 14.1% in Cyprus and 45.6% in Slovak Republic.[16]

Most of the statements disputing long-term financial sustainability of pay-as-you-go financed public pension systems are based on demographic data—and its incorrect interpretation. Thus, the European Commission at the presentation of the Green Paper on Pensions on 7 March 2010 stated: "The number of retired people in Europe compared to those financing their pensions is forecast to double by 2060—the current situation is simply not sustainable."[17] However, none of the European Commission's many studies on future developments is predicting that the ratio between pensioners and contributors will double over the next decades.

There is another highly problematic consequence of the incorrect interpretation of pure demographical figures. Equalizing the number of people of working age with the number of people in employment distorts the view of "the most effective strategy with which countries can prepare for population ageing"[18]; which is improving the employment integration of those of working age.

Labour market data clearly indicate that there is an enormous potential for better labour market integration across Europe—in all age groups and not just at higher ages, as it is often stated in the sustainability debate on public pensions. According to Eurostat figures, in 2016 only 65.6% of the age group 15–64 were in employment (including many millions only marginally employed), with rates varying between only 51.8% in Greece and 76.4% in Sweden.[19]

In order to shed light on the difference between pure demographic and economic dependency the Austrian Chamber of Labour (AK) developed a so-called 'dependency ratio calculator'.[20] The tool uses graphics of the age structure and people's economic status to calculate demographic and economic dependency ratios. Against the background of demographic projections, the impact of different labour market scenarios on the future evolution of the economic dependency ratio can be calculated. In a further step the impact on welfare state spending can also be determined.

The definition of 'economic dependency' used in the tool focuses on social transfers replacing former income. Recipients of public pensions and unemployment benefits are categorized as economically dependent and contrasted with people in employment.[21] As the level of earnings should be sufficient to enable decent living through own income and to contribute to the financing of social transfers for

---

[16]European Commission (2015b), Tab III.1.80.

[17]https://ec.europa.eu/social/main.jsp?langId=en&catId=89&newsId=839&furtherNews=yes

[18]European Commission (2008), p. 144.

[19]European Commission (2018a), III.1.48.

[20]See Wöss and Türk (2011, 2014).

[21]As children, students, house-wives and—husbands and other people without income are also economically dependent, the tool also allows calculations based on a broader concept of economic dependency—the total economic dependency ratio. Here the focus shifts from social transfers to total transfer needs within a society as a whole.

assessing economic dependency mini-jobbers are not rated as employed, provided available data allows for such a distinction.

The tool clearly shows that mobilizing existing employment potential in all age groups could help to considerably reduce future increases in the economic dependency ratio, thereby alleviating the financial burden of ageing.[22]

White Paper on Pensions

In 2012, the EU Commission's White Paper on Pensions[23] was published. In the analytical part of the document, both the limited relevance of purely demographic data and the need to look at economic dependency are clearly stated: 'The ageing challenge is often illustrated by the doubling of the old age dependency ratio ... Yet, the real issue is the economic dependency ratio, defined as the unemployed and pensioners as a percentage of the employed.' Then, the White Paper points to the huge impact of employment levels on the future evolution of the economic dependency ratio and on considerable scope for improvement: 'If Europe achieves the employment goal of the Europe 2020 strategy of 75% employment rate in the age group 20–64 and further progress is made in the period 2020–2050 the economic dependency ratio will only increase from the current level of 65–79% in 2050.[24] Many countries have considerable scope for improving the future adequacy and sustainability of their pension systems by raising employment rates, and this not just in higher age groups, but also for groups with lower employment rates such as women, migrants and youths. Reaching the EU employment target or catching up with the best-performing countries could almost neutralize the effects of population ageing on the weight of pensions in GDP.'[25]

Unfortunately, the key recommendations in the White Paper do not reflect this analysis. In line with World Bank and OECD, in order to combat the increase of dependency ratios, the Commission simply proposes to increase the legal retirement age. For whatever reason, the much broader approach of improving the labor market integration in all age groups, recommended in the analytical part of the White Paper, has not been taken up.

---

[22]Calculations based on the Dependency Ratio Calculator also reveal a huge impact of employment rates on public budgets (Türk et al. 2012).

[23]European Commission (2012).

[24]These calculations in the White Paper refer to AK's , dependency ratio calculator'.

[25]European Commission (2012), Sect. 2.3.

5   Impact of Labor Markets on the Economic Dependency Ratio: Case Study on Germany

In 2018, together with three German researchers, the authors of this text published a study on the impact of different labour market scenarios on the future evolution of the economic dependency ratio in Germany.[26] The calculations are based on "The 2015 Ageing Report". As in this report, the study uses 2013 as base year and the projection period extends to 2060.

As a starting point, in order to calculate the current level of the economic dependency ratio the study analysed the Labour Force Survey's data (LFS) for Germany.

According to LFS total employment in Germany was about 39.6 m in 2013. Bearing in mind that in LFS all persons who work at least 1 h for pay or profit during the reference week are counted as employed, this number does not help a lot when assessing economic dependency. According to German administrative data in 2013 5.3 m people exclusively worked in a mini-job. As the mini-jobbers'income (max € 450 per month) is not sufficient to ensure decent living through own work, let alone contribute to the financing of social transfers, to determine a realistic economic dependency ratio mini-jobbers are not allocated among those employed. As a consequence, the employment rate of men aged 15–64 decreased from 78.1% to 72.8%. As almost two thirds of the Mini-jobbers are women the reduction in female employment rates is even higher—from 69.0% to 57.8%. The total employment rate decreased from 73.6% to 65.4%.

While, from an economic point of view, LFS data tends to over-estimate employment figures, this data, simultaneously, tends to massively under-estimate the phenomenon of economic dependency due to unemployment. In 2013, the number of people registered as 'unemployed' by the German Federal Labour Office was about 3 m compared to 2.2 m according to LFS. The difference mainly results from the fact that in LFS unemployed people who, in conformity with German unemployment insurance legislation, work in a mini-job are not classified as unemployed. Furthermore, it has to be taken into account that not all groups of unemployed people are covered in the official unemployment figures, such as people over a certain age, participating in measures of ALMP or being temporarily unable to work due to sickness. With the concept of "Unterbeschäftigung im engeren Sinn" the German Federal Office of Labour offers a broader and more appropriate demarcation of unemployment for the aim of correctly calculating the economic dependency ratio. It includes all these groups and is a total of 3.8 m (2013), thus, exceeding the LFS number of unemployed by 75%.

The comparison of 24 m benefit recipients (3.8 m unemployed and 20.2 m pensioners[27]) and 35.2 m people in, more than marginal, employment the study

---

[26]Türk et al. (2018).

[27]European Commission (2015b).

reveals a 68% level of the 2013 economic dependency ratio[28] against an old-age dependency ratio of only 32%. The huge difference between these two ratios clearly demonstrates how misleading it is to only focus on demographic data.

The key part of the study is the calculation of three scenarios. The first two scenarios are based on the baseline demographic projections (europop2013) used in the EU's 2015 Ageing Report. From today's perspective these projections look over-pessimistic. Therefore, the third scenario is based on Eurostat's more recent and more optimistic demographic projections from 2017.

Standard Scenario
First, in order to establish a reference scenario, the so-called "standard scenario"is calculated. Starting from adjusted labour market data—as mentioned above—the calculations are exclusively based on the Ageing Report 2015 projection trends. Besides pessimistic demographic assumptions this scenario is characterised by little change regarding employment rates. Over the next few decades the employment rate of 15–64 years olds would only increase by 1.2 percentage points, from 65.4% (2013) to 66.6% (2060).[29] Little change in employment rates combined with the assumed huge decrease in the number of people of working age results in a massive decrease of the number of people in employment. As the unemployment rate is assumed to remain at a rather high level the decrease in the number of unemployed is mainly driven by demographic shifts, which simultaneously cause a huge increase in the number of pensioners. Using the "standard scenario", in comparison to the 2013 level, the economic dependency ratio would increase considerably—by 42% by 2040 and 51% by 2060. None the less these increases are significantly lower than the underlying increases in the demographic dependency ratio (75% and 86% respectively).

Building on its initial in-depth analysis of the current situation of Germany's labour market, the study judges the "standard scenario" as being far from making full use of existing employment potential.

High-Employment Scenario 1: Based on Pessimistic Demographic Projections
In contrast to the "standard scenario", in the "high-employment scenario 1" we assume a significantly improved use of existing employment potential. The main assumption is that, by 2050, activity rates by age groups and sex gradually align to current (2016) activity rates in Sweden, while the unemployment rate (based on the broad concept mentioned above) declines to 4% over the same period. This would result in a significant increase in employment rates of 15–64 years olds to 75.1% by 2040 and to 78.7% by 2060.

Compared to the "standard scenario", despite the unchanged assumption of a massively shrinking working age population, in this scenario the decrease in the number of people in work is much lower. While the number of employed in the standard-scenario reduces to 29.7 m (2040) and 26.3 m (2060) the corresponding

---

[28]Compared to only 56% based on unadjusted LFS data.
[29]Revised figures.

figures in the "High-employment scenario 1" are 34.0 m and 31.9 m. While declining unemployment rates go hand in hand with a further reduction in the number of unemployed, the number of pensioners is slightly higher than in the standard scenario. Higher activity rates, especially amongst the elderly, reduces the number of those in early retirement, but also result in a gradual decrease in the number of older people without pension rights, especially among women.

Overall, in the "high-employment scenario 1" the increase in the economic dependency ratio amounts to 19% by 2040 and to 18% by 2060, which is markedly less than the "standard scenario" increase of 42% and 51% respectively. While, obviously, the underlying increase in the demographic dependency ratio remains unchanged.

High-Employment Scenario 2: Based on More Optimistic (and More Recent) Demograhic Projections

The "high-employment scenario 2" is calculated based on Eurostat's more recent and more optimistic demographic projections from 2017. These projections also assume that there will be a considerable shrinking of the working-age population, but with -16% the reduction is significantly lower than assumed in the pessimistic demographic projection from 2013 (-28%). On the other hand, a higher increase in the number of older people is also expected. The demographic old-age dependency ratio is expected to increase by 55% by 2040 and 73% by 2060, compared to 75% and 86% in the pessimistic scenario.

While the number of pensioners increases even more than in the first 2 scenarios, the shrinking working-age population is over-compensated by increasing employment rates, therefore, the number of employed increases to 38 m by 2040 and to 37 m by 2060.

Under the "high-employment scenario 2", the economic dependency ratio only increases 8% by 2040 and 10% by 2060.

The figure below shows the evolution of demographic and economic dependency ratios in the 3 scenarios. It clearly illustrates both the enormous difference between demographic and economic ratios and the huge potential of better employment integration to curb future increases of the economic dependency ratio (Fig. 1).

The study summarizes: "The far-reaching removal of existing shortcomings in employment integration proves to be a promising strategy to beneficially tackle demographic change, both socially and economically"[30]

---

[30]Türk et al. (2018), p. 17 (own translation).

Germany 2013 – 2040 – 2060
Demographic vs economic dependency ratios

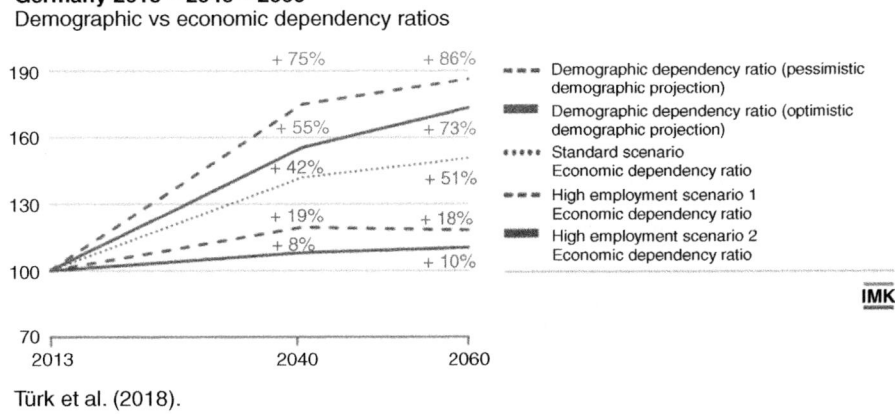

Türk et al. (2018).

Fig. 1 Evolution of demographic and economic dependency ratios

6   Concluding Remarks

- Better labour market integration of vulnerable groups such as women, immigrants and the elderly would help significantly to achieve adequate pensions and to avoid negative fragmentation of our societies.
- Mobilizing the full employment potential in all age groups would considerably alleviate the financial burden of ageing and thus significantly support financial sustainability.
- The economic dependency ratios of unemployed and pensioners relative to people in employment is much more meaningful than demographic ratios and should be brought to the fore in long-term projections and in public debate.

References

Blank F, Logeay C, Türk E, Wöss J, Zwiener R Ist das österreichische Rentensystem nachhaltig? in: Wirtschaftsdienst 3/2018 (only available in German)
European Commission (2008) Demography report 2008
European Commission (2012) An agenda for adequate, safe and sustainable pensions. White paper
European Commission (2015a) The 2015 pension adequacy report, volume 1
European Commission (2015b) The 2015 ageing report. Economic and budgetary projections for the 28 EU member states (2013–2060)
European Commission (2018a) The 2018 ageing report. Economic & Budgetary Projections for the 28 EU member states (2016–2070)
European Commission (2018b) Recommendation for a council recommendation on the 2018 National Reform Programme of Austria
European Commission (2018c) Pension adequacy report 2018, volume 1
ILO (2018) Reversing pension privatizations. In: Ortiz I, Duran-Valverde F, Urban S, Wodsak V (eds) Rebuilding public pension systems in Eastern Europe and Latin America

OECD (2015) Pensions at a glance 2015

Türk E, Wöss J, Zuleeg F (2012) 1000 billion euros at stake: how boosting employment can address demographic change and public deficits. European policy center, issue paper no 72

Türk E, Blank F, Logeay C, Wöss J, Zwiener R (2018) Den demographischen Wandel bewältigen: Die Schlüsselrolle des Arbeitsmarktes. IMK-Report 137 (not available in English)

World Bank (1994) Averting the old age crisis: policies to protect the old and promote growth

Wöss J, Türk E (2011) Dependency ratios and demographic change. The labour market as a key element, ETUI policy brief 4/2011

Wöss J, Türk E (2014) Demographie und Sozialstaat. Arbeitsmarkt hat zentrale Bedeutung, in: Wirtschaft und Gesellschaft, No. 3/2014 (only available in German)

Josef Wöss is head of the Social Policy Department at the Chamber of Labour in Vienna, member of the Austrian Social Partners' Advisory Council for Economic and Social Affairs and member of the EU-Commission's High-Level Group of Experts on Pensions.

He was a member of the Cabinet of the Minister of Finance of Austria in 1995/1996 and a member of the Cabinet of the Federal Chancellor in 1998/1999.

Some of his publications:

Wöss/Türk (2011): Dependency ratios and demographic change. The labour market as a key element, ETUI Policy Brief 4/2011

Wöss Josef (2011): Stellenwert der Mindestsicherung im österreichischen Sozialsystem, in: Pfeil/Wöss (Hrsg.). Bedarfsorientierte Mindestsicherung. ÖGB Verlag

Türk/Wöss/Zuleeg (2012): 1000 billion Euros at stake: How boosting employment can address demographic change and public deficits. EPC Issue Paper No. 72, November 2012

Blank/Logeay/Türk/Wöss/Zwiener: Alterssicherung in Deutschland und Österreich: Vom Nachbarn lernen? WSI-Report No 27, 1/2016

Redl/Thurnher/Wöss (2015); So sicher ist ihre Pension. Falter Verlag. Wien 2015

Wöss (2018): Austria: Occupational Welfare at the edge of statutory social insurance; in: Natali/Pavolini/Vanhercke (ed.), Occupational Welfare in Europe. Risks, opportunities and social partner involvement. OSE/ETUI

Türk/Blank/Logeay/Wöss (2018), Den Demographischen Wandel bewältigen: Die Schlüsselrolle des Arbeitsmarktes. IMK-Report137

Blank/Logeay/Türk/Wöss/Zwiener (2018), Ist das österreichische Rentensystem nachhaltig? In: Wirtschaftsdienst 3/2018

Erik Türk is an economist and pension expert in the Social Policy Department at the Chamber of Labour in Vienna.

Some of his publications:

Wöss/Türk (2011): Dependency ratios and demographic change. The labour market as a key element, ETUI Policy Brief 4/2011

Türk/Wöss/Zuleeg (2012): 1000 billion Euros at stake: How boosting employment can address demographic change and public deficits. EPC Issue Paper No. 72, November 2012

Mum/Türk (2014); Implizite oder „echte" Staatsschuld? Eine kritische Würdigung des Generational Accounting, WISO 3/2014

Blank/Logeay/Türk/Wöss/Zwiener (2016): Alterssicherung in Deutschland und Österreich: Vom Nachbarn lernen? WSI-Report No 27, 1/2016

Türk/Mum (2016); Excessive expectations. OECD and EU Commission Should Revise their Return Assumptions; in: WISO DISKURS 18/2016

Türk/Blank (2017), Niedrigrenten, Mindestsicherung und Armutsgefährdung Älterer. Ein Vergleich zwischen Österreich und Deutschland (Teil 2), in Soziale Sicherheit 9/2017, Bund-Verlag, 328-334.

Türk/Blank (2017), Niedrigrenten, Mindestsicherung und Armutsgefährdung Älterer. Ein Vergleich zwischen Österreich und Deutschland (Teil 1), in Soziale Sicherheit 7-8/2017, Bund-Verlag, 286-289.

Türk/Blank/Logeay/Wöss (2018), Den Demographischen Wandel bewältigen: Die Schlüsselrolle des Arbeitsmarktes. IMK-Report137

Blank/Logeay/Türk/Wöss/Zwiener (2018), Ist das österreichische Rentensystem nachhaltig? In: Wirtschaftsdienst 3/2018

Pensions in the Fluid EU Society: Challenges for (Migrant) Workers

Ivana Vukorepa, Yves Jorens, and Grega Strban

Abstract For majority of people, pensions are the most important income replacement benefit, when the ability to work is reduced (or no economic activity is expected anymore) due to old age. Moreover, equal access to social protection, regardless of the type and duration of employment, is one of the goals of the European Pillar of Social Rights, aiming also at adequate income in retirement. Hence, the paper focuses on old-age pensions and highlights potential national and mobility linked problems and challenges for future pension adequacy concerning persons working in non-standard forms of employment and self-employment. After the introductory part in which also the fluidity of the EU society is being explained, paper focuses on three aspects: 1) necessary changes in the pension systems due to new working arrangements, 2) appropriateness of the EU legislation on free movement and social security coordination in relation to public and supplementary (occupational) pension schemes, and 3) importance of combating fraud and error.

1 Introduction

Pensions are important source of income when the ability to work is reduced, or no economic activity is expected anymore due to old age. Hence, pension adequacy, i.e. the sufficiency issue of pension benefits referring both to the absolute level of preventing old age poverty and to the relative level of replacing life—time earnings (especially in work related income replacement pension systems) is very important and is given special attention not only in the Council of Europe (Strban 2015), but also in the EU (European Commission 2018b, c). However, reaching that goal is

I. Vukorepa (✉)
Faculty of Law, University of Zagreb, Zagreb, Croatia
e-mail: ivana.vukorepa@pravo.hr

Y. Jorens
Faculty of Law, University of Ghent, Ghent, Belgium

G. Strban
Faculty of Law, University of Ljubljana, Ljubljana, Slovenia

© Springer Nature Switzerland AG 2019
N. da Costa Cabral, N. Cunha Rodrigues (eds.), *The Future of Pension Plans in the EU Internal Market*, Financial and Monetary Policy Studies 48,
https://doi.org/10.1007/978-3-030-29497-7_18

aggravated in today's changing societies. Primarily due to demographic changes in the form of increased life expectancy, improvements in mortality and low fertility rates, that affect financing side and long-term sustainably of all pension systems. Secondly, and not less importantly, due to changes in the working arrangements caused by market pressures and new technologies. In addition, contrary to other international organisations, mobility within the EU is promoted, including labour mobility, which should contribute to the functioning (and positive effects) of the internal market. We can only mention the Erasmus mobility programs, researchers´ mobility and providing the best possible social security coverage to intra-EU migrants (e.g. the Decisions of the Court of Justice of the EU, hereafter CJEU, in the cases C-24/75 *Petroni* EU:C:1975:129, C-352/06 *Bosmann* EU:C:2008:290, and others).

Increased life expectancy means that we live longer, which is not necessarily something negative. It is a reflection of welfare and quality of life, which should be maintained at a highest attainable level also in old-age. Hence, pension adequacy is an ongoing concern, especially in the EU society that has become more and more fluid. With the notion of "fluid society" we are aiming at challenging the traditional norms of work, stability and social security (including pension systems) continuum. Adjective fluid could mean a person, thing or situation that moves or changes easily (https://www.yourdictionary.com/fluid, March 2019). However, we shall refrain from personal fluidity, e.g. age (a man of 69 claiming that should be recognised as 49 years of age; Turner 2018) or gender, colour of the skin, racial or any other individual fluidity. Hence, by using fluid society we are trying to indicate changes of traditional patterns of (organising) work and mobility, which used to be considered as a norm (standard), also when shaping social security systems after the Second World War. According to the ILO Convention 102 concerning minimum standards of social security from 1952, standard beneficiary is a man with a wife and two children in a stable (full-time and open-ended) employment relationship. Pension benefits should suffice for such a beneficiary. Nowadays, some authors discuss fluid borders, fluid services, work without boundaries, and fluid communications (Hoencamp et al. 2014). Indeed, work (organisation), movement and social security have become more non-standard or unstable, i.e. fluid, especially within the EU.

Therefore, we are of the opinion that societal fluidity is reflected mainly on three levels. Firstly, on the level of new working arrangements and acceleration of job polarization. Standard full-full time open-ended employment relationship is being on decline, falling to below 60% in 2016 (European Commission 2018a, 56). It is being more and more replaced by some known and already regulated non-standard forms of work (e.g. fixed-term contracts, part-time work, temporary agency work, telework, traineeships and student work), as well as with some new forms (e.g. on-demand work, platform work), all being associated with various elements of precariousness, in the form of job insecurity, employment record discontinuity and lower earnings (Schoukens and Barrio 2017; Eurofound 2015, 2018; ILO 2016). Noticeable is also slow but steady increase in the involuntary temporary employment (for EU 28 from 7.2% in 2008 to 7.8% in 2017), however with significant difference among Member States (Eurostat 2018). In order to earn additional source of income, some persons combine employment with additional self-employment activities, which is problematic if undeclared. In addition, there are categories of work force whose employment status is blurred, such as dependent solo self-employed (also referred to as bogus self-employed), that are in-between two basic standard categories: on the one side, employees (dependent and subordinated) and on the other side, independent self-employed (entrepreneurs), and can fall outside the scope of pension protection. In addition, there are situations of career mobility and transitions from employment to self-employment and backwards (sometimes fostered by active labour market policy measures and tax advantages) associated with possible loss of pension entitlements, especially when it comes to occupational pension schemes. Hence, noticeable is research on international and EU promotion of adequate social protection and coverage, for all workers, including those in non-standard forms of employment and self-employment, as important precondition for adequate income in retirement (e.g. principles 12 and 15 of the European Pillar of Social Rights; OECD/ ILO 2018; Spasova et al. 2017; De Micheli et al. 2018; Schoukens et al. 2018).

Secondly, fluidity can also be associated with the problem of fraudulent forms of underdeclared work, especially its grey zone, in the form of under-reporting of wages (so called envelope-payments) or hours worked (including full time jobs declared as part-time). All this can lead to formal underpayment, and hence tax and contributions evasion, resulting in lower pension entitlements. In the areas of crowd work linked to digital platforms and IT networks, noticeable is undeclared own-account work, i.e. self-employed work (Reinhard 2018, 577); On-demand economy income is often not declared and tax authorities find it hard to retrieve, because platform workers have limited incentive to declare income, large percentage is not even aware that the income needs to be declared, and platforms are still not required to report the earnings of the workers. Platform workers might even be inclined not to report their workers' earnings to avoid being considered employers or to discourage workers from being active on the platform (EESC 2017, 54).

Thirdly, fluidity of EU society is reflected on the rising and changing trends in intra-EU mobility, counting roughly to 11.8 million EU-28 movers in total in 2016 (Fries-Tersch et al. 2018, 12). Patterns of mobility of workers and self-employed have become more diverse. In addition to traditional long-term mobility scenario of moving from home country to host country and working there for a longer period of time, nowadays mobility is marked also by multiple shorter-term stays in other Member States (Fries-Tersch et al. 2018, 14, 37, 38, 59).

Therefore, the aim of this research paper is to highlight potential national and mobility linked problems and challenges for future pension adequacy concerning persons working in non-standard forms of employment and self-employment. After an overview of developments in the social risk of old-age, pension systems and pension coverage for standard and non-standard workers and self-employed in EU Member States, the second part of the paper focuses on problems in the case of cross-border mobility. In this area, the rules on social security coordination (Regulation (EC) 883/2004 and implementing Regulation (EC) 987/2009) are being analysed, mainly relevant for statutory public pension schemes. In addition, we evaluate the Union acquis developed for supplementary (occupational) pension schemes, aiming to prevent loss of pension rights as a consequence of mobility (Directive 98/49/EC and Directive 2014/50/EU). The third part deals with the importance of combating fraud and error in the domain of pensions, also by providing some examples of measures taken by Member States. In the final part are presented concluding research observations.

2 Social Risk of Old-Age, Pension Systems and Non-standard Forms of Employment

2.1 Social Risk of Old-Age

Historically, the changing nature of a certain social risk could be observed. In the light of the topic of this paper, it could be argued that also social risks could be "fluid". When first modern pension insurance was introduced, the social risk of old-age was based on the presumption of invalidity, i.e. disability to work due to old-age. Acquisition of the right to an old-age pension, e.g. in Germany at the end of nineteenth century was possible only after completing the age of 70. According to paragraphs 9 and 29 of the 1889 Pension and Invalidity Insurance Act (*Gesetz, betreffend die Invaliditäts- und Altersversicherung.* Deutsches Reichsgesetzblatt Band 1889, Nr. 13, Seite 97—144) an old-age pension could be provided only from the first day of the age of 71 years onwards. Interestingly enough, life expectancy at that time was 58 years of age and the average time of receiving a pension was 2 years (Dawson 1912, 128). Hence, in the case of defining old-age much above the average life-expectancy, there was no need of proving invalidity anymore.

Over the time, purpose of providing an old-age pension has changed. Apart from poverty prevention in the old-age due to inability to work, its purpose has been more linked to preserve a certain standard of living also in the old-age. Behind that idea is also a common and very general perception that pension systems should enable receiving a well-deserved pension, based on prior contributions, at normal health state of the beneficiary. Most importantly, the age at which a person can or should retire presents an agreement in the society at which society no longer expects economic activity from old-aged person. Retirement should be a happy moment in a person's life (*risque heureux*) and not an unhappy one (*risque malheureux*). Therefore, it has been advocated that old-age pensions should protect the previous standard of living of the beneficiaries (although within certain limits) and should not be reduced to a mere social assistance. In this context, through decades (and more than a century) the trend of extensive juridification (legal regulation) and institutional specialisation (special pension insurance carriers), but also of deprivatisation or socialisation of old-age risk and enhanced solidarity could be observed (Bley et al. 2007, 14). More and more were risks (including the risk of old-age) perceived as in need of societal protection, when individual and his or her family could not be left alone with his or her savings and private insurances. Hence, social insurances are used as a means of solidarity by dispersing individual risks as social risks to larger parts of a society (i.e. mainly working population), thus enabling existence and free development of every individual and the society as such.

In the recent years, we could witness a reverse trend. The States are reducing their responsibility for providing social security to their inhabitants. The risks (also of old-age) are being privatised or desocialised and solidarity reduced. This is resulting in higher pensionable ages, as a rule from 65 years of age, but also higher, e.g. raising it to 67 (in Greece, Germany from 2029, Belgium from 2030, the Netherlands from 2021, the UK from 2028) or even 68 (in Denmark from 2030, Ireland from 2028, Italy from 2021), while also discussing the long-forgotten but original age of 70 in some Member States, e.g. in Italy it should reach 69 years and 9 months by 2050, in Norway it is flexible between 62 and 75 and in the Netherlands the legal retirement age should be linked to the remaining life expectancy as of 2023 (MISSOC 2019). Moreover, the pensionable ages are being equalised for men and women as equal parts of human society. Unfortunately, the retirement age is not being reduced for men, but raised for women, who should be disburdened before retirement, when they actually care for children, disabled family members or those reliant on long-term care (Strban 2012).

Old-age pension is linked to a certain age. However, many Member States require certain qualifying (insurance or pension) period to open the entitlement (seniority pension). Also, ceasing of economic activity might be required (retirement pension), although some member States allow working and receiving a pension at the same time, some of them from a certain age onwards (MISSOC 2019). Nevertheless, the notion of old-age pension is being used in a broad sense, including also seniority and retirement conditions. It goes without saying that each member State is shaping their social security (including old-age insurance) system distinctively.

2.2 Pension Systems

Pension system is an important part of every country's social security system with a function of poverty alleviation in the old-age and life-time consumption smoothening. The design of the pension system, usually encompassing several layers of pension protection, depending on historical, cultural, economic and production backgrounds. It can be organised through public and/or private providers. Public pension schemes are often referred to as statutory, because they are regulated by legislative acts. Conversely, private schemes can be provided on a collective basis through occupational schemes (hence usually linked to the employer, based on the concept of deferred wage and sometimes involving social partners or professional organisations for self-employed in their designing and implementation) or on an individual basis through individual schemes in the form of personal accounts or insurance contracts (where participation is not linked to employment).

Furthermore, pension schemes can be subcategorised based on various specific criteria, such as legal regulation (statutory or contractual), management (state, insurance companies, pension funds, banks), participation (mandatory, quasi-mandatory or voluntary), personal scope (work-related or non-work-related, insurance based or residence based, general or special), sources of financing (tax-financed or contributory that can be financed by employer's and/ or employees contributions), financing modalities (pay-as-you-go, funded, book reserves or insurance contracts), eligibility conditions (e.g. pensionable age, qualifying periods, also in the form of waiting periods as eligibility periods for membership in the pension scheme, and vesting periods as minimum periods of scheme membership for the acquisition of rights), as well as types of pension promise, i.e. "defined benefit (DB) schemes" where benefit depends mainly on years of service and salary, and where pension plan provider bears the investment risk; "hybrid DB", where benefits depend on a rate of return credited to contributions, where this rate of return is either specified in the plan rules, independently of the actual return on any supporting assets, or is calculated with reference to the actual return of any supporting assets and a minimum return guarantee specified in the plan rules, or "defined contribution (DC) schemes", which are usually funded, and where the future benefit depends mainly on the accrued value of saved capital and the investment risk is born by the scheme member (Vukorepa 2012, 170–186). In the last two decades predominantly due to population aging, economic turmoil, changes in the labour markets and thereto related changes in the employment leading to more atypical jobs and nonstandard employment careers, the adequacy and sustainability concerns gained prominence among a wide circle of scholars and collective actors (such as the European Commission, World Bank). There has been a strong trend of shifting the underfunding risks, investment risks and longevity risks from pension providers to individuals. This individualisation process has been marked by several changes: partial privatisation of public pension systems, transfers from pay-as-you-go schemes and schemes financed by book-reserves, towards funded schemes, and regarding pension promises from defined benefits to defined contribution (Vukorepa 2012, 34–55, 142–164; Vukorepa 2015, 280–281). In occupational schemes, in addition to these changes further individualisation trends can be spotted, in the form of further moves towards individual retirement schemes and sometimes even removal of compulsory life-time annuitisation, e.g. in UK and Netherlands (Stevens 2017).

Important challenge for pension adequacy today presents integration of non-standard forms of employment and self-employment in contributory work-related pension schemes. "Non-standard form of employment" is an umbrella term for different employment arrangements that deviate from standard employment, which typically refers to full-time work under a permanent contract. In the comparative literature other terms can be found as well, such as 'atypical work' (Schoukens and Barrio 2017), "flexible work arrangements" (Grgurev and Vukorepa 2018), or "new forms of work" (Eurofound 2015). Non-standard forms of work may include some already known and regulated forms of work (such as temporary or short-term contracts, part-time work, agency work, domestic work, apprentices and student work), as well as some new forms such as on-demand work, intermittent contracts, casual work (including zero-hour contracts), voucher-based work, platform work (i.e. people working for digital platforms without having a fixed workplace, also known as crowd-work), portfolio workers, interim management work, owner managers together with bogus self-employment and dependent self-employment (Eurofound 2015; ILO 2016). Most of these alternative working arrangements are considered to provide weaker pension protection due to participation obstacles, such as limited personal scope of schemes (excluding some groups, e.g. self-employed), waiting and vesting periods, and various thresholds (minimum hours worked, or salary thresholds). On the contrary, residence-based schemes providing non-contributory basic pensions are not perceived as problematic, since they cover all residents, including all types of workers and self-employed. Hence, in the further elaboration we will focus only on contributory work-related pension schemes, both public and occupational.

2.3 Non-standard Forms of Employment

According to extensive comparative report by Spasova et al. (2017), all non-standard workers have access to public (statutory) pension schemes. However, some specific categories of workers may have only partial access to these schemes, for example casual workers (e.g. in Bulgaria, Malta and Romania) and seasonal workers (e.g. in Bulgaria, Hungary and Romania), on-call workers (e.g. in Hungary and Luxembourg), temporary agency workers (e.g. in Malta), and marginal freelancers and marginal part-timers, which e.g. in Austria are not covered by mandatory insurance but they can opt-in at rather low contribution levels. Partial access to statutory pension schemes is also linked to eligibility conditions which differ from those for standard workers, such as contribution periods, a flat-rate benefit instead of a pension based on a replacement rate (Spasova et al. 2017, 35). Another problem might be lower contribution rates at which some groups of non-standard workers pay pension contribution. Such situation is e.g. in Croatia, where for casual forms of work based on contract for service and authors contract (since 2017) the pension contribution rate is paid at reduced level (10% instead of 20%), while for student work no regular pension contribution is paid, only special contribution of 5% covering disability benefit in the case of injury at work (Grgurev and Vukorepa 2018; Vukorepa et al. 2017, 9, 12, 22). Since such labour force is cheaper, this can lead to labour market distortions, as well as lower accrual of pension benefits.

Although most countries provide full coverage for self-employed in their pay-as-you-go (PAYG) statutory public pension scheme, there are still some countries who do not cover them, or cover them partially, e.g. Germany, Spain, Romania, Netherlands, UK (Spasova et al. 2017, 36). For instance, in Germany, some categories of the self-employed are compulsorily insured ("employee-like persons" who are dependent self-employed without employees, as well as artists, publishers and craftsman) while others (traders and liberal professionals) may only opt-in voluntarily (Schoukens et al. 2018, 227; Spasova et al. 2017, 36), so there are continuous discussions for full inclusion of self-employed (Kress-del Bondio 2018, 608). In some countries where the self-employed have access to statutory public pensions (e.g. Switzerland, Norway, Romania, UK), they may have only partial access due to tighter eligibility conditions compared to standard workers, based on the contribution period, assessment base or replacement rates (Spasova et al. 2017, 36). As for statutory funded schemes, in countries who have established such schemes, the self-employed usually have the right to access them (e.g. Bulgaria, Croatia, Estonia, Poland,). They may be subject to mandatory insurance or can only join voluntarily (Spasova et al. 2017, 36).

Regarding occupational schemes access of non-standard workers may be hampered by some conditions and thresholds, while self-employed are usually not covered or may have access under less favourable conditions. According to Spasova et al. (2017, 37) in Denmark there are no schemes that cover self-employed, while in France, supplementary schemes for the self-employed are subject to different, heterogeneous rules within the same professional category. In Norway, self-employed are offered tax-subsidies in relation to supplementary retirement savings, but the degree of subsidy and the tax-exemption of contributions are less favourable than for wage earners.

Specific problem represents undeclared work, especially noticeable in on-demand economy forms of work, including platform work. Income is often not declared and tax authorities find it hard to retrieve it, because platform workers have limited incentive to declare income, large percentage is not even aware that the income needs to be declared, and platforms are still not required to report the earnings of the workers. Platform workers might even be inclined not to report their workers' earnings to avoid being considered employers or to discourage workers from being active on the platform (EESC 2017, 54). However, if platform work declared their position, and hence pension protection differs from country to country. For example, in Netherlands platform work is mainly carried out as solo-self-employment offering only limited coverage in the form of state-old age pension, while in Belgium special schemes have been established for self-employed platform workers, that are exempted from taxation and social security contributions as long as their income does not exceed a specific threshold, however outside these schemes, they can be treated as traditional employees or self-employed (Schoukens et al. 2018, 232–243).

Hence, it seems to us that there are several important improvements that need to be considered if we want future pension adequacy in the on-demand economy. Firstly, countries should consider providing for full integration of emerging new forms of employment and self-employment within the scope of pension protection by eliminating all participation thresholds, hence including also marginal work. Secondly, pension contributions (as well as other social security contributions) should cover all types of income equally (regardless whether from dependent work, self-employment or other gainful activities). This would result in a larger circle of persons paying contributions (i.e. larger solidarity circle), which is important both for the sustainability of pension system, and hence could lead to higher incomes in retirement, i.e. pension adequacy (similarly Grgurev and Vukorepa 2018,

259). Thirdly, it is necessary to simplify administrative procedures and provide for automatic collection of contributions and taxes, also through online and mobile services (ILO/OECD 2018, 10). This is especially necessary in the case of all online payments for platform provided work and services. In the case of other on-demand casual work, payment through vouchers that would guarantee automatic payment also of taxes and social security contribution, i.e. pension contributions, might be a good solution.

3   EU Legislation on Pensions and its Appropriateness for Free Movement of Non-standard Migrant Workers and Self-Employed

In the field of pension systems, it is up to the Member States to set them in place and to shape them in the way they deem appropriate. EU law only influences the substance of pension systems directly by ensuring equal treatment of men and women (e.g. Directive 79/7/EEC, Directive 2006/54/EC, Directive 2004/113/EC) and indirectly by supporting and complementing activities of the Member States (Article 153 TFEU) and encouraging cooperation between the Member States (Article 156 TFEU), to which end so-called social Open Method of Coordination was developed (Pennings 2015, 323–327). Most importantly, since 1950s recognised was the need to adopt rules on coordination of territorially organised social security systems due to the fact that national rules could hamper the exercise of the right to free movement of workers and, nowadays, all EU citizens. Hence, from the perspective of free movement of workers and protection of pension rights today three group of rules are relevant: 1) directly applicable Art. 45 TFEU on free movement of workers, that was used by CJEU in several free movement cases dealing with pension rights and Regulation (EU) 492/2011, 2) Art. 48 TFEU and directly applicable rules on coordination of social security systems, i.e. relevant for all public (statutory) pension systems are coordinated, that are provided in Regulations (EC) No 883/2004 (basic Regulation) and (EC) No 987/2009 (implementing Regulation), and 3) rules relevant for supplementary (occupational) pension schemes that are provided in Directives 98/49/EC and 2014/50/EU).

Hence, in this part we are presenting and analysing EU *acquis* relevant for pensions in the field of free movement from the perspective of non-standard migrant workers and self-employed.

3.1 Article 45 TFEU

Directly applicable Article 45 TFEU on free movement of workers has been used by CJEU in several free movement cases dealing with pension rights, both in the sphere of statutory and non-statutory pension schemes.

For example, in *Commission v Cyprus* (C-515/14, EU:C:2016:30) the CJEU ruled that an age-related criterion which deters workers from leaving their Member State of origin in order to work in another Member State, or within an EU institution, or other international organisation and which has the effect of creating unequal treatment between migrant workers, on the one hand, and civil servants who have worked in Cyprus, on the other, is contrary to Articles 45 TFEU and 48 TFEU and under Article 4(3) TEU.

The case *Pöpperl* (C-187/15, EU:C:2016:550) dealt with civil servant of a Member State who has left the public service in order to be employed in another Member State. The CJEU adjudicated that national legislation providing in that case for loss of the retirement pension rights acquired in the civil service and for retrospective insurance under the general old-age insurance scheme (conferring entitlement to a retirement pension lower than the retirement pension that would result from those rights in a pension scheme for civil service) was contrary to Art. 45 TFEU. Furthermore, CJEU pointed out that Article 45 TFEU must be interpreted as meaning that such person must have retirement pension rights which are comparable to those of the civil servants who retain retirement pension rights corresponding, despite a change in public-sector employer, to the years of pensionable service that they have completed, or, if such an interpretation is not possible, by disapplying any contrary provision of domestic law in order to apply the same arrangements as those applicable to those civil servants.

The *Erny* case (C-172/11, EU:C:2012:399) concerned a top-up amount paid by the employer in addition to a part-time pay, which was a scheme established for older workers switching from full time to part-time working with the purpose to enable such employees to make a gradual transition from working life to a retirement pension. Specificity of the case was that Mr. Erny was a cross-border worker working in Germany and residing in France, whose income earned in Germany and after deduction of the social insurance contributions paid in Germany was subject to French taxation rules. Since the taxation rate on wages was lower in France than in Germany, and since in determining the top-up amount employer applied German tax on wages, Mr. Erny was in the effect receiving lower top-up amount than a comparable worker residing in Germany. The CJEU pointed out that "the principle of non-discrimination requires not only that comparable situations must not be treated differently but also that different situations must not be treated in the same way" (para 40). The result of the *Erny* ruling is that any collective and individual agreements in setting up remuneration schemes (i.e. we are of the opinion also occupational retirement schemes, since they fall under the concept of deferred wage), must avoid treating mobile workers in a less favourable, otherwise risking breach of Article 45 TFEU and consequently being null and void pursuant to Article

7 (4) of Regulation (EEC) No 1612/68.[1] Interestingly, the Court rejected any justification arguments based on the increase in financial burdens and possible administrative difficulties for the employer (paras. 47–48), although exactly these arguments are underlying some of the provisions of the secondary EU acquis provisions regarding public statutory pension schemes (e.g. so called "less than one-year rule" prescribed by Article 57 of Regulation 883/2004) and regarding occupational pension schemes (e.g. possibility of the outgoing worker to withdraw retirement savings below a certain threshold, provided in Art. 5(3) of Directive 2014/50). For more see in subchapters below.

In *Casteels* (C-379/09, EU:C:2011:131) which concerned supplementary (occupational) pension rights of a worker employed successively by the same employer in several Member States. The CJEU adjudicated that a non-inclusion of the years of service completed by a worker for the same employer in establishments of that employer situated in different Member States and pursuant to the same coordinating contract of employment is not compatible with Article 45 TFEU. It is interesting to note that *Caseels* case dates from before the entrance into force of the Directive 2014/50 on minimum requirements for enhancing worker mobility between Member States by improving the acquisition and preservation of supplementary pension rights. Nevertheless, it is reasonable to expect that it will keep its relevance, especially in specific intragroup mobility cases, since new Directive 2014/50 still allows waiting and vesting periods of up to 3 years.

3.2   Relevant EU acquis and Challenges in the Field of Social Security Coordination

Regardless whether public pension schemes are general or special, contributory or non-contributory, they are covered by Regulation (EC) No 883/2004 on the coordination of social security systems (Article 3(1) and (2)).[2] Pursuant to Article 1(w), for the purpose of the coordination rules, the term "pension" is defined broadly, covering not only pensions but also lump-sum benefits which can substitute pensions, and payments in the form of reimbursement of contributions and, subject to the special provisions concerning the various categories of benefits (Title III), revaluation increases or supplementary allowances. In 2009, Regulation (EC) No 883/2004 was amended by Regulation (EC) No 988/2009 and adapted in order to take into account recent developments in some Member States, i.e. reduction of some contributory pay-as-you-go schemes and development of contributory funded

---

[1]Now corresponding to Article 7(4) of Regulation (EU) 492/2011.

[2]Private contractual pension schemes fall only exceptionally under the material scope of Regulation (EC) No 883/2004, provided that Member States have made a declaration to that effect (Article 1 (l) of Regulation 883/2004). So far, only France made such declaration for workers of ARRCO and AGIRC.

defined contribution schemes, that are often operated by private pension funds and provide benefits in respect of which periods of time are of no relevance for the benefit calculation. Hence, Article 52(5) of Regulation (EC) No 883/2004 was amended so that it excludes the *pro-rata* calculation of benefits, subject to such schemes being listed in part 2 of Annex VIII.[3] In addition to some horizontally applicable rules and principles (e.g. equality of treatment, aggregation rule, equality of treatment), specific rules on coordination of old-age and survivor's benefits are provided in Articles 50–60 of Regulation 883/2004. Nevertheless, there are some open issues concerning social security coordination in relation to non-standard migrant workers and their right to an old-age pension.

Aggregation rules concern the legal qualification of facts (Pennings 2015, 135) and ensure that persons who have used their freedom of movement may access social security benefits under the legislations of other Member States. These rules should be differentiated from the rules on the calculation of benefits (especially the pro rata rule) which purpose is to ensure a fair share of payment of benefits between institutions of various Member States.

In relation to pensions, in addition to the general rule on aggregation of periods provided in Article 6, Articles 45 and 51 of Regulation (EC) No 883/2004 contain special provisions on the aggregation of periods for old-age, survivors' pensions and invalidity benefits. It is specified that if granting certain benefits is conditional upon the periods of insurance having been completed only in a specific activity as an employed or self-employed person or in an occupation which is subject to a special scheme, then periods completed in another Member State under the corresponding scheme have to be taken into account. Otherwise, these periods should be taken into account for the purpose of providing the benefits of the general scheme. Furthermore, if the right to entitlement is conditional upon the person being insured at the time of the materialisation of the risk, then this condition shall be regarded as having been satisfied if that person has been previously insured under the legislation or specific scheme of that Member State and is, at the time of the materialisation of the risk, insured under the legislation of another Member State for the same risk or, failing that, if a benefit is due under the legislation of another Member State for the same risk. Hence, it seems that these specific aggregation rules for pensions are flexible enough, and would cause no specific problems in relation non-standard workers or self-employed, which was confirmed by experts of majority of member States (Strban et al. 2018, p. 56).

However, in relation to the obligation to provide pension and calculation of the benefit, several potential problems could be identified. Some are related to the precarious nature of the work and sometimes lower remunerations,[4] while others

---

[3]Member States having such schemes are: BG, CZ, DK, EE, FR, HR, LT, HU, AT, PL, PT, SI, SL, SE, and UK.

[4]As indicated above, first problem arises if non-standard form of work is not covered in earning-related pension schemes, hence no pension benefit is being accrued. A second problem relates to the pension adequacy since certain forms of non-standard employment or self-employment usually provide a lower income and are less stable, hence also resulting in less contribution density

could be connected to the existing coordination rules in relation to benefit calculation, especially when it comes to insurance periods of less than 1 year. Namely, pursuant to Article 50 of Regulation (EC) No 883/2004, the total amount of pension may consist of several pensions based on the periods of insurance completed in each of the Member States of employment or self-employment. Hence, each country applies the so-called partial pension method (Pennings 2015, 216).[5] For the calculation of the actual pension amount from each of the Member States, Article 52 prescribes a two-step process: a) calculation of the "independent benefit" based on the national legislation alone, and b) calculation of the "pro-rata benefit" based on the "theoretical benefit" which a person could claim if all insurance or residence periods would be completed under the legislation of that State.[6] The person is entitled to the higher amount of the two (independent benefit and pro-rata benefit).[7]

Nevertheless, in the case of insurance periods of less than 1 year, Article 57 of Regulation (EC) No 883/2004 contains a special rule in order to simplify the administrative procedure and reduce costs related to the payment of very low pensions (Janda 2018, 452–456). The so called "less than one-year rule" prescribes that the Member State is not required to provide benefits in respect of periods completed under the legislation it applies which are taken into account when the risk materialises, under two cumulative conditions: 1) the duration of the said periods is less than 1 year, and 2) when taking only these periods into account no right to benefit is acquired under that legislation. These periods of less than 1 year are not to be lost, since Article 57(2) stipulates that they are proportionally taken over by all the other Member States concerned, since they have to take them into account for when calculating a theoretical benefit (i.e. a basis for the pro rata benefit that will actually be paid).

(e.g. fixed-term employment, casual work, agency work). Thirdly, where the insurance period is an important element in the benefit calculation, application of a recalculation method to full-time equivalents or averaging it to some pecuniary threshold or a specific type of time-related threshold might seems might seem necessary and as a fair solution compared to 'standard' workers, but nevertheless can affect the future level of benefits.

[5]Since retirement ages and other qualification requirements (e.g. insurance period) are not harmonised within EU, differences between Member States might cause deferral of a pension by an insured person. In that case, pursuant to Article 50(2) of Regulation 883/2004, the Member State which conditions are satisfied, when calculating benefit, shall not take into account periods completed under legislations of a Member State whose conditions are not satisfied (or if person concerned expressly requests deferment of the award of old-age benefit under the legislation of one or more Member States).

[6]Member States can waive the right to a pro rata calculation provided that the "independent benefit" invariably results in being equal to or higher than the pro rata benefit. Such situations are listed in Part 1 of Annex VIII and concern the following countries: DK, IR, CY, LT, LI, NL, AT, PL, PT, SK, SE, UK. In addition, a pro rata calculation is not applied in schemes that provide benefits in respect of which periods of time are of no relevance for the benefit calculation. In practice, this manly concerns contribution-funded schemes operated by pension funds. Such schemes are listed in Part 2 of Annex VIII and concern the following countries: BG, CZ, DK, EE, FR, HR, LT, HU, AT, PL, PT, SI, SL, SE, and UK.

[7]Article 52(3) Regulation (EC) No 883/2004.

However, it seems that in practice there could be a problem of 'losing' these periods of insurance of less than 1 year in the event that these other Member States waived the pro rata calculation.[8] Taking into account the exact wording of Article 57 (2), it obliges the competent institutions of each of the other Member States to take these short periods into account only for the purpose of Article 52(1)(b)(i), i.e. for the pro rata benefit. Therefore, it can be concluded that Member States which waived the pro rata calculation of the benefit are excluded from sharing the financial burden of taking over the short periods of insurance.

Furthermore, if the effect of Article 57(1) of Regulation (EC) No 883/2004 were that all the institutions of the Member States concerned would be relieved of their obligations to provide benefits, then Article 57(3) specifies that benefits shall be provided exclusively under the legislation of the last of those Member States whose conditions are satisfied, as if all the periods of insurance and residence completed and taken into account in accordance with the aggregation rules had been completed under the legislation of that Member State. Hence, as a final solution to the problem of several 'mini-periods', the Regulation previews a transfer of the burden of pension payment to the last Member State (i.e. the Member State of last employment or self-employment).

As pointed out by Strban et al. (2018), p. 57–58), this final rule provided by Article 57(3) might also be perceived as problematic in some extreme examples of high mobility and short non-standard working assignments under the applicable legislation of various Member States, since the last Member State of employment or self-employment would have to pay the benefit for all the other Member States in which the person worked but has accumulated less than 1 year of insurance. Since the current coordination system in this area neither provides for the reimbursement of contributions between Member States nor from the worker (*Vermaut*, C-55/81, EU:C:1982:68, paragraph 15), such a result might not equitably distribute the financial burden among the Member States (in the case of high mobility). Hence, there are two potential solutions to the problem. A first solution might be the introduction of an additional rule which would still keep the rule that the last Member State should pay the total pension benefit, while at the same time providing for a proportionate reimbursement of benefits by the competent institutions of the other Member States to the institution of the 'last' Member State, which has actually been paying the benefit. However, this solution might bring more administrative complexity. The second solution would be to abolish the 'less than one year' rule, which could contribute to legal clarity and a fair distribution of the financial burden, especially in the event of high mobility. From the mobile worker's perspective, it would also ensure that no period is lost. However, a potentially negative side of the coin would be increased administration for very low benefits.

---

[8]Waiving is allowed pursuant to Article 52(4) and countries are listed in Part 1 of Annex VIII: DK, IR, CY, LT, LI, NL, AT, PL, PT, SK, SE, UK.

3.3   Relevant EU Acquis and Challenges Regarding Supplementary (Occupational) Pensions

At the outset it is worth mentioning that in theory the notion of supplementary pension schemes covers both occupational and individual pension arrangements which supplement state-provided social security pension schemes (OECD 2005, 29; Social Protection Committee 2008, 5–8; European Commission 2010, 6; Vukorepa 2012, 19). However, EU secondary legislation in the area of free movement (Directive 98/49/EC and Directive 2014/50/EU) uses the notion of supplementary pensions in a narrower sense, covering only occupational pension schemes for employed and/or self-employed persons. Therefore, we will continue using the term occupational schemes, i.e. occupational pension.

Occupational pensions are intended to provide supplementary income in the old-age, complementing coverage provided by statutory schemes. However, labour mobility through full portability of occupational pension benefits is not yet achieved, and might be very difficult in reality since occupational pension schemes between countries and within a country can differ significantly, e.g. based on the payment and calculation of contributions, calculation of benefits and risk sharing.

In trying to reduce obstacles to the cross-border mobility, Directive 98/49/EC on safeguarding supplementary pension rights represents an initial specific measure. It is applicable to both public and private, as well as voluntary and compulsory occupational schemes (excluding only occupational schemes covered by the Regulation on coordination of social security), and regarding personal scope it covers both employed and self-employed persons. It provides only limited protection in the form of equal treatment regarding preservation of vested pension rights (Art. 4 imposes the obligation that persons in respect of whom contributions are no longer being made to the scheme be treated equally regardless weather moving to another Member State or remaining within the same Member State), and by insuring the receipt of pension payments net of any taxes and transaction cost (Art. 5 on cross border payment). Another important aspect of Directive 98/49/EC is obligation to provide adequate information to scheme members when moving to another member State, regarding their pension rights and choices which are available to them (Article 7). Regarding cross-border membership, it contains rules only for posted workers by imposing obligation to enable payment of contributions by or on behalf of a posted worker during the period of posting to another member State, and by allowing to remain in the scheme of origin during the time of posting even in the case of mandatory occupational schemes in the host country (Article 6). It seems to us that from the wording of Article 6, it can be concluded that the right to be exempted from any obligation to pay contributions to an occupational scheme in the host state extends to the whole period of posting, while from the recital 12 of the Directive it seems that such exemption could be interpreted in a limited way, since recital points to the old regulation on coordination of social security system. According to the currently valid rules, in statutory schemes this exemption applies only for a limited period of time, i. e. max 24 months (Article 12 of Regulation 883/2004). Hence, in practice some problems might occur in the case of prolonged posting, above 24 months. In order to avoid any doubts, some Member States have Article 6 of Directive 1998/49 implemented in such a way that they have linked the exemption of paying contributions to supplementary schemes in host member State (i.e. country of employment) with the maximum duration of posting set in the coordination Regulation (e.g. Estonia and Lithuania, according to Christodoulou-Varotsi 2017, 14).

Directive 2014/50/EU represents a second step for enhancing worker mobility between Member States, on the one hand, by improving preservation of vested occupational pension rights and provision of information (already partially regulated by Directive 98/49/EC), and on the other hand by setting new standards regarding acquisition of pension right.[9] Regarding personal scope, it is worth mentioning that Directive 2014/50/EU is narrower than Directive 98/49/EC since it formally targets only workers and not the self-employed,[10] which might be perceived as its defect taking into account the fact that on-demand and platform workers are often employed as bogus self-employed, or solo self-employed. Nevertheless, since probably in many countries both Directive 98/49/EC and Directive 2014/50 are being transposed in the same pieces of legislation, it can be reasonably expected that some Member States will decide to apply broader personal scope also for Directive 2014/50.[11] Regarding material scope, pursuant to Articles 2 and 3, Directive 2014/50 covers "any occupational retirement pension scheme established in accordance with national law and practice and linked to an employment relationship, intended to provide a supplementary pension for employed persons", with the exception of schemes covered by Regulation (EC) No 883/2004. It applies only to periods of employment falling after its transposition, and covers only cross-border situations. It does not apply to workers moving within a single Member State hence does not deal with the transferability of pension entitlements between employment statuses, although, based on recital 6, member States may choose to extend Directive's applicability also to intra-country situations.

As already indicated above, Directive 2014/50 tries to remove obstacles to worker mobility between Member States by improving the acquisition (Article 4) and preservation (Article 5) of occupational pension rights linked to an employment relationship. It also contains provisions on information standards (Article 6) for active scheme members prior to their termination of employment, as well as for "deferred beneficiaries", i.e. former active scheme members who have vested pension rights in a supplementary (occupational) pension scheme and are not yet in

---

[9]According to Article 8(1), Member States had to adopt the laws, regulations and administrative provisions necessary to comply with Directive 2014/50/EU by 21 May 2018, or ensure that the social partners introduce the required provisions by way of agreement by that date.

[10]This can be concluded by comparison of definition for „supplementary pension scheme" defined by Article 3(1)(b) of Directive 2014/50/EU and by Article 3(1)(b) of Directive 98/49/EC.

[11]The final conclusions on the personal scope of Directive 2014/50/EU in the national context will be available only after comparative legal analyses conducted within the MoveS network of experts scheduled for second half of 2019, and after formal report of the European Commission due by the 21st May 2021 (pursuant to Article 9(2) of Directive 2014/50/EU).

receipt of a pension from that scheme. Rules on the content of information and their issuance upon request (which can be also limited by member States that such information upon request do not need to be provided more than once a year) are meant to be complementary to provisions of Article 11 of Directive 2003/41/EC (now replaced by Articles 37–44 of the recast Directive (EU) 2016/2341) and Article 7 of the Directive 98/49/EC, which all adds to the complexity of rules. Although correct and full information is very important for both active and passive (dormant) scheme member, nevertheless, in this paper we will not deal further with the problems of information provision, but choose rather to concentrate on potential challenges regarding the right to acquisition and preservation of pension rights.[12]

Regarding acquisition of occupational pension rights relevant is Article 4 and recitals 17 and 18. It is provided that "waiting period"[13] for starting acquiring rights and "vesting period"[14] as minimum periods of scheme membership for the acquisition of rights should not exceed 3 years in total, or combination of both. Furthermore, it is prescribed that minimum age for vesting of pension rights should not exceed 21 years, while Directive does not deal with the age limits for becoming a scheme member, as it is considered that minimum age requirements for scheme membership do not constitute obstacle to free movement (see also recital 17).

In relation to these rules, several problems can be expected. Namely, although Directive still allows for setting waiting and vesting periods of up to 3 years as well as setting minimum age for vesting (but not exceeding 21), it is reasonable to expect that such rules could nevertheless represent an obstacle to cross-border free movement. Hence, CJEU might be faced with litigations in which parties could not invoke breach of Directive 2014/50, but rather again breach of directly applicable Art. 45 TFEU on free movement of workers. Hence, the *Casteels* ruling will certainly still keep its relevance in the intragroup mobility cases. However, it is to be see if the CJEU would be inclined to spread its application, i.e. application of Art. 45 TFEU also to other cross-border cases. As put forward by Del Sol and Rocca 2017, 152–153), this might depend on the Court's assessment if shorter waiting and vesting periods could be presumed to be a hindrance to free movement of workers, or on the other hand, exactly because allowed by the Directive, perceived by the CJEU as too uncertain and indirect to be liable to hinder freedom of movement of workers (*Graf*, C-190/98, EU:C:2000:49, 25). Further on, since Directive does not cover minimum age requirements for scheme membership, it is likely that such membership conditions would more severely hit workers inclined to perform work in atypical employment arrangements during their younger age (e.g. student work, "click-work" as a specific sort of crowd work performed via platforms), hence in

---

[12]For more critical approach to the right to information see Sol and Rocca, 2017, 146–148.

[13]Waiting period is defined as the 'period of employment, required under national law or by the rules of a supplementary pension scheme or by the employer, before a worker becomes eligible for membership' (Article 3(d) Directive 2014/50/EU).

[14]Vesting period is defined as the 'period of active membership of a scheme, required under national law or the rules of a supplementary pension scheme, in order to trigger entitlement to the accumulated supplementary pension' (Article 3(e) Directive 2014/50/EU).

the future there might be cases involving both cross-border and age-discrimination issues.[15]

Regarding acquisition of rights, Article 4(1)(c) of Directive 2014/50/EU also sets a rule that if an outgoing worker did not yet acquire pension rights, s/he has a right to reimbursement of contributions. From the wording of Directive, it can be concluded that there is no right to reimbursement of employer's contributions, but only contributions paid by the outgoing worker, or paid on his/her behalf. Further on, the amount of reimbursement depends on the pension scheme type: in schemes in which the scheme or the employer bears the investment risk (in particular defined benefit schemes) there is a duty to reimburse the contributions, while in schemes in which the outgoing worker bears the investment risk (in particular in defined contribution schemes), there is option between reimbursement of the sum of the contributions or reimbursement of the investment value arising from these contributions. This means that if for defined contribution schemes, a Member State chooses reimbursement of the investment value of contributions, in practice this could result in the reimbursement of the amount that can be higher or lower than the sum of contributions paid-in (see also recital 19). Possible problem to these rules on reimbursement can be linked to the fact that the wording of directive is not clear regarding employer's contributions. Namely, since occupational pensions are perceived as "deferred wage", employer's contributions can be further perceived as contributions on behalf of the worker. Hence, taking into account the specificities of operating pay-as-you-go defined benefit schemes, and funded defined- contribution schemes, it is likely that from funded DC schemes outgoing workers would get investment values of all contributions (if this option chosen), while in other cases the obligation to return the "sum of contributions" would obligatory result in return of workers contributions, while regarding employer's contributions, only if they perceived as being paid on worker's behalf. Therefore, we are of the opinion that this

---

[15]However, this potential form of age discrimination might be considered justified if allowed by national legislation, since Article 6(2) of Directive 2000/78/EC establishing a general framework for equal treatment in employment and occupation prescribes the following: "*Member States may provide that the fixing for occupational social security schemes of ages for admission or entitlement to retirement or invalidity benefits, including the fixing under those schemes of different ages for employees or groups or categories of employees, and the use, in the context of such schemes, of age criteria in actuarial calculations, does not constitute discrimination on the grounds of age, provided this does not result in discrimination on the grounds of sex.*" By comparing the wording of Article 6(1) that is general provision on justification of difference in treatment on the grounds of age, and of Article 6(2) which represents a special rule for occupational schemes, it seems that Member State's discretion to allow difference in treatment based on age pursuant to Article 6(2) is larger, since that provision does not provide for objective and reasonable justification by a legitimate aim (unlike the wording of Article 6(1)). The only outspoken concern of Article 6(2) is that discrimination on the grounds of age in occupational schemes should not result in discrimination on the grounds of sex. Hence, it is worth reminding that differences in pensionable age and access conditions to an occupational retirement scheme can represent indirect discrimination based on sex, and hence fall under the scope of Art 157 TFEU on equal pay between man and women (se e.g. Bilka-Kaufhaus (C-170/84) and Barber (C-262/88)).

rule on reimbursement of contributions is not clear enough and might cause some future interpretation litigations.

Concerning vested pension rights, general rule is preservation of dormant pension right in the former employer's pension scheme. So called "dormant members" should be treated on par with active members (Article 5). However, preservation may vary depending on the nature of the pension schemes (e.g. regarding pension accrual modalities and indexation rules; some rules are more fit for schemes with defined benefits, while other for funded defined contribution schemes). Furthermore, in order to reduce managing and administrative costs of low-value dormant pension rights (recital 23), Member States may prescribe an exception from the preservation rule, i.e. they may stipulate withdrawal of capital sum subject to established national ceilings and worker's informed consent (Article 5(3)). It is reasonable to expect that cross-border atypical workers with lower wages and career interruptions would be more inclined to take this possibility, and thus use this financial means to bridge some financial problems. Hence, this rule can be perceived as helping their present financial situation (when going out of the scheme and a certain member State) while at the same time potentially frustrating their future pension adequacy, since early withdrawal of pension right (before retirement age) in practice usually leads to the risk of spending money for other purposes much before the old-age risk occurs.

4   Combating Fraud and Error

Restrictions to the free movement of persons can and do appear in many different respects, not in the least in the field of social security, where both fraudulent and erroneous situations can put a strain on the free movement of persons. Pensions are not an exception to this. There is a growing awareness in the Member States of the EU concerning the necessity to tackle cross-border social security fraud and error.

With respect to social security coordination, fraud is defined as "any act or omission to act, in order to obtain or receive social security benefits or to avoid obligations to pay social security contributions, contrary to the law of a Member State" while error is defined as "an unintentional mistake or omission by officials or citizens" (see Communication from the Commission (COM(2013) 837 final). Although both fraud and error often end up having the same effects, the capital difference between them is the fact that fraud cases require proof of intent, whereas error is unintentional. At the same moment we have to admit that often national legislations do not make a distinction between fraud and error.

Since still most of the controlling and monitoring actions happen at the national level, a close cooperation and data exchange between the Member States is crucial in order to prevent and combat fraudulent and erroneous situations in the realm of social security coordination. However it is rather surprising in this respect that only once, i.e. in Recital 19 of Regulation (EC) No 987/2009—a reference to fraud and error is made in these coordination Regulations. In a recent study on fraud and error in the coordination regulations in the EU (Jorens and de Coninck 2018), only a limited number of countries provided figures on fraud and error in the domain of pensions. In absolute figures, the number of cases involving fraud and error is rather small, with only Spain reporting around 1000 cases and Poland reporting 792 cases. In terms of money involved in these cases, the United Kingdom stated that around € 150 million was involved and Switzerland reported that more than € 3 million was involved. In relative figures, however, the impact of fraud and error cases is rather small.

With respect to pensions, two main types of fraud and error can be noticed: payment of pension rights after the death of pensioners whose rights were exported abroad and pensioners submitting false or incorrect information (e.g. incorrect civil status, incorrect income declaration, or incorrect statement of address). It is interesting to find out which steps Member States do in general take to prevent or to combat fraud and error in the domain of pensions. When the death of a pensioner is not reported (in time), the payment of the pension continues, which can cause problems. This problem can occur when the pensioner dies in the period between annual checks carried out based on life certificates. Moreover, this problem arises when relevant institutions abroad or relatives of the deceased have informed the competent institutions late or have failed to inform them.

In this respect it is wide spread practice in the Member States of the EU to require an annual life certificate from recipients of old-age or survivor's benefits living in another (Member) State in order to verify whether these persons are still alive and thus entitled to those benefits. In Austria, e.g., if the certificate is not received, the payment is suspended until it is received in order to prevent overpayments. In Romania, on top of such a life certificate, also a declaration of honour, provided for in the internal implementation of instructions relating to the implementation of the coordination Regulations, has to be filled in and returned to the territorial pension houses, in order to prevent the creation of different pension dossiers relating to the same beneficiary. In Switzerland the standard control procedure involves sending a standard letter with a barcode and reply envelope inviting several hundred thousand of pensioners to certify their life status with a qualified authority. If there is no reaction within 90 days, the payment of benefits is immediately suspended until the case had been clarified. Germany combines the life certificate method with automated cross-checking of registered deaths. More and more countries currently lay emphasis on the development of the exchange of data on pensioners (dates of death, marital status, amounts allocated etc.).

By the electronic exchange of data, institutions aim at both administrative simplification and an intensified fight against social fraud. A nice example is Denmark where in 2015 a new legislation was introduced according to which the procedure of adjusting pension rates to match the level of income for the beneficiary was restructured from a yearly check-up to an automatic monthly check-up on the basis of the Danish National Income. With this procedure, the built-up of large amounts due for recovery is to a significant extent avoided. This helps to prevent situations where errors occur due to the fact that claimants may not have been aware of their obligations to inform about changes in circumstances on a continuous basis as well results in cases of fraud being detected at an earlier stage. It is therefore not surprisingly that in order to avoid this risk a growing number of Member States (start to) exchange data. For instance, Belgium electronically exchanges data on the date of death with Germany, France and Luxembourg, and they are negotiating with the Netherlands, Italy, the United Kingdom and Spain to do the same. Denmark also signed new agreements with Germany and Poland for a regular exchange of data, and Croatia, have similar agreements with competent institutions in Slovenia, Germany and Poland. Furthermore, Germany regularly carries out automatic death data crosschecks for pensioners with several EU Member States. Notwithstanding these actions, there is still room for improvement (see Jorens et al. 2017; Jorens and de Coninck 2018).

The implementation of regular checks and monitoring activities is a substantial step in the prevention of and fight against fraud and error. Data matching and data mining are found to be very useful techniques to partly fulfil these tasks. However in order to be able to fully make advantage of these techniques, extensive corresponding databases and registers are needed. Member States should keep establishing, improving and updating their databases and registers and to facilitate consultation of these databases and registers by relevant parties, if possible even by institutions of other Member States etc. The fact that cross-border cooperation is in practice fully based on the goodwill of the Member States leads to the finding that some Member States are not always cooperative (they do not respond to questions, do not share data etc.) and that other Member States report they cannot do anything about that. These investigations are often subject to long response times, if a response is received at all.

It is important to notice that the European coordination rules do not include procedures for the cross-border investigation of suspected cases of fraud and error which is problematic. The cross-border cooperation between Member States' national institutions of social security is therefore to be facilitated, with due regard for enforcement. But there is still a long way to go. The discussion on the European Labour Authority also in the domain of social security, and possible introduction of the European Social Security Number (ESSN) are paramount examples of this.

5   Conclusion

The migrant worker at the beginning of the European Union (or of the three founding communities at that time) is no longer the migrant worker of today. The growing pan-European labour market with an increasing flexibility is at the origin of a new kind of a "fluid" worker. The migrant worker is not only constantly on the move between countries and jobs of a short nature but also between jobs with an uncertain outcome with respect to his or her concrete social protection situation due to different kinds of emerging non-standard forms of employment and self-employment. This leads to dangerous situations for the migrant worker who is, not in the first place, an economic person, but a human being looking to improve his or her living and working conditions.

Moreover, also social security, and in particular pensions systems, have developed at varying intensities, and are suffering to fulfil their role of supporting "happy old people". The breakdown between statutory and occupational schemes leads to important issues for the implementation of the policy of equal treatment, not just between men and women, but also more recently between standard and non-standard employees and self-employed, as well as all other issues in relation to the coordination of social security systems. This contribution has sketched some of these problems. It is our belief that further attention should be paid to these problems of a fluid society and that perhaps courageous steps have to be taken if the European integration wants to remain successful.

References

Bley H, Kreikebohm R, Marschner A (2007) Sozialrecht, Luchterhand

Christodoulou-Varotsi I (2017) Reply to an ad hoc request for comparative analysis - implementation of Directive 98/49/EC on safeguarding the supplementary pension rights of employed and self-employed persons moving within the European Union (July 2017), FreSsco, European Union. https://ec.europa.eu/social/BlobServlet?docId=18223&langId=en

Dawson WH (1912) Social insurance in Germany 1883–1911, its history, operation, results, and a comparison with the National Insurance Act, 1911, Unwin London

De Micheli B et al (2018) Access to social protection for all forms of employment: assessing the options for a possible EU initiative. Publications Office of the European Union, 2018, Luxembourg.   http://ec.europa.eu/social/main.jsp?catId=738&langId=en&pubId=8067& furtherPubs=yes, or directly to pdf http://ec.europa.eu/social/BlobServlet?docId=19160& langId=en

Del Sol M, Rocca M (2017) Free movement of workers in the EU and occupational pensions: conflicting priorities? Between case law and legislative interventions. Eur J Soc Secur 19 (2):141–157. https://doi.org/10.1177/1388262717711776

EESC – European Economic and Social Committee (2017) Impact of digitalisation and the on-demand economy on labour markets and the consequences for employment and industrial relations. Publications Office of the European Union, Luxembourg. European Economic and Social Committee, Brussels. https://www.eesc.europa.eu/sites/default/files/resources/docs/qe-02-17-763-en-n.pdf

Eurofound (2015) New forms of employment. Publishing Office of the European Union, Luxembourg. Available at: http://www.eurofound.europa.eu/publications/report/2015/working-condi tions-labour-market/new-forms-of-employment

Eurofound (2018) Overview of new forms of employment – 2018 update. Publications Office of the European Union, Luxembourg. https://www.eurofound.europa.eu/publications/customised-report/2018/overview-of-new-forms-of-employment-2018-update

European Commission (2010) Private pension schemes: their role in adequate and sustainable pensions. Publications Office of the European Union, Luxembourg. http://ec.europa.eu/social/ BlobServlet?docId=4853&langId=en

European Commission (2018a) Employment and social developments in Europe: annual review 2018. Publications Office of the European Union, Luxembourg. https://doi.org/10.2767/ 406275., http://ec.europa.eu/social/BlobServlet?docId=19719&langId=en

European Commission (2018b) The 2018 pension adequacy report, volume I. https://publications. europa.eu/en/publication-detail/-/publication/f0e89c3f-7821-11e8-ac6a-01aa75ed71a1/lan guage-en

European Commission (2018c) The 2018 pension adequacy report, volume II, country profiles. https://doi.org/10.2767/653851., https://publications.europa.eu/en/publication-detail/-/publica tion/62f83ed2-7821-11e8-ac6a-01aa75ed71a1/language-en/format-PDF/source-search

Eurostat (2018) Involuntary temporary employment (this indicator represents employees who could not find permanent job as a percentage of total employees). http://ec.europa.eu/eurostat/tgm/ table.do?tab=table&init=1&language=en&pcode=tesem190&plugin=1

Fries-Tersch E et al (2018) The 2017 annual report on intra-EU labour mobility, European Union, 2018.   https://publications.europa.eu/en/publication-detail/-/publication/cd298a3c-c06d-11e8-9893-01aa75ed71a1/language-en

Grgurev I, Vukorepa I (2018) Flexible and new forms of employment in Croatia and their pension entitlement aspects. In: Sander Gerald G, Vesna T, Nada B-V (eds) Transnational, European, and   national   labour   relations.   Springer,   Cham.   http://www.springer.com/gp/book/ 9783319022185

Hoencamp J et al (2014) The fluid society, working without boundaries, The perspective series, new insights into the UK workplace. Circle Research, Vodafone. https://www.yourreadybusiness.co. uk/wp-content/uploads/2014/02/Fluid%20Society_Report.pdf

ILO (2016) Non-standard employment around the world: understanding challenges, shaping prospects. International Labour Office, Geneva. Available at: http://www.ilo.org/global/publica tions/books/WCMS_534326/lang%2D%2Den/index.htm

ILO/OECD (2018) Promoting adequate social protection and social security coverage for all workers, including those in non-standard forms of employment. https://www.ilo.org/wcmsp5/ groups/public/%2D%2D-dgreports/%2D%2D-inst/documents/publication/wcms_646044.pdf

Janda C (2018) Alters und Hinterbliebenenrenten. In: Fuchs M (Hrsg.) Europäisches Sozialrecht, 7. Auflage, Nomos 2018, pp 452–456

Jorens Y, de Coninck M, (2018) Quantative data collected and analysis written by Frederic De Wispelaere and Jozef Pacolet "Fraud and error in the field of EU social security coordination: reference year 2017, European Commission, 2018. https://ec.europa.eu/social/main.jsp? catId=1098&langId=en#navItem-relatedDocuments

Jorens Y et al (2017) Analytical report 2017 on mutual assistance and sincere cooperation. An inquiry into the cooperation to enforce the coordination regulations and to combat fraud and error, 2017. https://ec.europa.eu/social/main.jsp?catId=1098&langId=en#navItem-relatedDocuments

Kress-del Bondio J (2018) Challenges to old-age social security in Germany. In: Hohnerlein EM, Hennion S, Kaufmann O (eds) Erwerbsverlauf und sozialer Schutz in Europa. Springer, pp 601–615

MISSOC (2019) Mutual information system on social protection. www.missoc.org

OECD (2005) Private pensions, OECD classification and glossary. http://www.oecd.org/finance/ private-pensions/38356329.pdf

Pennings F (2015) European social security law, Intersentia 2015

Reinhard H-J (2018) Adjusting old-age pensions to match employment biographies – the German case. In: Hohnerlein EM, Hennion S, Kaufmann O (eds) Erwerbsverlauf und sozialer Schutz in Europa. Springer, pp 571–579

Schoukens P, Barrio A (2017) The changing concept of work: when does typical work become atypical? Eur Lab Law J 8(4):306–332. https://doi.org/10.1177/2031952517743871 (open access direct pdf link: http://journals.sagepub.com/doi/pdf/10.1177/2031952517743871)

Schoukens P, Barrio A, Montebovi S (2018) The EU social pillar: an answer to the challenge of the social protection of platform workers? Eur J Soc Secur 20(3):219–241. https://doi.org/10.1177/ 1388262718798393, or http://journals.sagepub.com/doi/10.1177/1388262718798393

Spasova S et al (2017) Access to social protection for people working on non-standard contracts and as self-employed in Europe - a study of national policies; ESPN synthesis report. Publications Office   of   the   European   Union,   Luxembourg.   http://ec.europa.eu/social/BlobServlet? docId=17683&langId=en

Stevens Y (2017) The silent pension pillar implosion. Eur J Soc Secur 19(2):98–117. https://doi. org/10.1177/1388262717711777

Strban G (2012) Gender differences in social protection, MISSOC analysis 2012/2, MISSOC Secretariat, p 45. http://missoc.org/MISSOC/INFORMATIONBASE/OTHEROUTPUTS/ANALYSIS/2012/MISSOC_Analysis_2_FINAL_EN.pdf

Strban G (2015) Vpliv nadzornih inštitucij na uresničevanje pravice do socialne varnosti – imamo v Sloveniji (ne)ustrezne dajatve? (influence of the supervisory institutions on the implementation of the right to social security – are benefits in Slovenia (in)adequate?), Delavci in delodajalci, Vol. XV, 2015, 4, 477–499

Strban G, Carrascosa Bermejo D, Schoukens P, Vukorepa I (2018) Social security coordination and non-standard forms of employment and self-employment: Interrelation, challenges and prospects, MoveS analytical report 2018

The Social Protection Committee (2008) Privately managed funded pension provision and their contribution to adequate and sustainable pensions. http://ec.europa.eu/social/BlobServlet?docId=743&langId=en

Turner J (2018) If identity politics win, a man of 69 can be 49, when self-identification trumps biology, men can be women, white can be black and age really will be just a number, The Sunday Times, 10 November 2018

Vukorepa I (2012) Mirovinski sustavi: kapitalno financiranje kao čimbenik socijalne sigurnosti (Pension Systems: Funded Schemes as Social Security Factors). Pravni fakultet Sveučilišta u Zagrebu, Zagreb

Vukorepa I (2015) Vukorepa, Ivana. Lost between sustainability and adequacy: critical analysis of the Croatian pension System's parametric reform. Revija za socijalnu politiku 22(3):279–308. https://doi.org/10.3935/rsp.v22i3.1307. http://hrcak.srce.hr/149857?lang=en

Vukorepa I, Tomić I, Stubbs P (2017) ESPN Thematic Report on Access to social protection of people working as self-employed or on non-standard contracts, European Union, 2017. http://ec.europa.eu/social/BlobServlet?docId=17687&langId=en

Legal Acts

Communication from the Commission to the European Parliament, the Council, the European Economic and Social Committee and the Committee of the Regions: Free movement of EU citizens and their families: Five actions to make a difference; (COM(2013) 837 final)https://eur-lex.europa.eu/LexUriServ/LexUriServ.do?uri=COM:2013:0837:FIN:EN:PDF

Council Directive 98/49/EC of 29 June 1998 on safeguarding the supplementary pension rights of employed and self-employed persons moving within the Community, OJ L 209, 25.7.1998, p. 46–49, https://eur-lex.europa.eu/legal-content/EN/ALL/?uri=CELEX:31998L0049& qid=1552049108931

Directive 2014/50/EU of the European Parliament and of the Council of 16 April 2014 on minimum requirements for enhancing worker mobility between Member States by improving the acquisition and preservation of supplementary pension rights, OJ L 128, 30.4.2014, p. 1–7, https://eur-lex.europa.eu/legal-content/EN/ALL/?uri=CELEX:32014L0050&qid=1552049349499

European Pillar of Social Rights, OJ C 428, 13.12.2017, p. 10–15

Proposal for a Council Recommendation on access to social protection for workers and the self-employed, COM(2018) 132 final., http://ec.europa.eu/social/BlobServlet?docId=19158& langId=en

Regulation (EC) No 883/2004 of the European Parliament and of the Council of 29 April 2004 on the coordination of social security systems, OJ L 166, 30.4.2004, p. 1–123 (consolidated text from 11.4.2017, https://eur-lex.europa.eu/legal-content/EN/TXT/?qid=1552048989245& uri=CELEX:02004R0883-20170411)

Ivana Vukorepa is associate professor of labour and social security law at the University of Zagreb. She has completed her LL.B. studies at the University of Zagreb in 1999, while LL.M. at the College of Europe in 2001. In 2002 she did the Croatian Barr exam. From 2007 to 2008 she was Fulbright Visiting Researcher at the Georgetown University Law Center. In 2011 she earned her doctoral degree at the University of Zagreb. In the negotiations for the accession of Croatia to the EU she was Head of the Working group for negotiating chapter "Freedom of movement for workers". She has collaborated on several research projects, as well as in the European independent experts' networks such as: ESPN (from 20014-2018) and FreSsco (that in 2018 became MoveS). In social security law she has a particular interest in pensions. She is proficient user in English, independent user in German, good user in French and basic user in Italian.

Full bibliography list is available via: https://bib.irb.hr/lista-radova?autor=258330&lang=EN, or https://www.bib.irb.hr/pregled/znanstvenici/258330

Yves Jorens is professor of European social law and social criminal law at the Faculty of Law, Ghent University (Belgium) and director of studies. After nearly 20 years of research in the specific area of EU coordination of social security for migrant workers, he is acknowledged as one of the main international experts in this field. Throughout the years, he has participated in or directed numerous projects in the field of international employment and European social law. For more than 10 years he has been project director of the network on social security and free movement for migrant workers (trESS, FreSsco). He has written several articles and books on European social (security) law issues, international employment, international social fraud and European health care. Professor Jorens has a solid track record in managing large scale (research and training) networks. He is also director of IRIS, the International Research Institute on Social Fraud, a knowledge centre that gathers relevant information of regional, national and international interest regarding social fraud in the broadest sense of the word. Full bibliography is available at https://biblio.ugent.be/person/801001176383

Grega Strban is Full Professor and Dean-elect of the Faculty of Law University of Ljubljana. He studied also at the University of Cambridge (with distinction) and KU Leuven (magna cum laude), is external correspondent of Max-Planck Institute of Social Law and Social Policy, Munich, President of Slovenian Association for Labour Law and Social Security and as such member of the Executive Committee of the International Society for Labour and Social Security Law, Geneva, Vice-President of EISS, Leuven, Vice-President of Judicial Council of the Republic of Slovenia, coordinator of EU project MoveS and a Humboldtian. He is member of several editorial boards and author of many articles and book (chapters) in the area of (national, international and European) social security law. He passed the State (bar) exam for lawyers and received Roger Dillemans Award for Excellence in Social Security, KU Leuven (2004) and recognition of Best Young Lawyer in Slovenia (2001). http://izumbib.izum.si/bibliografije/Y20180923145808-A4808803.html

Printed by Printforce, the Netherlands